NORTH UIST

ITS ARCHÆOLOGY AND TOPOGRAPHY

WITH NOTES UPON THE EARLY HISTORY OF
THE OUTER HEBRIDES

BY

ERSKINE BEVERIDGE, LL.D.

AUTHOR OF

'THE CHURCHYARD MEMORIALS OF CRAIL,'
'COLL AND TIREE,' ETC.

WITH ONE HUNDRED AND FIFTY FULL-PAGE ILLUSTRATIONS
AND TWO MAPS

ORIGIN

This facsimile edition published in 2018 by
Origin, an imprint of
Birlinn Limited
West Newington House
10 Newington Road
Edinburgh EH9 1QS

www.birlinn.co.uk

First published in 1911 by William Brown

ISBN 978 1 91247 614 5
eBook ISBN 978 1 788851 22 0

British Library Cataloguing-in-Publication Data
A catalogue record for this book is available from
the British Library

Printed and bound in Great Britain by Clays Ltd, Elcograf S.p.A.

PREFACE

THE writer's earliest introduction to North Uist dates back to the autumn of 1897, when he visited the island for the purpose of comparing its ancient duns or forts with those found in Coll and Tiree. Since that period he has had frequent opportunities of exploring its various districts, and there are now but few with which he is not more or less familiar.

A stranger, upon landing at Lochmaddy—the principal harbour of North Uist—is apt to receive an unfavourable impression from the vast expanse of bogs occupying its east side, which is also absolutely treeless and relieved only by a few hills of no great elevation and by the tortuous recesses of salt-water lochs penetrating its seaboard. A fuller acquaintance, however, reveals various, and in some respects, unique attractions, as the north and west shores present a marked contrast to the forbidding aspect of the east. The rugged declivities of North and South Lee (near Lochmaddy) and those of Eaval (to the south of Loch Eford) are exceptional features in the scenery of North Uist, differing wholly from the general conditions which prevail. Among the less frequented districts is that of Portain (immediately north of Lochmaddy Bay), covering an area of about eight square miles and no doubt containing many pre-historic sites within its trackless waste. Here are only three cottages, two of them occupied by shepherds and the other by a tailor.

The writer well remembers his first visits to the tidal islands of Baleshare and Kirkibost, and the impression conveyed by Grimsay and Vallay when viewed across their still wider fords, giving

the idea that these were places apart, habitable only by the most
adventurous of mankind. In point of fact, with the partial exception
of Kirkibost Island, all the more important tidal annexes of North
Uist are easily accessible during well-defined periods, but always
subject to the interference of unusually rough weather.

North Uist, although commonly regarded as one island, is in reality
a group of islands; the main portion being greatly predominant as to
size, but surrounded by many others of considerable extent, among
them several which are now either uninhabited or occupied by a single
family.

Our first chapter deals with the general topography of North
Uist; climatic changes involving the total absence of trees, without
any prospect of re-afforestation under existent conditions; and also
the relative levels of land and sea in pre-historic times, with special
allusion to a 'lost continent' which is said to have linked St. Kilda
with the Long Island, and the Outer Hebrides with the Scottish
mainland. There is reason to believe that the same geological process
still continues, although so gradually as to be imperceptible unless
over a long cycle of years.

In this connection it is significant to find that in 1542 the valued
rental of North Uist was officially reduced by two or three 'merk-lands'
on account of encroachment by the sea, presumably at some period
then quite recent, no particular locality, however, being specified.
Up to that time the total valuation stood at sixty merks, including
twelve merks belonging to the Church, and it seems well to quote the
full reference to this subject as given in the *Exchequer Rolls*, vol. xvii.
p. 557, under date 3 August 1542, viz.—' Memorandum quod tota
insula de Oist extendit ad sexaginta mercatas terrarum, de quibus
duodecem mercate pertinent ecclesie, relique vero domino regi, de
quibus due mercate distructe existunt per fluxum maris. Et sic
restant quadraginta sex mercate fertiles.' On 31 July 1542 (*Ibid.*,
p. 649) a new lease had been granted to Archibald, 'the Clerk,' of the
'North Ile off Oyest, extendens ad xlv mark land, preter terras

ecclesiasticas ejusdem' for a term of five years at the rental of
£66, 13s. 4d.[1] For whatever reason, another merk is here deducted
from the forty-six given in the entry of 3rd August.

Nearly two centuries later, history seems to have repeated itself,
as we find a document addressed from North Uist in 1721 to the
Forfeited Estates Commissioners, wherein ' We, the wadsetters, tacksmen, and possessors undersubscrivers attest and deliver—That in
regarde of the extreme poverty reigning amongst the haill tennants
and possessors within the Barony of North Uist occasioned by a
murain in our cattle first in 1717 but more especially this year by a
second murrain whereby a great many of our cattle have perished to
the number of seven hundred and fourtie five cows, five hundred and
seventy three horse, eight hundred and twentie sheep. . . . And
moreover we attest and deliver that about Candlemass last the sea
overflowed severall parts of the countrie breaking down many houses
to the hazard of some lives which hase impaired the lands to such a
degree as its possible it may happen more and more that they cannot
answer to the worst sett in former times.'[2] Here again no specific
locality is given, but from the signatures to this ' attestation ' the
lands affected in 1721 evidently lay at the west and north shores of
North Uist, including the districts from Paible to Kilpheder on the
west, and those of Griminish, Vallay, Dunskellor, and Boreray on the
north.

With regard to the earlier devastation of about the year 1540,
when lands to the value of two or three merks per annum were so
completely lost as to be deducted from the rental, we would conjecture
that the principal damage was farther south,—perhaps chiefly at
Baleshare Island, where so recently as July 1859, through a high tide
accompanied by a south-westerly gale, ' the soil was washed away and
channels formed that had never existed before.'[3]

---

[1] See p. 142, postea, note 3.
[2] The Clan Donald, vol. iii. p. 664.
[3] Sailing Directions for the West Coast of Scotland, 1885, part 1, p. 88. See also p. 76,
postea, for the apparent discrepancy of a ' penny-land ' at Heisker in the seventeenth century.

In Chapter II. some attention is devoted to the primitive inhabitants of North Uist, although the evidence upon this subject is so debatable as to be rather inconclusive.   Unfortunately we are without any definite knowledge as to the racial affinity of the Picts, nor is the region identified from which they first reached our shores; while it also seems improbable that these questions can ever be fully solved. Not until the period of Norse supremacy in the Hebrides (ca. A.D. 850-1266) is any historic basis reached, and even then the Sagas contain merely a few references to 'Uist' in general.

The immediately following Clan times supply much fuller information, though often so obscure or contradictory as to be quite unreliable. This subject abounds in pitfalls, and it is hardly possible that all have been avoided, notwithstanding every endeavour towards accuracy. Each clan has recorded, from an individual standpoint, not only its own history but that of the various other clans with which it came most in contact, the natural results being hardly reconcilable upon a comparison of two or three independent accounts dealing with the self-same area and period.

The history of North Uist—for nearly six centuries after the cession of the Hebrides by King Magnus IV. of Norway to the Scottish crown in 1266—is intimately associated with the descendants of Somerled through his grandsons Donald and Roderick, the sons of Reginald.   Clan MacRuari held the island, together with other territories, until 1346, when John of Islay (chief of Clan Donald south, and usually known as 'First Lord of the Isles') acquired the Uists and Garmoran through his first wife Amie MacRuari, who then became sole heiress of the collateral branch, Clan Donald north.   In Chapter III. it is shown that John of Islay managed to divert the succession in Clan Donald south and in the lordship of the Isles to the issue of his second marriage.   The descendants of Amie MacRuari, as Clan Ranald, retained Garmoran and practically the whole of South Uist from ca. 1401 until these lands were sold during the period between 1813 and 1838; while another section—Clan Gorrie—pos-

sessed North Uist from 1373 to 1469, when that estate was transferred to Hugh MacDonald (of the Islay branch, half-brother of the
forfeited last Lord of the Isles), being thereafter held by his lineal
successors for almost four centuries until 1855, in which year it finally
passed from the MacDonalds of the Isles.

With regard to the chiefship in the various divisions of Clan
MacDonald, it would seem that the ancient Celtic law of Tanistry (or
tribal selection 'within three degrees of relationship to the main line')
took effect in at least four or five cases upon record;[1] once indeed
following and approving a nomination made by authority of the
crown. Reference is here made to Alexander (d. 1308, fourth in
lineal descent from Somerled) whose sons were rejected in favour of
their uncle, Angus Og, a staunch supporter of King Robert the Bruce
both at the Battle of Bannockburn and elsewhere. It would also seem
that the law of Tanistry cannot be held accountable for another
striking instance—already mentioned—where the eldest son[2] of John
of Islay by Amie MacRuari was excluded from his rightful succession
to the lordship of the Isles. This was evidently due to the personal
influence of a powerful chief, backed by royal authority and his policy
accepted by the clan either tacitly or perhaps with real approval. It is
interesting to note that Amie MacRuari, first wife of John of Islay,
was cousin-german to Lady Isobel of Mar, queen of Robert the Bruce;
his second wife being Lady Margaret Stewart, daughter of the 'High
Steward' of Scotland, afterwards King Robert II. For each of these
alliances it had been necessary for John of Islay to obtain a papal
dispensation on the point of consanguinity.

During the fifteenth century it is abundantly clear that marriages
were often contracted by the Hebridean chiefs from motives of
expediency, without any question of individual preference. Thus we
find in *Acta Dominorum Concilii* (Edin. 1839, pp. 346-347) the confirmation of an Indenture signed at Dingwall 6 Feb. 1474-75, by

[1] *The Clan Donald*, vol. iii. pp. 156-163.
[2] Whether Ranald or Godfrey, a matter which is not fully ascertained.

which David Ross—second in line as heir-apparent of Balnagown, and obviously of near kin to John, last Lord of the Isles—was taken bound, under money penalties, to marry a daughter of Hector MacLean of Lochbuie.   Since the confirmation bears date 30 June 1494, more than nineteen years after that of the original Indenture, this deed must have been executed at a period when the contracting parties were of tender years.   Even apart from this point, all individuality was completely ignored; David (son of Alexander, and grandson of 'Johnne of Rosse of Balnago') being bound to marry Margaret, or (failing her) Christian, or some other daughter of Hector MacLean. Moreover, in case David should fail, the obligation to marry one of these girls devolved upon his younger brother Hugh, or 'quhat vthir sone that sall happin to be aire to the said Alexr. of Rosse.'   The whole arrangement was thus a business transaction, its object relating to property, altogether regardless of the more personal interests concerned.

It seems noteworthy that the Garmoran territory—comprising Moydart, Arisaig, Morar, and Knoydart—together with the islands of Barra and South Uist, are to this day the main strongholds of the Roman Catholic faith in Scotland; a fact which shows the influence of a chieftain as associated with conservatism of creed on the part of his clansmen.   This becomes all the more significant when we find that these lands virtually include the entire possessions of Clan Ranald from the fourteenth until nearly the middle of the nineteenth century; although the island of Barra, and Boisdale in South Uist, had been transferred in 1427 [1] by Alexander, third Lord of the Isles, to 'Gilleownan Rodrici Murchardi Makneill.'   Glengarry, another district noted for its adherence to Roman Catholicism, was also held by a branch of Clan Ranald.   This persistence of 'the old faith' is still further remarkable since all the chiefs of Clan Ranald, after Ranald MacDonald who died in 1776, have been Protestants.

---

[1] *Reg. Mag. Sig.*, confirmation of 12 Nov. 1495.

The various crown-charters—chiefly noted from *The Register of the Great Seal of Scotland*—which refer to the lands of North Uist, are not seldom expressed in terms of direct contradiction to each other. In particular, during the period between 1542 and 1618, North Uist was claimed by Clan MacLeod of Dunvegan and Harris as against the MacDonalds of Clan Huistein; both sides being dispossessed under contrary charters, a state of affairs evidently due to alternating influence at court.

With regard to the conditions embodied in these grants from the crown, there is one peculiar clause, stipulating for the culture of trees, which we do not find in reference to North Uist before 17 August 1596 (*Reg. Mag. Sig.*). This provision is copied from a Linlithgowshire grant of 18 July 1595 (*Ibid.*), being again quoted in Uist charters of 20 July 1610, 21 July 1614, and 12 March 1618. In full, it runs: ' necnon habendo bonum largum hortum bene fossatum et septum cum esculis (*hauthorne*), salicibus (*sauch*), alnis (*aller*), tremulis (*esp*), cum fraxinorum (*asch*) plantatione, platanorum (*plane*), et ulmorum (*elme*) ad ratam dicte assedationis, viz. pro merca argenti tres arbores, pro completo circuitu hortorum ; cum seminatione mericarum (*brwme*), sustentatione nemorum et lucorum per fossationem et *lie haning* ; et ad seminand. canapem et linum extra hortos caulium et non infra.' While the object was excellent, the result in the Uists and Benbecula proved a complete failure, if indeed any serious attempt was made to fulfil the stipulations imported thither from a very different locality. Although the clause reads well, *ore rotundo*, it was beyond the power, even of a crown ordinance, to compete successfully with the gales of the Outer Hebrides.

It may appear venturesome, with only a slight knowledge of the Norse and Gaelic languages, to include a chapter upon the Place-Names of North Uist and their meanings. These, however, are by no means suggested as final, but rather for the purpose of serving as a basis from which more definite results may be attained ; and the writer is indebted for much practical assistance to friends of recognised

authority upon the subject.   There is nothing more easy to criticise than
a list of such derivations ; and conversely, few tasks seem harder than
that of reaching a fair standard of accuracy in dealing with new ground.

The Gaelic tongue, with its varying dialects and numerous gram-
matical inflections, has given much difficulty.   Upon this point we are
tempted to record the procedure of an author, himself unfamiliar with
Gaelic, who had occasion to quote from documents in that language.
His method was to take four or five exact copies of any troublesome
passage and submit these to independent experts, then striking an
average from the replies obtained.   After all, this plan had its advan-
tages, since, if a majority of specialists agreed they were probably
in the right.

With regard to place-names, an absolutely uniform treatment
seemed impracticable, and the compromise has been made of adopting,
as a rule,[1] the form in which they appear upon the six-inch Ordnance
map, which generally coincides with the spelling in ordinary use.
Even this map is not quite consistent, often giving the Anglicised
'Ben,' 'Craig,' 'Garry,' or 'Knock,' and elsewhere the correct vernacular equivalent.   Perhaps no compromise can satisfy the exact
scholar, although he will admit that to print, and consequently to
index, Uist as *Uibhist*, and Sleat as *Slèttr* or *Slèibhte* (according to its
derivation, whether from the Norse or Gaelic) would be most objection-
able, besides laying many a trap for the innocent lowlander.   All
that can be expected of the *Sasunnach* (this word itself being a pitfall)
is to adopt the recognised form, and in dealing with root-words to
follow one authority throughout,—in the present case MacBain's
Etymological Dictionary of the Gaelic Language (Inverness, 1896),
supplemented by MacLeod and Dewar's *Dictionary of the Gaelic
Language* (Edin., 1893).

It is interesting to note that many words are almost identical
in the Norse and Gaelic languages.   For example, the Norse *ey, gerði,
ajá, hólmr, hóp, klettr, kví, sker, vaðill,* and *vágr* are represented in

---

[1] The Gaelic accents are omitted, except in the case of words for which italic type is used.

Gaelic by *eilean, gearraidh, geo, tolm, ob, cleit, cuithe, sgeir, faodhail,*
and *bàgh*; the loan in all these cases being evidently from the Norse.
It is quite otherwise with the Gaelic *àiridh* (old Irish, *áirge*) or
'shieling,' which was borrowed by the Norsemen in the form of *-erg*
and afterwards corrupted into *-ary*.   The true Norse word for 'shieling' is *setr*, modified by the Hebrideans into *shader*, while in Orkney
the original form is closely retained as *setter*.   With hardly any
exception, two rules may be followed in this district of mixed tongues.
First, that bi-lingual derivatives, apart from pleonasms, are to be
rigidly avoided; and second, that in Gaelic (as explained on p. 11,
note 1) the generic or 'substantival' element almost invariably forms
the prefix, and the qualifying or 'adjectival' portion the suffix,
whereas a directly opposite arrangement prevails in the Icelandic or
old Norse language.   Thus we have in North Uist the precisely
equivalent place-names, *Balnacille* and *Kirkibost*; while the Gaelic
beinn, eilean, and *loch,* nearly always come first, as distinguished from
the Norse terminations in *-fjall*, (or *-val*), *-ey*, and *-vatn*.

Until the close of the fifteenth century little is known as to separate
holdings in North Uist, with the perhaps doubtful exception of
Balranald, which is said to have remained in the direct line of Clan
Gorrie (descendants of John of Islay and Amie MacRuari) for two or
three centuries from about the year 1400, its name recording that of
Ranald (son of Godfrey) who died in 1440.

The Clan Donald (vol. iii., Inverness, 1904) gives, however, much
information concerning the occupants of lands from *ca.* 1500.   In one
case—that of Boreray—a branch of the MacLeans succeeded in lineal
descent from 1498 (or even earlier) to so recent a date as 1865.
Griminish, with Scolpaig, can be accounted for, in a family of Mac-
Donalds, for nearly three hundred years from *ca.* 1500; and Oransay,
under the MacQueens, from 1619 until at least 1718.   The not uncommon Hebridean tack of 'three lives and three nineteens' goes a
long way in explanation of this continuity of tenure, the average term
of such a lease being about a hundred and forty years.

There are also found combinations of widely separate lands included under the same tack. For instance, Boreray and Grimsay—at the northern and southern extremities of North Uist—were held togeth r; while Oransay (near Trumisgarry, North Uist) was coupled with the salmon fishings of Kilmartin in Trotternish, Skye. In like manner, until about 1850, the island of Ronay formed a grazing pendicle of Baleshare, while Knock-Cuien was similarly attached to Carinish, and the hill of Burrival to Hougary. The south side of Loch Eford was then equally shared by the crofters of Knockline, Balmore, and Knockintorran (all in the Paible district), its north side being apportioned between various farms and townships; viz.,—part of Cainish to Balamartin, the remainder of Cainish and all Airidh Ghocmain to Scolpaig, Sponish to Baleloch, Breinish to Balelone, and Langass to Tighary and Hosta.

Wadsets take a somewhat prominent place in the tenancy of North Uist during the seventeenth and eighteenth centuries. A wadsetter held the position of a bondholder, though apparently in most cases occupying the lands upon which money had been advanced by him; while, on the other hand, there does not seem to be a single record of fore-closure, or any provision for that contingency. The wadset thus practically amounted to a loan by the tenant, in return for which he sat free of rent, apart from a nominal feu-duty, until the capital sum was repaid.

Not the least interesting of the results yielded by the excavation of ancient inhabited sites, has been the discovery of several structures —at Machair Leathann, Cnoc a' Comhdhalach, and Eilean Maleit—representing a little known variety of Earth-House. These are circular, with an internal arrangement of radial partition walls, of which the only example previously on record was that described by Captain Thomas at Ushinish, South Uist.

Of the eighty-six Duns or pre-historic forts enumerated in Chapter VI., hardly one is at all doubtful as to character. Other sites, less definitely vouched, receive merely incidental notice, though among them are several which almost certainly deserve to be accorded a better status.   Our list includes no fewer than seventy island-forts; each, as a rule, provided with a causeway from the neighbouring shore, while in exceptional cases it would seem that the only access was by means of a boat.   The causeways show considerable divergence in type, and most of them have evidently been submerged to the extent of 12 or 18 inches, though others stand at about the normal surface of the loch.   It was of special interest to find seven of these approaches interrupted by structural gaps, obviously arranged so as to give additional security.   Again, and no doubt with a similar purpose, the causeways display much irregularity of outline, in general taking a curvilinear form, but sometimes that of a zig-zag, or of a double curve shaped like the letter 'S.'

The typical Broch is represented in North Uist by at least five examples, and it seems highly probable that others might yet be revealed by more thorough investigation.

It would appear that some of the ancient forts continued in occasional if not regular use as dwellings to a distinctly later period in the Outer Hebrides than elsewhere.   According to tradition, three Duns in North Uist—those of Scolpaig, Steingarry, and Aonghuis— were occupied about the years 1505 to 1520; Dun an Sticir serving as a temporary refuge ca. 1601-1602.   Dun Ban, in Loch Caravat near Carinish, the only Hebridean fort which we know to have lime-cemented walls, may also date, even as to its construction, from comparatively modern times.

As to methods of warfare, we learn incidentally that archery was practised in North Uist ca. 1520, and at the Battle of Carinish— fought in May 1601—the bow and arrow, together with the sword, seem to have been the only weapons employed.

Of the Sand-hill sites, perhaps the most important is that at Udal near Ard a' Bhorain; though specimens of primitive tools or ornaments, fashioned of bone, horn, and bronze, are also to be found in other parts of North Uist where like conditions prevail, more especially on the north and west shores. It seems probable that several of these localities were casually inhabited throughout many centuries, their occupation no doubt overlapping with the Duns in point of antiquity, and on the other hand persisting until some not very remote period.

The distinctively Pagan remains in North Uist are confined to burials and monuments associated therewith. In this class are four or five Stone Circles, and eighteen or twenty Chambered Cairns and Long Megalithic Cists, including several massive cairns which retain much of their original character and are generally known in the Outer Hebrides under the local name of 'Barp.' Among the smaller cairns are a few which must be referred to Viking times in the category of boat-burials. Notice is also taken of several cup-marked rocks and loose stones, in one locality situated close to a Holy Well, whether or not these cups may have had an earlier and independent pagan origin.

The parish of North Uist has been well provided with ecclesiastical buildings, among them apparently a monastery and a nunnery (upon Shillay and Ceann Iar in the Heisker group), five or six churches which bear the special name of *Teampull*, and at least a dozen other chapels or cells, apart from two or three burial-grounds now without any trace or tradition of a former chapel, though perhaps in each case this once existed.

In a remote island such as North Uist, it is only natural to find a marked contrast between the mediæval and present conditions. To take a single example, the parish now contains fourteen schools; whereas Archibald 'the Clerk' (presumably educated for the Church), guardian to the young chief of Clan Huistein from 1539 to 1545, was unable to write; and James MacDonald of Castle Camus (acting in a similar capacity for the next heir) was equally illiterate, his signature being recorded in 1576 as 'with my hand at the pen led by W. Cuming, notar-publick, be mi speciale desirit thairto.' We also find, of date 3 March 1566-1567, a contract subscribed in like manner by Donald Gormson, then chief of his clan, 'de mandato dicti Donaldi scribere nescientis manu propria.' This is the more remarkable since Donald

Gormson had spent some years in England, 'verie well entertained by Queen Marie,' and therefore before 1558.

The writer cannot adequately express his gratitude to Dr. Joseph Anderson for invaluable assistance rendered in connection with the whole subject of the present volume; and he must also record sincere thanks to Dr. W. J. Watson, of high authority upon place-names, both Gaelic and Norse. The editors of *The Clan Donald* (an important work, completed in 1904) and Dr. Alex. Carmichael (whose *Carmina Gadelica* contains many notes as to old customs in North Uist) have freely given information upon various difficult points. Acknowledgment is further due to Mr. Angus MacIntyre—formerly U. F. Missionary at Lochmaddy, but now at Pirnmill, Arran—as also to Dr. M. T. Mackenzie, Scolpaig, and Mr. H. H. Mackenzie, Balelone, both of whom are thoroughly familiar with the district. Among other friends who have been most helpful are Mr. A. A. Chisholm, Lochmaddy, and Mr. Peter Morrison, Edinburgh; while Mr. J. B. Mackie, Dunfermline, has kindly assisted by reading the proof-sheets.

ERSKINE BEVERIDGE.

St. Leonard's Hill,
  Dunfermline.

The Publisher would like to thank Mike and Cathleen Russell
for the use of their copy of the original edition.

CONTENTS

CONTENTS

LIST OF ILLUSTRATIONS

MAPS

FULL-PAGE PLATES

d

NORTH UIST

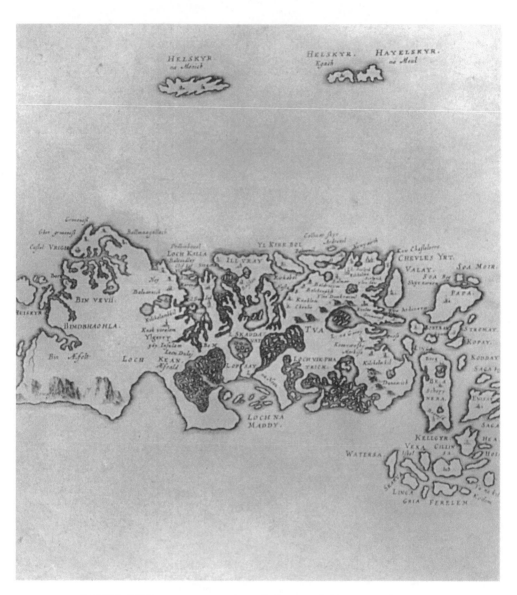

NORTH UIST; REDUCED FROM BLAEU'S ATLAS OF 1654.

FRONTISPIECE.

CHAPTER I

TOPOGRAPHICAL

NORTH UIST occupies a central position in the Outer Hebrides,[1] that continuous chain of islands which lies off the west coast of Scotland ; the whole extending from the Butt of Lewis to Barra Head in a total length of nearly 130 miles, and popularly known under the single designation of 'The Long Island.'

Together with its subsidiary islets, North Uist forms a self-contained parish in the county of Inverness, and has an area of 103,274 acres, the main island alone comprising 86,856 acres.[2] This is bounded upon the west and north-west by the Atlantic Ocean ; on the north and north-east by the Sound of Harris ; on the east by the Little Minch (there a channel about fifteen miles in breadth) ; and upon the south, separating it from Benbecula,[3] by a shallow but wide and complicated strait, studded with islets, and fordable at low water.

The main island measures in its extreme dimensions some eighteen miles east and west, by twelve miles north and south ; averaging however not more than about eleven miles in each direction.

Among the more important of the numerous islands associated with North Uist are Boreray, in the Sound of Harris, at the distance of barely a mile ; Ronay, situated half a mile south of Eaval ; and the

---

[1] Mentioned as *Hebudes* by the elder Pliny, and Ἔβουδαι by Ptolemy ; the *Inis Cat* or *Innse Gall* of Irish annalists, and *Suðreyjar* (southern isles) of the Norse Sagas. The 'ri' in *Hebrides* is understood to have originated in a copyist's error for 'u,' much in the same manner as *Ioua* took the form of *Iona* and *Mons Graupius* became *Mons Grampius* (Sir Herbert Maxwell's *Scottish Land-Names*, p. 52). 'Inis Cat' probably bears some relation to Caithness—the Norse *Kata-nes*, or 'point of the Catti,' a tribe whose name also survives in *Cataibh*, the Gaelic term for Sutherland.

[2] These figures are taken from the official 'Book of Reference' to the 25-inch Ordnance Survey Map, and include, for the whole parish, 8000 acres covered by fresh-water lochs, in addition to nearly 20,000 acres of foreshore and tidal waters.

[3] A large island, formerly a separate parish, but now included in that of South Uist.

A

Heisker or Monach group, lying out in the Atlantic, eight miles due west from Baleshare.

In addition to these are thirteen less independent island-annexes, each still occupied by one or more families,[1] but all of them insulated only at high water, being accessible by easy fords up to half-tide.

This class includes :—

EILEAN LIERAVAY, a little west from Lochmaddy pier, and connected with the peninsula of Stromban by a massive causeway or *stairseach*.

GRIMSAY, situated half-way across the precarious 'North Ford'[2] which leads to Benbecula. Grimsay is a low-lying island, boggy and somewhat unfertile.

SEANABAILY nearly adjoins the north-east corner of Grimsay, of which, although the two are distinctly separated at high water, it is usually considered as forming part.

The five islets next mentioned are all situated (together with many others of less extent) in the same Ford, to the north and west of Grimsay. These, in their semi-isolated condition, have a peculiarly quaint appearance, capped as they are by a few scattered cottages.

EILEAN STEAPHAIN lies nearest the shore of North Uist proper, off Ard a' Mhaide, the south-west extremity of Knock-Cuien. This islet is unnamed upon the Ordnance map, which, on the other hand, quite erroneously gives the title of *Eilean Steaphain* to the outer portion of Cailternish—a peninsula, not an island—directly opposite Seanabaily. South of the true Eilean Steaphain are

EILEAN LEATHANN, and

GARBH-EILEAN ; while south again of this latter is

EILEAN A' GHIORR, easily recognisable by a large conical mound near its centre.

EILEAN NA H-AIRIDH, the last of this group, lies at the west end of Grimsay, exactly half-way across the North Ford.

---

[1] In nine cases literally by one or two families, although Grimsay and Baleshare have each about three hundred inhabitants.

[2] This serves, unless during very stormy weather, as part of a regular thoroughfare between the islands of North and South Uist. First comes the 'North Ford,' with its devious route of fully three miles from Carinish to Gramisdale in Benbecula, followed by five miles of road across the last-mentioned island to Creagorry, and thence continuing for another mile through the deeper 'South Ford' to the shore of South Uist.

SEANABAILY and RONAY, from Eilean a' Ghiorr.

LOCH IOSAL AN DUIN and SOUND OF HARRIS.

Turning now to the west side of North Uist, we there find a range of three islands extending in line at no great distance from the shore, so as to occupy a total length of about three miles.   These are—

BALESHARE, with ILLERAY, sometimes regarded as separate islands, although in reality but one.   The original name for the whole was Illeray, a title now applied only to the north end of Baleshare :

VOROGAY : and

KIRKIBOST.   This latter is approached by the West Ford, regarded as the most dangerous of its class.

Two other tidal islands lie off the north coast ;—

VALLAY, opposite Griminish and Malaclett; and

ORANSAY, on the mid-north; the largest of seven islands in North Uist which bear this name.

Were an attempt made to enumerate the whole of the islands in the parish, this list might be extended a hundred-fold and still be incomplete.   All round the coast-line, but especially towards the north and east, are scattered innumerable rocky islets, uninhabited and uninhabitable, unless in some cases by a few black-faced sheep of hardy breed.   In the Atlantic Ocean, eight miles out from Griminish Point [1] (the north-western extremity of North Uist), are two very conspicuous islands, a mile apart, and known as Haskeir and Haskeir Eagach, the latter being composed of five bare rocks with deep-water channels between.   Among the smaller rocks those which present most individuality of character are Maddy More, and Maddy Gruamach, at the mouth of Loch Maddy, to which they give its name, literally ' Loch of the dogs.'   Both consist of dark columnar basalt; Maddy More with a ' cliff 85 feet high, showing the perpendicular face inshore and a green sloping face to seaward,' although, on the contrary, under the water-surface ' the outside is steep-to, but the inner side runs off shoal for one-third of a cable,' [2] while Maddy Gruamach, 600 yards to the south-west, is of very similar appearance. [3]

From a geological point of view, North Uist, in common with the whole Long Island, belongs to the Archæan formation, representing

[1] The St. Kilda group lies forty miles west of Griminish Point, the two larger islands being clearly visible from North Uist in fine weather.

[2] *Sailing Directions for the West Coast of Scotland*, 1885, part 1, p. 156.

[3] Near the north side of the entrance to Lochmaddy Bay is a small flat rock known as Maddy Beg.

the oldest rocks of Scotland. Although gneiss largely predominates, argillaceous schist also occurs throughout nearly the whole east shore, interspersed by numerous veins of trap, while Maddy More and Maddy Gruamach are remarkable as the only rocks of columnar basalt which exist either on this coast or in any part of the Long Island. These eruptive intrusions of the Tertiary period were no doubt contemporary with the still greater volcanic activity displayed in the neighbouring island of Skye, to which, indeed, it seems most probable that their origin is directly due.

The central portion of the Long Island, more especially North Uist and Benbecula, show a general configuration which may be described as unique. To quote Dr. Macculloch,[1] in particular reference to the southern and eastern sections of North Uist, 'This tract, comprising nearly half the area of the island, is apparently so equally occupied by land and water that the eye can scarcely determine which of the two predominates. . . . Such is the surface of the flat eastern land of North Uist; a brown, peaty, and boggy tract so interspersed with lakes and rocks as to be nearly impassable, and producing a scanty and wretched herbage for a few animals during the driest months of summer.' While this statement fully applies to the greater portion of the island, it must be added that the case is quite otherwise in the more sandy and pastoral districts adjoining the north and west shores, where a dry summer receives a doubtful welcome from the crofters.

Although so much of its surface is flat and ramified by large patches of water, North Uist possesses several ranges of hills, these lying chiefly towards the north and east, but also near its centre. The highest elevation is Eaval (1138 feet) at the south-east, while midway between this and the village of Lochmaddy are North and South Lee (823 and 920 feet respectively). Towards the northern shore are Crogary na Hoe (502 feet), Beinn Mhor (625 feet), Crogary Mor (588 feet), and Maari (562 feet); while Marrogh (552 feet), Beinn na h-Aire (503 feet), and Marrival (757 feet), in the central portion of the island, exhaust the list of hills over 500 feet in height, although several others nearly approach that elevation. It may be further noted that, at Balranald, a hillock of only 72 feet is dignified by the title of Beinn a' Bhaile.

[1] *A Description of the Western Islands of Scotland*, London, 1819, vol. i. p. 119.

The climate of the Outer Hebrides is more equable than that of any other part of Great Britain, the temperature ranging between very moderate limits throughout the whole year, while snow and ice seldom remain beyond a few days at a time.[1] For the west coast, the rainfall of this district can hardly be considered excessive, a forty-five years' average showing 52 inches at Lochmaddy, as compared with Fort-William 78·6, Stornoway 48·6, and Dumfries 40·2 inches, over the same period.

Apart from the large proportion of water-logged soil, the most unfavourable characteristic of North Uist is probably its exposure to a nearly continuous series of storms during the winter and spring months, gale after gale then arising; a condition of matters which too frequently recurs when summer weather might be expected. Mainly to this cause, but in some degree also to the salt-laden atmosphere, is no doubt attributable the almost total absence of trees not only throughout the Long Island, but even among the Inner Hebrides, with a few local exceptions in sheltered parts of Skye and Mull. Yet in former times, and presumably under other climatic conditions, it is certain that the oak, fir, and birch have flourished in North Uist, as is proved by the frequent disclosure of their remains within the peat. These are said to be specially common at Garry Tighary, and quite recently the writer noted several roots of trees in a moss-hole by the roadside at Loch Eford, there resting upon rock at least six feet below the present natural surface.

Such remains must however be regarded as accidental, having themselves contributed in but small degree to the formation of peat-bogs, which are mainly due to the decay of mosses, rushes, and other semi-aquatic plants. It may be added that the peat of North Uist, often from ten to twenty feet in depth, is of very compact texture, being in a state of extreme decomposition

[1] With regard to the Atlantic coasts of both Scotland and Ireland, it is a well-attested fact that the summer isotherms cross the British Islands in parallels east and west, with a gradual northward fall of temperature; while, on the other hand, the winter isotherms run approximately north and south, falling at that season from west to east. This noticeable elevation of the winter temperature on our western shores is evidently due to the impact of the Gulf-stream. West Indian shells, beans, and seeds, together with cocoa-nuts (even in bunches), bamboos, and Sargasso weed from the Equatorial Sea, are (some of them frequently, others occasionally) cast ashore upon the west coast of North Uist, while the arrival of at least one turtle is chronicled about the year 1900. In *Sailing Directions for the West Coast of Scotland*, these tropical seeds are specified as including *Guilandina bonduc*, *Dolichos ı ens*, and *Mimosa scandens*.

at its lower parts, and therefore possessing excellent qualities as a fuel.[1]

Upon the northern shore of Vallay, in two small bays nearly a mile apart,[2] the roots and branches of trees may usually still be found embedded within a layer of peat, disclosed here and there through the continually shifting sands. This feature is observable down to low-water mark, and even slightly beyond that point, and certainly testifies to great changes both in climate and in the relative levels of land and sea. Without pressing any extreme theory, the fact remains that for forty miles out to St. Kilda, the ocean is comparatively shallow, nowhere exceeding a depth of about seventy fathoms. 'The stack of Rockall, some 180 miles west of St. Kilda, rises from near the verge of the submerged platform on which the British Islands rest. A few miles to the west of it the sounding line goes down abruptly from one hundred to two hundred fathoms, and thereafter with swift descent down to the abysmal depths of the Atlantic.'[3]

---

[1] Macculloch's *Description, etc.*, vol. i. pp. 127-131. Captain Thomas (*Proc. Soc. Antiq. Scot.*, vol. vii. p. 194) favoured a theory that peat accumulates at the rate of about one inch in fifteen years, which would give a date of *ca.* 800-900 A.D. for the original erection of the Stone Circle and Avenues at Callernish in Lewis, where peat had formed to a depth of 5½ feet. Its rate of growth however is undoubtedly more variable than constant, and especially so in different localities; while in any case a much greater antiquity must be assigned to the Callernish Stones as representing a monument of the Bronze Age. At p. 5 of *The Sailing Directions, etc.* (already quoted), a period of about fifteen centuries is suggested for the growth of peat in North Uist.

[2] *Camas Mór*, and *Bàgh nan Craobhag* or 'bay of small trees.' At this latter spot the writer has often seen trunks and branches lying in peat at a level about twelve feet below high-water mark. These measured up to a diameter of about fourteen inches, and apparently represent the birch. It is to be noted that elsewhere the island of Vallay now contains no peat, and is even practically without heather.

At Kilpheder, on the Atlantic shore of North Uist, a solid layer of peat also shows under the stones on the beach near low-water mark. The old *Statistical Account*, vol. x. pp. 373-374, refers to Pabbay island in the Sound of Harris, 'where the sea ebbs out in spring tides to a great distance, there are visible, at the very lowest ebb, large trunks of trees; the roots of which, spread out widely and variously, are fixed in black moss, which might be dug for peat to a great depth. Nor is this peculiar to Harris. The same, and other phenomena of the like kind, are observable along the whole sandy shore of the Long Island.' See also the *New Statistical Account*, Inverness-shire, p. 191, for similar conditions in South Uist. The wide Sound of Harris (separating North Uist from Harris) is both shallow and dangerous, studded with numerous islets, the whole Long Island—from the Butt of Lewis to Barra Head—having evidently been continuous at a period not remote as viewed from the geological standpoint. It must be added, however, that there is no proof that these changes have occurred within the time during which any part of Scotland was inhabited by man.

[3] W. C. Mackenzie's *History of the Outer Hebrides*, Paisley, 1903, p. 569. The existence of the 'Maury' or 'Telegraph' plateau, reaching almost across the Atlantic from Ireland to Newfoundland, may here be noted; as also the fact that a gneiss very similar to that of the Long Island reappears in Labrador, Newfoundland, and at the mouth of the St. Lawrence, whence indeed this geological formation derives its name as 'Laurentian.'

Dr. James Croll,[1] endeavouring to account for not one but several periods of partial submergence and elevation of the British Isles (together with the rest of Northern Europe) during the Glacial epoch, holds that these were due to an increase in the eccentricity of the earth's orbit, which caused 'a simple oscillation of sea-level resulting from the displacement of the earth's centre of gravity by the transference of the ice-cap from the southern to the northern hemisphere'; and further that 'when the country was covered with ice, the land stood in relation to the sea at a lower level than at present, and that the continental periods or times when the land stood in relation to the sea at a higher level than now were the warm interglacial periods, when the country was free of snow and ice, and a mild and equable condition of climate prevailed. . . . The great submergence, as well as the great elevation or continental period, occurred during the earlier or more severe part of the Glacial epoch, and as the climate grew less severe these changes became of less extent, till we find them terminating in our submerged forests and 25-foot raised beach. . . . At the time when the ice would be on the southern hemisphere during the Glacial epoch, and the northern hemisphere enjoying a warm and equable climate, the sea-level would be several hundred feet lower than at present, the North Sea would probably be dry land, and Great Britain and Ireland joined to the continent, thus opening up a pathway from the continent to our island.'

To apply the above statements locally to North Uist (though also to Great Britain in general) it would follow that the 25-feet or 30-feet raised beaches, to be observed in many parts of the west coast of Scotland, indicate a period of greater cold succeeded by a comparatively modern and milder cycle; while the existence of submerged peat-mosses at the present day upon the shores of North Uist—notably at Vallay and Kilpheder—testify to a long past epoch of still more genial and equable climatic conditions than now prevail.[2]

---

[1] *Geological Magazine*, 1874. The facts, as to the succession of alternating glacial and warm interglacial periods, are universally admitted, although Dr. Croll's cosmic explanation is not so completely endorsed.

[2] In Dr. Croll's *Discussions on Climate and Cosmology* (Edin., 1885, pp. 185-188) it is reasonably asserted that during inter-glacial periods the climate was (1) more equable than at present as regards local variation between the summer and winter temperatures (perhaps no warmer during summer, but certainly much more genial in winter); that throughout all regions

Dr. Croll's theory, and the fact that submerged forests still exist in the ocean off the western shores of the Long Island, equally point to former circumstances more suitable for the growth of trees, and this in two separate directions : firstly, as testifying to a milder climate, and secondly, as inferring a considerable westward extension of the coast-line. This latter feature would in more or less degree involve a 'lost continent' with perhaps even the legendary hunting-ground of a 'Princess of Harris,'[1] which is said to have reached from Harris (and therefore presumably also from North Uist) so far out as St. Kilda, a distance of forty or fifty miles.

The whole subject is a most difficult one, though we may add that ascertained facts, alike from archæological and topographical points of view, would prove no appreciable change to have occurred in the present shore-level of North Uist as compared with that of about a thousand years ago. Such is emphatically the case from the period of Norse occupation onwards, as evidenced by descriptive place-names (particularly those of islands) and the causeways to island-forts in tidal waters, whatever conditions may have prevailed during some far distant era of pre-historic times.

Quite apart from pre-historic changes which have occurred in the relative levels of land and ocean, the continual drifting of sand before the wind has been a powerful factor as affecting the surface conditions near the west and north shores of North Uist ; while under water, off the west coast, an even more important influence must be ascribed to the action of the tides and ocean currents in scooping out the sea-bottom at some parts, and depositing it elsewhere in the form of sand-banks. Both processes exert themselves to-day, and will naturally persist throughout all time.

Reference has already been made to the peculiar interlacement of land and water which characterises the main portion of North Uist, a feature due in almost equal degree to the multitude of fresh-water lochs and to complicated arms of the sea, which indent the east coast of the island. Two of these latter, Loch Maddy and

—sub-tropical, temperate, and polar,—(2) a greater uniformity of climate then existed, not differing so much with latitude as now ; these conditions resulting in (3) a general mildness or comparative absence of high winds, together with a higher mean temperature ; and (4) more humidity of atmosphere.

[1] This tradition is still preserved in North Uist, a very similar legend being also quoted by Martin Martin in *A Late Voyage to St. Kilda*, London, 1698, p. 23.

Loch Eford, are especially large, each penetrating as far as five or six miles.

Loch Maddy is both wide and tortuous, containing a very labyrinth of islets and with a shore-line two hundred miles in length.[1] Loch Eford, on the other hand, is comparatively straight and narrow, running due east and west, so as nearly to intersect the main island, leaving an isthmus of less than four hundred yards at its inner extremity.

Among the innumerable fresh-water lochs of North Uist, the largest and most eccentric in outline is Loch Scadavay,[2] a widely branching sheet of water more than four miles long, yet hardly anywhere exceeding half a mile in breadth. This statement, however, conveys no real idea of its extraordinary shape, which may be likened to that of an octopus furnished with a profusion of additional limbs.

Along part of the north shore of North Uist, and almost continuously on its western side, the soil and other conditions are entirely different from those of the boggy tracts previously described, being (in common with much of the Atlantic margin of the Outer Hebrides) of a flat, sandy, and comparatively fertile nature, in a more or less restricted belt which follows the coast line. It is consequently in these districts that the bulk of the population and almost the only cultivated parts of the island are to be found.

Upon the Atlantic side there is no safe harbour, owing chiefly to its exposed situation, but also to the shallow sea abounding in reefs and skerries. The east coast of North Uist, off the Little Minch, is provided with several excellent and commodious anchorages, of which that in Loch Maddy is the most frequented; Cheese Bay, at the mouth of the Sound of Harris, not affording accommodation for other than the smaller craft; while Loch Eford, although visited weekly by a steamer from Glasgow, has so narrow an entrance as to be avoided by strangers.

The village of Lochmaddy is practically the only inhabited spot on the east side of North Uist, and, though possessing but a small population, is the seat of local government for the southern half of the Long Island, that is, for the whole district extending from North

---

[1] Macculloch's *Description*, etc., vol. i. p. 120.
[2] Covering 1135 acres, and locally said to contain 365 islets.

Harris to Barra Head.   Lochmaddy, in addition to its fine natural
harbour and a daily steamer from Oban, is thus furnished with many
of the resources of civilisation, including a public water-supply, a good
hotel, a bank, and—less enviably—a court-house, prison, and large
poorhouse, although it is satisfactory to note that the last three are
in very little demand.   The whole parish contains a comparatively
stationary population of about four thousand, some three-fourths
belonging to the main island itself.

Apart from its marked individuality in general appearance, North
Uist has little to offer by way of natural curiosities.   Notice must,
however, be taken of two sea-caves, both of them near the north-west
corner of the island.   The more remarkable is *Sloc a' choire*, or 'pit
of the cauldron,' situated in the north side of Tighary Point, and
directly facing the ocean.   In its roof, at a distance of about ten yards
from the edge of the cliff, an opening has been worn through the
upper portion of the rock in the form of a perpendicular shaft measuring from six to eight yards across, and during westerly storms the
Atlantic rollers here break with so much force as to spout upwards
through this vent to a height of more than two hundred feet.[1]   Local
tradition adds a prophecy to the effect that the sea-arch which covers
the outer portion of *Sloc a' choire* is destined to give way beneath the
weight of a newly married couple.

The second cave is of much greater extent, completely traversing
the neck of Griminish Point in a length of nearly 150 yards.   This is
known both as *Sloc Roe* (in the vernacular, *sloc-a-rodha*) and 'the
Pigeon Cave,' a name clearly derived from the many rock-pigeons
which frequent it, obtaining access not only at both ends but also
through a wide gap in its roof towards the north, where masses of soil
and rock have been washed away.

From Tighary Point northwards, the west coast of North Uist is
bordered by a range of cliffs, for the most part of no great height,
but interrupted by a succession of narrow and precipitous gullies,
each locally bearing the distinctive name of *Geo*;[2] as, for example,

---

[1] *New Statistical Account*, Inverness-shire, p. 161.   Much to his regret, the writer has never
had an opportunity of witnessing this phenomenon.

[2] The Icelandic *gjá*, 'a cleft or chasm'; one of the numerous loan-words which might be
quoted as showing the permanent influence exerted upon the Gaelic language by five centuries of
Norse supremacy.   Although *sloc* is the original Gaelic equivalent of *geo*, and both forms occur
close together in North Uist, it is noticeable that *geo* is much the commoner of the two, being
marked upon the Ordnance map in connection with no fewer than nineteen separate places at the

SLOC A' CHOIRÈ, TIGHARY POINT.

GEO NAN CALMAN, TIGHARY.

Fiarigeo, Geo an Fhàraidh, Geo na Tairgne, Geo Fionnaghal, Geo nan Calman, Geo an t-Simileir, etc., etc. It seems worthy of special remark that although *Fiarigeo* and *Geo an Fhàraidh* closely adjoin each other, with names which would at first sight appear to be phonetically related, there are good grounds for suggesting a wide difference both in their meaning and derivation. Thus *Fiarigeo* must be taken as of purely Norse origin, representing *fjara gjá* or 'beach-gully'; while *Geo an Fhàraidh* is Gaelic for 'gully of the ladder,'[1] in obvious allusion to a partly artificial slope in its cliff which was used within comparatively recent times as an access for conveying seaweed from the rocks below.

Two of this class—*Geo a' Chleibh* below the cattlefold at Bala-martin, and *Geo a' Steall* immediately to the north of *Geo nan Calman*—are also reported as 'spouting-caves,' although upon a much smaller scale than *Sloc a' choire,* and without any landward vent.

Mineral wells no doubt exist in many parts of North Uist, although only two can here be recorded from personal observation, these including a chalybeate spring near the roadside to the north of Crogary Beg, and a sulphur-well in the marsh west of Vallay Loch. At a shieling-mound close to the southern base of Marrival is *Tobar Chuithairidh,* known locally also as *Tobar an déideidh,* with reference to its supposed efficacy as a cure for toothache; while still another well, situated just above high-water mark at Vallaquie, may also be mentioned on account of its bearing the peculiar name of *Tobar Di-domhnuich* or 'Sunday well.'[2]

The marine zoology of North Uist,—and especially that of the western shore, tempered as it is by the gulf-stream,—exhibits a

north-west corner of this island, while side by side with these are fifteen others, all of them un-marked, but bearing local names which contain the same descriptive title.

Throughout the whole Scottish area the term *geo* (or *geòdh*) is practically confined to the Hebrides, Caithness, and the Orkney and Shetland groups, with a Hebridean range extending so far south as Islay, while it also occurs in the Isle of Man. On the east side of Mingulay, near Barra Head, the Admiralty Chart gives *Slochd chremis Geo,* a clear case of reduplication in bilingual form.

[1] Perhaps most weight ought to be attached to the fact of *geo* serving as a suffix in one case, but as a prefix in the other, an inversion fully explained by the opposite structural forms which characterise the Teutonic and Celtic languages. 'The composition of Norse names differs from that of Gaelic names, in that the specific or qualifying part, which in Gaelic comes after the generic term, is in Norse invariably prefixed to it.'—Dr. W. J. Watson's *Place-Names of Ross and Crom-arty,* Inverness, 1904, p. liv.

[2] Three 'Holy Wells' are also noted in Chapter IX., *postea,* as associated with the chapels at Sand, Carinish, and Ard a' Bhorain.

profusion of zoophytes and mollusca, amongst them some of great
rarity; but the writer is unable to enter into this subject, and would
refer any interested inquirer to a paper contributed by Professor
W. C. McIntosh to the Royal Society of Edinburgh (*Proceedings*,
1865-1866).

In much the same way the botany of the parish must be dismissed
with the remark that the sandy meadows of the north-west present
a gay aspect during the month of June, as regards both quantity and
variety of plant life, to the extent, indeed, of the wild flowers seeming there to predominate over the pasturage.   On the other hand,
it is understood that, speaking generally, no island in the Outer
Hebrides is noteworthy from a botanical point of view,—that is, with
respect to the occurrence of rare plants,—since the flora of the
Long Island (as of the Inner Hebrides) is distinctly non-oceanic in
character, having evidently been carried over a former continuity of
surface from the Scottish mainland during some remote period of
upheaval.

The *Osmunda regalis* is strikingly abundant in some parts,
luxuriating upon many islets in fresh-water lochs, and occasionally
also upon the shores of the latter.   This fern is however very
capricious, being plentiful in several lochs though totally absent from
others not far distant, where the conditions seem otherwise to be
identical.

The honeysuckle and bramble, as also the whin, thrive to some
extent, and the wild rose has been noted in six or seven widely
separate places, these chiefly near the east side of North Uist.   Upon
two island forts *Salix repens* was observed, and upon other two we
were surprised to find the red-currant, although this latter probably
represents a garden escape of old standing; while garlic, angelica, and
the foxglove also occur upon pre-historic sites.

It has already been stated that indigenous tree-life is practically
absent from North Uist in common with the rest of the Outer
Hebrides.   Slight exceptions are afforded by specimens of the moun-
tain ash (never more than about six feet high) growing upon a number
of islands, and also, less frequently, upon the faces of inland cliffs.   In
this last-named position, at Portain and also upon the island of Ronay,
the aspen was found; and under like conditions native ivy flourishes
at the south edge of Eaval.   The alder is somewhat common, and

small patches of juniper show at intervals upon the drier moorland, though nowhere exceeding a height of about three inches.

But at least two place-names—*Beinn na Coille* and *Bàgh nan Craobhag*—record the former existence of woods in North Uist, while tree-roots and hazel-nuts are occasionally disclosed in its peat-bogs.

A fairly level road completely encircles the main island, always keeping near the shore except where it crosses the southern portion between Lochmaddy and Clachan-a-gluip.

From Malaclett to Dusary a supplementary road[1] serves as a short cut across the north-west corner of the island, with a length of about four miles as compared with double that distance by the regular highway, which passes Scolpaig and Tighary.

On a clear day the heights of North Uist command a wide panorama. For example, the writer has from Unival viewed the Monach islands, St. Kilda, Barra, and Skye, while from the summit of Treacklett were visible parts of Harris and Lewis, together with the Flannan Islands or 'Seven Hunters,' distant forty miles to the north.

[1] Known as the 'Committee Road' from its origin as a relief-work during the potato famine about the year 1846.

GEO CEANN A' 'GHEARRAIDH.

BORERAY, LOOKING NORTH.

CHAPTER II

NORTH UIST IN PRE-HISTORIC AND VIKING TIMES

THAT a very early civilisation prevailed in the Outer Hebrides is amply proved by the Chambered-Cairns of Neolithic times, which are not uncommon throughout North Uist, and also by the Stone Circles and other Megalithic remains which there exist. These latter appear to represent a devolution from the still earlier and more massive type, and are generally attributed to the Bronze period, although it is not to be supposed that there was any marked line dividing the Stone and Bronze ages, but rather that the one became merged into the other by a very gradual and imperceptible process of transition.

History is entirely silent with regard to the aboriginal inhabitants of Scotland, and even as to its less primitive occupants up to about the Christian era. There seem however to be good grounds for suggesting that both Britain and Ireland were peopled by a race of Iberian origin long before the arrival of the Celts, and that the Gaelic tongue has been indirectly influenced in its vocabulary and grammar by some non-Aryan language like the Basque. [1]

Dr. John Beddoe [2] refers to 'two or three' strongly contrasted ethnological types as occurring in Lewis :—'There is the large, fair, comely Norse race, said to exist almost pure in the district of Ness, at the north end of the island; the short, thick-set, snub-nosed, dark-haired, often even dark-eyed race, probably aboriginal, and possibly Finnish, whose centre seems to be in Barvas; and the West Highland

[1] Professor Sir John Rhys, in *Proc. Soc. Antiq. Scot.*, vol. xxvi. pp. 305-306; who also (in the same contribution, pp. 307-351) draws a close parallel between the Pictish and Basque languages. Professor A. H. Keane, LL.D., another ethnographical authority of high repute, goes even farther in the same direction, associating the cave-dwellers of the Riviera with the Basques, the Gaulish Pictavi (Pictones), and the British Picts, all of whom he classes as of remote Afro-European or Hamito-Iberian type, speaking languages derived from that Hamitic family of which the nearest surviving representatives are the Basque in Europe and the Berber in Africa. See Professor Keane's *Man : Past and Present*, pp. 459-463, 523-526, Cambridge, 1900; also his *Ethnology*, pp. 378-379, Cambridge, 1901.
[2] *The Races of Britain*, p. 240, Bristol, 1885.

type which has gradually filtered in,' etc. This last we take to be the Gaelic or Celtic element.

Commenting upon the above statement, Mr. W. C. Mackenzie quotes local tradition to the effect that 'a race of low stature—so-called fairies and pigmies—inhabited Lewis in pre-historic times.'[1]

Passing allusion may be made to the fact that, especially in Orkney and Caithness, the Broch (a massive and well-marked type of fort confined, with few exceptions, to the extreme northern and western parts of Scotland) is popularly known as a 'Pictish Tower'; while, in like manner, the title of 'Picts' House' is often applied to the underground structures or Earth-Houses which have a much wider distribution, being common also throughout the eastern counties. Each of these very distinct classes is represented in North Uist by several examples, although there unaccompanied by any local tradition as to Pictish origin; and it must be further admitted that little weight has been given to this suggestion when found current in other districts.

The purpose of the Brochs can be readily understood as providing a secure retreat for both human beings and cattle, but the Earth-Houses show peculiar features which are much more difficult of explanation.

Wherever situated, these Earth-Houses generally present a striking similarity of plan, consisting of a long, low, and narrow gallery which gradually widens and increases in height from the entrance inwards. Dr. Joseph Anderson,[2] in comparing the dimensions of fifteen typical examples in different parts of Scotland, quotes their length as varying from 21 to 80 feet, with an average of 50 feet, and an individual greatest roof-height ranging from 2½ to 8 feet, and averaging 5½ feet. It is usually considered that this class was not built for use as

[1] *History of the Outer Hebrides*, p. xxv.

The Bannatyne Miscellany, vol. iii. p. 33 (1855), reprints a manuscript which at one time belonged to Robert Reid, Bishop of Orkney (who died in September 1558), and which was evidently written about the year 1460. This MS. runs :—

'De Orcadibus Insulis.

' Istas insulas primitus Peti et Pape inhabitabant. Horum alteri scilicet Peti parvo superantes pigmeos statura in structuris urbium vespere et mane mira operantes, meredie vero cunctis viribus prorsus destituti in subterraneis domunculis pre timore latuerunt.'

'Peti' in the above evidently refers to the Picts, and 'Pape' to Priests.

Martin Martin, in *A Description of the Western Islands of Scotland*, 1703, p. 105, mentions the ancient inhabitants of the Hebrides in similar terms, and evidently from the same authority ;— 'It is reported of them that they wrought in the Night time, and rested all Day.' Mr. David MacRitchie elaborates this subject in his *Fians, Fairies, and Picts* (London, 1893).

[2] *Proc. Soc. Antiq. Scot.*, vol. xii. p. 353.

dwellings in the common sense of the term, but rather as store-rooms or hiding-places in case of need. Nevertheless, even upon this footing, when we find at Safester in Shetland an underground gallery 45 feet in length, but measuring only 16 inches across its entrance and 30 inches at the widest part of its interior, with a roof-height nowhere exceeding 30 inches, it seems difficult if not impossible to avoid the conclusion that, whatever its purpose, this was not intended for use as a habitation by men of our ordinary stature.[1] It is believed by some that the 'fairies' or 'brownies' of Celtic folk-lore represent a race inhabiting subterranean dwellings whether in level ground or hillocks, these latter becoming associated with their name as *sìthean* or 'fairy-knolls.'

Although Earth-Houses are usually ascribed to the first four centuries of the Christian era, and several examples yield evidence of occupation during Roman or even post-Roman times,[2] the present writer would be inclined to attribute the origin of this class of ancient constructions to a still earlier period.

Of the various Earth-Houses known to exist in North Uist, particular descriptions, as far as available, are noted in Chapter v., so that no more need here be added, unless to remark that they include at least one which wholly differs from the normal underground gallery type, consisting of a circular chamber about thirty-five feet in diameter and from four and a half to six feet in height. This has evidently been adapted for the express purpose of habitation by a series of cubicles arranged side by side around the outer portion of its area, and separated from each other by short radial walls so as to form compartments about six feet in length; most of them closed towards the central portion of the chamber, but all accessible from a narrow passage which runs next the encircling wall throughout practically its whole circumference.

The Picts themselves, of whom so much has been written and so little is definitely known, were united with the Scots under Kenneth MacAlpin (Kenneth I. of Scotland) in A.D. 844, thereafter becoming entirely absorbed in the Scottish nation, and losing what individuality

---

[1] In Labrador the Eskimo still use a form of underground dwelling termed 'Igloshuak.' This is entered through a narrow passage, about twelve feet long, into a chamber where it is impossible for an ordinary European to stand upright, although the natives, being small in stature, experience no difficulty on this point.

[2] Dr. Joseph Anderson's *Scotland in Pagan Times: The Iron Age*, pp. 298-304.

they had previously possessed as a race.   Just at this period the Norse occupation of the Hebrides begins to be historically recorded, and it seems in every way probable that the disappearance of the Picts as a separate nation was due to two coincident agencies ; namely, that they were crushed out, between (on the one hand) the expansion of the Scottish kingdom, and (on the other) the growing domination of the Vikings, who had then begun to appear in numbers upon our shores.

Allusion has just been made to 'historical records,' and yet it must be confessed that what we do know of the arrival of the early Vikings in the Hebrides has mainly to be derived from the ancient Sagas of Iceland, Norway, and Orkney.   But from these, corroborated as they are by the scanty annals of Scotland and Ireland during the eighth and ninth centuries, it may be affirmed with some certainty that from A.D. 798, if not earlier, the Norsemen had been accustomed to visit and plunder the Hebrides or Sudreys [1] almost every summer, while it is reasonable to suppose that these raids commenced long before the first date which can be specifically quoted.   It is further a matter of fact that from about the year 852, the Sudreys, or parts of them, were ruled by Ketil Flatnef (Flat-nose), son of Bjorn Buna, lord of Sogn, near Bergen in Norway.   Little more is known of Ketil Flatnef, except that he died in the Sudreys not later than A.D. 884, and that his family (notably his daughter Aud Djupaudga, 'the deeply wealthy,' and her children by Olaf the White, King of Dublin) played an important part in the colonisation of Iceland about A.D. 886. Harald Harfagri, King of Norway, visited the Hebrides ca. A.D. 884, and thenceforward these islands remained an appanage of the Norwegian crown until the year 1266, when, as a consequence of the Battle of Largs, they were formally ceded by King Magnus IV. to Alexander III. of Scotland.   During these four centuries—A.D. 884-1266—it is evident that the Norse control was both lax and incomplete, with intervals of partial rebellion, but upon the whole, the Hebrides were throughout that period under Norwegian rule.   This was represented at the very first by subsidiary 'Jarls' who acted as collectors of tribute or 'scatt'; but latterly for nearly three centuries by a succession of outstanding chiefs who received or assumed the

---

[1] This general term of *Suðreyjar* comprehended the whole of our western isles from the Butt of Lewis to Islay.

title of 'King of the Sudreys,' and seem to have been in the position of governors with even greater than vice-regal power, subject to little beyond formal homage and a fixed annual payment as vassals to the Norwegian crown.

In the printed, and therefore comparatively accessible, Sagas (which are more numerous than might be expected) we have found only two distinct references to Uist, with another which is somewhat doubtful, while it must be further kept in mind that the Norse term of 'Vist' or 'Ivist' was a general one, including the separate islands of North Uist, Benbecula, and South Uist, as also probably that of Barra.

Both of these definite notices occur in connection with one of the voyages made by King Magnus Barelegs to the Hebrides (evidently that of A.D. 1093-1094 [1]) ; the first appearing in *Heimskringla edr Noregs Konunga Sögor* [2] as a quotation from Biörn Kreppil-hendi ; and the second in James Johnstone's *Antiquitates Celto-Scandicæ*,[3] upon the authority of another Icelandic 'Scald' or poet, Gisl Illugis-son, who fought under King Magnus at the Isle of Anglesey on his later expedition in A.D. 1098-1099.

Thus we have from Biörn Kreppil-hendi :—

'Lék of Lióðhús fíkjom lim-sorg nær himni ;
(vítt bar ferð á flótta fús) [gaus eldr or húsom] :
ærr skiæoldungr fór eldi Ivist ; buendr misto
(róg-geisla vann ræsir rauðan) lífs ok auðar ;'

translated—'Fire played fiercely to the heavens over Lewis ; he went over Uist with flame ; the yeomen lost life and goods.' [4]

[1] According to the dates affixed by Professor P. A. Munch in *The Chronicle of Man and the Sudreys*, Christiania, 1860, pp. 54-58.
[2] Copenhagen, 1777-1783, vol. iii. p. 209. Written by Snorri Sturluson, who died in 1241, and first printed at Stockholm in 1697.
[3] Copenhagen, 1786, p. 233.
[4] Here quoted from *Corpus Poeticum Boreale*, Oxford, 1883, vol. ii. pp. 243-244, as probably coming nearest to the original ; while, on the other hand, the translation seems unduly compressed, and an alternative may be given from *The Saga Library*, edited by William Morris and Eirikr Magnusson, vol. v. pp. 221-222, as representing the opposite extreme :—

'Wood-sorrow all through Lewis
Played wildly nigh the heavens ;
Wide were the folk flight-eager ;
Fire gushèd forth from houses.
Farèd the king fight-eager
Wide with the flame Vist over ;
The lord wan fight-beam ruddy ;
And life and wealth lost bonders.'

It is with this raid that W. C. Mackenzie (in his *History of the Outer Hebrides*, p. 23), asso-ciates the Lewis tradition of the burning of forests by the Norsemen.

Also from Gisl Illugisson :—

'Tók fyr Skíði, enn Skottar flýðo,
iaofra œgir Ivistar gram :
hafði fylkir, sá-es frami tœði,
Laogmann konung í liði síno ;'

thus rendered—'The king took the lord of Uist off Skye ; the Scots fled ; he kept King Lawman in his company.'[1]

In the text of *Heimskringla*[2] it is further stated :—'þa flýdi Lögmadr undan her oc hvar um eyar, en at lykdom tóko menn Magnus konongs hann med scipsögn manna, þá er hann villdi flýia út til Irlandz'; that is to say, 'Lawman fled away here and there about the islands, but at last King Magnus' men took him, together with his crew, whenas he would flee to Ireland.'[3] This Lagman, 'Ivistar gram,' was the eldest of the three sons of Godred Crowan (King of Man and the Sudreys, who died 1095), and is said to have ruled the northern portion of the Hebrides for seven years, his reign being assigned by Munch to the period from 1089-1096, on the assumption that he had received a delegated authority in the northern isles during his father's lifetime. King Lagman died while on a pilgrimage to Jerusalem, undertaken in self-imposed penance for the cruelty with which he had treated his brother Harald, and was succeeded, though not until after the death of King Magnus Barelegs in 1103, by his youngest brother Olaf Bitling, who reigned over the Sudreys for fifty years, dying in 1153.[4]

Olaf Bitling (also known as Olaf the Red) was murdered in the Isle of Man by his nephew Reginald, who usurped the sovereignty for perhaps less than a year, being deposed in 1154 by the rightful heir, Godred, son of Olaf, who reigned until his death in 1187. Ragnhild,[5] a daughter of Olaf Bitling (or 'the Red'), was married to Somerled Hold (the famous ancestor of the MacDonalds of the Isles), and between Godred[6] and his brother-in-law Somerled was fought, in

---

[1] *Corpus Poeticum Boreale*, vol. ii. pp. 241-242.
[2] Edition of 1777-1783, vol. iii. p. 211.   [3] *The Saga Library*, vol. v. p. 223.
[4] Munch, pp. 4, 54-58, 73.
[5] According to Gregory's *History of the Western Highlands and Islands of Scotland*, Edin., 1836, p. 12, *ca.* A.D. 1140. Somerled is in Gaelic *Somhairle*, now used as representing the Hebrew-English 'Samuel.'
[6] Gregory, p. 7 *et seq.*, uniformly styles him 'Godred the Black'; although the *Rolls* edition of the Sagas (vol. ii. p. 148) reserves this appellation for his grandson Godred, son of Reginald. This latter Godred reigned for a year or less, and was killed in Lewis A.D. 1230 (Munch, pp. 20, 93, 190, there named 'Godred Don'). Godred is 'Godfrey,' or in Gaelic, *Goraidh.*

1156, a great sea-battle, which resulted in a treaty dividing the Sudreys, the islands south of Ardnamurchan Point being yielded to Somerled, while Godred retained only the Isle of Man and the northern Hebrides as his portion. It appears moreover that in 1158 Somerled wrested these also from Godred, who retired to Norway until Somerled's death in 1164,[1] after which event he succeeded in resuming possession of all the islands reserved to him by the above-mentioned treaty.

Godred, son of Olaf the Red, left three sons, Reginald, Olaf, and Ivar, of whom, shortly before his death, he recognised Olaf (born in 1173, and afterwards known as Olaf the Black) as his lawful heir. Olaf the Black being thus a boy of fourteen when his father died in 1187, the reins of government were seized by Reginald, his elder but illegitimate brother, who assigned the island of Lewis as Olaf's share of the patrimony—Lewis here evidently including the whole Long Island or Outer Hebrides.[2] It is under these circumstances that we find the third Saga notice, to which allusion has already been made, as probably, though not quite certainly, conveying a further reference to North Uist. For this we are indebted to one of the minor Sagas, which tells in considerable detail how Gudmund Arason (Bishop-elect of Holar) and Rafn Sveinbjarnarson, while sailing from Iceland to Norway in the year 1202, were carried by successive storms far out of their course; first to 'Hirtir' or St. Kilda, and thence to Ireland, afterwards reaching Cape Wrath, only to be driven back and compelled to take refuge at 'Sandey,' in the Sudreys, where they found King Olaf residing.[3] A special point in this narrative is that Olaf the Black levied a fine upon the distressed voyagers, thus proving that his authority extended southward from Lewis, whether or not 'Sandey' be identified (according to Munch) with Sandray near Barra Head,[4] or (according to Captain Thomas) with the district and former parish of Sand, in North Uist,[5] which latter, both from its

---

[1] Munch, pp. 10-13, 80-81.   [2] Ibid., pp. 14-17, 83-84.
[3] Guðmundar Saga, in Biskupa Sögur, Copenhagen, 1857, vol. ii. pp. 563-564. Other references to this eventful voyage are contained in Ibid., vol. ii. pp. 481-485 ; Sturlunga Saga, edited by Dr. Gudbrand Vigfusson, Oxford, 1878, vol. i. p. 125, also vol. ii. pp. 291-292 (Hrafns Saga); and Corpus Poeticum Boreale, vol. ii. pp. 280-281.
[4] Munch, p. 83.
[5] This theory is favoured by Dr. Vigfusson in the Rolls edition of Orkneyinga Saga, London, 1887, vol. i., p. xxxvii. Captain Thomas's caution and sagacity bespeak great confidence in any statement made by him. Should his identification of Sandey be accurate, it follows that Olaf the Black must have been very intimately associated with the island of North Uist.

central position and comparative fertility, would appear in every way the more likely residence to be chosen by a ruler of the Long Island.

In 1208, soon after the incident just recorded, Olaf the Black made an appeal to his brother Reginald for an enlargement of territory, but in response was treacherously captured and sent to William the Lion, King of Scotland, by whom he was held prisoner in Marchmont Castle for nearly seven years, not being released until after Alexander II. came to the throne in 1214.

Olaf died 21st May 1237, and was succeeded by his son Harald, who (with his bride, Cecilia, daughter of Hakon, King of Norway) perished by shipwreck off the Shetlands on his voyage home from Bergen in the autumn of 1248. After Harald's death the rulership devolved upon his younger brothers, Reginald (assassinated within a month of his accession) and Magnus, who died at Russin Castle, Isle of Man, towards the end of 1265.[1] It may added that for a hundred years after Somerled's death in 1164, a large portion of what is now Argyllshire, together with the Inner Hebrides south of Ardnamurchan Point, seems to have continued under the rule of his descendants, who had thus to yield a double allegiance,[2] as holding their island possessions from the King of Norway, and those upon the mainland from the Scottish crown.

Such were the general arrangements which apparently existed throughout the western isles, until in 1266 (three years after the Battle of Largs) the Treaty of Perth was concluded between Alexander III. of Scotland and Magnus IV., King of Norway, whereby the latter resigned all control over the Hebrides, which thenceforth became an integral part of the Scottish kingdom, even if, for several centuries, the authority there exercised was hardly more than nominal.

[1] Munch, pp. 16-17, 27, 88, 100, 103, 190.
[2] *Ibid.*, p. 94 ; Gregory, p. 19 ; and Skene's *Celtic Scotland*, second edn., vol. iii. p. 293.

CHAPTER III

THE CLAN HISTORY OF NORTH UIST

TRIBAL rule certainly prevailed in the Hebrides, as elsewhere throughout the Scottish Highlands, from a very early period until interrupted by the Norse domination of nearly four centuries, during which it must necessarily have suffered a distinct check. Upon the withdrawal however of this alien supremacy in 1266, the clan system soon reasserted itself with greater vigour and prominence than at any previous time, the chiefs holding an arbitrary control of the remoter districts in open defiance towards the Scottish crown. This state of affairs continued until 1609, in which year King James VI. secured the reluctant signatures of the Island chiefs (Neil MacLeod of Lewis alone excepted) to 'The Band and Statutes of Icolmkill,' a series of enactments which imposed restrictions upon their autocratic power by introducing various social reforms, and further contained a definitely expressed submission to the authority of King and Parliament.

These 'Statutes' form a landmark in Hebridean history, not only as the first step to gradually improving conditions, but strangely enough (when we consider how they were forced upon the islanders) it would appear that from them is also to be dated 'the commencement of that ·remarkable attachment to the Stuart dynasty, and cohesion in a common cause, which, in after years, characterised the Highland chiefs. The agreement carried in its train political and economic results of far-reaching significance.'[1]

It is true that one of the most important clauses, forbidding the use of fire-arms, seems to have been practically ignored, the feudal custom of military service only terminating with the Battle of Culloden in 1746, a defeat immediately followed up by Acts of Parliament abolishing heritable jurisdiction and enforcing disarmament throughout the Highlands, thus dealing a final blow to the clan

---

[1] Mackenzie's *History of the Outer Hebrides*, p. 242 ; also Gregory, p. 333.

system, which thereafter ceased to exert its once prominent influence. Among the numerous Scottish clans, that of MacDonald of the Isles was one of the most outstanding, and it is with this and the collateral Clan Mac Ruari that we are mainly concerned in North Uist, both branches clearly proving their descent from Somerled Hold, 'regulus Herergaidel,'[1] a famous Hebridean chief to whom brief reference has been made in the preceding chapter. It seems here unnecessary to enter into the legendary accounts[2] of Somerled's genealogy, which trace this back to Colla Uais, King of Ireland, A.D. 327-332.[3] No more can be stated, with any certainty, than that his father was Gilli-Bride, son of Gilli-Adomnan,[4] it being fairly evident that Somerled came of a mixed race with both Celtic and Norse blood in his veins —mainly Celtic on the paternal side—while there is also a strong presumption that his ancestors in direct line had already for several generations held the lordship of Argyll,[5] to which in 1156 Somerled himself added the southern half of the Hebrides.

Upon Somerled's death at the Battle of Renfrew in 1164, these wide possessions were divided amongst his three sons, Dugall,[6] Reginald, and Angus. Dugall thus inherited Lorn, Morvern, Mull, and Jura; Reginald had Kintyre, Islay, and half of Arran; while Angus received Bute and the other half of Arran, together with the mainland district from Ardnamurchan to Glenelg.

Reginald died in 1207,[7] being succeeded by his sons Donald and Roderick, who also, after the death of their uncle Angus (in 1210, and evidently without surviving issue), acquired the territories which he had held. It was through the descendants of these sons of Reginald that the Somerled line afterwards obtained possession of both North and South Uist, Donald giving his name to Clan MacDonald

---

[1] Munch, p. 7.

[2] Fully detailed in 'The Book of Clanranald,' *Reliquiæ Celticæ* (Inverness, 1892-4, vol. ii. pp. 151-155), and also quoted in *The Clan Donald*, vols. i. and iii.

[3] Dates given in *The Annals of the Four Masters*, Dublin, 1846, pp. 2-3.

[4] According to *The Clan Donald*, vol. iii. p. 178, a daughter of Gilli-Adomnan married Harald Gilli, King of Norway,—son of King Magnus Barelegs.

[5] *The Clan Donald*, vol. i. pp. 36-38 : Munch, pp. 74-75 ; and Gregory's *History*, pp. 10-12. Throughout this chapter *The Clan Donald* (3 vols., Inverness, 1896-1904) is very generally quoted, even where no specific reference is given.

[6] From whom, or (according to the MacDonald version) from another Dugall, son of Reginald, is descended Clan MacDougall of Lorn.

[7] This Reginald (or Ranald) founded a Benedictine monastery and a nunnery of the same order, at Iona in 1203, his sister Beatrice (or Bethog) being mentioned as the first prioress of that island ; Skene's *Celtic Scotland*, second edition, vol. ii. pp. 415-416 ; see also *Reliquiæ Celticæ*, vol. ii. p. 157.

of Islay (latterly 'of the Isles') and Roderick to Clan MacRuari of Garmoran[1] and the North Isles.

Following upon the Treaty of Perth in 1266, it became necessary for King Alexander III. to deal with the sub-tenure of the Hebrides, and particularly with that of the Long Island which till then remained under control of the Norwegian King of Man. We find that little interference ensued as to the southern portion of the isles, King Alexander confirming Angus Mor (son of Donald, the founder of Clan MacDonald) in Islay and Kintyre, as also Dugall and Allan (sons of Roderick) in Garmoran, although these representatives of Clan MacRuari had to resign Bute and Arran to the Stewart family, receiving, evidently in compensation, the Uists and Benbecula, while Lewis and Skye were granted to William, Earl of Ross. Very little is known of the Uists during the eighty years, from 1266 to 1346, when they were held by Clan MacRuari in the male line. It is however recorded that in 1285-1286 Allan, son of Roderick, 'committed an act of piracy on a Spanish ship with a valuable cargo, which was driven ashore on the Outer Hebrides,'[2] and according to another authority, 'the MacRuari family seem to have inherited a large share of the piratical tendencies of the ancient Vikings, . . . in 1297 invading and carrying slaughter and depredations into the islands of Skye and Lewis, and burning the ships in the service of the King.'[3]

Upon the death of Dugall MacRuari in 1268, his brother Allan assumed the sole lordship of Garmoran and the North Isles; while we also find that, in the next generation, King Robert the Bruce granted a crown-charter[4] to his wife's uncle, Roderick, son of Allan, in part of the lands of Garmoran and of Kilpheder in South Uist, 'in parochia de Kilpedire blisen,' together with the islands of Eigg, Rum, Barra and Uist (here apparently North Uist), all of which 'Cristiana de

---

[1] Garmoran is understood to have represented the districts of Moydart, Arisaig, Morar, and Knoydart—the *Garrw Morwarne* of a confirmation granted by David II. in 1343; and *Garbh-mór earrain*, or 'rugged mainland,' of the *New Statistical Account* (Argyllshire, p. 164). Professor D. Mackinnon describes Garmoran as the western sea-board from Morvern northwards, stating the name to be in part still preserved in that of Morvern itself,—*a' mhór earrann*, or 'great portion.' Dr. Alex. MacBain has however rejected this derivation of Morvern in favour of *Mór-bhearna* or 'the great passes' (*Transactions, Gaelic Soc. of Inverness*, vol. xxv. pp. 65, 72); while *Mór-bhearna*, 'sea gaps, or passes,' might equally serve.   [2] Mackenzie's *Outer Hebrides*, p. 69.
[3] *The Clan Donald*, vol. i. p. 87. We also find that in the year 1212 Roderick, grandson of Somerled, had harried the Irish coast with an armament of 76 galleys; *Ibid.*, vol. ii. p. 6, quoting *The Annals of Ulster*.
[4] *Origines Parochiales*, vol. ii. p. 363,—referring to a manuscript in the Advocates' Library (A.4.16, 34.2.1.) 'A Collection of Charters Evidents and Antiquities, collected by E. Hadinton';

Marr filia quondam Allani filii Roderici''[1] had resigned for conveyance to her brother Roderick and his heirs-male, failing whom, to Christina's own son Roderick. There is also stipulated the provision 'unius navis viginti et sex remorum cum hominibus et victualibus pertinentibus' for the king's service.

This charter is variously attributed either to the year 1309 or 1320, and must be of earlier date than 28 March 1325, when Roderick (brother of Christina MacRuari), was forfeited by the Scottish Parliament sitting at Scone.[2] In 1343[3] however David II. reinstated Ranald (son of Roderick) who only survived for three years, being killed in 1346 at Elcho, near Perth, by William (O'Beolan), Earl of Ross. But indeed, during the unsettled ages (of prolonged duration in the Hebrides) the tenure of these islands is full of complications—forfeitures alternating with renewed grants. It would be practically impossible to follow these details, and, since matters usually resolved themselves *in statu quo*, there is fortunately small occasion for the attempt.

Ranald being the last direct representative in the male line of Clan MacRuari of Garmoran and the North Isles, these lands passed to his sister Amie (otherwise Anna or Algive),[4] wife of John of Islay, then head of Clan MacDonald.

vol. ii. pp. 48-49. The actual document (noting all contractions) appears thus to run—'Insulam de Barr(ay) cu(m) p(er)tinen(ciis). et Insula(m) de Guy(ste) cu(m) p(er)tinen(ciis). quasquidem terras Cristiana de Marr,' etc. The word which we take to be Guyste (see *Guiste* in Thomson's *Acts of Parliament of Scotland*, anno 1292, vol. i. p. 447, the red pagination being here quoted throughout), is usually read as Harris, although this seems incorrect, both from the MS. itself and from the absence of any proof that Harris was ever possessed by Somerled's descendants. 'Herce' (*Reg. Mag. Sig.*, 1 Jan. 1372-1373) has indeed also been read as Harris, but is evidently a copyist's error for 'Herte' or St. Kilda.

[1] As noted in *The Clan Donald*, vol. ii. p. 18, Christina, daughter of Allan MacRuari, became through her marriage with Donald, Earl of Mar, 'the mother of Bruce's wife, and thus the progenetrix of a long line of sovereigns, the first of whom was her great-grandson Robert II.' She was fourth in lineal descent from Somerled, being grand-daughter to Roderick, of Garmoran and the North Isles, from whom Clan MacRuari took its name. King Robert the Bruce, during the critical period which followed his accession to the Scottish throne, received substantial aid from his mother-in-law, Christina of the Isles, who had succeeded her father Allan in the MacRuari lands at his death, probably soon after the year 1286. Amie MacRuari was Christina's niece, and fifth in direct line from Somerled, being also cousin-german to Isobel of Mar, the first wife of King Robert the Bruce.

[2] *Acts of Parliament*, vol. i. p. 483, 28 March 1325.

[3] *Ibid.*, vol. xii. p. 7, 12 June 1343. This crown-charter specifically includes the whole islands of Ywest, Barra, Egghe and Romme, and their pertinents, together with 'octo vnciatas terre de Garrw Morwarne videlicet Mudeworth Mordhowor Aresayg Cnudeworth cum suis pertinenciis'; these latter names of course representing Moydart, Morar, Arisaig and Knoydart.

[4] *Reliquiæ Celticæ*, vol. ii. p. 158; *Origines Parochiales*, vol. ii. p. 370; *The Clan Donald*, vol. i. pp. 111, 127, and vol. iii. p. 184, thrice mentions her as Euphemia, but Amie is the name by which she is best known.

D

Here it becomes necessary to trace the succession in the last-named clan from its founder Donald, son of Reginald and grandson of Somerled. We have already seen that it was to Angus Mor, son of Donald, that King Alexander III. confirmed possession of Islay and Kintyre after the Treaty of Perth in 1266. This Angus Mor died *ca.* 1293, and was succeeded by his son Alexander, who however rebelled against King Robert the Bruce, with the result of his capture in 1308 at Castle Swen (North Knapdale), and imprisonment in Dundonald Castle, where it is said that he died shortly afterwards.[1] Alexander left several sons, but of these and their descendants nothing more is heard in the western isles, both lands and chiefship passing to Angus Og, younger brother of Alexander.

Angus Og was a staunch supporter of the Bruce, and with his followers, 'variously estimated at from 5000 to 10,000 men,' played an important part in the victory of Bannockburn. For this and other services the king rewarded him with large additional grants, including the islands of Mull, Jura, Coll, and Tiree, and the districts of Glencoe and Morvern.[2] Angus Og died in 1330 and his tombstone may still be seen at Iona. To him succeeded his son John, 'the good John of Islay,' although the adjective does not seem very appropriate. John MacDonald of Islay was at least a shrewd and prosperous man, and commenced his long rule of fifty-six years by making, in 1335, a treaty of alliance with Edward Balliol by which he was confirmed in most of the lands above-mentioned, with the important additions of Skye and Lewis;[3] Skye however being omitted in a charter of 1343 granted by David II.[4]

It has already been mentioned that John had married Amie MacRuari, heiress of her brother Ranald, the last of the male line of MacRuari of Garmoran and the North Isles. Upon Ranald's death in 1346 the possessions of Clan MacDonald and Clan MacRuari thus became united for a time into one vast territory, John of Islay acquiring control of all the Outer Hebrides in addition to other islands and a wide mainland area. He was thereafter known as 'First Lord

---

[1] *The Clan Donald*, vol. i. p. 89.
[2] *Gregory*, pp. 24-25.
[3] *Rotuli Scotiæ*, vol. i. pp. 463-464, where King Edward III. 'ratificat indenturam inter Edwardum de Balliolo, suum pseudoregem Scotiæ, et Johannem de Insulis,' Morvern being included as 'terram de Kenalbadon et de Ardinton,' the 'Kinbaldein and Ardnamurchin' granted by King Robert the Bruce to Angus Og, father of John (Robertson's *Index of Charters*, p. 2).
[4] *Acts of Parliament*, vol. xii. p. 6.

of the Isles,'[1] the title 'Dominus Insularum' being given him in a document of 1354.[2]

John of Islay and Amie MacRuari were third cousins, their great-grandfathers having been brothers, and the necessary dispensation for this marriage was obtained from Pope Benedict XII. in 1337.[3] For his conduct towards Amie no excuse is forthcoming on behalf of John, Lord of the Isles, nor does any seem to have existed. While readily accepting his wife's inheritance, he did not hesitate, within three or four years at the most, to divorce[4] (or perhaps more exactly, to *repudiate*) her in order to marry Lady Margaret Stewart, great-granddaughter of King Robert the Bruce and daughter of the 'High Steward' of Scotland, afterwards King Robert II. The date of this second marriage is approximately known from a letter of the then Pope, Clement VI., 14th June 1350, 'to dispense John de Insulis, Lord of the Isles, and Margaret, daughter of Robert called Steward . . . to intermarry, they being related in the third and fourth degrees of affinity.'[5] All accounts agree that the *quasi* divorce of Amie MacRuari was due to no fault on her part; even Hugh MacDonald— the Sleat historian of his own clan—describing her as 'a good and virtuous gentlewoman.'[6] She had three sons, John, Ranald, and Godfrey, the eldest of whom (with his only son Angus) predeceased his father. By his second wife (Lady Margaret), John, first Lord of the Isles, had also three sons, Donald (his successor in the lordship of the Isles), John Mor, and Alasdair Carrach.

According to tradition, it was Amie MacRuari who built 'the little oratory in Grimsay' and Teampull na Trionaid at Carinish (both situated in North Uist), as also the parish church of St. Columba and Borve Castle in Benbecula.[7] With regard to the castle of Borve, its

---

[1] It is claimed by historians of the Clan MacDonald that John of Islay was not the first of the family to assume this title. There is at least no doubt that his lineal ancestors, Gilli-bride, Somerled, Reginald and Donald, of the twelfth and thirteenth centuries, were styled 'King' or 'Lord' of the Isles in ancient chronicles of these periods.

[2] Hailes' *Annals*, second edition, vol. iii. p. 381. It is interesting to note that John of Islay fought at Poitiers (1356) against the Black Prince, by whom he was captured and held prisoner for fifteen months. [3] Given at Avignon, 4th June 1337; *Scot. Hist. Review*, 1911, pp. 249-250.

[4] We can find no evidence of any divorce, simply that Amie was superseded.

[5] *Register of Papal Letters*, vol. iii. p. 381; the date being given as '18 Kal. Julij.'

[6] *The Clan Donald*, vol. i. p. 117; quoting from an old manuscript, of which a copy is preserved in vol. iv. of the 'Gregory Collections'—ten MS. volumes in the Library of the Society of Antiquaries of Scotland. A large portion of this particular record was printed in *Collectanea de Rebus Albanicis*, pp. 282-324, where Amie is mentioned (p. 298) in the above terms.

[7] *Collectanea*, p. 298; although Teampull na Trionaid was probably built long before. Amie MacRuari is also said to have erected the castle of Eilean Tioram in Moydart.

name would denote a Scandinavian or possibly even earlier origin ; although the existing ruins (of mediæval or feudal style) may well be those of a later keep built by the deserted Amie, who is believed to have spent the rest of her life in Benbecula and North Uist.

'John of the Isles' received from David II. in 1362 a general confirmation of all the lands then held by him,[1] very possibly intended to cover Amie's inheritance, as no details whatever are expressed ; while, soon after the accession of his father-in-law to the Scottish throne (as Robert II.) he was careful to obtain a further royal grant[2] securing to himself personally the whole MacRuari territory, so as to fortify his title therein.

John, first Lord of the Isles, died at Ardtornish Castle in 1386, and although Donald (the eldest son by his second wife) was to succeed him both in the Clan Donald lands and the lordship of the Isles, it is satisfactory to find that within a year of receiving the last-mentioned charter, John had the justice to settle upon Ranald (or Reginald)[3] eldest surviving son of his first marriage, most of the MacRuari territory. This resignation took the form of a crown-charter given by Robert II. :—'Confirmasse donacionem illam et concessionem quas dilectus filius noster Johannes de . yle fecit ; Reginaldo de yle filio suo de Insulis . terris et castris infrascriptis videlicet de terra . de Mudewort cum castro . de Elantirym de terra de Arrasayk, de terra de Morowore, et de terra de Cnudeforde . de Insula de Egge . de Insula de Rume de Insula . de Huwyste . cum Castro de Vynvawle de Insula de Barre et de Insula de Herce, cum omnibus aliis minutis Insulis ad dictas Insulas pertinentibus,' with other lands in Sunart, Ardgour, and Lochaber.[4]

According to one authority, the 'Huwyste' of this charter refers only to South Uist, Godfrey, younger brother of Ranald, having

[1] *Reg. Mag. Sig.*, 4 July 1362 (folio volume, p. 30). John, first Lord of the Isles, was evidently favoured by David II., since he is found acting as High Steward of Scotland in 1364 ; *Exchequer Rolls*, vol. ii. pp. 129, 141, 173.

[2] *Reg. Mag. Sig.*, 9 March 1371-2 (pp. 90 and 125) ; also *Acts of Parliament*, vol. i. p. 560 It is very noticeable that the lands are here described as those 'quondam Alani filii Rodorici, who seems to have died before 1292 ; any reference to Roderick, son of Allan, or to his children Ranald and Amie (through all of whom the inheritance had intermediately passed) being significantly avoided.

[3] It is said that Ranald also died in 1386, leaving five sons, of whom Allan, the eldest, succeeded him as heir (*The Clan Donald*, vol. iii. pp. 226-227).

[4] *Reg. Mag. Sig.*, 1 Jan. 1372-3 (folio volume, p. 117). 'Herte' or St. Kilda is known to have belonged to Clan MacRuari. It may be noted that in *Origines Parochiales*, vol. ii. p. 372 and elsewhere this charter is erroneously quoted as of the year 1392.

obtained a grant of North Uist as his portion, which he held even in his father's lifetime.[1]

It is true that Godfrey, in a 'donation' of 1389 confirming the chapel of the Holy Trinity at Carinish and various lands in North Uist to the Monastery of Inchaffray,[2] describes himself in plain terms as 'Gothfridus de Insulis dominus de Wyste.' Still the point is by no means clear, especially as Godfrey was at that very time dispossessing his nephews from part at least of their rightful territory of Garmoran; this document itself bearing to be sealed by him, 'apud Castrum nostrum de Elane tyrym,' which fortress, together with the rest of Moydart, etc., had been expressly secured to Ranald and his heirs by the crown-charter of 1373.

Ranald and Godfrey, sons of John of Islay by Amie MacRuari, were the founders of Clan Ranald[3] and Clan Gorrie respectively, Ranald's eldest son Allan evidently regaining possession of Garmoran after Godfrey's death in 1401.

Clan Gorrie held the lordship of North Uist for nearly a hundred years, Godfrey being followed by his sons Angus (died ca. 1430) and Ranald (died 1440), the latter giving his name to Balranald, where he resided.[4] Ranald 'Mac Gorrie' was succeeded in turn by his sons Alexander and John, after whose times (John dying ca. 1469) this sept fell into decay, its representatives becoming tenants, under Clan Huistein, in part of the lands which had been ruled by their predecessors.

We must now follow the main line of Clan Donald from John, first Lord of the Isles, to his great-grandson, Hugh MacDonald of Sleat, who played an important part in the history of North Uist,

---

[1] *The Clan Donald*, vol. i. pp. 135-136 ; vol. iii. p. 360. Gregory, p. 30, contends that Godfrey was the eldest son of the first marriage of John of Islay, but was superseded because of his 'maintaining his mother's prior claims, and his own as her heir'; although *The Clan Donald*, vol. i. p. 133, seems to prove Ranald as having been the elder of the two, and he it was who undoubtedly received much the largest portion of the MacRuari lands.

[2] *Charters of Inchaffray Abbey*, Scot. Hist. Soc., Edin., 1908, p. 136 :—'sicut melius liberius honorificencius et vtilius Cristina filia alani bone memorie vera heres et Reginaldus dictus m'Rodry verus dominus et patronus dictam capellam cum prefatis terris dictis monasterio et conuentui contulerunt'; 7 July 1389.

[3] Garmoran, together with South Uist, Eigg, and Benbecula, continued to be held by various branches of Clan Ranald until early in the nineteenth century, when these estates were gradually dispersed, South Uist and Benbecula being purchased in 1838 by Colonel Gordon of Cluny. None of the ancient territories of Clan Ranald were retained by its chief, except 'the Islands of Tyrim and Risgay or Risca, in Loch Moidart . . . extending to about 30 acres,' and even these were offered for sale in *The Scotsman* so recently as July 1904, the above being a quotation from the brief advertisement. [4] *The Clan Donald*, vol. iii. p. 362.

he and his lineal descendants in Clan Huistein holding possession of that island for nearly four centuries, viz. from *ca*. 1469 until 1856.

The fact has already been noted that John was succeeded in 1386 by Donald, eldest son of his second marriage (with Margaret, daughter of Robert II.) both in the Clan Donald estates and the titular lordship of the Isles. It was this Donald who in the attempt to enforce a not unwarranted claim (through his wife) to the earldom of Ross, led an army of 10,000 men of his own and other clans across the Scottish mainland, penetrating so far as Aberdeenshire, where, on 24th July 1411, he fought the memorable Battle of Harlaw against the royal forces.

Upon Donald's death, *ca*. 1423, his eldest son Alexander became third Lord of the Isles, ultimately also obtaining full recognition as Earl of Ross, although this right seems to have been withheld from him until the accession of James II. in 1437. Alexander, indeed, twice suffered the indignity of imprisonment at the hands of James I., but latterly enjoyed undisturbed possession of his double inheritance, which, after his death in 1449, passed to his son John as fourth Lord of the Isles and Earl of Ross.

John, fourth (and last) Lord of the Isles, who was then a mere lad of eighteen, soon became embroiled in rebellion, to which in 1462 he added the still more serious offence of making a treasonable compact with Edward IV. of England for the subjugation of the Scottish kingdom. This secret agreement was not divulged until thirteen years later, when James III. took prompt action with the natural consequence of John's forfeiture in December 1475, although on 1st July 1476 he was reinstated as Lord of the Isles, at the sacrifice of Kintyre, Knapdale, and the earldom of Ross.

After this crisis it appears that John completely changed his attitude towards the Scottish crown, to the extent indeed of becoming wholly out of touch with the younger element in Clan Donald, and of thus losing any control over the ambitious schemes devised by his son Angus Og, and latterly by Alexander of Lochalsh, his nephew. The next outstanding event in his career was the Battle of Bloody Bay, a naval engagement fought between the clans *ca*. 1482 or 1484 off the north end of Mull, where John, with his Island supporters, was defeated by his own son Angus Og, who led the main portion of Clan Donald in rebellion against the royal supremacy. Although, subsequent to the year 1475, his personal loyalty can hardly be called in question, John was evidently held responsible for all offenders over whom he had nominal rule. Only thus can we account for his second forfeiture in May 1493, a penalty which closely followed the invasion of Strathconan by Alexander of Lochalsh, and which he survived for less than five years, dying in lodgings at Dundee in January 1497-8, a pensioner on the bounty of King James IV.[1]

With regard to the succession in North Uist, we come now to Clan Huistein,[2] which derived its name from Hugh MacDonald of Sleat in Skye, an illegitimate son of Alexander, third Lord of the Isles (by a daughter of Patrick O'Beolan, an abbot who held Carloway in Lewis)[3] and consequently half-brother to John, fourth (and last) Lord of the Isles.

It would seem that Hugh's investiture in North Uist followed soon after the death of John (chief of Clan Gorrie, and great-grandson of Amie MacRuari), already mentioned as having been the last of the MacRuari line to retain possession of that island. The earliest known document bearing upon this subject is a royal charter of James IV. (10 Nov. 1495) confirming to Hugh MacDonald of Sleat the lands of North Uist, together with others situated in South Uist, Benbecula, and Sleat, all as previously granted to Hugh on 28 June 1469[4] by his brother John, then Earl of Ross and Lord of the Isles.

[1] *The Clan Donald*, vol. i. p. 282—'Item (Feb. 5, 1497-8), to Pate Sinclair, to send to Dunde to pay for Johnne of Ilis furthbringing and berying, and to loues his gere . . . *ls.,—i.e.* to settle with his landlady.—The High Treasurer's Accounts.' Through the courtesy of the Rev. A. J. Macdonald, joint-editor of the *The Clan Donald*, we are able to quote an earlier entry of 10 January 1497-8, 'to Johnne of Ilis, liand seik in Dunde. . . *xxviijs.*' The original MS. of the Lord High Treasurer's accounts has unfortunately one or more leaves here amissing, and the only remaining authority for both of the above is an old volume of extracts from the records during the reigns of James III. and IV., a quarto consisting of 139 pages, with an introduction of 33 pages by James Paterson, of apparent date about 1840. John, last Lord of the Isles, was buried in Paisley Abbey, and according to the *Exchequer Rolls*, vol. vi. p. 158, must have attained his sixty-seventh year, since he was a minor for three years after his father's death in 1449.

[2] Sometimes termed 'Clan Donald north' of Skye and North Uist, to distinguish it from Clan Donald south' of Islay and Kintyre (Gregory, p. 61). [3] *Collectanea*, p. 304.

[4] *Reg. Mag. Sig.* in the confirmation of 10 Nov. 1495, more fully detailed in Chapter IV. *postea*, where reasons are given for attributing this original grant to the year 1469. Although Hugh is styled 'dominus de Slete' in the charter of 1469, apparently inferring his previous possession of that territory, there are other facts which present some difficulty. According to *Reg. Mag. Sig.*, 21 Aug. 1464, Celestine had received from his brother (John, fourth and last Lord of the Isles) in the preceding year (8 Nov. 1463) a grant '28 marcarum dominii de Slete,' whereas the charter of 1469, in favour of Hugh, included lands which seem to have been identical, viz., 'unacum terris 28 merc. de Slete, in dominio suo Insularum,' the former grantee (Celestine 'de Insulis de Lochalche') himself acting as a witness. It would almost appear that Celestine, between the years 1464 and 1469, had resigned these lands of Sleat in favour of his brother Hugh, who only now acquired a formal title to them.

Hugh (otherwise *Uisdean* or *Austin*) evidently made his home at Dunskaith Castle in Skye, tradition adding that he was buried 'in Sand in North Uist,'[1] his death having certainly occurred before August 1498.[2]

Hugh MacDonald of Sleat is said to have have had six sons[3] by as many different mothers, the eldest being John (through his marriage with Fynvola, daughter of Alexander MacIain of Ardnamurchan), who inherited the Clan Huistein lands. This John died without issue in 1505 or 1506,[4] and was succeeded in Sleat and North Uist by his half-brother Donald Gallach[5] for only about a year, when Donald was treacherously murdered by Gilleasbuig Dubh,[6] another of Hugh's sons.

After Donald Gallach's death *ca.* 1506, the clan territory passed from father to son in regular succession for four generations, through Donald Gruamach[7] (d. *ca.* 1537), Donald Gorm (killed at the siege of Eilean Donan Castle in 1539), Donald Gormson[8] (d. 1573), and Donald Gorm Mor (d. 1616), the latter being one of the nine Highland chiefs who signed 'The Band and Statutes of Icolmkill' on 23 August 1609. Donald Gorm Mor left no issue, and was followed by his nephew Donald Gorm Og as next heir, who received a knighthood from James VI. in 1617, and a baronetcy of Nova Scotia from Charles I. in 1625.

At this point ought to be noticed a group of four crown-charters

---

[1] *Collectanea*, p. 316.   [2] *Reg. Mag. Sig.*, 5 Aug. 1498.

[3] *The Clan Donald*, vol. iii. pp. 467-468.

[4] Not before 23 Aug. 1505 (*Reg. Mag. Sig.*), the date of a crown-charter granted upon his resignation in favour of Ranald Alansoun, chief of Clan Ranald, although this transfer seems never to have taken effect. It would appear that John wished to divert the succession in North Uist and Sleat from Clan Huistein to Clan Ranald, an object which he had already accomplished by two similar charters of 5 Aug. 1498 (*Reg. Mag. Sig.*) as to the lands in South Uist and Benbecula secured to his father by the confirmation of 1495.

[5] Probably without any legal title, *The Clan Donald*, vol. i. p. 311. Donald Gallach was born *ca.* 1461, his mother being Elizabeth Gunn, daughter to the 'crowner of Caithness,' *Collectanea*, p. 307, and *Reliquiæ Celticæ*, vol. ii. p. 213. From him is lineally descended the present Baron MacDonald of Sleat.

[6] *The Clan Donald*, vol. i. p. 312; vol. iii. p. 12.

[7] During the minority of Donald Gruamach, from *ca.* 1506-1517, North Uist was the scene of much bloodshed, for which Donald's unscrupulous uncle and guardian, Gilleasbuig Dubh, seems to have been responsible.

[8] Donald Gormson spent some years in England, 'verie well entertained by Queen Marie in tyme of his being banished out of Scotland,' according to a letter from his son Donald Gorm Mor, *The Clan Donald*, vol. ii. p. 760. A contract dated 'the ferd day of Marche' 1566-1567, was signed by Donald Gormson 'with my hand at the pen led be the notar under writtin at my command. Ita est Jacobus Hoppringille notarius de mandato dicti Donaldi scribere nescientis manu propria.'—*Collectanea*, pp. 147-149.

which date from 1596 to 1618. By the first of these, King James VI.
'intelligens Donaldum Gorme de Slait ejusque predecessores fuisse
favorabiles et nativos tenentes et hereditarios possessores terrarum
subscriptarum, et originales cartas ejus progenitoribus pertinentes
occasione depredationum et crudelium inimicitiarum ac temporis
injuria perditas esse . . . ad feudifirmam dimisit dicto Donaldo,
etc.,' certain lands in Sleat, North Uist, Benbecula, and South
Uist.[1]

Further, in 1610, Donald Gorm Mor conveyed the portions of
South Uist and Benbecula included in this charter of 1596 to
'Donaldo M'Callane V'Eane de Ilentirime,' his distant cousin, who
was then chief of Clan Ranald.[2]

In 1614 was recorded a somewhat contradictory charter, by
which 'Rex confirmavit et . . . de novo ad feudifirmam dimisit
Donaldo Gorme de Slait' the whole lands enumerated in that of
1596, and in identical terms (even including those portions of
South Uist and Benbecula transferred to Clan Ranald in 1610),
all of which had been resigned into the king's hands by the said
Donald (Gorm Mor) for the purpose of his obtaining this new
title.[3]

Here it must be noted that from 1542 until 1618 the tenure of
Sleat and North Uist was in a very curious position. The MacLeods
of Dunvegan and Harris had, in 1542, received from King James V.
a charter of these very lands, and in 1613 Sir Roderick Mor MacLeod
was served heir to his uncle William MacLeod in the same, obtaining
a charter on 11 December of that year.[4] This disputed possession
naturally involved many troubles, until a settlement was reached by
a crown charter of 1618, through which Sir Donald (Gorm Og)
MacDonald—as representing Clan Huistein—was 'de novo' confirmed in all the lands specified in the previous grants of 1596 and
1614 (except those in South Uist and Benbecula) 'quas terras de

[1] *Reg. Mag. Sig.*, 17 Aug. 1596. Further reference to this document is made in Chapter IV.
postea.
[2] The original deed was signed 'apud Eige, 4 Jun. 1610,' and confirmed by King James on
20 July of the same year, *Reg. Mag. Sig.* This Donald MacAllan received four days later a royal
charter to other lands in South Uist, Garmoran, and Eigg, incorporated 'in liberam tenandriam
de Casteltirrim,' *Reg. Mag. Sig.*, 24 July 1610.
[3] *Reg. Mag. Sig.*, 21 July 1614. We can only suggest that this new charter was sought in
protection against the MacLeod claims, while it also inferentially cancelled the conveyance of 1610
to Clan Ranald.
[4] *The Clan Donald*, vol. iii. pp. 21, 50-51. These deeds are not recorded in *Reg. Mag. Sig.*

E

Sleat et North Wist idem Don. et D. Rodericus M'Cleod de Dun-vegane miles, ceteras idem Don., resignaverunt.'[1]   In this transaction certain money payments were stipulated from Sir Donald to Sir Roderick, pending which the lands of Trotternish were to be held as security by the last-named.[2]

Sir Donald Gorm Og MacDonald seems thereafter to have held undisturbed possession of the lands of Sleat and North Uist until his death in December 1643,[3] being then followed in the baronetcy and estates by his son Sir James, who died in 1678 and was succeeded by his son Sir Donald as third baronet.   Donald, son of this Sir Donald, led his clan under Claverhouse on the side of James VII. at Killie-crankie in July 1689, for which offence the young chief was promptly forfeited by Parliament, although this penalty appears never to have taken effect, notwithstanding an attack upon Sleat by two govern-ment frigates in 1690.[4]

Sir Donald, third baronet, died in 1695, and was followed in succession by his son and grandson as fourth and fifth baronets, who both bore his own baptismal name, and died in 1718 and 1720 respectively.   The fourth baronet had been forfeited in 1716 (on account of support given to the Earl of Mar), and his son, Sir Donald, leaving no issue, the title devolved upon an uncle, Sir James MacDonald, until then 'of Orinsay' (brother of the fourth baronet), who only survived his inheritance of this somewhat barren honour for a few months, the sixth baronet of Sleat dying in the autumn of 1720.   This Sir James Macdonald had served with the Highlanders both at Killiecrankie and Sheriff-muir, but afterwards became thoroughly loyal to King George I., endeavouring to keep the men of Sleat from joining in the insurrec-tion of 1719.[5]

---

[1] *Reg. Mag. Sig.*, 12 March 1618,—'D. Donaldo M'Connald de Slait, militi.' From the *Retours* (as hereinafter noted) we find that, on 6 May 1617, 'Donaldus Gorme de Slait *hæres* Donaldi Gorme de Slait, *patrui*,' was served heir to the whole of the lands enumerated in these crown-charters of 1596 and 1614.

[2] *The Clan Donald*, vol. iii. pp. 55-57 ; referring to a document in the Sleat charter-chest.

[3] The *Retours*, 20 Feb. 1644, show that Sir James MacDonald was duly served heir to his father, Sir Donald, in all the lands of Sleat, North Uist, South Uist, and Benbecula, mentioned in the royal grants of 1596, 1614, and 1618 (*Reg. Mag. Sig.*), together with others in North Uist, now first shown in any charter of Clan Huistein, and apparently to be identified as having formerly belonged to the church (see p. 45, *postea*).

[4] *The Clan Donald*, vol. iii. pp. 69-74.

[5] *Ibid.*, vol. iii. pp. 83-84 ; the 'Orinsay' here mentioned is Isle Ornsay in Sleat, Skye.

We have now reached a critical period[1] in the history of Clan Huistein, their forfeited estates being offered for sale in October 1723, and purchased by Kenneth Mackenzie, an Edinburgh lawyer acting on behalf of the Sleat family. The price was £21,000 sterling, which included the the three baronies of Sleat, Trotternish, and North Uist, with a rental officially given as £1550. What with a grant from Parliament of £10,000 to the children of Sir James (sixth baronet), and another of smaller amount to the daughters of Sir Donald (fourth baronet), added to the claims of 'wadsetters and others' (who allowed these debts to remain upon the security of the property), it is stated that only £4000 went to the Crown.

This transaction was followed in 1726 by a contract of sale between Kenneth Mackenzie and Sir Alexander MacDonald (seventh baronet, elder son of Sir James, and a minor at the time), ratified in February 1727 'by a crown charter of his lands erecting the whole into a barony to be called the Barony of MacDonald.'[2]

Sir Alexander (seventh baronet) married in 1739, as his second wife, Lady Margaret Montgomery, daughter of the Earl of Eglinton, and died in November 1746, his widow surviving until 1799.[3] There will be occasion in Chapter x. for some reference to Lady Margaret and her endeavour to foster the manufacture of textiles in North Uist, but meantime it need only be added that her two sons, Sir James and Sir Alexander, successively inherited the baronetcy and lands in 1746 and 1766, the last-named, Sir Alexander (ninth baronet), being also created Baron MacDonald of Sleat by King George III. in 1776.

---

[1] With regard to the northern branches of Clan Donald we may here note the interesting coincidence, that a crisis in their fortunes seems to have recurred with some regularity at intervals of little over a hundred years. Six prominent events are enumerated, all of them to be characterised as turning-points in the annals of the clan, even if we minimise the feud with the Dunvegan family—though this appears to have been no light matter.

1164. Somerled died.
1266. The Hebrides ceded to Scotland by the King of Norway.
1373. Clan Ranald founded ; the male line of Clan MacRuari having failed in 1346.
1469. Clan Huistein founded.
1475 and 1493. John, last Lord of the Isles, forfeited.
1613-1618. Disputed charters (from 1542) between Clan Huistein and Clan MacLeod, settled in 1618. The Battle of Carinish, 1601.
1716-1723. Forfeiture and sale of Sleat and North Uist ; purchased on behalf of the heir.
1826-1838. Sale of the Clan Ranald estates, followed by North Uist in 1855.

[2] *The Clan Donald*, vol. iii. pp. 84-85.

[3] *History of the Macdonalds and Lords of the Isles*, by Alexander Mackenzie, Inverness, 1881, pp. 237-239.

North Uist continued in the possession of the same family (lineal descendants of Hugh MacDonald, the founder of Clan Huistein in 1469) until the year 1855, when it was sold by Godfrey William, fourth Baron MacDonald of Sleat, to Sir John Powlett Orde, Bart., whose grandson, Sir Arthur J. Campbell-Orde, Bart., still owns almost the whole island.[1]

[1] This estate was advertised for sale in October 1908.

CHAPTER IV

THE PLACE-NAMES OF NORTH UIST, WITH THEIR ASSOCIATIONS, TOPOGRAPHICAL AND PERSONAL

In ancient documents dating from the thirteenth until well into the seventeenth century, it is to be noted that the term 'Uist' comprehends the whole of North Uist, Benbecula, and South Uist, together with their islet pendicles; the 'Vist' or 'Ivist' of the Norsemen apparently including Barra[1] also, or in other words, all the Long Island up to the Sound of Harris.

Great caution is thus necessary when quoting from old charters which refer to Uist in general, and thence deducing a particular application to any one of its three (or even four) main component islands, and especially with regard to the minor place-names, which are in several cases duplicated, occurring in Benbecula or South Uist and again in North Uist. As so commonly happens with regard to other cases of the same class, the derivation of 'Uist' affords very debatable ground. It is usually explained as representing the Norse *vestr* or 'west,' a term always employed in the Sagas when describing voyages to the British Isles; while it has alternatively been derived from *vist*, signifying in the same language 'an abode, a dwelling.'

Many are the disguises under which the name of Uist appears in ancient times. The Saga form has already been noted as Vist or

---

[1] In the Scottish chronicles from the year 1292 onwards, Barra is always treated as a separate entity. Thus we read in Thomson's *Acts of Parliament of Scotland*, vol. i. p. 447 *anno* 1292, 'Egge et Rumme Guiste et Barric cum minutis Insulis,' and again (*Ibid.*, vol. i. p. 560, 9 March 1371-1372), 'Ovyste Barreh Rumme Eggeh et Hỳrce.' 'Hyrce' seems a copyist's mistake for 'Hyrte' or Hirta, now St. Kilda, being apparently the first reference to that island in our own ancient records; although it is mentioned as 'Hirtir' in a Saga relating to the year 1202, as already noted at p. 20, *antea*. Hirta is explained by Captain F. W. L. Thomas (*Proc. Soc. Antiq. Scot.*, vol. vii. p. 172) as *h'Iar-Tir*, 'the west land or country,' its later name of St. Kilda being supposed to represent *Eilean ceile-Dé* or 'island of God's servant.' Dr Alexander MacBain (*Transactions of the Gaelic Society of Inverness*, vol. xxv., p. 79) derives Hirta from *Irt*, an old Irish word for 'death,' and Kilda from the Norse *kelda*, 'a well.'

It may be added that the record of 1292 also mentions 'Skey et Lodoux,' in obvious allusion to Skye and Lewis.

Ivist,[1] but in immediate succession the following occur, only the earliest date being given at which each variant spelling is found :—

A.D. 1282, Iuist (*Acts of Parliament*).[2]

1292, Guiste (*Ibid.*).

ca. 1309, Guy[ste] (*Hadinton's Collections*; MS. in the Advocates' Library).

1343, Uwest (*The Clan Donald*, vol. ii. p. 743).

1343, Ywest (*Acts of Parliament*).

1372, Ovyste (*Ibid.*).

1372, Oviste (*Reg. Mag. Sig.*, but 'Ouiste' in Robertson's *Index of Charters*).

1373, Huwyste (*Reg. Mag. Sig.*).

1389, Wyste and Wuyste, also Uuyst and Hwyste (*Inchaffray Charters*).

1495, Wist (*Reg. Mag Sig.*).

1498, Ewist and Ewyst (*Ibid.*).

1505, Euist (*Ibid.*).

1532, Oest (*Ibid.*).

1540, Owist (*Exchequer Rolls*).

1542, Oist and Oyest (*Ibid.*).

1545, West [3] (*Reg. Mag. Sig.*).

[1] Captain Thomas (*Proc. Soc. Antiq. Scot.*, vol. xi. p. 476) prefers '*I-fheirste* = Crossings-island, Fords-island,' which, if phonetically admissible, would well apply not only to North and South Uist but even in fuller degree to the intervening island of Benbecula. This is the solution favoured by Sir Herbert Maxwell in his *Scottish Land-Names*, p. 85. In treating of Benbecula Captain Thomas derives its name from '*Beinn-dha-Fhaoghailaichean*, pro. Ben-a-Oo-a-la, Hill of the Two Fords' (*Archæologia Scotica*, vol. v. p. 236). A simpler and perhaps even better explanation may be *Beinn na faodhlach* or 'hill of the ford.' Benbecula is much intersected by water, both salt and fresh, and is very flat except for the hill of Rueval (409 feet), from which the island has evidently received part of its title, this occurring in early charters as *Beandmoyll*, 1535, *Beanweall*, 1542 (both quoted from *Reg. Sec. Sig.* in *Origines Parochiales*, vol. ii. p. 370), and also as *Buchagla* and *Benvalgha* in 1549, Monro's *Description of the Western Isles*, Edin., 1774, pp. 34-35. Professor Munch, in *The Chronicle of Man and the Sudreys*, p. xix., suggests that the Norse forms of Lewis, Uist, and Skye, 'may only be substitutes for Gaelic names of a similar sound, but quite different signification.'

[2] Vol. i. p. 109, 'Littera regis Norwagie super terris de Iuist et Egyn'; although printed as 'Inist,' evidently through a clerical error.

[3] '30 mercat. de Kandes de West'; perhaps the northern half of South Uist as distinct from Boisdale (its southern extremity), which latter is represented by 'Baegastallis' (*Reg. Mag. Sig.*, 1495), 'Bowistill' (*Ibid.*, 1610), 'Benistill' (*Retours*, 1627, clearly an error for Beuistill), 'Beigistill' (*Ibid.*, 1627), 'Beagistill' (*Ibid.*, 1655), and 'Beuistill' (*Ibid.*, 1695). Kandes appears elsewhere in the *Reg. Mag. Sig.* as 'Kyndeis' (1610), and in the *Retours* under the name of 'Kennies vel Kendess' (1627), and 'Kyndies' (1695). The northern portion of South Uist (probably the whole district now known as Howmore) formerly went under the name of 'Skerehowg' (1495), 'Skeryhof' (1498), 'Skerihoif' (1532), 'Skerehoug' (1596), and 'Skirhuge' (1610), all in *Reg. Mag. Sig.*; while in the *Retours* it appears as 'Skerdhoug' (1617 and 1644), and 'Skeirchug vel Serehoig' (1695). Kandes is certainly the Gaelic *Ceann deas* or 'south head,'

1563, Uyst (*Reg. Mag. Sig.*).

1597, Wiest (sasine quoted in *The Clan Donald*, vol. ii. p. 756).

1607, Ust (*Reg. Privy Council*).

1610, Wyoist (*Reg. Mag. Sig.*).

1616, Eusta (*Ibid.*).

1617, Owyst (*Ibid.*).

1623, Wuest (*Ibid.*).

1648, Oust (*Acts of Parliament*).

1695, Vuist (*Retours*).

In addition to these, *Collectanea de Rebus Albanicis* has—

1561, Veist and Weist;

1576, Vyest and Vyist:

while we find various authorities quoted in *Origines Parochiales Scotiæ* for—

1549, Wyst;

1574, Ewyast;

1615, Yiest;

apart from the appearance of Viist, Vyist, Vistey, Vistus, Euste, and Eust, upon sundry old maps. Mackenzie's *History of the Outer Hebrides* (p. xxxix.) further gives Ouyst, Wistus, Ywist, and Wust.[1]

a term still applied in the vernacular to the whole of South Uist. The modern *Baghasdail* or Boisdale no doubt represents a Norse *Bœgisdalr* (cf. *Bœgisá*, the name of a river in Iceland,— noted in *Islands Landnámábok*, Copenhagen, 1774, p. 238, and also to be found in Dr. E. Henderson's *Iceland*, Edin. 1818, vol. i. p. 100; whereas Skeryhof in its various forms seems to be a bi-lingual compound, from *Sgire*, the Gaelic word for 'a parish,' and *hof*, which is 'a temple' in the old Norse language.

[1] We here add a few very similar place-names in Scotland, England, and France, which however may have no real bearing upon the Hebridean 'Uist' in its various forms.

In the parish of Latheron, Caithness, are marked upon modern maps 'Houstry' and 'Houstry Burn,' near Dunbeath. Of this property the earliest notices we can find are under the name of *Owist* or *Oust* (*Reg. Mag. Sig.*, 23 Nov. 1581 and 3 April 1592), also *Owstisdaill* (*Ibid.*, 2 Aug. 1616), and *Owist* in the *Retours*, 22 July 1605; Blaeu's atlas of 1654 showing the same place as *Ousdale* and *Ousdail*. In the Holderness district of Yorkshire is an *Owstwick*. Near Treport, in the north of France, are *Eu*, *Aouste*, and *Oust-marest* or *Aoust-marest*, all three explained in Joanne's handbook (*Normandie*, edn. of 1872, p. 202) as corrupted forms of Augusta. In the department of Morbihan (Brittany) a river *Oust* flows into the Vilaine; and at the southern extremity of France, close to the Pyrenees, we find *Oust* and *Ustou* in the department of Ariége. *Ust* is not uncommon in Russia, either as a prefix or a complete place-name.

Perhaps the above are hardly worth noticing, except for the fact that Yorkshire and the northern coast of France were favoured by settlers from Scandinavia. But indeed, all the French names quoted (except that of the river in Brittany, which seems more to the point) probably represent the Latin *Augusta*, while those in Caithness and Yorkshire may be derived from the Norse *austr* or 'east.'

Other variants such as Uidhist (evidently a corruption of the Gaelic form, *Uibhist* or *Uibhisd* [*Book of Clanranald*]), also occur, though it would be impossible to decide how many of these permutations are due, not to the original record, but to the transcriber,—or, for that matter, even to the compositor and the corrector of proofs.

Having thus dealt with the general title under which both North and South Uist have appeared at different times, it now remains to discuss the earlier references to specific localities in North Uist, gathered chiefly from printed copies of old charters and other legal documents.

In approaching this subject it seems well, by way of introduction, to quote in full the relative text of three crown-charters (from the Register of the Great Seal), and of two 'Brieves of Succession' or services of heirs, as they appear in that other useful government publication, 'Inquisitionum ad Capellam Domini Regis retornatarum . . . Abbreviatio,' London, 1811. It is from these five documents, here following, that we learn most as to the divisions and valuations of the lands of North Uist in early times :—

Reg. Mag. Sig., 1424-1513, 'No. 2286. Apud Striveling.' 10 Nov. 1495, confirming a previous charter of 1469, James IV.

'Rex confirmavit cartam Johannis de Yle, comitis Rossie, et domini Insularum,—[qua, cum consensu concilii sui, concessit fratri suo, Hugoni Alexandri de Insulis, domino de Slete,—terras

    30 mercarum de Skerehowg,
    12 merc. de Beanbeacla,
       denariatam de Gergremynis,
    60 merc. ex parte borientali de Wist,
    2 denar. de Scolpic,
    4 den. de Gremynis,
    2 den. de Talawmartin,
    6 den. de Orvinsaig,
    dimed. den. de Waynlis,
    et dimed. den. de insula Gillegerre,

unacum terris 28 merc. de Slete, in dominio suo Insularum : Tenend. dicto Hugoni et heredibus ejus masculis inter ipsum et Fynvolam Alexandri Johannis de Ardnamurchan legitime sive illegitime procreatis, . . . apud Aros, 28 Jun. 1469].'[1]

Reg. Mag. Sig., 1424-1513, 'No. 2873. Apud Striveling.' 23 August 1505, James IV.

'Rex concessit Ranaldo Alansoun de Ylandbigrim,[2] et heredibus ejus,
—28 mercatas terrarum de Sleit, una cum castro et fortalicio de Dunskahay; et 60 mercatas terrarum in capite boriali de Euist, viz. davatas Scotice dictas

    le Terung de Yllera,
    le Terung de Paible,
    le Terung de Pablisgervy,
    le Terung de Bailrannald,
    le Terung de Holf,
    le Terung de Watna, Scolping et Gremynis,
    le Terung de Wala,
    le Terung de Solos,
    1 ablatam terrarum de Walis,
    1 ablatam terrarum de Ylandgarvy,
    6 denariatas terrarum de Orwansay,
    2 den. de Talmertane,
    2 davatas Scotice dictas le Terungis de Sanda et Borwira, et
    1 den. terrarum de Gerrymare, infra dominium Insularum;
        quas Joh. Insularum, filius et heres quondam Hugonis Insularum, resignavit.'

The above-quoted charter of 1505 clearly proves that the Gaelic '*tir-unga*' (ounce-land) was an exact equivalent of the Pictish 'davach,' both of which have also been identified by Captain Thomas[3] with the better known 'ploughgate.' It moreover lends strong support to Captain Thomas's argument that the Norse 'unciata'—in other words, the *tirunga*—was, at the period in question and in the Outer

---

[1] This date reads in the manuscript *Reg. Mag. Sig.* as 'millesimo quadringentesimo nono,' but the difficulty caused by a word (sexagesimo) having by some accident been omitted in this record is fortunately capable of solution. Of the possible alternatives, the extreme dates (1449 and 1479) may be set aside, since John, last Lord of the Isles, was a minor until 1452 (*Exchequer Rolls*, vol. vi. p. 158), and three of the original witnesses—Donald of Dunnyveg, Celestine of Lochalsh, and John of Lochbuie—had died before 1479 (*The Clan Donald*, vol. iii. pp. 374, 466; *Reg. Mag. Sig.*, 4 Feb. 1478-1479). The year 1459 must also be excluded, Celestine not having become 'of Lochalsh' until 2 Feb. 1462-1463 (*Reg. Mag. Sig.*, 21 Aug. 1464). This original charter of 1469 was doubtless granted after the death of John (grandson of Godfrey, the founder of Clan Gorrie) in 1468-1469.

[2] *Caisteal Bheagram*, the chief fortress of Clan Ranald in South Uist, occupying an islet in a small loch at Howmore.   [3] *Proc. Soc. Antiq. Scot.*, vol. xx. p. 201.

Hebrides, worth from four to six merks, each merk representing thirteen shillings and fourpence. In the present case, ten 'terungs' and ten penny-lands are aggregated as equal to 60 merks, although this latter may perhaps have been a rough rather than an exact computation, especially as we find the earlier charter of 1469 quoting 60 merklands *plus* 15 penny-lands for what appear to be the same subjects. Captain Thomas (pp. 209-210) adds that in North Uist alone (apart from Caithness) there are indications that the ounce contained 18 pennies, as against the 20 pennies into which the Saxon ounce of silver was divided. It would further seem that the *tirunga* or 'davach' usually comprised about 100 to 120 acres of arable land, with no doubt a further allotment of pasturage;[1] its area varying however in different localities, the ounce being a measure of annual value, quite apart from definite extent.

We have it stated upon good authority that in North Uist, towards the close of the eighteenth century, a halfpenny land was sufficient to carry a stock of six full-grown cows and six horses, the tenant paying a rent of £5, 4s., this amount including public burdens;[2] while at the same period a pennyland in the parish of Reay (Caithness) was worth from £5 to £8 per annum.[3]

 Reg. Mag. Sig., 1593-1608, 'No. 472. Apud Falkland.' 15 August 1596, a fresh title granted by King James VI. (the original charters having been lost) in favour of Donald Gorm Mor MacDonald as to—

  '20 librat. terrarum antiqui extentus de Slait,
   40 libratas ant. ext. de North Wist,
   30 mercatas de Skerehoug,
   12 mercatas de Beambecula,
    denariatam de Gergremynis,
   2 den. de Scalpic,
   4 den. de Gremynis,
   2 den. de Tallawmartin,
   6 den. de Orvinsaig,
   ½ den. de Waynlis,
   ½ den. de Ile-Gillegerre,

---

[1] Professor D. Mackinnon (in *The Scotsman* newspaper, 28 Dec. 1887) practically agrees with this conclusion; stating the average *tirunga* to extend from about 120 acres as a minimum to 400 acres or more, according to the hill-pasture included.

[2] *Old Stat. Acc.*, vol. xiii. p. 311, *anno* 1794.   [3] *Ibid.*, vol. vii. p. 575.

cum castris, molendinis, silvis, piscationibus, libertatibus
tam per mare quam per terram consuetis, ...
—Reservando 40 solidat. dict. terrarum de Wist per
regem eligendas et possidendas per hujusmodi incolas
ut regi optimum visum esset ; sub provisione quod dicte
40 sol. nunquam disponerentur hominibus insulanis *lie
hielandmen* nisi prius oblate essent dicto Donaldo,'
subject to a yearly payment amounting to £257, 6s. 8d.
(*Scots*), together with a duplicand on the entry of heirs,
and sundry other stipulations.

It will be observed that this charter does not include the whole
of North Uist, appearing to be the first occasion when the king
reserved to himself part of that island, of which the total extent
is stated in 1542 as equal to 60 merks including 12 merks of church
lands.[1]

Retours (*Inquisitionum, etc.*), Inverness, No. 32. 'Maii 6. 1617.

Donaldus Gorme de Slait, *hæres* Donaldi Gorme de Slait,
    patrui,—in

        20 libratis terrarum antiqui extentus de Slait :—E. 80 l.
        et 6 l. 13s. 4d. in augmentationem :—

        40 libratis terrarum antiqui extentus de Northwist :—
        E. 120 l. et 6 l. 13s. 4d. in augmentationem :—

        30 mercatis terrarum de Skerdhoug ;

        12 mercatis terrarum de Beambeculla.

---

[1] *Exchequer Rolls*, vol. xvii. p. 557 ; the secular lands of North Uist,—at that time in the
hands of the king through the minority of Donald Gormson at his succession in 1539,—being
there stated as formerly extending to 48 merks, but since reduced to 46 merks through inroads by
the sea. In the same year a new lease gives them as only 45 merks (*Ibid.*, p. 649), perhaps owing
to very recent further damage from similar causes.
It is interesting to compare the extent of North Uist, as quoted in *The Exchequer Rolls* of
1542 and the crown-charter of 1596, with reference to the same lands in a tack of teinds
granted in 1630 by John, Bishop of the Isles, to Sir Donald Gorm Og, first baronet of Sleat.
This lease was limited to the bishop's share of 'the teind scheavis and utheris' accruing from lands
in Skye and from 'The Fourtie pund land of North Wist quhairof thair was aucht merkland
haldin of auld of the bischopes of the Isles . . . . . . exceptand and reserveand to me and my
successouris the teind fische of the haill seais and locheis perteining and adiacent to the saidis
landis.' This tack was for nineteen years, the rent (in addition to a 'girsume' or grassum of
unstated amount) being an annual payment of 'the sowme of ane hundreth pundis usuall money
of this realme togidder with twentie elnes of fyne plaiding at the feist of Mertimes' ; (*The Clan
Donald*, vol. iii. pp. 651-654, where this document is given in full). The bishop signed himself
'Johannes Leslaeus, Epus Sodorensis,' and we find that he only held the see of the Isles from
1628 until 1633, being then translated to Raphoe (Keith's *Scottish Bishops*, edn. of Edin., 1824,
p. 309).

1 denariata terrarum de Gergremynis ;
2 denariatis terrarum de Skolpick ;
4 denariatis terrarum de Gremynis (vel Greinynis) ;
2 denariatis terrarum de Tallowmartane ;
6 denariatis terrarum de Orwnsag ;
dimidio denariatæ terrarum de Wainlies ;
dimidio denariatæ terrarum de Ile Gilligerrie,
    jacentibus in dominio insularum infra vicecomitatum de
    Innernes :—E. 44 l.—proviso quod castrum de Camys
    semper pateat et in promptu sit S.D.N. Regi, locum tenen-
    tibus, camerariis, aliisque regiæ Majestatis servitoribus
    illic frequentantibus;—reservando 40 solidatas terrarum
    de Wist dicto S.D.N. regi et successoribus, possidendas
    per hujusmodi incolas ut sibi optimum visum fuerit, sub
    hac lege, quod nullo pacto disponantur hominibus insula-
    rum lie Heillandmen, nisi quod eædem prius offerantur
    dicto Donaldo Gorme, suis hæredibus et assignatis.—
    E. 257 l. 6s. 8d. *feudifirmæ, in integro.*'
Retours (*Inquisitionum, etc.*), Inverness, No. 68.   'Feb. 20.
    1644.
Dominus Jacobus McDonald de Slaitt miles baronettus, *hæres*
    Domini Donaldi McDonald de Slait militis baronetti, *patris*,
    —in
        20 libratis terrarum antiqui extentus de Slaitt :—
            E. 86 l. 13s. 4d.
        40 libratis terrarum antiqui extentus de Northwist :—
            E. 126 l. 13s. 4d.
        30 mercatis terrarum de Skerdhong ;
        12 mercatis terrarum de Beambecula ;
        1 denariata terræ de Gergriemyniss ;
        2 denariatis terrarum de Stalpit (vel Scalpit) ;
        4 denariatis terrarum de Greamnyss ;
        2 denariatis terrarum de Talbowmartein (vel Tallow-
            martein) ;
        6 denariatis terrarum de Orumseg ;
        dimidio denariatæ terræ de Waynelies ;
        dimidio denariatæ terræ de Ilegilligeir, cum molendinis et
            piscationibus, in dominio de Iles ;—E. 44 l.—exten-

dentibus in integro ad 257 l. 6s. 8d. *feudifir-marum* :[1]

  9 denariatis terrarum insulæ de Hilleskere in North-wist ;

12 denariatis terrarum de Ungnab ;

  2 denariatis terrarum de Caronies ;

  3 denariatis terrarum de Kirkibost ;

  1 mercata terræ de Castertoun in Illaroy in North-wist ;

  2 mercatis terrarum de Ardmidyllis in Slait :—E. 40 m. &c. *feudifirmæ* :

10 denariatis terrarum de Killibaxter in Trouterness.— E. 52s. *feudifirmæ.*'

With reference to this document and its variant readings

  'Stalpit (vel Scalpit),' *i.e.*, Scolpaig ;

  'Talbowmartein (vel Tallowmartein),' the Balamartin of to-day ;

  as also 'Skerdhong,' for Skeryhof ;

it may be remarked that ancient manuscripts are very liable to be mis-read in regard to some letters, particularly *u* and *n*, *c* and *t* (almost identical), and *b* for *l*.

The following is a fairly representative selection of North Uist place-names, including the most familiar in daily use and others which seem to deserve special notice. These have been arranged in alpha-betical order, together with remarks upon the various localities, and some attempt to trace their past history so far as references are available from old documents.

With much diffidence the writer also ventures to insert suggested derivations, these however being offered quite tentatively, and as a working basis for inquiry into a subject not yet fully discussed. Although considerable pains have been taken to secure general accuracy, many of these identifications will lay themselves open to criticism from students thoroughly versed in the root-languages. Even with this proviso, it is interesting to note how largely the Norse element here predominates over the Gaelic, a feature still more strongly marked in the neighbouring island of Lewis.

[1] The items from this point to the end of the charter had evidently been *church lands*, now for the first time included with the main portion of North Uist.

AHMORE (pronounced 'ah-vore,' the Gaelic, *àth-mhór*, or 'big kiln'), now the name of a farm which extends along the shore between Geireann Mill and Trumisgarry, opposite Ahmore Strand.

AIRIDH MHIC RUARIDH (Gaelic, 'shieling of the son of Roderick'), is situated immediately east of Griminish and to the north of several fairly good fishing lochs often known under this general term, although apparently in error. As a place-name it does not occur in any old charter, having no doubt been included under Griminish.

ALIOTER, a small promontory in one of the many recesses of Lochmaddy Bay, close to the roadside. Clearly the Gaelic *àth-Leòdair* for 'Leod's ford'; Leod (in early form *Leot*) representing the Norse *ljótr*, or 'ugly,' also used as a proper name.

ARD A' BHORAIN (Gaelic, 'point of the deer's grass,' from *boran*).[1] This is a promontory extending from the centre of the northern coast of North Uist towards the island of Boreray. 'The sandy isthmus which connects Ardavuran point with North Uist is so low as to be partially flooded at spring tides, and it is not easily discernible. On the pitch of the point is a solitary cottage, and on the inner side a burial-ground with a square mausoleum.'[2] The 'Row Ardineen' of Blaeu, 1654.

ARD AN RUNAIR (given as 'Ardrenil' in Blaeu's atlas of 1654). This is the extreme westerly point of North Uist, on the Balranald estate opposite the rocky islet of Causamul. Its name has been derived from the Gaelic as meaning 'point of the secretary, or clerk,'[3] although more probably to be associated with an earlier origin, especially since we find Loch Runavat about two miles to the east, this clearly representing *Rúna-vatn*, the Icelandic for 'loch of the counsellor.'

ARD SMEILISH, evidently Norse, perhaps to be explained as *smyl-nes* or 'point of the evil one.' An irregular promontory in the east side of Loch Scadavay, and one of four place-names in North Uist which end in *-lish*. See under Oilish, *postea*.

ARISAIG and ASHDAILL (*ár-óss-vik* or 'bay of the river's mouth,' and *askr-dalr*, both of them Norse) can hardly now be identified as

---

[1] Or possibly *Àrd a' mhurain*, 'point of the bent-grass.'
[2] *Sailing Directions for the West Coast of Scotland*, p. 75.
[3] In *Uist Bards*, Glasgow, 1894, p. viii.

to situation, although the former is supposed to have been at Claddach-Illeray and the latter near Bayhead. The 'Judicial Rental' of 1718 gives two tenants for Arisaig and six for Ashdaill, these last including 'John Laing, schoolmaster.'[1]

BAILE MHIC CONAIN is not marked upon the Ordnance map although its position is still known as having formed what is now the southern part of Newton farm, immediately to the north of Goulaby in the district of Sand. 'Balliviconen' appears in the 'Rental' of 1718 as then divided into four holdings of good size;[2] and we are informed that this was one of three townships—the others being *Baile Mhic Phàil* and *Caolas* (or Kyles Berneray)—which were cleared in order to make the single large farm of Newton, whence the very modern name of the latter.

BAILE MHIC PHAIL. This was immediately north of Baile Mhic Conain, and the map-name *Gearraidh Mhic Phàil* still appears a little to the east. 'Ballivicphaill' comprised fifteen small holdings,[3] probably extending eastwards to Cheese Bay, of which a branch is known as *Loch Mhic Phàil*.

BALAMARTIN, or 'Talamhartuinn' (Gaelic, *baile* representing the 'village' or 'homestead,' and *talamh* 'the land' of Martin), situated on the west side of North Uist between Hosta and Balelone, and now a crofters' township. The name frequently occurs in old charters, and always as '2 denariatæ' in valuation.

> 'Talawmartin,' *Reg. Mag. Sig.*, 1495, confirming a previous deed of 1469;
> 'Talmertane,' *Ibid.*, 1505;
> 'Tallawmartin,' *Ibid.*, 1596;
> 'Balmertein,' 'Belmertein,' and 'Belmerteine,' *The Clan Donald*, vol. ii. pp. 754-756, *anno* 1597;
> 'Tallowmartane,' *Retours*, 1617;
> 'Talbowmartein vel Tallowmartein,' *Retours*, 1644;
> 'Tallowmairtine,' and 'Tallowmairtin,' *The Clan Donald*, vol. ii. pp. 783-784, *anno* 1657.

---

[1] *The Clan Donald*, vol. iii. pp. 660, 662; also *Ibid.*, p. 372, for 'Rev. John Laing, Parochial Schoolmaster of North Uist.'
[2] *Ibid.*, p. 659. Some kitchen-midden remains are to be found upon a hillock at this site.
[3] *Ibid.*, p. 659.

BALELOCH (Gaelic), a farm at the north end of Loch Hosta. This is
the 'Ballekinloch. John M'Lean. 50 m. 2½ b. vict. 2½ st. b.'
noted in the 'Judicial Rental' of 1718.[1]

BALELONE (Gaelic, *bail' an lòin* or 'township of the marsh') lies immediately to the north of Balamartin. The name does not occur
in early documents, and it would seem that Balelone formed part
of either Scolpaig or 'Watna' during the sixteenth and seventeenth centuries.

In 1718 'Balloan' consisted of five crofts.[2]

BALESHARE (Gaelic, *baile sear*, 'east village or township,') is the
name of a large and comparatively level island, approached from
the south-west shore of North Uist by an easy ford at half-
tide. Like Balelone it is not mentioned in ancient charters,
although in this case evidently because of its former inclusion
under the general title of Illeray (which see). 'East village'
would seem at first sight to be peculiarly inappropriate as describing Baleshare, but we are told that this tidal annexe once extended
considerably seawards, where the waves now cover the site of a
'west village,'—*baile siar*;—an explanation which fully agrees
with reported encroachments by the ocean,[3] while it is even
said that the walls of ruined cottages may still sometimes be
seen under water off the western shore.

An official hand-book states that the channel between Baleshare
and North Uist 'in fine weather is left dry at high-water neap tides,
but during south-west gales it cannot be forded even at low-water
springs. Gales from this quarter cause the highest floods. One
which occurred in July 1859 occasioned much damage to the agricultural property of the tenants of Illeray and Baleshare; not only were
their crops of potatoes and barley destroyed, but the soil was washed
away and channels formed that never existed before. North-east
gales cause the best ebb and worst flow.'[4]

Ranald, a natural son of Sir James MacDonald the second baronet
of Sleat, and born in Skye *ca.* 1660, became tacksman of Baleshare
about the year 1700, also acting as factor of North Uist for some

[1] *The Clan Donald,* vol. iii. p. 660.
[2] *Ibid.,* p. 661.
[3] See remarks in Preface as to damage caused by the tides *ca.* 1540 and again in 1720; also
notes under Heisker, *postea.*
[4] *Sailing Directions* of 1885, p. 88, already quoted.

period until 1733, when he surrendered that office to Ewen MacDonald of Vallay. Ranald died in 1742, being succeeded in Baleshare by his eldest son Hugh, who prospered so well as to become the purchaser of an estate in Kintyre. Hugh MacDonald survived until 1769, and his son Donald held Baleshare together with the island of Kirkibost, also obtaining the factorship of North Uist.

This Donald was drowned in 1800, and his son William (afterwards Professor of Natural History at St. Andrews University) sold the Kintyre property, while it was doubtless about the same period (perhaps in 1799, 'three nineteens' after Ranald's death), that the tack of Baleshare came to an end.[1]

Baleshare is marked 'Balshen' upon Blaeu's map of 1654. It has now no peat, although we are assured that this was regularly cut there within the past century.

BALMORE (Gaelic, 'the large township') is the name of a hamlet at Paible. It appears (although too far north and east) as 'Balmoir' upon Blaeu's map of 1654; and in 1718 'Ballmore' was shared by eight crofters. In 1723 a 'Bond of Uist men and others' was signed at 'Ballimore.'[2]

An early occupant was 'Paul of the Thong,' who received these lands from the treacherous *Gilleasbuig Dubh, ca.* 1506, and held them until his own death *ca.* 1516.

Blaeu's atlas of 1654 shows two other place-names (south of 'Balmoir' and opposite the north end of 'Yl Kirkbol,' or Kirkibost Island) which ought here to be noted. These are—

BALDRICYM, now unknown;

BALCHENGHSH,[3] equally unknown, unless it may be identified with *Seanaval*, which occurs as a place-name upon the Balranald estate; or (according to *Origines Parochiales*, vol. ii. p. 373) with Kilmuir, although the reason is not very apparent.

---

[1] *The Clan Donald*, vol. iii. pp. 536-540. Ranald MacDonald appears in the 'Judicial Rental' of 1718 as paying '214m. 7½b. vict. 6st. b. t⅜t. ch.' for 'Ballshare' (*Ibid.* p. 662); and he also signed the Bond of 1723 as 'Ranald M'Donald of Balleshahr,' being evidently one of the wadsetters of North Uist (*Ibid.*, vol. ii. p. 792.)

[2] *Ibid.*, p. 792, and vol. iii. p. 662.

[3] Blaeu shows 'Balshen' in 'Ilvray,' and 'Balchenghsh' a little to the north, opposite 'Yl Kirkbol.' It may here be mentioned that this atlas of 1654 was evidently compiled at second-hand from loose or general descriptions. The maps appended to *Origines Parochiales* are also not strictly accurate,—the identifications being somewhat conjectural, as will be seen on comparing those which refer to the Outer Hebrides in vols. i. and ii. of that important work. Notwithstanding these discrepancies, both authorities have been found most helpful.

'BALNAKELIE,' or *baile na cille* (Gaelic, 'homestead of the chapel') in
Illeray, was a township at *Teampull Chriosd* towards the south
end of Baleshare island.   This name occurs as 'Ballienakill in
Eillera,' 1561 (*Collectanea*, p. 2); and again in a payment 'ffor
the landis of Balnakelie in Illera, sextene males,' 1576,
(*Ibid.*, p. 10).

BALRANALD (Gaelic, 'Ranald's village, or farm-town') is noticed as
'le Terung de Bailrannald,' *Reg. Mag. Sig.*, 1505 ;
'The 10 penny lands of Balranald,' in 1694, *The Clan Donald*,
vol. iii. p. 494 ;
and is marked 'Balrenil' upon Blaeu's map of 1654.

In Chapter III. it has already been noted that Clan Gorrie evidently
held the whole of North Uist from at least *ca.* 1389 to 1469.   Godfrey
(d. 1401, youngest son of John of Islay and Amie MacRuari) was the
founder of this clan, and it is from Ranald, younger son of Godfrey,
that Balranald is understood to derive its name, from the fact that he
there made his residence.   Ranald died in 1440, and the chiefship of
Clan Gorrie devolved in succession upon his sons Alexander and John,
the last-named dying *ca.* 1469.   After this period North Uist passed
to Hugh MacDonald of Sleat, younger brother of John, last Lord of
the Isles, and the founder of Clan Huistein.   John, son of Ranald
MacGorrie, seems to have been the last of Clan Gorrie who held North
Uist as a property, although his son Donald was tenant (or perhaps
tacksman) of Balranald *ca.* 1500-1515, while it is also said that this
estate remained in the occupation of his descendants for about two
hundred years thereafter.

In 1694, Alexander MacDonald (son of John, of Griminish, and
fifth in lineal descent from Donald Herrach, a younger son of Hugh
MacDonald of Sleat) advanced 3000 merks to Sir Donald MacDonald,
third baronet of Sleat, upon a wadset of 'the 10 penny lands of
Heisker, the penny lands of Peinmore and Peinnie Trynoid, and the
10 penny lands of Balranald.'   The 'Judicial Rental' of North Uist
(1718) compiled in connection with the forfeiture of Sir Donald
MacDonald (fourth baronet) in 1716, mentions Balranald as then
'vacant,' though Alexander MacDonald of Heisker must have still
held it up to almost exactly that time, surviving until 1723, while it
was not until 1727 that any part of this wadset seems to have been
discharged.   The next known occupant of Balranald was Captain John

MacDonald (fifth son of Major William MacDonald 'the Tutor,' a direct descendant of Donald Gallach and brother of the fourth baronet of Sleat) who received in 1740 a tack of Kirkibost, Kyles (Paible) and Balranald, and also became factor for the whole of North Uist, dying before 1750. His tenure seems merely to have been a life-rent, his only child, Margaret, receiving a tack of Paiblesgarry after her father's death.[1]

It was apparently about the year 1750, or somewhat earlier, that another Alexander MacDonald (who had been 'of Hougharie' from at least 1717) obtained a lease of Balranald and Kirkibost. This Alexander was drowned at Kirkibost ford in 1760, and has since been followed in Balranald by five generations of his descendants,[2] of whom Alexander MacDonald (d. 1901) purchased that estate together with Paiblesgarry and Penmore from Sir John Campbell-Orde, Bart., in 1894, and is succeeded by his only son J. A. Ranald MacDonald, the present proprietor and occupier.

BORERAY (Norse, *borgar-ey* or 'fort-island') lies in the Sound of Harris, separated from Ard a' Bhorain by a channel nearly a mile wide, and is the largest of the few islands in that sound which belong to the parish of North Uist. Boreray measures a mile and a half in length, and the earliest appearance of its name in old charters seems to be under '2 davatas Scotice dictas le Terungis de Sanda et Borwira,' *Reg. Mag. Sig.*, 1505.

Martin[3] writes :—'In the middle of this Island, there's a Freshwater Lake, well stock'd with very big Eels, some of them as long as Cod, or Ling-Fish; there is a passage under the Stony Ground, which is between the Sea and the Lake, through which it's suppos'd the Eels come in with the Spring Tides; one of the Inhabitants called *Mack-Vanish*, i.e. *Monks-Son*, had the curiosity to creep naked through this Passage.'

---

[1] *The Clan Donald*, vol. iii. pp. 362-365, 483-484, 494-495, 541. Captain John MacDonald was 'out in the '45.'

[2] *Ibid.*, vol. iii. pp. 487-494.

[3] *A Description, etc.*, p. 68. Boreray has also been derived as meaning 'bore-island,' no doubt from this underground connection between Loch Mor and the sea. The island, moreover, contains one *sloc* and five *geos*, but 'fort-island' is evidently the true explanation. It may be further noted that the northmost of the St. Kilda group is identical in name, while Boreraig or *borgar-vik* occurs twice in Skye.

According to Dr. Alexander Carmichael[1] the inhabitants of Boreray were accustomed to pasture their lambs upon a neighbouring islet
(named *Eilean nan Uan*) until it was entirely washed away in a
great storm early in the eighteenth century, being now represented
by a shoal known as 'Oitir nan Uan.' This tradition would seem to
be founded upon fact, and from another source we are informed that
the lost island lay between Lingay and Suenish Point in a part
still very shallow, while elsewhere, both to the east and south-east
of Boreray, the chart shows a depth hardly exceeding two fathoms at
low-water.

Boreray was held under successive long tacks by a junior branch
of Clan MacLean (of Ardgour) for several centuries, apparently indeed
from before the year 1498, this tenure remaining in the same family
until so recently as 1865. The earliest lease, although not proved by
documentary evidence, is fairly well vouched as having been granted
to Neil Ban MacLean, second son of Donald (the first MacLean of
Ardgour) by Hugh MacDonald of Sleat 'who from childhood had been
reared in MacLean of Ardgour's house.'[2] Hugh was half-brother to
John, the last Lord of the Isles, and died in 1498, a date which would
approximately fix that of the tack itself. Two subsequent leases were
certainly obtained by Neil's descendants in 1626 and 1712 (as noted
postea) and if the tack of *ca.* 1498 was in similar terms to that of
1712 it might easily stretch over the intervening period of 130 years,
in which case three leases would suffice for the whole MacLean tenancy.
We also find that three successive life-rents, with fifty-seven years to
follow, was 'the most favoured type of tack among the chiefs and
gentry of the Isles.'[3]

Concerning the first acquisition of Boreray by the MacLean family
there is a story told, which, although no doubt at least partly fictitious,
may here be recorded. It is said that the chief of Clan MacDonald,
while on a visit to MacLeod of Raasay, had lost to him at some
game of chance, a large portion of his lands. Thereupon MacLean, a
body-servant of MacDonald's, remarked, 'It is nothing; silver and
gold will buy them back.' MacLeod having assented to this view of
the matter, MacLean forthwith handed him two coins, one of them

---

[1] In a paper contributed to the *Scottish Geographical Magazine*, vol. ii. pp. 461-474.
[2] *An Historical and Genealogical Account of the Clan Maclean*, by a Seneachie, London,
1838, p. 277.
[3] *The Clan Donald*, vol. iii. p. 135.

silver and the other gold, claiming to have thus re-purchased the estates for his master. The sequel tells that this quibble was completely successful, MacDonald retaining his lands against the trifling payment, and subsequently granting to MacLean a long lease of Boreray as a reward for his ingenuity in saving the situation.

Upon 17th March 1626, Sir Donald (Gorm Og) MacDonald, first baronet of Sleat, granted a fresh lease to a later 'Neill Maclaine sone lauchfull to Donald Maclaine in Ust for all the dayes of his lyftyme and after his deceise to his nearest and lauchfull airis and assigneis quhatsumever for all the dayes, space, yeiris and terms of twentie ane yeiris of all and haill my aucht penny land of Burray and ane penny land in Solas with partes pendicles and pertinentis thereof, lyand in North Ust . . . Togidder also with the office of baillerie of the Loches of North Ust, the said Neill his duteis thereof quhilk sall begyn at the terme of Whitsonday nixt immedetlie following the deceis of the said Donald Macleane quhilk sall happin at the pleasur of God,' paying as yearly rental 'the sowme of Forty punds monie of this realme with ten bollis bere of the countrey mett and ten merkes of teynd dewtie, togidder also with the Kingis Majesties Maills and taxationes yeirlie at Mertinmas in Winter . . . and also the said Neill and his forsaids doand service to me baith by sea and land, according to use and want,' etc., etc.[1]

Sir Donald MacDonald, fourth baronet of Sleat, four years prior to his forfeiture of 1716, granted on 13 August 1712 a much longer tack to Archibald MacLean of Boreray 'for 3 lives and 3 nineteens for certain gratitude and pleasure and good deeds paid and done,' while in 1734 a fourth life was added by Sir Alexander MacDonald, seventh baronet.[2] To this tack reference is made by the old *Statistical Account* in stating of Boreray (the island of Grimsay near Benbecula being included in the same lease) in 1794 : 'It is presently possessed by a gentleman of the name of MacLean, whose predecessors have been in possession of it for several generations back, one of whom, for services done to the family of MacDonald, obtained, for the small yearly rent of

---

[1] *The Clan Donald*, vol. iii. pp. 650-651. This Neil MacLean 'of Boray' in 1657 signed himself 'N. McLeane, witnes,' *Ibid.*, vol. ii. p. 786. He was either the sixth or seventh MacLean of Boreray, and his son John was tacksman of that island about the year 1700 (Martin's *A Description, etc.*, p. 57).

[2] *The Clan Donald*, vol. iii. p. 135. Archibald MacLean appears in the 'Judicial Rental' of 1718 as paying annually '184m. 12½b. vict. 4st. b. 4st. ch.' (*Ibid.*, p. 662), these contractions representing merks Scots, bolls of oats, stones of butter, and stones of cheese.

£12 Sterling, a very long lease of it, 57 years of which are to run after the present possessor's demise.'[1] This tenant of 1794 was John MacLean, as twelfth or thirteenth of Boreray in family succession. He died in April 1821 at the age of sixty-two ;[2] and his son Donald was the last MacLean of Boreray, resigning his lease at Martinmas 1865, when the long tack of 1712 with the eke of 1734 had yet thirteen years to run, upon receipt of £3000 as against the unexpired period. The site of the mansion-house and garden occupied by the MacLean family is still shown immediately to the north of *Cladh nam Manach.*

Although the full text of the lease granted in 1626 to Neil MacLean is printed in *The Clan Donald,* the tack of 1712 for 'three lives and three nineteens' seems of sufficient additional interest to justify quotations at some length from a manuscript copy dated 1790 :—'Registered in books of Lords of Session, Edinburgh, 6 Oct. 1722.' 'Sett in rentall Tack and assedation,' by 'Sir Donald McDonald of Sleat, Knight Baronet,' to 'Archibald McLean of Barorary. . . . for all the days of his own lifetime and to his assigneys and subtenants of no higher degree than himself during the said space and after his decease to his heire male next of lynn duely served and retoured as to him for all the days space and years of his lifetime and to his assigneys and subtenants during the said space and after the decease of said heir to that heir his heir male which failing as said is and his assigneys and subtenants for all the days of his lifetime Together also for the space of three nineteen years, next and immediately following the expiration of the said liferents to their succeeding successors fynally one after another All and Haill the Eight penny lands of Baroray and the penny lands of Sollos with the Island of Lingay adjacent thereto and All and Haill the Lands of Meikle and Little Grimsayes with the Isle called Island Yirr and all the other smaller islands belonging thereto and as presently possessed by the said Archibald MacLean with all and sundry houses biggings mosses muirs meadows sheallings pasturages annexis connexis parts pendicles and pertinents thereof as well by sea as by Land not named as named together also with the Just and equall half of the multure and Dutys of the miln of Lochgarine all lying within the Barrony of

---

[1] Vol. xiii. pp. 303-304.
[2] Tombstone in the burial-ground at Ard a' Bhorain. This date would agree with the expiry of the tack in 1878.

Northeast and Sheriffdome of Inverness together also with the office of Bailliary of the haill Loches of North crust and also the equall half of the ammerciaments of Court of the tenements and servants of the said Archibald McLean and his foresaids dwelling upon the said Lands Together also with the thrie shearing Days work yearly in harvest and three days of threshing in winter of each one of my tennants of my twenty penny Lands of Sand lying within the said Barrony during the haill space respectively above specified. And the entry of the said Archibald MackLean and his foresaids is hereby Declared to begin after the expiration of the old former right and tack granted by the deceased Sir Donald MackDonald of Sleat my great grandfather to the deceast Neil MacLean of Barroray Dated the (17) day of (March 1626) years in his option of the date of thir presents the one but prejudice to the other and so furth to continue the possession of the said Lands offices and others above specified to be peaceable bruiked joyed occupied laboured intromitted with used and disponed,' etc. etc.

'For the which cause the said Archibald McLean Binds and obliges him and his heirs and successors to content and pay to me the said Sir Donald or my heirs or assigneys yearly the sum of fifty-six pounds Scots money, ten Bolls bear seed of the country meatt and seven bolls and three merks money foresaid of teinds And that at the terms of payment underwritten vizt. The silver Duty at the feast and term of Martinmas And the said ten Bolls bear seed and the seven Bolls and three merks tiends betwixt the terms of Christenmass and Candlemass and thereafter and so furth yearly to continue during the haill space respectively above Specified together with the Kings maile due for the said Lands abovewritten, and to releive me and my foresaids of all taxations public burdens and impositions imposed or to be imposed upon the said Lands during the said haill space And sicklike the said Archibald McLean and his foresaids giving to me and my foresaids service both by sea and land Conform to use and wont and he and his foresaids bound to answer to the Courts to be holden by me or my successors or our Deputts and keeping his majestys peace as becomes And it is hereby declared that the foresaid seven Bolls and three merks of tiends payable yearly by the said Archibald McLean and his foresaids is in full satisfaction of all and what others I could seek or crave of him or his foresaids do hereby authorize and empower the said Archibald M'Lean and his foresaids to exact and uptake from their subtenants of the saids Lands the personage or viccarage tiends or otherwayes as they think,' etc. . . . 'In witness whereof written by Daniel MacKinnon writter in Sleat I have subscribed thir presents at Armidale the thirteen day of August One Thousand seven Hundred and twelve years Before these witnesses David Ross my servitor and the said Daniel M'Kinnon,' etc.

In the absence of any pier, Boreray has no settled landing-place, this being taken at whatever part of the sandy bay on its east side best suits the tidal conditions at the particular time.

For the Pagan and Monastic remains upon this island, see Chapters VIII. and IX.

CAINISH (Norse; with -nes, or 'point'). On the north side of Loch Eford, separating it from Loch Hunder.

CAILTERNISH (certainly Norse, perhaps kjalar-tré-nes, meaning 'keel-timber point'). A peninsula in the south end of North Uist, immediately opposite Seanabaily.

CALLERNISH (Norse); usually explained as kjalar-nes, or 'keel point.' This is on the north side of Griminish, facing Vallay island with a narrow sound between. We can see no topographical reason for the word 'keel' being applied either to this Callernish or to its more familiar namesake in Lewis. Both of these places are associated with ferries at the present day,[1] and kallaðr-nes or 'shouting-point' would seem in every respect a better derivation.

CARAGARRY; on the north side of the entrance to Loch Eford. Norse? kjarr-gerði, or 'copse-garry'—see under Loch Caravat.

CARINISH (Norse; either Káris-nes,[2] with Kari as the name of an individual; or less probably kjarr-nes, 'copse point,' the first syllable of Carinish being now long, although—as written in some old documents—there are indications that it may have been formerly short). A township at the south-west extremity of North Uist, and noteworthy for its two ancient and closely adjoining chapels.

---

[1] At Callernish in Lewis there is a ferry across Loch Roag to Linshader. That from Griminish in North Uist to the island of Vallay is now (whatever may formerly have been the case) half a mile farther up the sound at Glamaris, a place-name locally translated to the writer as 'safe harbour' which no doubt agrees in point of fact, although hardly with the original meaning. For Glamaris we would suggest the Norse glamr-hús or 'tinkling-house,' if not even glammaðr-hús or 'Tinker's house.'

[2] See also the neighbouring Loch Caravat, and Caragarry at South Lee. Knock-Cuien, to the south of Loch Caravat, is said to have been covered with trees, and on the north-west side of the same loch is Beinn na Coille, 'hill of the wood.'

The name of Carinish seems first to appear in one of the charters of Inchaffray Abbey, to which 'Gothfridus de Insulis dominus de Wyste' granted a confirmation 'pro salute anime nostre et nostrorum predecessorum in honore sancte trinitatis et beate marie virginis gloriose Monasterio sancti Johannis euuangeliste in Insulamissarum et conuentui eiusdem in puram et perpetuam elemosinam capellam sancte trinitatis in Wuyste et totam terram de karynche et quatuor denariatas terre in ylara inter hussaboste et kanusorrarath cituatas,' etc., 7 July 1389.[1]

The lands of Carinish, whenever their extent is stated, invariably occur as 'two pennylands,' belonging to the church from a very early period, although before 1644 they had been acquired by the MacDonalds of Clan Huistein."[2]

'Cairenische thair' is mentioned as among 'The Abbatis landis within Donald Gormis' boundis,' 1561; and again, 1576, is included in an obligation by 'James McDonill Growemych of Castell Cammes' to 'Jhone Bischop of the Ilis and commendatour of Ycolmekyill and Ardchattane, . . . ffor the landis of Carinche, aucht males and ane mart.'[3]

The 'lands of Carroniss and Iyllegilegeirie' are included in a sasine in favour of Donald MacDonald, younger of Sleat, anno 1657, and are there further detailed as 'the twa penny land of Carronys,' 'Iyllegillegeirie' being only a halfpenny land.[4]

There is a further curious reference in 1694 to 'the penny lands of Peinmore and Peinnie Trynoid'[5] (coupled in a wadset with Heisker and Balranald) which would seem to include half of the lands of Carinish once associated with Teampull na Trionaid.

Some description must here be given of the Battle of Carinish, fought in May 1601,—a sanguinary affair, although upon a comparatively small scale.

About the beginning of the seventeenth century a bitter quarrel arose between the MacDonalds of Sleat and North Uist, and the MacLeods of Dunvegan and Harris, petty warfare being already an almost normal condition between these two clans. The special cause

---

[1] *Charters of Inchaffray Abbey*, Scot. Hist. Soc., p. 136.
[2] *Retours*, Inverness-shire; 20 Feb. 1644.
[3] *Collectanea*, pp. 2, 10. Blaeu's map of 1654 shows the place-name as 'Kareness.'
[4] *The Clan Donald*, vol. ii. pp. 783-784.
[5] *Ibid.*, vol. iii. p. 494.

H

of this fresh trouble was that Donald Gorm Mor (MacDonald) had married and divorced Mary MacLeod, a sister of Siṛ Ruaridh Mor, sending her home to her relatives. After skirmishes in Skye and Harris, Sir Ruairidh sent his kinsman Donald Glas MacLeod with a force, variously stated at from forty to sixty men, to lay waste North Uist and bring thence the cattle and goods reported to have been placed for safety within the precinct of *Teampull na Trionaid*. The story runs[1] that Donald Glas was attacked at Carinish by *Domhnull Mac Iain 'ic Sheumais* (a famous warrior of Clan Huistein, and nearly related to his chief, Donald Gorm Mor)[2] with only sixteen followers, when a fierce battle ensued between the two companies at a place known ever since as *Féith na fala* (the ditch of blood), about four hundred yards north-east from the 'Temples.' Thanks to the tactics adopted by *Domhnull Mac Iain*, and notwithstanding his small following, he and his MacDonalds succeeded in almost annihilating the MacLeods under Donald Glas, of whom indeed five or six managed to escape for a time, though authorities agree that only two of the MacLeods ultimately reached safety at Loch Eford, where they had left their boats.[3] Three or four of this small remainder, including the son of Donald Glas, made for the island of Baleshare, but were overtaken as they reached the strand. Although offering surrender, all were slain, young Donald Glas receiving a sword-cut which cleft his skull above the right ear. He was buried in Carinish 'Temple' (presumably the larger one), but the others rest where they fell, at the foot of a green knoll, still known as *Cnoc Mhic Dho'uill Ghlais*, a little above the shore.[4] It is

---

[1] Gregory, pp. 295-296 ; *Archæologia Scotica*, vol. v. pp. 230-237 ; and *The Clan Donald*, vol. iii. pp. 40-48, 500-501. From all accounts it would seem that the bow and arrow and the sword were the only weapons used at the Battle of Carinish.

[2] This 'Donald, son of John, son of James,' was second-cousin to his chief, being a grandson of James MacDonald (Gruamach) of Castle Camus, elsewhere noted as in 1576 guardian during the minority of his grand-nephew Donald Gorm Mor who was afterwards championed by this grandson at Carinish in 1601, and again at Dun an Sticir in 1601-1602.

Donald Glas MacLeod was the first of the family of Drynoch in Skye (*History of Clan MacLeod*, by Alexander Mackenzie, pp. 65, 215). It would seem that both father and son fell at Carinish, but the traditional *Cnoc* and *Oitir Mhic Dho'uill Ghlais* certainly commemorate the son.

[3] Mackenzie's *History of Clan MacLeod* states that the boats of the invaders were left at Port nan Long, opposite Berneray, in the sound of Harris. Other accounts favour Loch Eford, which would give the MacLeods a very short journey to Carinish by land, although involving a considerable detour by sea.

[4] These particulars are to be found in a detailed account of the Battle of Carinish given by Captain Thomas, who mentions that he had heard the story 'fifty or a hundred times,' but

said that the MacLeods had just breakfasted within *Teampull na Trionaid*, and the whole narrative shows the pre-Reformation sanctuary limits to have been ignored by both parties. *Domhnull Mac Iain 'ic Sheumais*, the hero of this affair, was then resident in Eriskay, although it is understood that he afterwards settled at Carinish, dying *ca.* 1650. His descendants continued to occupy Eriskay (an island which lies between South Uist and Barra) for several generations, and it was in the house of this Donald's great-great-grandson —Angus MacDonald, tacksman of Eriskay in 1745—that 'Prince Charles Edward spent his first night on Scottish soil after disembarking from the *Doutelle*.'[1]

In 1718 the 'Judicial Rental' of North Uist shows 'Caranish' as then divided between nine tenants, with a tenth item 'Waste' valued at an almost equal total, being probably a commonty held jointly by the nine. 'Plaid' or 'Blanket' here figures as part of the rent in every case.[2]

CARNACH (Gaelic, 'place of cairns'), a locality on the west side of North Uist, opposite Baleshare.

CASTERTOUN, see Eastertoune.

CAUSAMUL[3] (Norse, with *-hólmr*), a group of small rocks lying out in the Atlantic, a mile and a half west from Ard an Runair; evidently the 'Collinar skyr' shown in Blaeu's atlas. There is a Kisamul or 'Chisamil' Castle[4] upon an islet in Castlebay (Barra), a former stronghold of Clan MacNeil.

never with any material difference. He further notes the discovery in later years of a skull, easily recognisable as that of the younger Donald Glas MacLeod from a gash shown above the ear, adding that this skull lay within the 'Temple' so recently as 'twenty years ago'—say *ca.* 1840 ; *Archæologia Scotica*, vol. v. pp. 230-237.

[1] *The Clan Donald*, vol. iii. pp. 502-503.   [2] *Ibid.*, p. 660.

[3] Martin in his *Description, etc.*, of 1703, pp. 61-63, mentions Causamul as '*Cousmil*, about a quarter of a mile in circumference, ... still famous for the yearly fishing of Seals there, in the end of *October*, this Rock belongs to the Farmers of the next adjacent Lands, there is one who furnisheth a Boat, to whom there is a particular share due on that account, besides his proportion as Tenant, the Parish Minister hath his choice of all the Young Seals, and that which he takes is called by the Natives, Cullen Mory, that is, the Virgin Marys Seal,' etc., etc. He proceeds to minutely describe the process of clubbing, and adds :—'I was told also that 320 Seals Young and Old have been killed at one time in this Place. The reason of attacking 'em in *October*, is, because in the beginning of this month the Seals bring forth their Young on the Ocean Side, but these on the East Side who are of the lesser stature bring forth their Young in the middle of *June*.'

The *Old Stat. Acc.*, vol. xiii. p. 322, states 'there are 2 rocks to the westward, the one at the distance of 16, and the other, of 4 miles from shore, inhabited only by seals,' with a similar description of their slaughter in October or November. Although the actual distance is here doubled, reference is evidently made to the Haskeir rocks and to Causamul, while we learn that the former are still visited for this purpose.

[4] Marked 'Chastel Kyslum' upon Blaeu's map of 1654; clearly also of Norse origin, with *-hólmr*.

'CHEVLES YRT' (Gaelic), appears in Blaeu's atlas of 1654 immediately to the north of Griminish Point, which is there named 'Kow' (presumably 'Row' or *Rudha*) 'Chastelorre,' meaning the 'point of Castle Orre,' to be identified with *Caisteal Odair* of the Ordnance survey. This 'Chevles' is clearly an error for *Caolas*, a 'strait,' while 'Yrt' refers to Hirta or St. Kilda. Upon Blaeu's map of North Uist, *Caolas* reappears in the mid-north as 'Keules,' and again in the south-west as 'Cheulis,' about which no difficulty need be made, since the spelling of Gaelic words is so often phonetic.

CLACHAN (Sand) comprised ten crofts according to the 'Rental' of 1718, and lies immediately to the east of St. Columba's, between Goulaby Burn on the north, and Reumisgarry on the south.

CLIASAY BEG and CLIASAY MORE (Norse, ? *klifs-ey* or 'cliff-island '), in Lochmaddy Bay.

DUNSKELLOR, a small farm at Sollas, named from the massive fort which stood there, but now shows as little more than a mound. Skellor seems to be of Norse derivation, perhaps representing *skjöldr*, 'a shield' or *skjálgr*, 'squinting,' (both also used as personal names), but quite possibly from *skeljar*, 'shells.'

It is recorded that Angus MacDonald had a tack 'of the lands of Dunskellor, and others, in Sand, from Sir Donald MacDonald of Sleat, the proprietor';—apparently Sir Donald Gorm Og, first baronet, who died in 1643.

In 1718 'Doun' (evidently Dunskellor) was tenanted by Lachlan MacLean of the Boreray family, who in 1721 signed a complaint on account of murrain and devastation by the sea as 'Lauchlin McLeane in Douin.'

About forty years later, we find Archibald MacDonald of the Griminish family as factor (or more probably ground-officer) on the North Uist estate, and residing at Dunskellor. He died *ca.* 1767.[1]

DUSARY (Norse, apparently *Dugfúss-erg* or 'the shieling of Dugfus'), a very small hamlet with a corn-mill, immediately north of Kirkibost. Perhaps included in the latter, certainly not mentioned in any of the old charters.

---

[1] *The Clan Donald*, vol. iii. pp. 388, 484, 662, 664.

EASTERTOUNE (or Castertoun—but more probably Eastertoune, which
exactly represents the Gaelic form of Baleshare) seems to appear
both in '1 mercata terræ de Castertoun in Illaroy in North-
wist,' *Retours*, 1644; and again as 'Eastertoune in Iyllaray,'
1657.[1]

Upon the divisional map appended to *Origines Parochiales*, vol. ii.
part 2, this is marked near the centre of Baleshare island.

EILEAN A' GHIORR (pronounced 'Yeeor'; Gaelic, ? *eilean a' ghior*, or
'island of the short cut'); see under Garbh-Eilean.

EILEAN LEATHANN (Gaelic, 'broad island'), in the North Ford,
between Carinish and Grimsay.

EILEAN LIERAVAY (? Norse, *hliðar-vágr* or 'slope bay,' from the same
root-word as the neighbouring hills, North and South Lee;
other possible derivations being *liri-vágr*, 'tern bay,' or *leiru-
vágr*, 'muddy bay'). Already noted as lying a little to the
south of Lochmaddy, and connected with the point of Stromban
by a massive causeway.

EILEAN NA H-AIRIDH (Gaelic, 'island of the shieling'), a tidal
island in the North Ford, close to the west side of Grimsay.

EILEAN NAN CARNAN (Gaelic, 'island of the little cairns'), a tidal
island between Baleshare and Carinish. There are indeed two
of this name in the Baleshare ford, although that to the north is
very small.

FLODDY BEG and FLODDY MORE (Norse, *fljót-ey* or *flot-ey*), off the
north-east of Ronay. There is also another Flodday, the largest
of the islands near the mouth of Loch Maddy.

FOSHIGARRY (Norse, *fjósa-garðr* or 'byre-yard') at Griminish.

GARBH-EILEAN (Gaelic, 'rough island'). So far as we can judge,
this island in the North Ford (opposite and close to Claddach
Carinish and Seanabaily), perhaps together with its neighbour
Eilean a' Ghiorr, may represent not only the 'Ylandgarvy,' but
also the 'Ile-Gillegerrie' of ancient charters. As to Ylandgarvy
there can be little doubt, although it only occurs (to our knowledge) in *Reg. Mag. Sig.* of 1505 as

       '1 ablatam terrarum de Ylandgarvy,'
following   '1 ablatam terrarum de Walis.'

---

[1] *The Clan Donald*, vol. ii. p. 783.

The context, and also the coincidence that Ylandgarvy and Walis are the only halfpenny lands recorded in this charter of 1505, together with the fact that a previous grant of North Uist (1469, confirmed in 1495, *Reg. Mag. Sig.*) also includes only two entries of halfpenny lands, viz., 'Waynlis' and 'Insula Gillegerre,'—seem to prove the identity of Waynlis with Walis, and of Insula Gillegerre with Ylandgarvy.   And this is all the more probable if we take into account the sequence of the various lands as conveyed in these charters ; a point which is further accentuated by the retour of 1617 (p. 44 *antea*), where

> 'dimidio deniariatæ terrarum de Ile Gilligerrie'

reappears, immediately following the only other halfpenny land mentioned—that of 'Wainlies'—while both of these again occur in the retour of 1644 (also quoted on p. 44).

So far, then, as inferences may be drawn from description and context, the above seems the only tenable solution.

The great difference in name is admittedly a *crux*, not lessened by our finding very contradictory identifications of Ile Gilligerrie upon the maps in *Origines Parochiales*, vol. ii. parts 1 and 2.   In part 1, 'Gilligerrie' is shown as an *alias* for Illeray (Baleshare), while part 2,—evidently upon second thoughts and recognising the difficulty—gives it as synonymous with Killigray,[1] an island in the sound (and parish) of Harris.

'Ylandgarvy' thus appears but once in the old records (*Reg. Mag. Sig.*, 1505), while three notices of 'Ile Gilligerrie' have been already quoted, viz. :—

> 'Insula Gillegerre,' *Reg. Mag. Sig.*, 1469 ;
> 'Ile Gilligerrie,' *Retours*, 1617 ;
> 'Ilegilligeir,' *Retours*, 1644.

To these may now be added (and always as a 'halfpenny land ')
> 'Ile-Gillegerre,' *Reg. Mag. Sig.*, 1596 ;
> 'Ile-Gillegerrie,' *Ibid.*, 1614 ;
> 'Ellangellegerrie,' or
> 'Ellen Gilligerrie,' *The Clan Donald*, vol. ii. pp. 754-756, *anno* 1597 ;

---

[1] The earliest undoubted reference which we have found to this interesting island of Killigray is contained in the *Retours*, Ross-shire, 17 April 1627, where it appears as 'Killigir.'

'Iyllegillegeirie' (associated with Carinish), *Ibid.*, pp. 783-784, *anno* 1567).

Notwithstanding the differences in form, we must conclude (for the reasons already given) that Garbh-Eilean is identical with both Ylandgarvy and Ile Gilligerrie ; the latter name perhaps representing *Eilean gille Ghoraidh*, 'the island of Godfrey's servant,' in some relation to the Clan Gorrie which held North Uist from about A.D. 1389-1469.

GARRY MAARI (apparently Norse, from the hill Maari, which see). In the charter of 1505, already quoted from *Reg. Mag. Sig.*, there appear—

'le Terungis de Sanda et Borwira
et 1 den. terrarum de Gerrymare.'

These lands are clearly to be identified with Garry-Maari,[1] near the centre of the northern district of North Uist. Here, a mile south of Trumisgarry (part of the ancient parish of Sand), and in a position almost equi-distant between lochs Aonghuis, nan Geireann (Geireann Mill), and Fada, is the hill of Maari (562 feet), with a pass, Bealach Maari, running northwards between it and Crogary More to Loch Aonghuis. Again, immediately to the south of Maari, are Buaile Maari and Bogach Maari. This is the furthest inland, and one of the most easterly localities specified in the old charters of North Uist, nor can it ever have afforded more than a mere trifle of arable soil as compared with pasturage.

GERRINACURRAN (Gaelic, 'garry of the carrots'), noted as a small farm in the 'Judicial Rental' of 1718.[2] There are two places of this name in North Uist, one at Sollas, and the other in Baleshare (near Rosamul), with the latter of which this entry ought apparently to be identified.

GOULABY (Norse, *gulr-bœr*, or 'yellow homestead'), south of Newton farm.

GOULAR (Norse, *gulr-á*, or 'yellow burn'), at Kilmuir.

GRENETOTE (Norse, *grœna-topt*, or 'green croft'), on the mid-north shore of the island, and within the past few years resettled under

[1] The tract of land stretching from *Allt Bà-finne* (a little east of Geireann mill) to Ahmore, and from the hill of Maari to the northern shore of the main island.

[2] *The Clan Donald*, vol. iii. p. 662.

the Crofters' Commission. Grenetote is immediately to the east of Sollas, in which 'terung' (*Reg. Mag. Sig.*, 1505), it was probably included.

GRIMINISH (Norse, 'Grim's point). This place-name refers to the north-west extremity of North Uist, and includes the portion nearest St. Kilda, only forty miles due west.

Here we meet an undoubted difficulty in regard to the ancient records. Griminish, wherever its extent appears, is invariably described as a fourpenny land, and for this reason—apart from the slight distinction in name—can hardly be confounded with Ger-Griminish in Benbecula, which was only a penny land.[1] Some uncertainty however seems to exist upon another point, viz., that although various documents, dating from 1469 to 1657, clearly define Griminish as in North Uist, nevertheless Blaeu's atlas of 1654 shows both 'Gher Grimeness' and 'Grimeness' in Benbecula, and we find these repeated in the same positions (no doubt following Blaeu) upon the map appended to *Origines Parochiales*, vol. ii.; while in the current Ordnance map, Griminish (though rather as the name of a district than a definite spot, and without any Ger-Griminish) also appears in Benbecula, in addition to the better-known Griminish at the north-west corner of North Uist.[2] To meet these apparent contradictions a hypothesis of error seems at best unsatisfactory, although Blaeu is by no means immaculate, and the *Origines Parochiales* (*cf.* the maps in parts 1 and 2 of vol. ii.) gives internal evidence of partial conjecture. The solution may possibly be that Ger-Griminish (the *garðr* or 'garth' of Griminish) in Benbecula was an appanage of the Griminish twenty miles farther north—or *vice versâ*. *The Register of the Privy Council*[3] couples 'the four penny land of Greymins' with properties undoubtedly situated in Benbecula and South Uist, as being in 'questioun and contraversie' between 'Sir Donald Gorme

---

[1] 'Gergremynis,' *Reg. Mag. Sig.*, 1495 ; 'Gerrygremynis,' *Ibid.*, 1498 ; also in *Retours* (Inverness) of 1617 and 1644, etc.

[2] It is to be noted that a stretch of moorland, immediately to the south of Griminish in North Uist, is still locally known as 'Garry Griminish,' although not thus marked upon the map.

[3] Vol. xiii. p. 742, 30 July 1622,—'The thirty merk land of Skeirhoug, twelve merk land of Beainbecula, one penny land of Gerrogreyninis, and four penny land of Greymins' (elsewhere 'Gray mynes,' p. 37) in letters of caption following upon a horning of 20th July, and also mentioned (*Ibid.*, pp. 37-38, 1 Aug. 1622) without enumeration of extent.

of Slaitt, and Johnne M'Donald M'Allane V⁰ Eane, Capitane of the Clanrannald.'

We now come to the notices in ancient records which undoubtedly apply to Griminish in North Uist :—

> '4 den. de Gremynis,' *Reg. Mag. Sig.*, 1495, confirming the charter of 1469 ;
> 'le Terung de Watna, Scolping et Gremynis,' *Ibid.*, 1505 ;
> '4 den. de Gremynis,' *Ibid.*, 1596 ;
> 'quatuor denariatas terrarum de Grimineis,' *The Clan Donald*, vol. ii. pp. 754-756, *anno* 1597 ; [1]
> '4 den. de Greminys,' *Reg. Mag. Sig.*, 1614, and also 1618 ;
> '4 denariatis terrarum de Gremynis (vel Greinynis),' *Retours*, 1617 ;
> '4 denariatis terrarum de Greamnyss,' *Ibid.*, 1644 ;
> 'the ffour penny land of Gremineyse,' *The Clan Donald*, vol. ii. p. 784, *anno* 1657.

As in the cases of the neighbouring Balamartin and Scolpaig, it would seem that the notaries adopted a thoroughly congenial rule of never (when they could avoid it) spelling the same name twice alike.

The first recorded occupant of Griminish is Donald Herrach, a younger son of Hugh MacDonald of Sleat (the founder of Clan Huistein), by a daughter of MacLeod of Harris. For almost exactly three hundred years (from *ca.* 1498-1770) he and his descendants appear to have held Griminish, together with Scolpaig which indeed was probably their place of residence throughout that long period. Dun Scolpaig [2] is said to have been erected by Donald Herrach, and in any case it seems certain that he was

---

[1] This sasine in four places mentions 'quatuor denariatas terrarum de Grimineis,' but in another repetition speaks of 'triginta libratarum terrarum de Greminis' (p. 756), which would however seem a clerical error, and not to be founded upon ; more especially as other lands conveyed by the same document—*e.g.* those of 'Gar-gramnis' in Benbecula—are also inconsistently enumerated first as a pennyland and afterwards as a 'dawata.' This deed partly follows *Reg. Mag. Sig.* of 17 August 1596, to which it also explicitly refers.

[2] *The Clan Donald*, vol. iii. pp. 479-481 ; also Mackenzie's *History of the Macdonalds*, pp. 253-256.

murdered within this fort *ca.* A.D. 1506, through the treachery of his step-brothers Gilleasbuig Dubh and Angus Collach.[1]

Donald Herrach was succeeded in Griminish by his son Ranald, who served in Ireland with the MacDonalds of Antrim, being there severely wounded and returning to North Uist only to meet a violent death, in or before 1537, while on his way to spend the New Year at Kirkibost with his cousin and chieftain Donald Gruamach.[2] Angus, son of Ranald, died in 1586 and was followed in Griminish (as also evidently in Scolpaig) by his son Hugh and grandson John, the latter dying *ca.* 1700,[3] while Archibald (son of John) received a tack of both Griminish and Scolpaig from Sir Donald MacDonald (third baronet of Sleat) in 1715.[4] Archibald died in 1740, though even during his lifetime (1723) we find his son John described as 'in Scolpig,' afterwards holding both Griminish and Scolpaig until he died in 1765. Angus, eldest son of John, emigrated to North Carolina, returning before 1771 to North Uist, although he seems never to have there possessed any lands, his brother Archibald succeeding instead. It was evidently at the death (without issue) of the latter that this long tenure ceased, Griminish passing to Lieutenant Ewen MacDonald of the Vallay family[5] (a great-grandson of William 'the Tutor'), who seems to have held it from about 1770 to 1785.

Martin[6] writes, 'the Natives affirm that Gold Dust has been found at *Griminis* on the Western Coast of the Isle of *North Uist*, and at *Copveaul* in *Harries*; in which, as well as in other parts of the Isles, the Teeth of the Sheep which feed there, are died yellow.' We are told however that this is a purely natural condition as regards the teeth of old sheep.

GRIMSAY (Norse, ' Grim's island '), in the extreme east of the North Ford (to Benbecula), does not appear—under this name at least—

---

[1] See Dun Scolpaig in Chapter VI. If this date for the occupation of Dun Scolpaig be correct, that of *ca.* 1520 for Dun Aonghuis in connection with Angus, son of Donald Herrach, seems quite reasonable.

[2] *The Clan Donald*, vol. iii. pp. 482-483; Mackenzie's *History of the Macdonalds*, p. 256. Ranald is said to have been murdered at a spot marked by a cairn on Druimard in Balmore, a little west of Bayhead.

[3] 'John M'Donald in Grimines his marke following Q,' in an agreement of 1678, *The Clan Donald*, vol. ii. p. 787.

[4] *Ibid.*, vol. iii. pp. 479-485. Archibald MacDonald paid a yearly rent of '180m. 16b. vict. 8st. b. 8st. ch.' ('Judicial Rental' of 1718, *Ibid.*, p. 660). 'Archibald M'Donald of Griminshe,' 1721 ; *Ibid.*, vol. iii. p. 664.

[5] *The Clan Donald*, vol. ii. p. 792 ; vol. iii. pp. 485-486, 543.

[6] *A Description, etc.*, p. 339.

in any old charter. The earliest reference seems to be contained in a long tack of Boreray together with Grimsay, granted to Archibald MacLean in 1712 and lasting until 1865.[1]

GROATAY (Norse, *grjót-ey* or 'gravel island'), near the south entrance to Cheese Bay, with a small annexe upon which stand the remains of Dun Mhic Laitheann.

HAMERSAY (Norse, '*Hamarrs-ey*'); a small island in Loch Maddy, not far from the village.

HASKEIR includes two separate clusters of rocks, a mile apart, which lie in the Atlantic Ocean, at a distance of nearly eight miles west from Griminish Point. The derivation is obviously Norse, representing *haf-sker*, or 'deep-sea skerry.'[2] Of these groups, the southern (ten miles due north from its much more important congener named Heisker, with the Monach lighthouse) consists of 'five bare rocks with deep water channels between; they are without a blade of grass‖ or any fresh water, and can only be landed on in fine weather. The highest is 83 feet above the sea.'[3] This is known as Haskeir Eagach or 'the notched Haskeir,' a title thoroughly descriptive of the group when viewed from the nearest shore. Blaeu's atlas of 1654 marks these islets as 'Helskyr Egach' and 'Hayelskyr na Meul' (? the lumpy ocean-skerry); while Martin (p. 66), writes, 'About Three Leagues and an half to the West, lies the small Islands called *Hawsker-Rocks*, and *Hawsker-Eggath*, and *Hawsker-Nimannich*, id, est, *Monks-Rock*, which hath an Altar in it, the first called so from the Ocean as being near to it, for *Haw* or *Thau* in the Ancient Language signifies the Ocean, the more Southerly Rocks are 6 or 7 big ones nicked or indented, for *Eggath* signifies so much. The largest Island which is Northward, is near half a Mile in Circumference, and it is covered with long Grass.' Apart from the name thus given to the northernmost Haskeir (which is certainly confused with that of *Heisker nam Manach* in the 'Monach' group, ten miles to the south), Martin here fairly maintains his usual accuracy.

---

[1] *The Clan Donald*, vol. iii. p. 135; *Old Stat. Acc.*, vol. xiii. p. 304; also under Boreray, *antea*. The MacLeans held previous tacks of Boreray from about the year 1498, but we can find no mention of Grimsay in connection with any of these before 1712.

[2] The local pronunciation is 'Ha-sgeir,' quite distinct from that of Heisker, which may be phonetically rendered as 'Eys-sgeir.'   [3] *Sailing Directions*, 1885, part 1, p. 15.

The northern rock—*Haskeir na Meul*—is described as containing two parallel ranges of cliffs, which are from eighty to a hundred feet high, and traverse nearly its whole width. Here are also three natural arches and several caves.[1] It is evidently to Haskeir and Causamul that reference is made in Sir John Sinclair's *Statistical Account of Scotland*, although in both cases the distances from the main island are greatly overstated:—'There are 2 rocks to the westward, the one at the distance of 16, and the other, of 4 miles from shore, inhabited only by seals, which the possessors of the farms these rocks belong to attempt to kill once a year, either in the month of October or November. . . . These rocks have once been very valuable,' etc.[2] The *New Statistical Account*,[3] treating of the same subject, mentions three large rocks which 'from time immemorial, have been attached to the farms opposite to them, in various divisions. These are still retained possession of, not for their pasture,—for pasture there is none,—but for the seals they produce. In the proper season, under certain regulations, a boat is sent to each rock, the crew being furnished with large clubs, which they use dexterously,' etc. Reference to this systematic killing of seals on the Haskeir rocks is made both by Archdeacon Monro in 1549 and by Martin Martin in 1703, the former mentioning 'Haysker, quherin infinit slaughter of selchis is';[4] and we are told that the practice even yet continues to some extent.

In connection with these rocks, a curious story may here be given as evidently founded upon fact. It seems that, one autumn about eighty years ago, a tinker, 'desiring to exercise some self-restraint,' laid in a stock of provisions as also of materials for his trade, and sailed with these to the northern Haskeir. There he was left for a whole winter, having arranged with the boatmen to return for him early in the following year. Distinct traces of a rude stone hut may still be seen, not far from a small spring of fresh water, so that the general conditions fully agree with this account, even if it be hard to imagine how any one could choose such winter quarters, and very certain that the experiment was never repeated.

[1] Harvie-Brown in *A Vertebrate Fauna of the Outer Hebrides*, 1888. 'Towards the west end are 3 or 4 acres of rich soil and coarse grass, but in winter the waves cast their spray over the whole surface.'—*Sailing Directions*, 1885, part 1, p. 15.
[2] Vol. xiii., p. 322 (1794). [3] Inverness-shire, p. 164 ; written in 1837.
[4] Monro, pp. 35-36 ; and Martin, pp. 60-61.

CEANN EAR, HEISKER.

CEANN IAR, HEISKER.

HASTEN (Norse, *há-steinn* or 'high stone,') was an old township at Paible, on the west side of North Uist, marked 'Hasta' in Blaeu's map of 1654.

In 1718 this appeared as 'Hausten,' then consisting of seven crofts.[1] Here stands a rugged hillock capped by Creag Hasten, a peculiar isolated rock somewhat resembling a ruined castle when seen from a distance.

HAUNARY (Norse, *hafnar-ey* or 'haven-island,') an islet north of Ronay.

HEISKER[2] (Norse, probably *hellu-sker*,[3] 'flat skerry').

This general name is applied to a group of five islands which stretch east and west through a total length of between four and five miles, lying out in the Atlantic Ocean, eight miles due west of Baleshare, although distant barely four miles south-west from Rudha Mor at Paible, the nearest promontory on North Uist. The group includes Stockay, a low barren rock to the north-east, and on its west extremity another separate rocky islet named Shillay, where now stands the Monach lighthouse. Between these are three sandy islands of no great elevation, two of them much the largest of the group, and known respectively as *Ceann Ear* (east head) and *Ceann Iar* (west head), united at low water by the smaller intervening islet of Shivinish, which is usually joined to Ceann Iar and fordable from Ceann Ear at half-ebb, thus together forming two islands at ordinary high-water, but three at the flood of spring-tides. Ceann Ear covers by far the greatest area, measuring at its extremes nearly two miles by half a mile, or quite double the size of Ceann Iar.

Apart from the lighthouse establishment on Shillay and two dwellings at Ceann Iar, the whole population is domiciled upon Ceann Ear in a very small village which is provided with a missionary and a school-mistress, as also with a post-office served by weekly mails from Bayhead in North Uist.

[1] In the 'Judicial Rental,' *The Clan Donald*, vol. iii. p. 660.

[2] Also known as the 'Monach Isles,' although this latter title ought to be restricted to Shillay as *Eilean nam Manach* or 'Island of the Monks,' with reference to an early monastery which occupied the site of the present lighthouse.

[3] A form which closely agrees with that of 'Helsker' given by Archdeacon Monro in 1549. *Heilagr-sker* or 'holy skerry' would well suit the circumstances, if otherwise admissible as to its phonetics.

Both of the main islands are chiefly composed of sandy soil with wind-blown portions; Ceann Ear having two small lochs in its rocky south-western spur, while Ceann Iar shows a less broken surface and contains an outstanding hillock, Cnoc Mor, together with promontories which bear the distinctively Norse names of Hearnish and Hakinish. Upon Ceann Iar is a large cattlefold with a range of seven adjoining huts, these latter serving as temporary accommodation for the crofters of Ceann Ear.

Shivinish is of but small extent and normally connected with Ceann Iar by an elevated spit of sand. We here witnessed the picturesque sight of the crofters' sheep and cattle being driven across to Shivinish from Ceann Ear at half-tide, so soon as the ford became available.

In Croich harbour, on the north-west of Ceann Ear, is a large isolated rock known as *Heilleam*,[1] partly clothed with scanty turf, and also bearing some appearance of walls, which the writer now much regrets not to have more closely examined.

With reference to an interesting (though probably untenable) derivation of Heisker offered by Dr. Alexander Carmichael, it now becomes necessary to make several lengthy quotations, the first of these bearing official authority :—

'About 70 years ago the islands were well covered with good pasturage, with machirs or sandhills of considerable height. At half-tide all the islands except Shillay and Stockay, were connected, as at present, by a sandy beach, and they were inhabited by eighteen families, besides cottars, who were enabled to keep 1000 head of cattle, sheep, etc. About 10 years after, without any apparent cause, the whole of the surface of the islands was denuded of soil and grass, except two very small portions on each end. The inhabitants were consequently obliged to leave, and for nearly 15 years the islands were uninhabitable, except by one family, and a channel of 6 or 8 feet was scoured out on each side of Shevenish island.'[2]

In a communication printed as an Appendix to the 'Napier'

---

[1] Certainly Norse; perhaps *heill-hólmr*, or possibly from the same root-word as Heisker itself, but including *-hólmr* instead of *-sker*.

[2] *Sailing Directions*, part 1, p. 82. The expression '70 years ago' apparently refers to a date about the year 1800.

Crofter Commission Report,[1] Dr. Alexander Carmichael (who has an intimate knowledge of the Outer Hebrides) takes Heisker to represent *Aoi-sgeir*[2] or 'isthmus-skerry,' although 'partly through the gradual subsidence of the land, and partly owing to the gradual dislodgment of the friable soil forming the isthmus, the isthmus by degrees gave way to fords, and the fords broadened into a strait four and a half miles wide and four fathoms deep. Tradition still mentions the names of those who crossed these fords last, and the names of persons drowned in crossing.' The same writer adds (*ca.* 1884) 'I know men who ploughed and reaped fields now under the sea,' though this latter statement may apply to Harris instead of North Uist.

The Admiralty Chart of 1865 (corrected to the year 1900) tends to confirm Dr. Carmichael's description of the strait which now separates Heisker. This map shows a range of shallow water extending in a curve along the west shore of North Uist from the south end of Baleshare to Ard an Runair, with a narrow submerged strip reaching directly out from the centre of this shoal (opposite Kirkibost island) for nearly five miles to Ceann Ear, and nowhere exceeding a depth of four fathoms (that is, at low water). On the other hand, the same chart gives a very regular depth of nearly twenty fathoms between the Scolpaig shore and the two northern skerries (known as *Haskeir Eagach* and *Haskeir na Meul*), ten or eleven miles north of

[1] *Blue Book of* 1884, No. C.-3980, 'Report of Her Majesty's Commission of Inquiry into the condition of the Crofters and Cottars,' etc., pp. 464-465. While mentioning Dr. Carmichael's derivation of Heisker as from *Aoi-* (otherwise *Uidh-*) *sgeir* we may add that the same authority in another paper (*The Scottish Geographical Magazine*, vol. ii. pp. 461-474) cites local tradition to the effect that Heisker was at one time joined both to North Uist and Benbecula ; further adding —'Intelligent crofters informed the writer of having seen fragments of iron bolts sunk into certain low-water rocks in the Atlantic between Benbecula and h'Eisgeir. These rocks lie at a distance of some miles from the land on either side, and are believed to have been the sites of embankments. . . . It is interesting and curious to find various submerged sites over the now wide and open sea still called by their place-names, as Sgeir a Chloidhean ("the barrier rock," the site of a flood gate), Ceardach Ruadh ("the red smithy"), and others.' But Ceardach Ruadh still exists as a sand-hill site on Baleshare island, immediately above its west shore and close to Sgeir Husabost. In this connection may be noted the existence of a very small tidal rock off the west shore of North Uist, close to Dig Mhor, at the mouth of Loch Paible, and still known as *Airidh Nighean Ailein*, or 'the shieling of Allan's daughters.' This is locally said to be an ancient pasturage, and the inference remains that when it acquired this name the coast-line extended distinctly further out into the ocean.

It may be further stated that, six miles south-west of Canna is a skerry marked *Oigh-sgeir* or 'Hysker' on different maps. *Sgeir* invariably refers to a rock in the sea, never to one situated upon the land.

[2] The Icelandic form *Eiŏ-sker* would equally serve, both *uidh* and *sgeir* being words borrowed from the Norse into the Gaelic language.

Heisker; and still farther west, an average of some fifty fathoms out from the Haskeirs to St. Kilda. Thus the ocean between North Uist and the Heisker group is characterised by a remarkably uniform shallowness.

The earliest record of the lands of Heisker is of very uncertain date. According to *Collectanea de Rebus Albanicis*, p. 289, Donald, son of Reginald (and grandson of Somerled of the Isles), mortified 'the Island of Heisker to the Nuns of Iona' sometime before 1289. *The Clan Donald* (vol. i. pp. 72-73) however, in referring to this account by 'the historian of Sleat,' notes that Donald's death occurred 'very probably prior to 1249, for before that date we find his son Angus giving a charter for part of his lands in Kintyre.' The same authority, vol. ii. p. 229, credits Reginald MacRuari, son of John, first Lord of the Isles, with bestowing, among other gifts, 'the Island of Heisker, in North Uist, to the Monastery of Iona.' As Reginald died *ca.* 1386, there is here far too wide a margin of chronology, and it is no doubt safer to ascribe this mortification to the fourteenth rather than to the thirteenth century.

The next is a merely incidental reference in *Collectanea*, p. 320, as to a sister of Sir Donald Gallda (last of the MacDonalds of Lochalsh) who 'was such an idiot, that she was sent to Heiskier, a remote island, lest she should be seen of strangers, to the care of a gentleman living there, a Macdonald called Donald Du Maclauchlane'; which, if authentic (as may likely be the case), would infer a date of somewhere about the year 1500 for this episode.

Then we come to Archdeacon Monro's *Description* of 1549:—
'Helsker Nagaillon. Be aught myle of sea, frae this ile towards the west, lyes ane ile four myle and haff myle braid, laiche maine land, callit Hesker Nagaillon, it has abandance of corne and elding for fire, it perteins to the Nuns of Columnkill.'[1] This notice may fitly be taken in connection with another quoted by Mr. Cosmo Innes[2]:—
'In 1574, Mary Nikillean, prioress of the monastery of Saint Mary the Virgin in the island of Yona, granted to Hector M'Clane of Doward in heritage the nunnery lands, including the four pennylands of Ballienangalleach[3] and the lands of Hellsker in the isle of Ewyast.'

[1] Monro, p. 35.
[2] *Origines Parochiales*, vol. ii. p. 372 ; quoting the 'Protocol Book of Gavin Hammiltoun.'
[3] In Benbecula ; *Baile nan Cailleach*, literally represented by the modern 'Nuntown.'

If the place-name 'Helsker Nagaillon' is correctly transcribed[1] from the MS. of Archdeacon Monro, its origin may be due to some association with the Clan MacLean, whether through Agnes or Mary MacLean of the Duart family, who successively held the office of prioress of Iona from at least A.D. 1509 to 1574,[2]—*Nic Gillein* representing in Gaelic 'daughter of Gillean,' with reference to the founder of Clan MacLean (*Gille-Eòin* or 'servant of John') said to be lineally descended from Fergus I., King of Scotland.

In an obligation dated 17th March 1575-1576,[3] reference is made to an annual payment 'for the third of the fermes of Halskienagallechie, tuentie males grane, and the third part of ane maill,[4] due by 'James McDonill Growemych of Castell Cammes' to the Bishop of the Isles, 'in tyme cuming to be yerlie maid in Ycolmkyll, betwix Petersmess and Beltane'; this 'Halskienagallechie' clearly representing Heisker under the form of Dr. Carmichael's '*Heisgeir nan Cailleach.*'

Next comes an incidental notice in a crown-charter of 7th March 1610, by which King James VI., 'pro servitio sibi impenso et impendendo, concessit D. Thome Ker militi, . . . insulam appellatam Hirta, cum tribus insulis portui ejusdem adjacentibus, que fuerunt pendicule dicte insule, jacen. ex boreali occidentali parte de Owist et Halkster circiter 60 miliaria maris . . . Solvend. unum argentum nummum nomine albe firme.'[5]

[1] If this authority fails us (or indeed, in any case), there are strong reasons for favouring Dr. Carmichael's identification of 'Heisgeir nan Cailleach' in the same way that Shillay even more certainly bore the descriptive title of 'Heisgeir nam Manach,' referring to the former existence of a nunnery upon the one island and of a monastery upon the other. A very possible solution might be that during the fifteenth century the Heisker group was known as 'Heisker Nagaillon,' while latterly a particular portion acquired the name of 'Heisgeir nan Cailleach.'

[2] From *Origines Parochiales*, vol. ii. pp. 295-297, we find that in 1509 the prioress of Iona was 'Agnes, daughter of Donald Makgillane,' otherwise styled 'Anna, the daughter of Donald M'Terlet,' who evidently died in 1543. In 1548 Queen Mary admitted to the temporalities of Iona 'the lady Mary Farquhardson or M'Gilleone, prioress of Icolmkill, promoted by His Holiness the Pope (Julius III.) to the monastery or nunnery of the same'; while, on 15th February 1566-1567, this queen also granted to Marioun Makclane for her lifetime 'the prioressie and nvnrie of the abbey of Ycolmkill liand within the diocie of the Ylis, now vakand throw deceis of vmquhile Agnes M'Clane, last priores thairof.'

A charter of 1427 was witnessed by 'Terleto Ferchardi Makgilleoin,' confirmed 12th November 1495, *Reg. Mag. Sig.*

[3] *Collectanea*, pp. 9-12.

[4] According to *Collectanea*, p. 173, the *male* or *maillia* was 'a measure of grain of Scandinavian origin, formerly much used in Orkney. . . . The *male* of meal is valued in this charter at 3s. 4d., the *large boll* at 6s. 8d. The *male* was therefore equal to half a boll.' It is to a Tiree charter of novodamus, dated 19 March 1587-1588, that reference is here made.

[5] *Reg. Mag. Sig.* This is of special interest, being perhaps the only record of St. Kilda as an individual property.

K

Seven years later,[1] 'Rex . . . concessit et de novo dedit Rodorico McKenzie de Cogeauche' certain lands which 'Hector McCleane de Dowart' had resigned for that purpose. Amongst these were included '4 den. de Ballienangalleache et terras de Helsker in insula de Owyst,' for which a curious form of rent was stipulated—'pro Ballienangalleache 12 maleas grani, et pro Helsker 50 maleas grani et 20 maleas ordei, mensure de Owyst (vel 6 sol. 8 den. pro malea), martam (vel 10 sol.), pro sustentatione unius noctis 2 maleas manseti ordei (vel 6 sol. 8 den. pro malea), 4 mensuras casei a ballivo dicte insule (vel 5 sol. 4 den.).'

The Register of the Great Seal, 19 December 1623, contains a grant from James VI. infefting William Stirling[2] of Auchyle 'in terris de Kilmorie in Wuest . . . . 11 den. terrarum de Skeirnakillach et Ylskeanacwissage in Wuest,' with the statement that these latter had belonged to '*lie Nunrie* de Ycolmkill.'[3] This charter conveys other lands in various parts of Scotland, including '4 den. de Ballincayloche in Beanveill' or Benbecula, which are thus shown to have been quite distinct from the eleven pennylands of 'Skeirnakillach et Ylskeanacwissage,' again mentioned in the same document as 'Skeirnacaliche' and 'Yliskeanacuschage' respectively, while a footnote adds that the latter name appears in *The Register of the Privy Seal* as 'Ylskermacwissag.' From these notices it is evident that, early in the seventeenth century, the Heisker group was known under this pair of unwieldy names which present so marked a contrast to the simple and geographically descriptive Ceann Ear and Ceann Iar of modern times. The statement made by Dr. Carmichael that one of these (from the context, presumably Ceann Iar), was once occupied by a small nunnery 'the site of which can still be traced,' would fully account for 'Skeirnakillach' as *Sgeir nan Cailleach* or 'skerry of the nuns'; leaving Ceann Ear, with its profuse growth of bent-grass, to be identified as 'Ylskermacwissag' or the Gaelic *Heisgeir nan cuiseag*, signifying 'Heisker of the stalk-grass.'

A charter of Charles I., *Reg. Mag. Sig.*, 24 July 1630, grants to Lachlan MacLean of Morvern, upon the resignation of his brother

---

[1] *Reg. Mag. Sig.*, 11 April 1617.

[2] We elsewhere find that this William Stirling was factor to the then Earl of Argyll.

[3] Supplementing a resignation by Andrew, bishop of the Isles, 'tunc Episc. Rapotensis in regno Hibernie, cum consensu Thome tunc Episc. Insularum, filii sui,' of other lands also formerly belonging to the nunnery of Iona.

Hector, '4 den. de Ballinangalloche' (clearly Nuntown in Benbecula) 'et terras de Heisker in insula de Wist,' although here no details are given.

The *Reg. Mag. Sig.* is not available (in printed form) beyond the year 1659, and the next references to Heisker—apart from the 'Helskyr na Monich' upon Blaeu's map of 1654—are to be sought in the *Retours* of Inverness-shire. Here, 20 February 1644 (No. 68), occur in the succession of Sir James MacDonald, Bart., of Sleat,

'9 denariatis terrarum insulæ de Hilliskere in North-wist,'

while again (No. 88, 22 January 1662) Sir George Mackenzie of Tarbert, Bart., was served heir to his grandfather, Sir Roderick MacKenzie of Coigeach, in various lands, all differing from those above-mentioned, with one exception (and that perhaps only in appearance), viz. :—

'4 mercatis terrarum de Ballienaugalleache, et terris de Helsker in insula de Wist.'

Our final quotation, dating between these two retours, is from *The Clan Donald*, vol. ii. pp. 783-784, where a sasine of the lands of Sleat, January 1657 (granted by Sir James MacDonald, Bart., in favour of Donald MacDonald, his eldest son), includes 'the nyne penny land and Isle of Hallesker,' or 'Halleskeir,' together with many other portions of North Uist, etc.

This of course seems to directly contradict the succession recorded in 1662; but in the first place it must be acknowledged that the period was one of conflicting and inoperative charters, while secondly, there is at least a possibility that Heisker may then have been shared between MacDonald of Sleat and MacKenzie of Coigeach.

In 1692, Alexander MacDonald (son of John MacDonald of Griminish and fifth in lineal descent from Donald Herrach) was tacksman of Heisker. This Alexander, 'or, as he was known in his day, and is still known in tradition, *Alistair Bàn Mac Iain 'Ic Uisdein*,' deserves to be honourably remembered for his generosity in sending prompt assistance to the survivors of the massacre of Glencoe. We are told that upon hearing in remote Heisker the news of this calamity, he filled his 'birlinn' with meal and sailed for Ballachulish, there bestowing his cargo in relief of pressing necessities.[1]

---

[1] *The Clan Donald*, vol. ii. p. 222.

Two years later, the same Alexander MacDonald advanced 3000 merks to Sir Donald MacDonald (third baronet of Sleat) upon a wadset of 'the 10 penny lands of Heisker, the penny lands of Peinmore and Peinnie Trynoid, and the 10 penny lands of Balranald.'[1] He died in 1723,[2] and this wadset remained undischarged until the repayment of 2000 merks to account in 1727 by Kenneth Mackenzie (the Edinburgh advocate), and a further payment in 1748, which probably closed the transaction.

John, son of Alexander, seems to have died soon after this settlement, and is nowhere described as of Balranald, but simply ' of Heisker.' The 'Judicial Rental' of 1718 states the annual payment for Heisker at '220 m. 75 b. vict. 22 st. b.'; and in 1723 the signature of 'Jo. McDonald of Heillskire' appears in a 'Bond of Uist men and others.'[3]

HOLF ; see Hougary.

HONARY (Norse, ? *horn-erg* or 'corner shieling'), south of Honival, near Loch Mhic Phail.

HOSTA (Norse; perhaps *Högni-staðr* or 'Högni's stead'; but more probably *haug-staðr*, from *haugr*, 'a mound or cairn,' as in Hougary.[4] This is the name of a township between Tighary and Balamartin, close to Loch Hosta, a sheet of water half a mile in length.

A curious local tradition is recorded, in which Hosta plays an important part as to a feud between Siol Gorrie and Siol Murdoch, both of them septs of Clan MacDonald and inhabiting North Uist, of which island the Siol Gorrie had held possession from *ca.* 1389-1469. To quote Dr. Carmichael:[5]—'It would seem

---

[1] *The Clan Donald*, vol. iii. p. 494. It is to be noted that a sasine of 1657 mentions the 'nyne penny land and Island of Hallesker,' *Ibid.*, vol. ii. p. 783. Here is the discrepancy of a penny land, perhaps due to encroachments by the sea.

[2] His daughter Anne was married in 1696 to James MacDonald of Eriskay, a grandson of Donald, the Carinish hero of 1601, *Ibid.*, vol. iii. pp. 494-495, 503.

[3] *Ibid.*, vol. ii. p. 792 ; vol. iii. pp. 495, 662. The tenancy of Heisker is thus noted only from 1692-1748. Reference has already been made to the 'seclusion' of a sister of Sir Donald Gallda of Lochalsh upon Heisker in the first half of the sixteenth century. It is curious to note that, almost exactly two hundred years later, history repeated itself in the case of the unhappy Lady Grange, who was in 1732 to 1734 also 'secluded' upon Heisker, being afterwards removed to St. Kilda, and there held prisoner for nearly eight years (Seton's *St. Kilda*, p. 50).

[4] The recently disused 'Hough Mill' stands about midway between Hosta and Hougary.

[5] *Proc. Soc. Antiq. Scot.*, vol. viii. pp. 278-279.

that the Siol Murdoch (*Siolach Mhurachaidh*), the descendants of Murdoch, were the stronger, and consequently that the Siol Gorrie (*Siolach Ghoirridh*), the descendants of Gorrie,[1] were as much indebted to their stratagems as to their strength in maintaining the unequal contest. The greater part of the Siol Murdoch lived in the valley of Hosta. About three-quarters of a mile from, and in the hill above this, there was a lake. The Siol Gorrie upon one occasion came under cover of night and cut away the embankment of this lake, whereupon the water rushed down the glen and drowned the inhabitants of the valley beneath. The scene of this tragedy has remained the site of the lake ever since. During calm, clear weather, I believe, the remains of houses can still be discovered in the bottom of the lake. To revenge this outrage, the rest of the Siol Murdoch marched in a body against the Siol Gorrie, who lived at Udal, on the north-east side of the island. It is said that Udal was the largest township in the Long Island at that time. The Siol Murdoch found the Siol Gorrie at their tillage in the fields, when they came upon them unawares, and put them all to the sword, except one man who escaped by swimming and wading across to the island of Oirisey, whence he escaped to Boisdall, in S. Uist, where it is said some of his descendants are still. After putting all their foes to the sword, the Siol Murdoch pursued their course to the hamlet of Udal, the whole of which they gave to the flames, sparing neither young nor old, male nor female, in their savagery.' The township of Udal is said to have been at that time occupied by eighteen families.

Another version of this story makes Siol Murdoch the first aggressors and Siol Gorrie the avengers. It is further said that a shallow loch already existed at Hosta, containing an island-fort in the possession of Siol Murdoch, who were drowned by a sudden rise in the level of Loch Hosta when the waters of a former *Loch Clettraval* had been let loose. If we are to accept this tradition as containing some basis of historical fact, it must refer to a period at about the middle of the sixteenth century.

The rental of Hosta in 1718 was '100 m. 5 b. vict. 5 st. b.,' and the

---

[1] Gorrie or Godfrey was a son of John of Islay by Amie MacRuari, and obtained the North Uist portion of his mother's inheritance in or before 1389. Murdoch (who gave his name to Siol Murdoch) is said to have been a natural son of Angus Mor of Islay, who died *ca.* 1293 (*The Clan Donald*, vol. i. p. 84, vol. iii. p. 366).

tenant or tacksman at that period (1718-1723) was Hector MacLean, who seems to have held a wadset.[1]

HOUGARY (pronounced 'Hoe-gary;' Norse, *haugr-gerði*, meaning 'how-'[2] or 'mound-enclosure'). A township at Kilmuir on the west side of North Uist, close to the parish churchyard, and not far from Balranald.

This no doubt represents the 'Holf' of 1505, and is certainly the 'Howyairth' marked upon Blaeu's map of 1654 ;—

> 'le Terung de Bailrannald, le Terung de Holf, le Terung de Watna Scolping et Gremynis,' *Reg. Mag. Sig.*, 23 Aug. 1505.

The 'Judicial Rental' of 1718 shows fourteen tenants as then occupying 'Howgarie,' but only one of these with any considerable holding.[3] Alexander MacDonald appears as one of the small tenants, and afterwards became factor of North Uist at some date about 1750 to 1754.[4]

HURIVAG (Norse, with -*vágr* or -*vik*), near Cheese Bay.

ILE-GILLIGERRIE or YLAND GARVY ; see under Garbh-Eilean, *antea*.

ILLERAY (Norse, ? *illr-ey* 'bad island,' perhaps in allusion to repeated encroachments by the sea[5]) ; the present name for the northern portion of Baleshare island, though in old charters we find only two notices of its extent :—

> 'quatuor denariatas terre in Ylara,' *Charters of Inchaffray Abbey*, 1389 ;
> 'le Terung de Yllera,' *Reg. Mag. Sig*, 1505.

At that period Illeray must have included the whole of Baleshare, which finds no individual mention in any of the earlier records quoted in the present chapter.

In addition to the above references, Illeray is further named as containing *Baile na cille* and *Eastertoune* (which see, *antea*).

---

[1] *The Clan Donald*, vol. ii. p. 792 ; vol. iii. pp. 662, 664. It is stated that Lachlan Og MacLean had a tack of Hosta after losing the farm of Havisgarry near Sollas.

[2] The neighbouring island of South Uist was formerly divided into two parishes, that which occupied the northern portion bearing the name of Howmore, and representing the 'Skerehoug' or 'Skeryhof' of old charters.

[3] 'Angus McDonald, 120 m. 12 b. vict.' ; equalling about one-third of the whole valuation of the fourteen tenants ; *The Clan Donald*, vol. iii. pp. 661-662.

[4] *Ibid.*, pp. 487-488.

[5] See Baleshare, *antea*.

HOUGARY, FROM SOUTH.

PERFORATED SLAB FROM ILLERAY.

'Ballienakill in Eillera,' 1561;

'Balnakelie in Illera,' 1576;

'Castertoun in Illaroy' (a merkland), 1644;

'Eastertoune in Iyllaray,' 1657;

also 'Kirkapost in Eillera,' *Collectanea*, p. 2, *anno* 1561, though this ought probably to read as 'near Illeray.'

According to the 'Judicial Rental' of 1718 'Ulleray' was then occupied by thirteen small tenants, with a fourteenth item of 'Waste,' as in the case of Carinish.[1] Indeed Illeray and Carinish are in other respects very similarly treated, each tenant paying part of his rent in plaid or blanket, a feature which occurs nowhere else in North Uist at that period. As regards the four pennylands in Illeray conveyed by the charter of 1389, the description 'inter Hussaboste et Kanusorrarath cituatas'[2] is difficult to follow. A manuscript copy of various MacDonald charters[3] in the Library of the National Museum of Antiquities, Edinburgh, bears opposite this line a marginal note 'inter Kirkibost et Balvanich' evidently suggesting Kirkibost in North Uist and Balivanich in Benbecula, though thus inferring two serious and consecutive errors on the part either of the notary or transcriber. The true explanation seems to lie in the fact that a rock off the west shore of Baleshare is still known as *Sgeir Husabost* so that Husabost was evidently once a place-name on that island, while *Ceann* (or *Camas*) *-eararaidh*, 'head (or creek) of the parching'—that is, of corn, preparatory to the grinding process—may also there have existed.

In making the foundations of a new cottage near the north end of Illeray, the ground-officer recently unearthed, at a depth of about four feet, a peculiar slab measuring about twenty-two by twenty inches, and perforated near its centre by a clearly cut hole four and a half inches in diameter. Even stranger is the fact that near óne corner of this stone (figured upon the accompanying plate) is a well-formed cup-mark two and a half inches across.

KALLIN (Gaelic, from *na ceallan*, 'the cells, or churches') see under Grimsay, in Chapter IX.

---

[1] *The Clan Donald*, vol. iii. pp. 660-661.

[2] More fully quoted under Carinish.

[3] Two MS. volumes of *MacDonald Collections*, bearing the autograph of John Dillon; vol. ii. p. 1185.

KEALLASAY MORE and KEALLASAY BEG (Norse); two islands in the north-west branch of Loch Maddy.

KEANVAROCHY (Gaelic, *ceann a' mhargaidh*). This and Markisa are placed close together upon Blaeu's map of 1654, both names evidently referring to a former market-stance on the south-east slope of Blashaval, three miles north from Lochmaddy. The last market there held—*ca.* 1840-1850—is still locally remembered.

KENTUACHE (better, Kentuath or *ceann tuath*) is an old Gaelic name for the 'north head' of Uist, which repeatedly occurs in Archdeacon Monro's *Description*,[1] although there mis-spelt 'Kentnache,' a troublesome error followed upon the maps in *Origines Parochiales*, vol. ii. parts 1 and 2.

KERAMEANACH (Gaelic), a township situated between Malaclett and Sollas; now known as 'Middlequarter' which is an exact translation of the Gaelic form.

Kerameanach appears in the 'Judicial Rental' of 1718 as then held by eleven small tenants.[2]

KERSIVAY (evidently Norse, perhaps including *ker* or 'tub,' and *vágr*, 'a bay'). An old place-name for the site occupied by the scattered village of Lochmaddy, which see.

KILMUIR (Gaelic, *cill Mhoire*, 'the church of St. Mary'). This occurs in an obligation of 1576 to pay 'for the third part of the personage of Kilmorie in Vyist, auchtene males';[3] and again in a crown-charter of 1623 infefting William Stirling of Auchyle in 'terris de Kilmorie in Wuest,' together with other lands.[4]

Kilmorie is an old form of Kilmuir, the chief of the two parishes into which North Uist was divided. Its ancient burial-ground, a little to the south of Hougary, is noticed under Ecclesiastical Remains in Chapter IX., where reference is also made to the fact that this particular locality bore the still earlier name of *Colasaidh*.

---

[1] Edinburgh, 1774, pp. 34-37. On page 35 we read 'Into this north heid of Ywst, ther is sundrie covis and holes in the earth, coverit with heddir above, quhilk fosters maney rebellis in the countrey of the north heid of Ywst.' *Ceann tuath* evidently included the whole of North Uist, as against *Ceann deas* for South Uist.

[2] *The Clan Donald*, vol. iii. p. 660.

[3] *Collectanea*, p. 10.

[4] *Reg. Mag. Sig.*, 19 Dec. 1623.

KILPHEDER (Gaelic, 'the church of St. Peter'), like Balelone, with which it now makes a single farm, does not appear in any old charter, both places having probably been included under Scolpaig until about the beginning of the eighteenth century.

According to the 'Judicial Rental,' Kilpheder was held in 1718 by Neil MacLean at '80m. 5b. vict. 6st. b.'; the same tenant or tacksman being a party to the complaint of 1721.[1] His signature as 'Neil M'Lean of Killpheder'—evidently a wadsetter—is appended to the Bond of 1723, a document also signed by the tacksmen of Valay, Hosta, Balleshahr, Keerkipost, Heskar or Heillskire, and Borreray.[2]

In Chapter IX. are described an old cross at Kilpheder, and the site of a former chapel there.

KIRKIBOST (Norse, *kirkju-bólstaðr* or 'church-stead') is a township upon the west shore of North Uist, having either taken its name from or given it to the neighbouring Kirkibost Island.   We have found only four references to this place-name in old charters :—

> 'Kirkapost in Eillera,' *Collectanea*, p. 2, *anno* 1561 ;
> 'ffor the landis of Kirkebost, auchtene males of grane, tua bollis beir, threttie cubakis quhite cheiss, and ane plaid, yerlie,' *Ibid.*, p. 10, *anno* 1576 ;
> '3 denariatis terrarum de Kirkibost,' *Retours*, 1644 ;
> 'the three penny land of Kirkibost,' *The Clan Donald*, vol. ii. p. 784 ; 1657.

Of these, the earliest has already been quoted in connection with Illeray, if only to point out that this notice seems inexact ; Kirkibost probably never having been included in Illeray although adjoining it upon the north.

The earliest notice of Kirkibost is merely incidental, telling how Ranald (a son of Donald Herrach) was murdered on his way thither to visit his cousin Donald Gruamach.[3]

Angus MacDonald was 'in Kirkibost' February 1678, and then appears as party to a document with 'his marke following Q.'

Archibald MacLean was the tenant in 1718, the 'Judicial Rental'

---

[1] *The Clan Donald*, vol. iii. pp. 660, 664.
[2] *Ibid.*, vol. ii. p. 792.
[3] *Ibid.*, vol. iii. p. 483.   Donald Gruamach had his chief residence at Dunskaith Castle in Skye ; he died in 1537.

of that year giving his payment as '£10 stg. 20 b. vict. 15 st. b.',—the only item in that report where pounds sterling occur.[1]

In 1740 Captain John MacDonald, younger son of William 'the Tutor,' received a tack of Kirkibost, Kyles, and Balranald, becoming also factor for North Uist in succession to his brother Ewen. He died before 1750, and his daughter Margaret afterwards had a tack of Paiblesgarry. Upon his death, Alexander MacDonald (of Hougary from at least 1717) succeeded to the factorship, likewise obtaining a lease of Balranald and Kirkibost. He was drowned at Kirkibost ford in 1760.

The next tacksman whom we find at Kirkibost was Donald (son of Hugh MacDonald in Baleshare) who also held the factorship of North Uist, and by a curious coincidence met the same fate as his predecessor 'at the back of the island' in 1800.[2]

KIRKIBOST ISLAND (Norse). This is a tidal island, a mile and a half long and comparatively flat, approached from Claddach-Kirkibost by a dangerous ford of a mile. It contains an Earth-House and traces of one or two other ancient sites. The 'Yl Kirkbol' of Blaeu.

Like Baleshare (a little to the south) Kirkibost Island seems to have suffered greatly from encroachments by the ocean.[3]

KNOCKINTORRAN (Gaelic, *cnoc an torruinn*, or 'hillock of thunder'), a township at Paible, midway between Hasten and Paiblesgarry.

We find only one occupant noticed as of 'Knocknatorran' or 'Knockintoran,' viz., Donald MacDonald, second son of John of Griminish. In 1718 this Donald paid a rent of '£100 Scots. 15 b. vict. 10 st. b.,' but is not mentioned after 1721.[4]

KNOCKLINE (Gaelic, *cnoc an lìn*, 'hillock of the flax') is another crofter township a little to the east of Knockintorran.

KNOCK-CUIEN (Gaelic, no doubt 'the hillock of MacQueen'). A new

[1] *The Clan Donald*, vol. ii. p. 787 ; vol. iii. p. 660. Archibald MacLean appears to have held a wadset in 1723, *Ibid.* vol. ii. p. 792.
[2] *Ibid.*, vol. iii. pp. 487-488, 539, 541.
[3] *Old Stat. Acc.*, vol. xiii. p. 304. The *New Stat. Acc.*, Inverness-shire, p. 163, records this island as 'at one time of considerable value. . . . a great part of it was literally blown away, and the sea now occupies fields which formerly produced fine crops of bear or barley.'
[4] *The Clan Donald*, vol. iii. pp. 484, 662, 664.

township on the north side of Grimsay ford, crofted within the past few years.

KYLES-BERNERA (Gaelic, 'the sound of Berneray'). As a place-name this seems to have been identical in position with Port nan Long, a little north of Newton and still the ferry to Berneray island, a fact conveyed by the old form above quoted.

The 'Judicial Rental' of 1718 includes 'Kyles, etc. Wm. M'Leod of Bernera. 200 m.'

Captain Donald Roy MacDonald (son of Ranald of Baleshare) served at Culloden, but afterwards settled in North Uist where he kept a school, also becoming tacksman of Kyles-Bernera about 1764.[1]

KYLES-PAIBLE (Gaelic), a hamlet of quaint appearance at the south-east extremity of Paible. This name seems to be associated with the ferry to the Heisker islands, and it is to the neighbouring bay that most of the Heisker boats come for the needful supply of peats.

It has already been noted that Captain John MacDonald had a tack in 1740 of Kirkibost, Kyles, and Balranald; 'Kyles' here being evidently Kyles-Paible.

Roderick MacDonald was successively tacksman of Kirkibost and Kyles-Paible at some period about the year 1800.[2]

LANGASS (Norse, lang-áss or 'long ridge'), in the mid-south of North Uist, adjoining Loch Eford. Here are a 'barp' and a stone circle, both of them described among Pagan Remains in Chapter VIII.

LIERNISH (Norse, líri-nes or 'tern point'), a large promontory on the south-east, opposite Grimsay and Ronay.

LINGAY (Norse, lyng-ey or 'heather island'). This lies near the extreme north-east, towards Boreray, of which township it is a grazing. Lingay is occasionally fordable by wading from Newton at the lowest tides. It has an excellent anchorage, and although now uninhabited, is said by Martin to contain the site of a chapel.[3]

[1] The Clan Donald, vol. iii. pp. 536-537, 662.   [2] Ibid., pp. 373, 541.

[3] Martin in his Description, etc., of 1703, p. 69, writes of Lingay 'it is singular in respect of all the Lands of Uist and the other Islands that surround it, for they are all composed of Sand, and this on the contrary, is altogether Moss covered with Heath, affording five Peats in depth, and is very servicable and useful, furnishing the Island Boreray, &c. with Plenty of good Fuel: This Island was held as Consecrated for several Ages, insomuch that the Natives would not then presume to cut any Fuel in it.' The Boreray crofters now bring their peats from the island of Stromay in Cheese Bay. There is another but much smaller Lingay, a tidal islet in Ahmore Strand.

LOCHMADDY (Gaelic, *loch nam madadh*, 'loch of the dogs,' in allusion to the three rocks, the Maddies, at its entrance), now the most important (though not the largest) village in the parish, seems to be unnoticed in old records until the year 1616. In this however it forms no exception to the whole east coast of North, Uist, which, up to the seventeenth century, is totally ignored. The reason is not far to seek, owing to the erratic configuration and boggy nature of all the east side. The early charters include —as may be expected—mainly or solely the more fertile strips upon the west and north-west shores, never mentioning the central portion nor the districts extending along the coast of North Uist from the north-east to south-east. The entry of 1616 refers to a complaint of piracy and murder in Lewis and specially names 'Lochmaldie on the coast of Uist' as a rendezvous of the pirates.[1]

Neil MacLean 'of Kerseva' or Kersivay (an old place-name at Lochmaddy village) is said to have been factor for North Uist,[2] but more probably was only ground-officer.

MALACLETT (Norse, from *klettr*, 'a rock,' coupled with *mjöl*, 'meal,' or *mala*, 'to grind'), a township on the north shore immediately west of Middlequarter. There was formerly a mill upon the small burn which runs past the smithy, and the remains of a dam are still visible higher up this stream.

'Malaglate'—as it is often written—was occupied by Donald Odhar (grandson of Godfrey MacDonald of Clan Gorrie) when he had to vacate Vallay at some period from about 1620 to 1650.[3]
Malaclett was held by five small tenants in 1718.[4]

MARKISA is a now obsolete place-name shown upon Blaeu's atlas of 1654 as near Keanvarochy (which see, *antea*) fully three miles north of Lochmaddy. Both words clearly indicate a market-stance, Markisa being derived from either the Norse *markaðr* or

[1] *Reg. Privy Council*, vol. x. p. 634.
[2] *The Clan Donald*, vol. iii. p. 539.
[3] *Ibid.* vol. iii. p. 371. This matter is fully discussed under Vallay, *postea*. It appears that the ruins of Donald's homestead at Malaclett were until recently known as *Totaichean Mhic Ghoraidh*.　　　　　　　　[4] *Ibid.*, p. 661.

LOCHMADDY FAIR.

ORANSAY, VALLAY, FROM SOUTH-EAST.

the Gaelic *margadh*, but in any case more remotely connected with the Latin *mercatus*.

MIDDLEQUARTER; see Kerameanach.

MONACH (Gaelic, *eilean nam manach* or 'island of the monks') is a title often applied to the Heisker group in general, although no doubt more specially belonging to Shillay, where it is said that a small monastery once stood.

OILISH (Norse), to the north of Udal on the west side of Ard a' Bhorain, normally shows as a jutting point, although converted into an island by high tides.[1] Locally pronounced 'Ooe-lish,' and indeed marked *Hulish* upon the Admiralty Chart, this is one of four North Uist place-names which terminate in *-lish*—the others being Ard Smeilish, Varlish, and Veilish—all of them equally obscure as regards derivation. The Norse *flis*, or 'slice,' might possibly here serve; although *nes*, 'a point' (assuming the letter *n* to be dropped after *l*),[2] would seem a more likely solution, especially as each of these names refers to a promontory or peninsula.[3] Earlish (pronounced Ar-lish), near Uig in Skye, evidently comes into the same class.

Together with Veilish, and perhaps the general district of Udal, Oilish seems to have been included in the half-penny lands of Walis or Waynlis. See under Veilish, *postea*.

ORANSAY or ORASAY is certainly Norse, representing *örfiris-ey* or 'tidal island,'[4] a description thoroughly applicable to all the Oransays visited by the writer in different parts of Scotland.

---

[1] There are traces of an enclosing wall, just above high-water mark on the north and west.

[2] Dr. Alex. MacBain, in treating of Gaelic phonetics, states that 'post-consonantal *n* disappears after *l*, leaving *ll*,' a rule which would support the above explanation—*An Etymological Dictionary of the Gaelic Language*, first ed., 1896, pp. xxviii-xxix.

[3] Since the foregoing was in type we have heard of two other place-names in North Uist with the same termination. These are *Ardvrialish* at Loch Portain, and *Ardvialish* near Breinish; both of them evidently promontories although not shown upon the Ordnance map.

[4] 'An island at ebb time connected with the mainland is called *Örfiris-ey*, mod. *öffurs-ey* (cp. Orfir in the Orkneys)'—Cleasby and Vigfusson's *Icelandic-English Dictionary*, p. 134. Also, '*ör-firi*, or *ör-fjara*, an out-going, ebbing,' *Ibid.*, p. 766. *Eilean Tioram* is the literal Gaelic equivalent for the Norse 'Örfiris-ey,' and is represented by *Castle Tioram* (of the Ordnance Survey) in Loch Moydart, the *Elantirym* of Clan Ranald charters. This is a case much in point, even though the map shows *Castle Tioram* as now attached to the shore at Dorlin by a narrow spit of land, corresponding with the neck which is also marked as leading to the Oransay at Vallay (North Uist), an instance where the island is usually joined on to the shore, but sometimes cut off by exceptional tides. It is no doubt upon similar grounds that *Castle Tioram* is elsewhere described as an island at high-water; *Vindication of the Clanronald of Glengarry*, Edin., 1821, p. 44; also *New Stat. Acc.*, Argyllshire, p. 147.

This name has been popularly derived as commemorating St. Oran, the friend and companion of St. Columba, but the frequency with which it recurs throughout the Hebrides—each of these islets evidently bearing the same general character—must practically exclude the assumption that so many as twenty-seven or twenty-eight tidal islands in the West of Scotland should have been named after this saint.[1] Treating as synonymous the varied modern spellings, Oransay, Orasaidh, Orasaig, Orasay (perhaps the commonest of all), Orinsay, Ornsay, Oronsay, Orosay, and Orsay,[2] with further equally slight deviations, we find islands of this general name distributed over the whole west coast of Scotland from Lewis to Islay.

The following are marked upon the six-inch Ordnance Survey map, although this list is almost certainly incomplete :[3]—

[1] The Oransay which is connected at low-water with the well-known Colonsay (' Orbhansaigh Colbhansaigh,' cf. *Reliquiæ Celticæ*, vol. ii. p. 210) can hardly be excepted, despite the tradition (and very possibly the fact) that it was the first landing-place of St. Columba and St. Oran upon Scottish soil. Colonsay is commonly derived from St. Columba, though probably it had possessed a somewhat similar name long before that saint trod its shores, being twice mentioned as *Colosus* in St. Adamnan's *Vita S. Columbæ*, which was written in the seventh century. It is at least certain that the two known dedications in Colonsay are to St. Cathan and St. Oran ; while the church of Oransay (according to Fordun, founded by St. Columba) is variously taken as commemorating The Holy Cross, St. Columba, and St. Oran, although this latter may well arise from the coincidence with the island's modern name.

Here may be noted (from *Origines Parochiales*, vol. ii. p. 281), a reference to the priorate of ' Orosai ' in 1554 or 1555 ; while the fine cross at Oransay bears an inscription variously given as ' Colini filii Cristi ' and ' Colini prior. Orisoi,' the letters in the third and fourth lines being so indistinct as to cause hesitation between these two readings. It seems certain however that the date (1510) usually attributed to this cross is incorrect.

[2] This last, off the Rhinns of Islay, is the most southerly and perhaps the only doubtful instance quoted. It appears in Archdeacon Monro's *Description* (p. 16) as ' Ellan Onersay, ane myle in lenthe, it hath ane paroch kirke, and is verey guid for fishing, inhabit and manurit, with ane right dangerous kyle and stream, callit Corey Garrache ; na man dare enter in it bot at ane certain tyme of the tyde, or ellis he will perish ' ; which remarks seem to imply that the narrows were fordable. This is the ' Island Ouirsa' of Martin, p. 243 ; and is elsewhere named Eorsay-Elan, Oersa, and Oversa or Oversay. Mr. T. S. Muir in his *Island Characteristics*, p. 128, quotes it as ' Eilean Oransay,' with a chapel dedicated to ' St. Orain,' but without stating his authority.

[3] Apart from the somewhat doubtful case of the Oransay attached to Colonsay (already discussed), and Mr. Muir's more categorical reference, we have found, amongst all these twenty-eight islands, only one instance of a chapel definitely marked upon the Ordnance map as dedicated to St. Oran. This exception is 'Teampull Orain, Remains of,' shown upon the Oransay which adjoins Vallay in North Uist ; and while it is just possible that an ' örfiris-ey ' might happen to be selected for a dedication to this particular saint, not much can be founded upon so isolated an example. Alternatively, of course, the near coincidence in name may have caused an erroneous association, whether in mediæval or only in recent times.

At Orphir in Orkney is (or was) an 'örfiris-ey ' ; in Shetland at the south end of Yell there is an *Orfasay* ; Iceland has at least one small island of almost identical name ; while in Scandinavia ' *Örfyrisey* occurs during the middle ages, and *Offersö* in three places in modern Norway.' For these northern identifications we are indebted to papers contributed by Mr. A. W. Johnston to the Society of Antiquaries of Scotland and to the Viking Club.

Lewis, five (one each in East Loch Roag, Loch Leurbost, and
Loch Erisort; besides two others,[1] *Orrasaidh Beag* and
Àird Orrasaidh in Loch an Stroim, a southern branch
of West Loch Roag).

North Uist, seven (one each at Vallay, Trumisgarry, Alioter,
Lochmaddy, and Langass; two at Aulisary).

Benbecula, three (east side).

South Uist, two (on the south-west, and in Loch Carnan,
north-east).

Barra, three (two near the south-east, one north-east).

Vatersay, one (north).

Skye, two (south-east and south-west).

Loch Sunart, one (at the mouth).

Kerrera, one (south).

Coll, one (east).

Colonsay, one (south).

Islay, one (at the Rhinns).

It is interesting to find that so many Hebridean islets of one (and
that a very separate) class, are known under such an equally distinctive name. Indeed, little exaggeration would be involved in the
statement that this, in one form or another, is the commonest of all
titles for any small tidal island in that district, while the form
'Orasay' seems to be the usual local pronunciation.

Having thus attempted, perhaps at unnecessary length, to explain
the derivation of this place-name, we now turn to the only Oransay in
North Uist (that near Vallaquie and Trumisgarry), which seems to be
recorded in old charters. This was a six-penny land, being mentioned
as :—

'6 den. de Orvinsaig,' *Reg. Mag. Sig.*, 1495 (confirming
charter of 1469).

'6 denariatas terrarum de Orwansay,' *Ibid.*, 1505.

'Sex denariatas terrarum de Orinstaig.'

'   ,,   ,,   Orinsack.'

'   ,,   ,,   Orwinsaig.'

---

[1] Both of them tidal-islands, although the larger is known as *Àird*. Two of the others
enumerated—those in Loch Leurbost, Lewis, and at the Rhinns of Islay—are shown upon the
six-inch Ordnance map as true islands at all states of the tide, though perhaps fordable at low-
water.

'Sex denariatas terrarum de Orumsage'—all in *The Clan Donald*, vol. ii. pp. 754-756, *anno* 1597.
'6 denariatis terrarum de Orwnsag,' *Retours*, 1617.
'   „   „   Orumseg,' *Ibid.*, 1644.
'the six penny land of Orvinsaig,' *The Clan Donald*, vol. ii. p. 784, *anno* 1657.

The treacherous Archibald MacDonald (*Gilleasbuig Dubh*)—a natural son of Hugh MacDonald, founder of Clan Huistein—seems to have resided upon this Oransay from *ca.* 1498 to 1516, with an interval of about three years between 1506 and 1510 when he joined a band of pirates in the southern Hebrides.[1] It was this Archibald who compassed the murders of his brothers Donald Herrach and Donald Gallach, *ca.* 1506, and was in consequence chased out of North Uist by Ranald Ban, chief of Clan Ranald,[2] who died in 1509 ; the dates thus fully agreeing with this piratic interval, *ca.* 1506-1510.

Out of the seven tidal islands named Oransay, which are to be found in North Uist, it was certainly this, near Trumisgarry, for which Kenneth MacQueen received in 1619 a tack of three lives and three nineteens—that is for his own life, two life-rents thereafter, and fifty-seven years beyond.[3] A clause which included 'the salmon fishing of the water of Kilwartain on both sides of said water from the sea flood to the shealing place of Grimsaig' gave some difficulty until the solution was forthcoming that both these places are in Trotternish (the Kilmartin river and its tributary Abhuinn Gremiscaig) on the north-east side of Skye.

The 'Judicial Rental' of North Uist in 1718 names a Kenneth MacQueen as occupant of this Oransay against a money payment of 240 merks Scots, and '8 b. vict. 24 st. b.'[4]

---

[1] *The Clan Donald*, vol. iii. pp. 12-13. *Gilleasbuig Dubh* seems also to have possessed the island of Scalpay (*Reg. Mag. Sig.*, 10 March 1516-1517). There are two islands of this name, one forming part of Skye, and the other of Harris.

[2] *Gregory's Collections*, vol. iv. of ten MS. volumes in the Library of the National Museum of Antiquities, Edinburgh. See also Chapter VI. under Dun Scolpaig.

[3] *The Clan Donald*, vol. iii. pp. 135-136. This was evidently the Kenneth MacQueen whose name occurs in a charter from Donald Gorm Mor, signed at Eigg, 4 June 1610, and witnessed . . . 'Kennetho McQuein servitore dicti Don. Gorme'; confirmed *Reg. Mag. Sig.*, 20 July 1610. Donald Gorm Mor died in 1616, being succeeded by his nephew Sir Donald Gorm Og, who, three years later, granted this long tack to the servant of his predecessor.

In 1648 the name of 'Kenneth Mcqueene of Orisay' appears amongst other tenants whose loyalty was guaranteed by Sir James MacDonald, second Baronet of Sleat, *The Clan Donald*, vol. ii. p. 781.   [4] *Ibid.*, vol. iii. p. 660.

A tradition is locally current to the effect that one of the MacQueens of Oransay buried a golden treasure in a foal's skin near the summit of Crogary More at a spot from whence the sun can be seen shining upon three forts at the same time.[1] These conditions infer a hiding-place on the north face of the hill, within view presumably of Dun na Mairbhe, Dun Aonghuis, and Dun Rosail.

ORIVAL Rock, in the sea north of Griminish Point. Evidently of Norse derivation, perhaps including *ör,* 'an arrow'; but different in origin from *Oreval,* the name of a hill two-and-a-half miles to the south.

OTTERNISH (Norse, *Óttars-nes* or 'Otter's point'). A promontory jutting out towards Berneray in the Sound of Harris; see also in Chapter VIII., under Pagan Burials.

PAIBLE [2] (Norse, *Papa* with *ból, bæli,* or *býli,* all meaning 'the priest's abode'). This is practically the modern Bayhead, although the name Paible is still in use, perhaps as applying to the whole district between Kirkibost island and Balranald, and thus including the townships of Balmore, Knockintorran, Knockline, and Kyles-Paible. In its simpler form we have found but one ancient reference to this name :—

'le Terung de Paible,' *Reg. Mag. Sig.,* 1505,

showing it to have been an ounce-land, doubtless containing (as usual) eighteen penny-lands.

An interesting tenant of Paible must here be mentioned—Hugh MacDonald of Clan Gorrie, who lived *ca.* 1740 to 1820. He was son of Donald MacDonald in Paiblesgarry, and is first noted as at Paible, though said to have occupied Balranald under a sub-lease after his father's death. In 1777 he left North Uist, and finally held a tack of Kilpheder and Daliburgh in South Uist. Hugh was known as *Uisdean Bàn,* and to him Donald Gregory was indebted for 'a genealogy of the MacDonalds of Sleat and Clanranald, which . . . was written down at Balranald in North Uist on the 10th August 1800,

---

[1] According to another version, the gold was enclosed in a bull's hide, and its exact locality is to be identified by a certain shadow cast by the full moon.

[2] Similar place-names are found in Lewis and Harris, and there is still a *Papýli* in Iceland. 'Priest's island' (Norse, *Papa-ey*) frequently occurs throughout the Hebrides as *Pabbay,* and in the Orkney and Shetland Isles as *Papa.*

M

and is preserved among the Gregory Collections.'[1]   The eldest son
of Hugh MacDonald (James, born at Paible in 1771), was author of
A General View of the Agriculture of the Hebrides, published in 1811.
See also under Kyles-Paible.

PAIBLESGARRY (Norse, the *gerδi* or ' garry' of Paible), now forms the
    southern portion of Balranald estate.   This was another ounce-
    land—

        ' le Terung de Paiblesgervy,' *Reg. Mag. Sig.*, 1505.

    Reference is given to an inventory of the effects of ' Alexander
MacDonald of Paiblisgarry,' who died in or before 1657, and was
youngest son of Sir Donald MacDonald, first baronet of Sleat.   He
married in 1653, and was followed at Paiblesgarry by his son Captain
Hugh MacDonald (who died before 1718) and his grandson John.   It
is evidently this John MacDonald who appears in the ' Judicial Rental '
of 1718 as of ' Pableskarry,' paying annually ' 100 m. 15 b. vict.
10 st. b.,' and whose signature is appended to the complaint of 1721.

    Donald MacDonald ' in Paiblisgarry,' who appears as a witness on
2nd August 1723, was of a quite different family, being a descendant
of Clan Gorrie, and the father of Hugh MacDonald, the 'seanachie'
of 1800, just mentioned under Paible.   Again, in 1750, Margaret
—daughter of another John MacDonald, who was tacksman of
Kirkibost, Kyles (Paible), and Balranald, being fifth son of William
' the Tutor'—received a tack of Paiblesgarry after her father's
death.[2]

PENMORE (Gaelic, *peighinn mhór* or ' the big penny-land '), is still a
    place-name upon the Balranald estate, between the mansion-house
    and Tighary.

    In 1694, Alexander (fourth son of John MacDonald of Griminish)
had a wadset upon ' Heisker, Peinmore, and Peinnie Trynoid,' to the
extent of 3000 merks, evidently discharged in 1748 by his son John.
Archibald MacDonald (great-grandson of Malcolm of Clan Gorrie)
was tacksman successively of Penmore and Kirkibost, apparently *ca.*
1800.[3]

    [1] *The Clan Donald,* vol. iii. pp. 367-368. This pedigree appears in the third of ten MS.
volumes of the *Gregory Collections* which have been already quoted as now in the library of the
Soc. Antiq. Scot. at Edinburgh.
    [2] *The Clan Donald,* vol. ii. p. 792 ; vol. iii. pp. 136, 366-367, 471, 541, 660, 664.
    [3] *Ibid.,* vol. iii. pp. 372-373, 494-495.

RONAY, FROM NORTH.

CATTLE AT MALACLETT ON VALLAY FORD.

PORT NA COPA (Gaelic, more correctly *port na caipe* or 'harbour of the foam') is a rocky creek four hundred yards south of Scolpaig Bay, though, judging from present appearances, it can never have been a harbour in the ordinary sense. The latter half of this name is thoroughly descriptive, since even in moderate weather the waves are here lashed into foam which thickly covers the pebbled beach, while we are told that during storms it attains a depth of from five to fifteen feet, also stretching inland over the whole field above the creek in a heaving viscous mass of foam two to five feet in depth.[1]

PORT NAN LONG (Gaelic, 'harbour of the ships'), already noted as the ferry to Berneray Island. Perhaps more correctly *Port na Luing* (in the singular), if we are to follow local tradition which derives the name of this bay from one of the Spanish Armada having there been lost. It is said that part of the wreck can still be seen at very low tides in shallow water between Port nan Long and Berneray.

REUMISGARRY (Norse, ? *Hrymrs-gerði*), immediately east of Vallaquie. This is the 'Rimskarry' of 1718, then divided between four tenants.[2]

RONAY[3] (Norse, *hraun-ey* or 'rough island'), lying at the south-east extremity of the parish, and separated from Grimsay by a narrow rocky channel. The 'Kilrona in Uist' mentioned in *Collectanea*, p. 192, *anno* 1628. Ronay consists of a series of steep hills, comparatively bare at the north, but more heather-clad towards the south. Otters are here plentiful.

Ronaybeg is a name used for the smaller northern portion of the same island, the whole being united by an isthmus, four hundred yards in width, between *Bàgh nan Uamh* and *Bàgh na Caiplich* on either side. In 1891 Ronay had a population of six.

SAND (Norse, *sandr*), the northern of the two former parochial divisions of North Uist, but now only a parish *quoad sacra* :—
'le Terung de Sanda,' *Reg. Mag. Sig.*, 1505.

---

[1] Dr. Alex. Carmichael in *The Scottish Geographical Magazine*, vol. ii. p. 470.
[2] *The Clan Donald*, vol. iii. p. 659.
[3] Malcolm MacDonald, (grandson of Donald, the third and last of the MacGorries who were tacksmen of Vallay up to *ca.* 1620 or 1630), farmed this island of Ronay 'in whole or in part' *ca.* 1680-1720 ; *The Clan Donald*, vol. iii. p. 372.

'perteining to the Abbatt of Ecolmkill . . . Item, the personage of Sand thair,' *Collectanea*, p. 3, *anno* 1561.

'for the kirklandis and teyndis of Sandey, tuentie bollis beir, of the mett and mesour of Vyest,' *Collectanea*, p. 10, *anno* 1576.

'Clachan' in the 'Judicial Rental' of 1718,[1] then held by ten small tenants, evidently corresponds with the farm of Clachan Sand, which adjoins that of Newton on its north.

(See also Chapter II. p. 20 *antea*, for a Saga reference which Captain Thomas believed to apply to Sand.)

SCOLPAIG (Norse, *skolpr-vik* or 'chisel bay') is at the north-west corner of the island, and is understood to have been the last rendezvous of smugglers in North Uist. A hillock close to the west of Scolpaig House, and within 150 yards from the bay, is still known as *Cnoc an Litich*, or 'the Leith-man's knoll,' popularly said to contain a cave or recess in which the lowlander hid his contraband goods. It seems evident that a cavity of some nature does here exist, and may have been used for this purpose; although excavation would probably reveal it as an Earth-House of pre-historic origin.

Scolpaig was a two-penny land :—

'2 denar. de Scolpic,' *Reg. Mag. Sig.*, 1495, confirming a previous charter of 1469 ;

'le Terung de Watna, Scolping et Gremynis,' *Ibid.*, 1505 ;

'2 den. de Scalpic,' *Ibid.*, 1596 ;

'duas denariatas terrarum de Scolpite alias Scolpick,' (and twice again as 'Skolpick' in the same sasine), *The Clan Donald*, vol. ii. pp. 754-756, *anno* 1597 ;

'2 denariatis terrarum de Skolpick,' *Retours*, 1617 ;

'2 denariatis terrarum de Stalpit (vel Scalpit),' *Ibid.*, 1644 ;

'the twa penny lands of Skalpac,' *The Clan Donald*, vol. ii. p. 784, *anno* 1657 ;

also 'John Macdonald in Scolpig,' *Ibid.*, p. 792, *anno* 1723.

John MacDonald, of the 'Bond' of 1723, was son of Archibald MacDonald of Griminish and Scolpaig, becoming settled in Scolpaig during his father's lifetime. This family of MacDonald seems to have

---

[1] *The Clan Donald*, vol. iii. p. 659.

held both of these farms in direct succession from the time of their ancestor Donald Herrach, probably from 1498 until about the year 1770. During these three centuries the history of Scolpaig was so closely associated with that of Griminish that we need not here repeat the list of tacksmen or tenants.

Four miles to the south, on Balranald estate near Ard an Runair, is Port Scolpaig, though its connection (if any) with this better-known Scolpaig seems hard to deduce.

SCOTVEN, a bay on the south side of Grimsay, where steamers some- times call. This name is a difficult one, but we are advised upon excellent authority to class it as a bi-lingual, from the Norse *skot* or 'shot,' and the Gaelic *bheinn* for 'hill'; originally no doubt altogether Norse—*skot-fjall*, a place where archery was practised —and thus affording one of those rare examples in which half of a Norse place-name has been translated into Gaelic, but the other half left untranslated.[1]

SCREVAN (? Gaelic). Elsewhere incidentally mentioned, in connection with the Earth-House near Port nan Long, as a hillock on the point of Otternish, opposite Berneray in the Sound of Harris.

SEANABAILY (Gaelic, *seana bhaile* or 'old town'), an island in the North Ford close to Grimsay, of which it is generally considered as forming part. At Balranald, and in the township of Middle- quarter, the place-name Seanaval also occurs.

SHILLAY (Norse, *selr-ey*, 'seal island'), the outer of the Heisker group, and the site of a fine lighthouse. This is said to be the true *Monach*, so named from a monastery which formerly stood there.

SHIVINISH (Norse, ? *syfjaðr-nes*, or 'sleeping-point'), a small island intermediate between Ceann Ear and Ceann Iar in the Heisker group, but joined to both of these at low-water.

SIGINISH (Norse, *sik-nes*, 'ditch or channel point'), north of Alioter.

SKIBINISH (Norse, *skipa-nes* or 'ship point'), a promontory at Grenetote.

SOLLAS (Norse, ? *söl-áss*, 'dulse ridge'), the most important town- ship on the northern shore of North Uist. We have found this mentioned but once in the early charters, viz. :—

'le Terung de Solos,' *Reg. Mag. Sig.*, 1505.

[1] See Dr. W. J. Watson's *Place-Names of Ross and Cromarty*, pp. lvi. and 224. The only point which troubles the present writer is that neither at Scotven, nor indeed elsewhere in Grimsay, does any elevation seem to deserve the name of *fjall* or *beinn*.

The present township includes the ancient holdings of Sollas, Havisgarry, Misigarry, Gerrinacurran, and Doun (Dunskellor), all of these formerly tenanted by MacLeans, no doubt through the Boreray connection. The tack granted by Sir Donald MacDonald of Sleat in 1627 to Neil MacLean includes his 'aucht penny land of Burray and ane penny land in Solas'; while the 'Judicial Rental' of 1718 gives 'Mrs. M'Lean of Boreray' as tenant of Sollas, paying a rental of '240 m. 16 b. vict. 16 st. b.' Since the next item in this document is Boreray itself, tenanted by Archibald MacLean, we take this Mrs. MacLean to have been Archibald's widowed mother, whose husband's Christian name was evidently John.[1]

SPONISH (Norse, *spói-nes* or 'curlew-point'), a long promontory a mile north of Lochmaddy pier. There is another Sponish in North Uist, half-way up Loch Eford.

SRUTHAN NA COMRAICH (*na Comaraig* of the Ordnance map, Gaelic, 'stream of the sanctuary'), is here noted as a significant name, commemorating the fact that the Carinish 'Temple' and its church-lands were once a place of refuge from the avenger of blood.[2] This stream is within the ford to Benbecula, just off the south extremity of Carinish (evidently the lands once known as Unganab), and thus shows only at ebb-tide, presumably representing the southern limit of the sanctuary.

STANGRAM (Norse; either *steinn-garðr-hólmr*, 'stone-wall-isle'; or perhaps *stangar-hólmr*, 'pole-isle').[3] An island in the Vallay ford.

STIG. Upon John Speed's map of 1610 this name is marked in North Uist east of Carinish, while Eskin also appears in the north-east part of the island, and Essir where we would expect to find Lochmaddy.[4] Trees are, moreover, indicated in three places on the west side of 'Eust.' Altogether this map is most inaccurate

---

[1] *The Clan Donald*, vol. iii. pp. 650, 662. See also under Boreray, *antea*.

[2] *Ibid.*, vol. i. pp. 471-472.

[3] Stangram has certainly been surrounded, just below high-water mark, by a dry-stone dyke, pierced both on the north and south by walled entrances sufficiently wide to admit a cart.

[4] In the old Norse language *stigr* means 'a path, a footway.' It seems probable however that these three words are hardly place-names in the ordinary sense, but rather to be taken as descriptive terms bearing upon the general appearance or products of various localities. Thus Eskin and Essir might be rendered as 'fishes' and 'oysters' respectively,— from the Gaelic *iasgan* and *eisirean* (old Irish, *eisir*). *Isginn* occurs as a place-name at Loch Shell in Lewis.

as to the Outer Hebrides, being evidently a loose compilation from earlier and unreliable sources.

STOCKAY (Norse, *stokk-ey* or 'stock-island'), a large and nearly barren rock, the most easterly of the Heisker group.

STOLIE (Norse, ? *stagl-ey*, 'rack isle'), an isthmus which separates the inner recesses of Loch Maddy from those of Loch Mhic Phail.

STROMAY (Norse, *straum-ey* or 'stream-island') at Loch Aulisary; separated from the mainland of North Uist by a very narrow channel. It is here that the Boreray crofters cut their peats.

Another but much smaller Stromay lies at the south end of Baleshare.

TEILEM is the name of a small island in Loch Mhic Phail, and near it are also Teilem Bay and Teilem Point. Norse, with *-hólmr*; perhaps the same word as *Heilleam*, p. 70.

TIGHARY (Gaelic, *tigh a' ghearraidh*, 'house of the enclosed arable land'). This is a township on the west side, between Hosta and Balranald. In 1718 'Tigheary' was farmed by the Rev. John MacLean, parish minister of North Uist, a son of Neil MacLean of Boreray.[1] It was afterwards occupied by the Rev. Allan MacQueen, who contributed a notice of his parish to the *Old Stat. Acc.* of 1794.

TOROGAY[2] (Norse, perhaps *törgu-ey*, 'target or buckler island'). There are two islets of this name, the smaller—in Vallay ford—belonging to North Uist, while the other, although only four hundred yards east of Otternish, forms part of Harris.

TRUMISGARRY (Norse, *þrumis-gerði*); a township towards the northeast of the island, in the district of Sand and immediately south of Vallaquie. John, son of Angus Glass (or Aonghas Fionn), whose name is associated with that of Dun Aonghuis *ca.* 1520, appears upon record in 1562. From him are descended the MacDonalds of Trumisgarry.

'Tromskarry' also figures in the 'Judicial Rental' of 1718 as a small holding tenanted by Hector MacLean.[3]

UDAL, close to Oilish at Ard a' Bhorain, is certainly Norse, whatever

---

[1] *The Clan Donald*, vol. iii. p. 662; also Scott's *Fasti*.
[2] Between two and three miles to the south of Torogay, and to the west of Ben Aricaiter, is a hill named *Toroghas*.
[3] *The Clan Donald*, vol. iii. pp. 481-482, and p. 662.

its meaning.   After rejecting several alternatives, *út-dalr* or
'outer valley' appears the more suitable, even if this promontory
is rather to be described as a plain than a dale.   There seems
indeed to remain a trace of 't' in the present local pronunciation.

See under Hosta, for a tradition as to the burning of Udal
township by the Siol Murdoch.

UNA, near Tighary.   Probably Norse, and from the same root-word as
Unival and Loch Huna.

UNGANAB (Gaelic, 'the abbot's ounce-land').   This seems to have
been at Carinish, where, about 600 yards south of Teampull na
Trionaid, we find the site of a former loch marked upon the
Ordnance map as *Loch an Aba*, or 'loch of the abbot.' [1]

Unganab is thus mentioned in early documents :—

'In the Ile of Weist the tuentie-four pennie land callit
Unganab,' *Collectanea*, p. 2, 1561 ;
'ffor the landis of Vngenab in Vyist, with the pendiclis and
pertinentis thairof, fourtie-aucht *males* of beir, of the
custome and vse of Vyist,' *Ibid.*, p. 10, *anno* 1576 ;
'12 denariatis terrarum de Ungnab,' *Retours*, 1644 ;
'the twelff penny land of Ungnab,' *The Clan Donald*, vol. ii.
pp. 783-784, *anno* 1657.

VALLAQUIE is the name of a grassy tract which lies between Sand and
Trumisgarry, immediately to the north of *Faodhail Vallaquie*.

Its derivation is certainly Norse, including *kví*, 'a fold or small
enclosure,' the 'quoy' of the Orkneys. [2]   From the existence of another
Vallaquie, a tidal island in the south-west corner of Lochmaddy Bay,
vaðill-kví or 'ford-enclosure' would seem the most suitable explanation in both cases.

In 1718 'Vallakuy' was held by four small tenants. [3]

VALLAY [4] is also Norse, representing '*vaðill* and *vöðull* [Shetl. *vaadle* ;
Dan. *veile*], a shallow water, especially places where fiords or
straits can be passed on horseback,' [5] from *vaða*, 'to wade.'

---

[1] Near Kallin, upon the island of Grimsay, another Loch an Aba still exists.
[2] Dr. Isaac Taylor, in his *Words and Places*, 1902, p. 153, notes *Ky* as representing 'a house'
in Cornwall, while in Brittany it frequently appears under the form of *Qui* or *Cae*.
[3] *The Clan Donald*, vol. iii. p. 660.
[4] In Rodil Bay, Harris, is a much smaller island which bears the same name, and is also tidal ;
while a little to its north are Rudha Vallarip and Loch Vallarip.
[5] *Icelandic Dictionary* (Cleasby and Vigfusson), p. 673.

Vallay consists almost entirely of sandy soil covered by grass, and seems to have formed a 'davata' or ounce-land :—

'le Terung de Wala,' *Reg. Mag. Sig.*, 1505.

It measures about two miles in length by an average of half a mile in width, and lies at the north-west corner of North Uist opposite Griminish, being very regularly accessible up to half-tide by a ford of nearly two miles across firm sands from either Malaclett or Claddach-Vallay.

This island is mentioned in Archdeacon Monro's *Description* of 1549 (p. 37), but only in a few lines, and apparently not from personal observation :—' ane ile callit Valay, twa myle lang from the north to the south, ane myle braid, a fayr mayne ile, inhabit and manurit, pertaining to Donald Gormesone.'

It is quite otherwise with Martin's account of the tour which he made through the Hebrides a few years prior to 1703, when his *Description of the Western Islands of Scotland* was first published. Martin writes of ' Valay' (which he certainly visited) :—' It is about 4 Miles in Circumference, arable and a dry Sandy Soil, very fruitful in Corn and Grass, Clover and Dasie' ;[1] then proceeding to note three Chapels and an Earth-House, as to which we quote his remarks in their respective connections.

The first recorded occupant of Vallay whom we are able to trace with any certainty was Godfrey MacGorrie, who held Vallay about the year 1516,[2] being there succeeded by his son Alexander and grandson Donald until after 1614, when the last-mentioned is found witnessing a sasine as 'Donald MacGorry in Valay.' The story is told how MacDonald of Sleat and North Uist (evidently Sir Donald Gorm Og of 1616-1643), while crossing the sands to collect his rents, observed a seal disporting itself in a deep pool, and sent for one of MacGorrie's sons to shoot it ; this lad, the youngest of three, taking so skilful an aim that his arrow passed through one eye and out of the other. It appears that Donald MacGorrie was then under notice to leave Vallay, but (on account of this episode) received a lease of Malaclett farm

[1] *A Description, etc.*, pp. 66-67.
[2] Then 'MacDonald of Vallay,' *The Clan Donald*, vol. iii. p. 369. This date is fixed by the death of Gilleasbuig Dubh, who had murdered his half-brothers Donald Herrach and Donald Gallach, *ca.* 1506. According to local tradition, 'Siol Gorrie' were responsible for the drowning of Hosta township, and in return met prompt punishment at the hands of 'Siol Murdoch,' who burned the village of Udal.

instead, where the ruins of his dwelling were known as *Totaichean Mhic Ghoraidh* until quite recently.[1]

In the same connection it is added that upon a slope in Vallay named *Leathad na Croise* formerly stood a stone cross pierced by three holes, and that the sons of Donald MacGorrie were here accustomed to practise archery, each selecting one of these holes through which he usually succeeded in passing his arrow.[2]

After this time there is a blank of about a century in the list of known tacksmen or occupants of Vallay, and we next find Lachlan MacLean as 'of Vallay' in 1718, 1721, and 1723,[3] the last entry proving that he held a wadset. It has already been mentioned that the estates of Clan Huistein were sold by auction in 1723 under the forfeiture in 1716 of Sir Donald MacDonald, fourth baronet, who died in 1718. The fifth and sixth baronets of Sleat, Sir Donald and Sir James, respectively son and brother of the fourth baronet, held the property for brief periods; Sir James dying in 1720, and leaving his younger brother William (third son of Sir Donald, third baronet) as guardian to his son Sir Alexander, the lineal heir, then only ten years of age. It was on behalf of this child, seventh baronet of Sleat, while yet a minor, that these estates were purchased in 1723 by Kenneth Mackenzie, the Edinburgh advocate, as a friend of the family. In this transaction it is recorded that Kenneth Mackenzie obtained assistance from the 'wadsetters' upon the property,[4] as also from Major William MacDonald, uncle and guardian of the young heir (and therefore commonly known as '*An Taoitear*,' or 'the Tutor'), who had been of Aird in Skye, but on the resettlement of the estates of Sleat, Trotternish, and North Uist in 1726-1727, received for himself 'a free grant of the farm of Aird during his lifetime, and a perpetual lease of the Island of Vallay, on the coast of North Uist, for his heirs and successors, for a shilling a year as feu. The Taightear

[1] *The Clan Donald*, vol. iii. pp. 369-371. Reference is evidently here made to the sea-pool which lies between Torogay and Eilean Dubh, half-way across Vallay Strand. Even at low-water this is so deep as to have caused the loss of life in recent years, the ford of nearly two miles being dangerous in misty weather or upon a dark night.

[2] *Ibid.*, vol. iii. p. 371. The situation of *Leathad na Croise* cannot be now identified, although most probably it was the broad slope at St. Mary's chapel on Vallay :—see Chapter ix. for a quotation from Mr. T. S. Muir as to a cross with *four* holes.

[3] *Ibid.*, vol. ii. p. 792, vol. iii. p. 664. The rent paid for Vallay in 1718 by Lachlan MacLean was 220 merks Scots, 20 bolls oats, and 13 stones of butter ; *Ibid.*, vol. iii. p. 662.

[4] *Ibid.*, vol. ii. pp. 791-792, 'Bond of Uist men and others, 1723,' signed by 'creditors on the Estate of the late Sir Donald MacDonald,' who had died in 1718.

lived and died at Aird, a place about two miles north of Duntulm Castle, and at the most northern point of Skye.'[1]

William 'the Tutor' married (first) Catherine, one of the twelve daughters of Sir Ewen Cameron of Lochiel, and (second) Janet, daughter of Lachlan MacLean of Vallay. He died in 1730, and was evidently held in the highest esteem, receiving a memorable funeral with a procession 'two miles in length, six men walking abreast' accompanied by seven pipers and a surely fabulous consumption of whisky.[2] In any case Ewen (third son of 'the Tutor') settled at Vallay in 1727, and was also factor of North Uist from 1733 to 1740. It was he who built the old house of Vallay, upon which a lintel (evidently displaced in alterations made long ago) bears in raised lettering his own initials and those of his wife, Mary MacLean, together with the date of their marriage :[3]

E.M.D.   M.M.L. 1742

This was one of the four slated houses in the parish noted in 1794, but had even then become ruinous.[4]

Ewen MacDonald was famed both as a performer upon the bagpipes and a composer of pibrochs; he died in 1769,[5] while it would seem that his widow survived him for nearly twenty years, their joint will being proved on 28th March 1789.[6] Ewen was followed at Vallay by his only child William (d. 1770) and his grandson Major Alexander (d. ca. 1820), another Alexander (son of the last named) leaving the island for Trotternish ca. 1825; this latter date confirming the suggestion already made that the long tack granted to William 'the Tutor' and his descendants was for three lives and three nineteens, the third life being that of William, who died in 1770, which would make the lease expire in 1827.[7]

[1] Mackenzie's *History of the Macdonalds*, p. 231. We must however come to the conclusion that this grant of Vallay was not a 'perpetual lease' or feu, but a very long tack, such as 'three lives and three nineteens,' which would in every way agree with its termination, ca. 1825, or perhaps more exactly, in 1827.

[2] *Ibid.*, p. 234, 'upwards of 300 gallons'; also *The Clan Donald*, vol. iii. pp. 540-541. William 'the Tutor' had served both at Killiecrankie and Sheriffmuir.

[3] *The Clan Donald*, vol. iii. p. 542.

[4] *Old Stat. Acc.*, vol. xiii. p. 325, 'the church, one mill, a house at Lochmaddie, that was intended for a public house, and another in the Island of Vallay in a ruinous condition.' Elsewhere it is stated (p. 308) that in 1794 there were only eight carts in the whole parish. This account was written by the Rev. Allan MacQueen, parish minister of North Uist, and married to a sister of Major Alexander MacDonald of Vallay.

[5] *The Clan Donald*, vol. iii. p. 542-543; also Mackenzie's *History of the Macdonalds*, p. 241.

[6] In the 'Commissariot of the Isles,' *Scottish Record Society*.

[7] *The Clan Donald*, vol. iii. pp. 543-545.

No manse is provided for the parish minister of North Uist, who receives a small money payment instead ; and it has long been the practice of successive incumbents to rent a small farm. Thus, the Rev. Finlay MacRae (missionary at Sand and Sollas for three years from 1815, and ordained to the charge of the parish in 1818) lived first at Baleloch, but in 1825 secured a tack of Vallay, which he occupied until his death in 1858, being succeeded in the tenancy by his son James, who died *ca.* 1873, and thereafter by his widow until 1877, when she left to reside in Edinburgh. Vallay was thus tenanted by two families from 1727 until 1877.

Mr. MacRae was born in 1792, and his contribution to the *New Stat. Acc.* (North Uist) is dated 1837. On the north side of the island, among the rocks just above high-water mark to the west of Traigh Himiligh, is a small well, which has been artificially enlarged, and bears on the face of the vertical rock the incised lettering D MR
1853

From internal evidence in his *Description* it is clear that Martin Martin visited this island shortly before 1703 ; while, just fifty years later, Captain Barlow, when engaged in confiscating arms and making a report to Government upon the Long Island, seems to have had his head-quarters in North Uist at Vallay, thence dating two letters of 30 June and 9 October 1753.[1]

VANNT ; see under Watna.

VARLISH (locally ' Ver-lish '), a small promontory at Kilpheder on the west side of North Uist. This is clearly of Norse derivation, although one of the four place-names ending in *-lish* which are specially difficult to explain. A little to the south is Traigh Verral, a wide sandy beach, and it seems highly probable that Varlish and Verral are related as to origin.[2]

VEILISH (pronounced ' Vei-lish ') is also certainly Norse,—? *væng-flis*, or ' wing-slice.' Situated near Udal, half-way out to Ard a' Bhorain, Veilish forms a promontory at the ebb, but an island at extreme tides ; while with Oilish and Udal it seems to represent the *Waynlis* or *Walis* of old charters.

---

[1] Mackenzie's *History of the Outer Hebrides*, pp. 598-605.
[2] There is also *Loch a' Vearal* close to the north-east shore at Teilem Bay.

The references are :—

> 'dimed. den. de Waynlis,' *Reg. Mag. Sig.*, charter of 1469
> (confirmed in 1495);
>
> '1 ablatam terrarum de Walis,' *Ibid.*, 1505; [1]
>
> 'dimidio denariatæ terrarum de Wainlies,' *Retours*, 1617;
>
> '$\frac{1}{2}$ den. de Waynles,' *Reg. Mag. Sig.*, 1618;
>
> 'dimidio denariatæ terræ de Waynelies,' *Retours*, 1644;
>
> 'dimidiam deniariatam terrarum Wainliss,' and
>
> 'dimidie denariate terraram de Uanilis,' *The Clan Donald*,
> vol. ii. pp. 754-756, *anno* 1597;
>
> 'the halff penny land of Waynlies,' *Ibid.*, vol. ii. p. 784, *anno*
> 1657.

As to the derivation of *-lish*, see also under Oilish, *antea*.

VOROGAY (Norse, perhaps *vargr-ey* or 'outlaw island'). This tidal islet is situated in the shallows between Baleshare and Kirkibost and contains a single cottage.

The *Mhorgay* of Groome's *Gazetteer* (1901) and *Vorgay* of Lewis' *Topographical Dictionary of Scotland* (1846).

On the east side of Vorogay the northern point of a small bay is locally known as *Rudh' a' Bhodaich*, as commemorating the tradition that it was formerly haunted by a ghost. The story runs that this *bodach* bore so close a resemblance to the tenant that the latter found his position unbearable and removed from the island, although it is added that he afterwards returned and ultimately died there.

WATNA (clearly Norse, derived from *vatn*, 'water, a loch,' presumably in the plural). Compare the place-name Watten, in Caithness.

There may here be some connection with 'the Bailliary of the Loches' an office conferred in 1712 upon a tenant of Boreray (see p. 55 *antea*), although the term 'Lochs' is so generally descriptive throughout North Uist that its special identification with any one locality would present a most difficult task.

---

[1] It may be specially noted that in this charter of 1505 appear 'le Terung de ·. . . Watna,' 'le Terung de Wala,' and also '1 ablatam terrarum de Walis,' thus making it absolutely certain that each of the three place-names is separate and distinct. 'Wala' clearly stands for Vallay (an ounce-land), and 'Walis' for Veilish or Oilish (a halfpenny-land).

Watna is mentioned in *Reg. Mag. Sig.*, 1505, under
'le Terung de Watna, Scolping et Gremynis.'

Since Scolpaig and Griminish always appear as twopenny and
fourpenny lands respectively, the deduction would follow that Watna
itself represented twelvepenny lands, if, as was reasonably held by
Captain Thomas,[1] the *tirunga* or 'ounce-land' of North Uist comprised
eighteen pennylands. It may be added that the same charter
separately enumerates the terungs of Vallay and Sollas ('Wala' and
'Solos') which are thus necessarily excluded from consideration in the
matter.

The 'Judicial Rental' of 1718 includes *Vannt* as a small farm held
by Angus MacDonald,[2] this being supposed to represent a tract north
of Hougary, while it would almost seem that *Vannt* ought to be
treated as a variation of the place-name *Watna*. 'Hector MacKinnin
in Vaninb' witnessed a document in 1723,[3] and though *Vaninb*
perhaps approximates more closely to Unganab than to *Vannt*, it is
at least noteworthy that the only Hector MacKinnon mentioned in
this rent-roll of 1718 was one of four tenants who shared 'Howgarie.'

Local tradition gives *Mánt* (otherwise *Am fearann Mántach* or
An sgìre Mhántach) as the ancient name of a district near the western
shore of North Uist, and representing part at least of the tract which
lies between Balranald and Scolpaig.

YLAND GARVY; see under Garbh-Eilean.

Here follow alphabetical lists of the principal Hills and Lochs in
North Uist.

NAMES OF HILLS

BEINN A' CHARNAIN (380 feet), in Ronay; Gaelic, 'hill of the little
cairn.'

BEINN A' CHARRA (235 feet), east of the 'Committee Road'; Gaelic,
'hill of the rock.'

BEINN AN T-SAGAIRT (176 feet), in Ronay; Gaelic, 'hill of the priest.'

BEINN ARICAITER (407 feet), near the north-west corner of North
Uist; Gaelic, *Àiridh Caitir*, 'hill of Catherine's shieling.'

---

[1] Already quoted at p. 41.
[2] *The Clan Donald*, vol. iii. p. 662.   [3] *Ibid.*, vol. ii. p. 792.

BEINN AULASARY (452 feet), a spur of Marrival; Norse, *Ólafs-erg* or
'Olaf's shieling,' quite distinct from the other *Aulisary* (with an
'i'), near the east side of North Uist.

BEINN BHREAC, near Newton; Gaelic, 'speckled hill.'

BEINN DUBH SOLLAS (330 feet), in the mid-north. See under Sollas.

BEINN LANGASS (295 feet), Norse, 'hill of the long ridge'; towards
the south-west.

BEINN MHOR (625 feet), Gaelic, 'great hill'; to the north-east,
near Trumisgarry.

BEINN NA COILLE (224 feet), west of Loch Caravat; Gaelic, 'hill of
the wood.'

BEINN NA H-AIRE (503 feet), part of Marrival; Gaelic, 'watch-
hill.'

There is another Beinn na h-Aire (475 feet) south of Eaval.

BEINN RIABHACH, east of Balelone; Gaelic, 'spotted hill.'

BEINN RISARY (397 feet), south-east of the last-named. Norse, *hrís-
erg*, 'brushwood-shieling,' or possibly *Hrings-erg*, 'Hring's shieling.'

BEINN RODAGRICH (but *Roideagich* in the *Sailing Directions*, p. 164),
(324 feet), at the south end of Ronay. Evidently Gaelic.

BEINN SCAAPAR; perhaps originally the Norse *skaptár-fjall*, or
'shaft hill.' At Portain on the east side of North Uist.

BEINN SCOLPAIG, at the north-west corner of the island. Norse,
from *skolpr-vík*, 'chisel-bay.'

BEINN VANISARY, a small hill in the same district. Norse, *Magnús-
erg*, Gaelicised into *Mhànas-àiridh*, or 'Magnus' shieling.'

BLASHAVAL (361 feet), towards the north-east; Norse, *blása-fjall* or
'bare hill.'

BURRIVAL (461 feet), south of the entrance to Loch Eford. Pronounced 'Beer-eval.' A flat topped hill; Norse, perhaps *bjöör-
fjall*, 'table-hill'; or 'the table of Eaval.'

CARRA-CHROM (380 feet), to the north-west; Gaelic for 'crooked rock.'

CLETTRAVAL (North and South Clettraval, 389 and 437 feet), also to
the north-west. Norse, *klettr-fjall*, 'craggy hill.'

CRAONAVAL, north of Loch Caravat. Norse, ? *krúna-fjall*, 'crown-
hill.'

CRINGRAVAL (129 feet), at Clachan-a-gluip. Norse, *kringr-fjall*, 'easy
(or smooth) hill'; or perhaps *kringla-fjall*, 'round hill.'

CROGARY BEG and CROGARY MORE (462 and 588 feet), near Trumisgarry. Norse, *krókr-gerði*, 'crooked garth (or enclosure).'

CROGARY NA HOE (502 feet), south of the entrance to Cheese Bay.
Norse, as above, but with *haugr*, 'a mound.'

EAVAL (1138 feet), at the mouth of Loch Eford. Pronounced 'ay-
val.' Norse, *ey-fjall* or 'island hill.'

FLISAVAL (162 feet), south of Loch Fada. Norse, ? *flesja-fjall*, 'hill
of the green places.'

HONIVAL, a small hill to the east of Beinn Mhor. Norse, perhaps
from *horn*, 'a corner,' like Loch Hornary in Grimsay.

LAIAVAL, near Trumisgarry. Norse, *lágr-fjall*, 'low hill'; or
possibly *laga-fjall*, 'law hill.'

LEE. North and South Lee, respectively 823 and 920 feet in height.
South of Loch Maddy. Norse, from *hlíð*, 'a slope.'

MAARI (562 feet), in the mid-north. Probably representing the
Norse *már-erg*, or 'gull-shieling.'

MARRIVAL (757 feet), quite distinct from the last, and near the
centre of North Uist, in a continuous chain with Marrogh, Beinn
Aulasary, and Beinn na h-Aire. Certainly Norse; perhaps
már-fjall, 'gull-hill.'

MARROGH (552 feet), the eastern spur of Beinn na h-Aire, which
separates it from Marrival. The origin of this name is quite
obscure.

OAVAL, a small hill between Trumisgarry and Newton; only here
noted because of its undoubtedly Norse derivation.

OREVAL (about 300 feet), between Carra-chrom and Beinn Vanisary.
Norse; perhaps *orri-fjall*, either 'moorcock hill' or 'Orri's hill';
but possibly from *ör*, 'an arrow,' as suggested for Orival Rock,
which however must have a different meaning in its second portion.

SKEALTRAVAL (332 feet), north of Loch Scadavay. Norse, ? from
skjöldr,—skjaldar-fjall, or 'hill of the shield';—probably
associated in name with Loch Skealtar, between two and three
miles to the south-east.

SLETTRAVAL, a hillock south of Sollas. Norse, *sléttr-fjall* or 'smooth
hill.'

TREACKLETT is the map-name for a western spur of Marrival, which
extends up to the Committee Road. The local pronunciation is
striochclett.

EAVAL, FROM EILEAN A' GHIORR.

LOCH A' GHLINNE D'ORCHA and SOUTH LEE.

UNIVAL (457 feet), immediately west of Loch Huna. Norse. No doubt to be associated in derivation with Loch Huna, which is locally understood to represent a woman's name (?) *Unnr* or 'Una.' *Húnn* means 'a young bear.'

NAMES OF LOCHS

Both fresh-water and sea-lochs, alphabetically arranged.

LOCH A' BHARPA; Gaelic, 'loch of the Barp (or barrow)'; but clearly a loan-word, from the Norse *varpa*, 'to throw, to cast in a heap.' There are two lochs of this name in North Uist, one at Langass, and the other near Carinish.

LOCH A' GHEADAIS; Gaelic, 'loch of the pike.' East of Eaval, near the shore.

LOCH A' GHLINNE DORCHA; Gaelic, 'of the dark glen.' East of Burrival.

LOCH AN AASTROM. Norse, *á-straumr* or 'tide-river.' A large tidal loch near Lochmaddy with a strong current through its narrow exit. Locally known under the Gaelicised form of *Stròm Mór*.

LOCH AN EILEIN; Gaelic, 'loch of the island.' A marshy loch at Griminish, containing two islets, each of them with the ruins of an ancient fort.

LOCH AN TOMAIN; Gaelic, 'of the hillock.' Very irregular in shape; east of Eaval.

LOCH AN T-SAGAIRT; Gaelic, 'of the priest.' South of Loch Aulisary.

LOCH AONGHUIS; Gaelic, 'loch of Angus.' At Ahmore, in the mid-north.

LOCH AULISARY; Norse, from *Ólafs-erg* or 'Olaf's shieling.' A sea-loch off Cheese Bay.

LOCH BRUIST (?) Gaelic; on the west side, near Horisary.

LOCH CARAVAT; Norse, perhaps *kjarr-vatn*, meaning 'copse-loch.' There are two lochs of this name, one near Carinish,[1] and the other on the island of Grimsay. See also under Caragarry and Carinish.

---

[1] It would seem probable that Carinish and the neighbouring Loch Caravat—little more than a mile apart—are to be derived from a common origin.

Loch Crogavat; Norse, *krókr-vatn* or 'crooked loch'; south of the entrance to Loch Eford.

Loch Deoravat; Norse, *dýra-vatn* or 'loch of the deer'; west of Loch Hunder.

Loch Eashader, south of Sollas, and pronounced 'Ee-shadr.' Norse; perhaps *æs-setr*, 'edge shieling'; or *ær-setr*, 'ewe shieling.' This seems to be the only instance where the word *setr* or *shader* is still preserved in North Uist.

Loch Eaval, at Tighary. Pronounced 'aya-val' much as in the *Beinn* thus named, although perhaps not derived from the same root, there being no hill in its neighbourhood.[1]

Loch Eford is obviously Norse, representing *ey-fjörðr* or 'island firth,' although often erroneously written 'Loch Eport' and taken as Gaelic for 'loch of the harbour.' This is a narrow inlet six miles in length, and all but intersecting the main island of North Uist to the south of Loch Maddy. The name seems first to appear in 1628 as *Lochewot*, coupled with 'Lochmadie' and 'Lochmᶜfaill.'[2]

Loch Eik, one of the Airidh Mhic Ruaridh group. (?) Norse, from *eik*, 'an oak.'

Loch Fada; Gaelic, 'long loch.' This is a very common name throughout the Hebrides, and occurs in at least four places in North Uist.

Loch Grogary; Norse, either *Gróas-gerði*, 'Groa's garry,' or perhaps from *gróðr*, 'fruitful.' Near Hougary and Kilmuir.

Loch Grunavat; Norse, *grunnr-vatn*, 'shallow loch'; a branch of Loch Eaval.

Loch Hacklett; Norse, from *há-klettr* or 'high rock.' This loch is at Portain, but another near Knock-Cuien also bears the same local name, although marked *Loch nan Garbh Chlachan* upon the map.

Loch Horisary, on the west side. Norse, *Þóris-erg* or 'Thori's shieling.' A general title also loosely applied to the chain of small lochs which are connected by the Horisary 'river.'

Loch Hornary, in Grimsay. Norse, *horn-erg* or 'corner shieling.'

---

[1] It is true that there is a *Cnoc Eaval* at the north end of this loch, possibly representing the Norse *ær-fjall*, or 'ewe hillock.'

[2] *Collectanea*, p. 192.

LOCH HACKLETT AND EAVAL.

CAVE AT BURRIVAL.

Loch Hosta, near Tighary; already noted under Hosta.

Loch Huna. Norse. To the east of Unival, the same derivation no doubt explaining both names.

Loch Hunda; Norse, *hund-á*, 'loch of the dog-stream.' West of Loch Scadavay, into which it flows.

Loch Hunder, at the west base of South Lee. Norse, either repeating the last noted place-name, or perhaps 'loch of the dogs.'

Loch Hungavat; Norse, *tunga-vatn* or 'tongue-water'; a small loch north of Loch Fada, near Lochmaddy.

Loch 'ic Colla, west from Loch Obisary. Gaelic, 'loch of the son of Coll.'

Loch Leodasay; Norse, with *Ljóts-ey*, 'the loch of Ljot's island.' Near the south-west shore, opposite Baleshare.

Loch Maddy (also noted under the village of Lochmaddy, officially the most important in North Uist). It is understood that before the year 1640 'The Company of the General Fishing of Great Britain and Ireland' (which received a royal charter in 1632) had built storehouses upon a small island[1] in Loch Maddy, and also upon Hermetray in Cheese Bay, close to North Uist, but belonging to the parish of Harris. 'The Company' met with a strong opposition from the inhabitants of the western isles, and this conflict of interests would readily explain why the strangers chose the smaller islands for their stores and curing-stations.

In describing Lochmaddy Bay, Martin writes[2]—'the Seamen divide the Harbour in two parts, calling the South-side *Loch-Maddy*, and the North-side *Loch-Partan*.[3] There is one Island in the South *Loch* which for its Commodiousness is by the *English* call'd *Nonsuch*.'[4]

It may be noted, as a matter of curiosity, that Blaeu's map of

[1] Mackenzie's *History of the Outer Hebrides*, pp. 312-326. This was Faihore, probably the same island to which Martin refers as *Nonsuch*.

[2] *A Description*, etc., p. 54.

[3] Loch Portain.

[4] This island is marked upon Moll's atlas of 1725. In the same connection, and certainly as to Cheese Bay, Martin adds (p. 55), 'In this Harbour there is a small Island called *Vacksay*, in which there is still to be seen the Foundation of a House, built by the *English*, for a magazine to keep their Cask, Salt, &c. for carrying on a great Fishery which was then begun there. . . . It also affords a good quantity of Oysters, and Clam-shell-fish, the former grows on Rocks, and are so big that they are cut in four peices before they are eat.' The island of *Vaccasay* belongs to Harris, not to North Uist.

1654 shows the Maddy rocks far out of their correct position, marking '3 Ylens na Maddy' off the coast of South Uist, midway between Loch Boisdale and Loch Eynort.

LOCH MHIC PHAIL (Gaelic, 'loch of the son of Paul') appears as 'Loch-mᶜfaill' in a document of 1628 (to which reference has already been made under Loch Eford), and is a well-sheltered branch of Cheese Bay, within the east entrance to the Sound of Harris. This is given as 'Loch Vik-Phatrick' by Blaeu in 1654. Two miles to the west, at Newton, was formerly the crofter township of *Baile Mhic Phàil*, still represented on the Ordnance map by a *Gearraidh* of that name.

LOCH MINISH; Norse, from *miᵈ-nes* or 'middle point.' An inner branch of Loch Maddy towards the north.

LOCH MOR; Gaelic. Upon the islands of Boreray and Baleshare.

LOCH NA CAIGINN; Gaelic, 'loch of the couple' or 'of the coupling.' At Portain. A hillock close to the west of this loch is marked *Caigeann* upon the map, at a place where the ruins of two cottages may still be seen.

LOCH NA CEITHIR-EILEANA; Gaelic, 'loch of the four islands.' This name occurs twice in North Uist, to the east of Langass and also south of Loch Eford.

LOCH NA COINTICH; Gaelic, ? 'loch of the mossy place.'

LOCH NAN ATHAN; Gaelic, 'of the fords (or kilns).' At Dusary.

LOCH NAN CLACHAN; Gaelic, 'of the stepping-stones.' This is the largest loch in the Airidh Mhic Ruaridh group.

LOCH NAN EUN; Gaelic, 'of the birds.' Near the centre of the main island, south-west of Loch Scadavay. The 'Loch na Neen' of Blaeu, although wrongly placed by him.

LOCH NAN GEARRACHAN,—Loch na Gearrachun and Loch Fada na Gearrachun of the Ordnance map. Gaelic, 'loch of the garries.'[1] Upon Airidh Mhic Ruaridh, close to the north, the place-names *Garry Iochdrach* and *Garry Uachdrach* are still preserved.

LOCH NAN GEIREANN; Gaelic, 'of the weirs.' A very large loch in the mid-north of North Uist; excellent for sea-trout in autumn.

[1] Dr. Carmichael states however (*Carmina Gadelica*, vol. ii. p. 284) that *Gearr* or *Gearr a' Chuain* represents the Gaelic for 'a grilse.' This explanation does not here agree with the facts, although it would fitly apply to both of the Lochs 'nan Geireann' afterwards noted.

This is generally known as 'Geireann Mill Loch'; the 'Loch na Gerry' of Blaeu. There is a smaller Loch nan Geireann connected with Loch Skealtar near Lochmaddy.

LOCH NAN STRUBAN; Gaelic, ? 'of the cockles.' On the west side, near Clachan-a-gluip.

LOCH OBISARY; Norse, *hóps-erg* or 'shieling of the harbour,' having an almost land-locked bay at its exit. The 'Loch Opsay' of Blaeu. A large sheet of water, with a depth of 151 feet near its north end, where salt water enters from Loch Eford at spring-tides.

LOCH OLAVAT; Norse, *Ólafs-vatn* or 'Olaf's loch.' At Griminish.

LOCH PORTAIN; Gaelic, 'of the little harbour.' A considerable arm of the sea, forming the north-east branch of Loch Maddy. In Moll's map of 1725, marked 'L. Patran, here 400 Sail have been loaded with Herrings in one Season.'

LOCH RUNAVAT; Norse, *rúna-vatn* or 'loch of the counsellor.' On the estate of Balranald, two miles south - east from Ard an Runair.

LOCH SANDARY; Norse, *sand-erg*, 'sand-shieling.' There are two small lochs of this name, one at Paible and the other at Sollas.

LOCH SCADAVAY; covering 1135 acres, the largest loch in North Uist and near the centre of the island; marked 'Loch Skaddavat' upon Blaeu's map of 1654. Of Norse derivation, apparently representing *skaða-vatn* 'loch of disaster,' or *skatt-vatn* 'tax-loch.'

LOCH SKEALTAR; Norse, ? from *skjöldr*, 'a shield.' See also under Skealtraval, a hill not far distant.

LOCH SKILIVAT; Norse, perhaps *skilja-vatn*, 'dividing loch.' Between Kilpheder and Scolpaig.

LOCH SNIOGRIVAT; Norse, *snjóigr-vatn* or 'snowy-loch.' A very small loch of crater-like appearance within the summit of Beinn Scolpaig. There is another *Loch Sniogravat* (of similar size) upon Ceann Ear in the Heisker group.

LOCH STEAPHAIN; Gaelic, 'Stephen's loch.' To the east of Balranald. Perhaps most of the six following lochs are to be derived from personal names.

LOCH STRINIVAT; Norse; east of Trumisgarry.

LOCH SURTAVAT; Norse, *svarta-vatn* or 'black loch'; in the Eaval district.

Loch TERGAVAT; Norse.   At Portain, south of Cheese Bay.

Loch TORMOSAD; Norse, *Þormóŏs-vatn* or 'Diarmad's loch.'   South
of Loch Huna.

Loch TROSAVAT; Norse.   One of the Horisary lochs.

Loch VAUSARY; Norse, perhaps from *Valdís-erg*, or 'Valdi's shieling.'
East of Balranald.

Loch VEIRAGVAT, near Blashaval.   Norse; probably *merki-vatn* or
'boundary loch,' the letter 'v' representing aspirated 'm.'

OBAN NAM FIADH; Gaelic, 'little bay of the deer'; a tidal loch south
of Loch Eford near its inner end.   *Oban*, as we are informed by a
Gaelic scholar of repute, means literally 'a bay within a bay,'
although otherwise taken as merely 'a little bay.'   Borrowed
from the Norse *hóp*, signifying 'a small land-locked bay or inlet,
connected with the sea so as to be salt at flood tide and fresh at
ebb.'[1]   Hence also the old Scottish word *hope*, for a haven or
safe anchorage.

[1] Cleasby and Vigfusson's *Icelandic Dictionary*, p. 281.   This description peculiarly applies to
the circumstances under which the name of *Oban* or *Ob* is found at fifteen different places in North
Uist.   Eight of these are tidal lochs connected with the sea by very narrow outlets through which
the current ebbs and flows; while the other seven are sheltered bays, almost completely land-locked
and more or less drained off at low water.

CHAPTER V

CAVES AND EARTH-HOUSES

FOUR sea-caverns upon the Atlantic shore of North Uist have already been noticed in Chapter I.—three of them distinguished as spouting-caves, while another crosses the whole neck of Griminish Point. It is however to a quite separate type that reference is now made, namely to a series of eight distinctly inland caves, all situated in cliffs towards the east side of the island. Of these eight, the writer can describe only six from personal observation, in each case finding evidence that the site had been inhabited at some period more or less remote. It may indeed be practically assumed that the aborigines (of whatever race) would at first prefer to occupy caves, as affording ready shelter with-out the initial labour of construction, so that here might be reasonably sought any traces of primitive man which still exist in North Uist, even if no such indication is now visible upon the surface of the deposits which they contain.

By far the finest in every respect is a large cave within a cliff at *Druim na h-Uamh*, half a mile to the south-east of Burrival and mid-way between Loch Obisary and Loch an Tomain. This recess faces due south, with a lofty entrance 8 feet 6 inches wide and reaching to about the same height above the débris accumulated upon its level base. It penetrates the rock in a direct line for 13 yards, forming a natural tunnel (although perhaps to some extent artificially aided) gradually contracting to half of these dimensions at its inner end, where was found a spring of clear water about 18 inches deep. Soil lies upon the floor in a thickness varying to a maximum of at least 2 feet, and on this being probed at several parts, it was found largely to consist of clay-like ashes including fragments of ancient pottery, charred bones and heather stems or roots, with a few shells, chiefly those of the limpet. The access to the mouth of this cave is by an almost perpendicular climb of some 20 feet, thus adding greatly to its original security.   From two independent sources we learned that according to local tradition Prince Charlie spent a night in this cave at Burrival.[1]

Within the same district, perhaps the most difficult of approach in all North Uist, is a small cave in an eastern spur of Eaval overlooking Loch a' Gheadais.   Here were also found traces of occupation, whether temporary or settled, and the place is still locally known as *Uamh mhic Cealtair*.[2]

At Portain, immediately to the north-west of Loch Gille-Ghoid, is the third inland cave to be noticed.   This lies well above the loch in a rocky gap betwixt two knolls, its entrance facing north, and consisting of twin openings which evidently communicated within.   Both accesses are narrow and awkward ; that to the east, occupying the lower position by about 6 feet, forms the main branch of the cave extending inwards upon a level for nearly 7 yards, and is lined against the rock to the west throughout its second half by a rudely built wall showing from three to five courses of small stones.   The floor here disclosed kitchen-midden remains, consisting of burnt stones, shells of the limpet and periwinkle, as also various small bones, one of them shaped with an oval spatulate end.   Close to the west is the second opening, which descends abruptly to its floor, the interior here extending for only 4 yards, at a level of about 3 feet above that of the other.

Ashes and shells were even more abundant in this upper division, together with a few fragments of coarse pottery, and it is stated that complete ' craggans ' have here been unearthed.

Half a mile to the south-east, at Gleann Seilisdeir among many fallen boulders in the south face of a rugged cliff, is another and much larger cave.   This penetrates the rock for 23 feet, measuring 15 feet across its mouth but diminishing inwards to a width of 11 feet, while its height in like manner falls from 5 feet to barely half of that elevation.   Among the accumulated soil upon the floor were found kitchen-

---

[1] Unfortunately Mr. W. B. Blaikie's *Itinerary of Prince Charles Edward Stuart* (Scot. Hist. Soc., 1897) proves this story to be a myth. The prince, during his wanderings of 1745-1746, never set foot upon North Uist, unless perhaps for a few hours at Ardmaddy on 28 June 1746 (*Ibid.*, p. 53).

[2] Pronounced 'mhic Cailter' and locally (though no doubt erroneously) said to be synonymous with ' Mac Alpin ' ; both remarks equally applying to an island in the mouth of Loch Eford nearly 3 miles farther north,—*Eilean mhic Shealtair*, a dark rounded lump of some elevation, drying off towards the south at ebb-tide. ' Cailter ' is probably of Norse derivation, as in the place-name Cailternish ;—see p. 56, *antea*.

midden remains consisting of pottery, ashes, shells, bones, and a few bristles.

The aspen was noted as growing on the west end of this cliff at the side of Abhuinn Loch Gille-Ghoid which here forms a series of slight waterfalls, most unusual features in the scenery of North Uist, and only to be found upon a very small scale.

Well up the south-east face of Beinn Bhreac is *Uamh Creag Eideann*, a small oblong cave, 7 feet wide by 4 feet high and recessed 5½ feet into the rock. Although this now stands fully open towards the south, its entrance has been partly blocked by a former wall of which some traces still remain. It may be further noted that upon a narrow plateau, close to this cave, is a group of slabs fixed in upright position and evidently marking the site of an ancient burial within a cist, once covered by a cairn of stones.

Four hundred yards south from Ardmaddy Bay, at the base of a crag on the eastern slope of North Lee, is a similar but larger cave which measures 8 yards in width by 3 or 4 feet in height and extends from 6 to 9 feet inwards. This is known as *Uamh a' Bhalbhain* (the dumb man's cave) and has certainly been inhabited, the floor towards its south end being thickly strewn with kitchen-midden shells (chiefly of the limpet, but also of the mussel) together with ashes and some fragments of pottery.

There remain two other caves which the writer cannot describe from a personal visit, although informed that both show traces of human occupation. One of these is situated in the base of a cliff upon an eastern spur of Eaval, its entrance facing northwards; this cave is a favourite haunt of the rock-pigeon, and as viewed from a knoll near Loch Surtavat, half a mile to the north, seems to be of considerable size. The other, half-way up the east face of South Lee, and locally known as *Uamh nic Còmhain*, is said to contain two large stones placed within its entrance.

In the island of Grimsay, close to the west of Loch an Aba, is a hillock named *Cnoc na h-Uamha*, with fallen rocks at its north base. This may indicate a former cave, though none could now be traced.

At Ronay is a large bay, *Bàgh nan Uamh*, but here also no evidence could be found for the origin of its name, unless indeed this may refer to the lairs of otters which abound in the island of Ronay.

In Chapter II., which deals with the inhabitants of North Uist in

P

pre-historic times, the general dimensions and arrangements of Earth-Houses upon the Scottish mainland have already been discussed, and we now turn to the examples of this class (about fifteen in number) which can be enumerated in the whole district now under consideration.

Commencing at the extreme north end of North Uist, the first Earth-House to be noted is in a sandy hillock at Screvan, on the east side of Port nan Long. This site was partially excavated in 1887, with the result that beneath a flagstone was found the entrance, consisting of a short curved stairway, which gave access to a long, low, and narrow passage, leading into a large circular chamber. The roof of the latter unfortunately fell in, thus causing any further examination to be abandoned.

We are informed that there was an Earth-House at Clachan Iosal near the south base of the hillock which is capped by Dun Rosail. Here some indistinct walls are to be seen, and kitchen-midden traces also exist.

Nearly a mile still farther in a south-westerly direction the Ordnance map gives at Vallaquie the double record, 'Erd-house,' and 'Druim na h-Uamha' or 'ridge of the cave.' In a long and interesting paper 'On the Primitive Dwellings and Hypogea of the Outer Hebrides,'[1] communicated to the Society of Antiquaries of Scotland in 1867, Captain F. W. L. Thomas includes a somewhat meagre notice of this Earth-House, together with 'a rough plan, taken from memory' showing it as a pair of circular chambers, each about 7 feet in diameter, connected by a short and narrow passage. These details were supplied from a partial exploration by the Rev. John Macdonald, parish minister of Harris, but must evidently be discarded as erroneous, since we have another and very different account from Mr. (now Dr.) Alex. A. Carmichael, who excavated the site much more thoroughly in April 1871.[2] According to the fuller description given by Dr. Carmichael, this underground structure at Vallaquie was a curved gallery of regular outline, measuring 20 feet in length by a width of 5 feet 8 inches at its base, and enclosed by walls 5 feet high, although these latter showed the unusual feature of sloping gradually inwards at each side of the gallery so as to leave a width of only 4 feet 8 inches between

---

[1] *Proc. Soc. Antiq. Scot.*, vol. vii. pp. 153-195 ; the special references occurring at pp. 170-171, and on plate xxxvii. figure 21.

[2] *The Anthropological Journal*, 1872, pp. 272-275, with three illustrations.

their tops. Two long slabs lay across this space, which had been roofed by overlapping stones at a maximum height of about 7 feet above the floor-level; while the entrance passage was from the south, through a doorway near the centre of the wall on that side, 34 inches high and narrowing upwards from 34 to 26 inches in width. The site is now recognisable as a sandy hollow in the surface of a mound, strewn with a few kitchen-midden shells.

At Portain, in the base of a cliff on the steep west bank of Loch Hacklett (its entrance now covered by a bush near the shore), is a curiously situated Earth-House which bears some resemblance to a cave, although it seems to come into the present class while possessing a certain amount of individuality.

The following is a quotation from the article by Captain Thomas,[1] to which we have already had occasion to refer :—

'A plan of another hypogeum (fig. 22) in North Uist, is sent by my enterprising correspondent Mr. A. Carmichael. He states—'Tigh Talamhant, by Loch Hackleit, Loch Portain, is very like a garry, or cairn, that otters would frequent; indeed, before venturing in, I took the precaution to introduce my little Skye terrier to ask who was at home. The narrow part goes backwards and upwards from the lake, and at the end there is a large opening. The small opening below is just enough to admit a man to pass. The whole of the passages are covered, and I have marked the position of one large rhomboidal roof-stone, weighing, as I calculate, about four tons. It is extraordinary that the builders of this Tigh Tal'ant should have been able to move so ponderous a stone. Over the Tigh are several feet of moss, and on this, but a few yards back, towards the foot of the cliff, is an old wall, 3 or 4 feet high, the remains of an old building over the Tigh Tal'ant.'

The sketch-plan and scale exhibit a winding passage about 40 feet in length, 30 inches wide, and 3 feet high, with two narrow entrances towards the loch and an opposite branch into the hill-side; while the inner extremity is shown as incomplete and there-fore extending beyond the 40 feet above-mentioned. It may be added that Captain Thomas proceeds to refer to other specimens at Ness, in Lewis, 'where they are known as Tigh fo Thalaimh.'[2]

---

[1] *Proc. Soc. Antiq. Scot.*, vol. vii. p. 171 ; also plate xxxvii. figure 22.
[2] Captain Thomas (p. 171) mentions the existence of Earth-Houses 'near Cladach, and on the east side of Ben Eval, near Loch Eport, North Uist.' In regard to these sites the present

In the north bank of Loch-an-Duin, Portain, facing the causeway towards the fine island fort which stands near, are some indications of another Earth-House, although perhaps merely representing a natural cavity. Here, now hidden by a luxuriant growth of wild roses, is the appearance of a doorway measuring 22 inches across its exterior, and then bending abruptly westwards where it narrows to 12 inches, all between what seem to be structural walls. No more can be added, except that, on probing with a stick, the way was found clear for a distance of nearly 2 yards within.

A cattle-fold near the west side of Kirkibost Island contains a ruined Earth-House which has evidently been of the normal type. A complete 'craggan' was here found several years ago, and upon the surface of the replaced soil are still to be seen kitchen-midden remains, including fragments of pottery and shells of various kinds.

On Balranald estate, close to the east edge of the high-road and opposite *Druim na h-Uamha* ('ridge of the cave'), is another example of the same class. This was partially excavated in 1896 by the late Mr. Alexander MacDonald of Balranald, but afterwards entirely filled in.

At Kilpheder, nearly three miles farther north, and close to the shore, the Ordnance map notes 'Site of Erd-Houses'—in the plural. Here the seaward margin has been gradually weathered so as to expose thin layers of kitchen-midden within its broken face, further revealing, in the upper portion of this sandy knoll, traces of a slight single wall which curves in a northerly direction for several yards and seems to represent part of the underground linings of one of the Earth-Houses here indicated.[1] From this site have recently been collected a few hammer-stones, together with many fragments of ancient pottery showing eight or ten varieties of ornamental patterns, both raised and incised, some specimens being unusually thick. Small pieces of iron slag and a single cut-marked bone were found, as also two stones of peculiar appearance, one of them having clearly formed part of the upper half of a quern cut down to a lozenge shape in order to serve some secondary purpose unknown ; while the other represents

writer has no information, unless the latter be one of the rock-caves already described as on the east of Eaval.

[1] Upon Varlish point, just to the north, a second Earth-House is said to have existed.

KILPHEDER EARTH-HOUSE, POTTERY.   ACTUAL SIZE.

EARTH-HOUSE NEAR SITHEAN AN ALTAIR, VALLAY; GROUND PLAN.

the broken half of an oval, 3 inches long when complete, and hollowed with a marked depression in the centre of each face.

Immediately behind Scolpaig House is a mound locally known as *Cnoc an Lìtich* or 'hillock of the Leith-man,' in supposed connection with the days of smuggling, when Scolpaig Bay is said to have been a favourite resort. This knoll evidently contains an underground chamber of some description, as, while the surface was being ploughed, the horses have partly sunk into a cavity, once perhaps an Earth-House, although definite proof is not available without thorough excavation.

Martin [1] notes an Earth-House upon the island of Vallay, near the chapels dedicated to the Virgin Mary and St. Ultan. His account thus runs:—' Below the Chappels there is a flat thin Stone, called *Brownies* Stone, upon which the ancient Inhabitants offered a Cows Milk every Sunday, but this Custom is now quite abolish'd. Some Thirty Paces on this side is to be seen a little Stone House under Ground, it is very low and long, having an entry on the Sea side; I saw an entry in the middle of it, which was discover'd by the falling of the Stones and Earth.' [2] Martin's account was written before the year 1703, and an endeavour to re-discover this site in the spring of 1904 proved not unwholly unsuccessful. Excavation of the sandy soil in a slight knoll between the modern tomb and the foundations of an old barn or dwelling (at a point about 30 yards south-west of St. Mary's chapel and its burial-ground) revealed a single and somewhat curved wall, running approximately north and south. The top of this underground dyke was 12 or 18 inches below the surface, and its slender nature, combined with a slight outward batter, showed it to be a mere subterranean lining without any independent stability.

---

[1] *A Description, etc.*, p. 67.

[2] Here is to be noted the juxtaposition of an Earth-House with a 'Brownie's stone.' With regard to the 'Ancient Customs' of the Hebrideans, Martin in his *Description, etc.*, p. 110, adds: —'They had an Universal Custom, of powring a Cows Milk upon a little Hill, or big Stone where the Spirit call'd *Browny* was believed to lodge, this Spirit always appeared in the shape of a Tall Man having very long brown Hair: There was scarce any the least Village in which this Superstitious Custom did not prevail.' Pennant's *Tour*, vol. iii. p. 437, describing 'The Gruagich Stones,' states that these 'as far as tradition can inform us, were only honoured with libations of milk, from the hands of the dairy maid, which were offered to *Gruagach* upon the *Sunday*, for the preservation of the cattle on the ensuing week.' Again, the *New Stat. Acc.* of 1845, Inverness-shire, pp. 275-276, affirms 'Even so late as 1770, the dairy maids who attended a herd of cattle in the Island of Trodda, were in the habit of pouring daily a quantity of milk on a hollow stone for the "Gruagach."' In this case (at Kilmuir, Skye) the 'Gruagach' is described as 'a female spectre of the class of Brownies.' There can indeed be no doubt as to the existence of this custom, whatever its origin.

Assuming, as is evidently the case, that this formed one side of an
Earth-House gallery, no trace of the opposite wall or of any roof
could be satisfactorily made out,[1] although the single outline was
followed in a length of at least 10 yards through the rising bank to
a point where it abruptly ceased. The height of this wall was found
to vary from 2 feet at the south (apparently the original entrance)
to a maximum of about 4 feet, and the excavation disclosed a few
kitchen-midden bones and shells, together with wood-ashes and some
fragments of ancient pottery which showed three different patterns,
these relics lending further support to the character suggested for
this structure. The only other outstanding features were two short
transverse walls abutting at right angles on the east, one of them
half-way along from the entrance, and the other near the northern
extremity. Both of these however were very weak, and showed for
little more than a foot above the foundation level of the supposed
Earth-House. Close to each was found a human skull, under
which circumstances, together with the proximity of a burying-
ground, it was considered best not to pursue the inquiry further in
that direction.

Another site upon the island of Vallay attracted notice from the
fact of its containing a few stones upon the surface of a very slight
mound, about 30 yards to the south-east of Sithean an Altair, which
is elsewhere described (in Chapter VIII.) as covering a group of burnt
burials. Careful examination of this mound first revealed traces of
two small cists immediately underneath the loose stones already
mentioned ; while at a lower level were discovered the remains of an
Earth-House, sufficiently complete to show the outline of its original
plan. The entrance was from the west, and the main passage (somewhat curved, but running approximately east and west) measured
2 feet wide and about 13 feet in length. No cap-stones were found
in position except at the outer end of this passage and across its
inner doorway, where it led into a short transverse gallery giving
access to three separate chambers which branched off towards the
south, east, and north-west. The work of excavation proved very
difficult, as it was through dry sand, the structural walls consisting
for the most part of irregular and comparatively small stones which

[1] Possibly the east wall and the covering stones were removed to build the neighbouring
chapels.

EARTH-HOUSE NEAR SITHEAN AN ALTAIR, VALLAY. FROM WEST.

EARTH-HOUSE, MACHAIR LEATHANN, GROUND PLAN.

were apt to slip down as soon as their faces were laid bare. For this reason, and from the general absence of roof-slabs, the original height of the passage could not be exactly ascertained, except that it appears to have been less than 2 feet at the outer entrance, and not over 3 feet at any other point.

The south chamber entered immediately to the right from the inner opening of the main passage, and was pear-shaped with its apex towards the east, measuring in greatest width about 5 feet north and south, with an extreme length of 8 feet east and west. The walls of this chamber were rather more substantial in character, especially near a slight recess at the north-east corner, where they consisted of long slabs firmly set on end, while in other parts the stones were smaller and less shapely, built to a height still showing as from 3 to 4 feet at different places. Upon its floor lay the crushed fragments of what was evidently a single craggan of large size and coarse material, with a thickness varying from half an inch to an inch.

Reference has been already made to a short gallery running at right angles to the inner doorway of the entrance passage. This gallery was 30 inches wide by only four feet in length, and led northwards, directly from the opening of the chamber just described, into both of the other chambers, which lay one at each side of it.

The east chamber measured about 7 by 3 feet, and was of oblong and almost rectangular shape, fully open at its west end, and with walls remaining to a height of 39 inches. Just within this oblong recess, and near its south wall, was found a vertebral segment of the whale set upright in the floor, and measuring 13 by 9 by 4 inches. Apart from the obvious fact that it had been here fixed by human agency, this relic bore several cut-marks from some sharp instrument, and was also artificially shaped towards one extremity. Close to it stood a small slab of stone, set on end in like manner and even more firmly fixed into the floor, having apparently formed the back of a hearth, the subsoil at this point consisting entirely of ashes with some limpet-shells.

Of the three chambers disclosed within this Earth-House, that towards the north-west was much the largest, and in shape bore some resemblance to a triangle with sides measuring about 17, 15, and 9½ feet respectively. The north wall of the main entrance-passage evidently also served as part of the southern boundary of this north-west chamber, which tapered off to a point near the outer doorway, although no direct access seems to have existed from that quarter.

Within the narrow western angle of this largest chamber was found a complete craggan, set on its base and measuring 12½ inches in height by a width of 12 inches across its mouth; a vessel so fragile as to require the utmost care in its removal. In all probability the other craggan, which had been found crushed by the sand (because lying upon its side) on the floor of the southern chamber, was originally of similar type.

The north-east corner of the same chamber contained a small recess of irregular outline which measured about 2 feet by 3 feet. Here was found a flat and curiously shaped object, carved out of the bone of some large cetacean (doubtless the whale), and measuring 5¾ by 4½ inches with a thickness of half an inch. Small rectangular niches had been cut into each of its corners in opposite pairs, at least one of these pairs being connected by a slight but sharp groove across the face. A leading feature indeed of the scanty finds at this site was that they chiefly consisted of fragments of bones of the whale, for the most part carved or sawn to some extent. In addition, there were several portions of deer-horn, a rude bone pin,[1] together with other bones partly cut or shaped, and three hammer-stones; also two fragments of pottery, one with a raised pattern, the other being a thick plain rim perforated by a small hole near its edge. It was further noticeable that the entrance-passage and each of the chambers contained kitchen-midden remains in the form of ashes and shells, the latter chiefly of the limpet, as also a few bones, apparently of the cow and the sheep.

The walls of the north-west chamber were found to be very badly preserved, having evidently suffered from interference at some period unknown. In the south and east chambers, as already noted, the walls still showed to a height of 3 or 4 feet, there remaining to a level of about 2 feet below the present surface, which in a general way stood 6 feet above the floor of the whole structure. No-where could be found any trace of the roofs which must once have covered the separate chambers, but the entire absence of roof-slabs

---

[1] It may be noted that several bone pins have been recently found upon the surface of the soil a little to the east of this Earth-House.

(except across the narrow entrance-passage), taken in conjunction with the width of the chambers—5, 3, and 9 feet respectively, in those to the south, east, and north-west—would strongly suggest that the coverings must have been of wood, long since entirely decayed. Owing to the loose nature of the soil, there was no alternative but to replace this after the Earth-House had been examined, so as to avoid unnecessary damage.

Upon Machair Leathann (Gaelic for ' broad plain '), half a mile north of Middlequarter and Sollas, are many grass-covered hillocks of blown sand. One of the largest of these contains an underground structure which may be classed as an Earth-House, although its interior arrangements differ greatly from the simple gallery plan usually associated with that term, while on the other hand it bears a marked resemblance to the radial chambers elsewhere described as existing within the structures at Cnoc a' Comhdhalach and Eilean Maleit.[1]

Though not more than 8 or 9 feet in height, this mound covers an area of about 110 by 75 yards, and had been noted as the site of an ancient dwelling, from the fact that the broken surface at its southern end was strewn with kitchen-midden remains of shells, ashes, and pottery. Further proof became available in the summer of 1906, when the Middlequarter cattle-herd carefully excavated a series of four underground chambers built side by side, each somewhat in the shape of a truncated wedge, and together appearing as the segment of a very regular arc enclosed between outer and inner walls, the former circular but the latter straight.[2] These outer and inner walls practically represent concentric circumferences about 6 feet apart, with the intervening space divided into separate (though communicating) chambers by lateral walls, each of which radiates as if from a common centre ; so that while the chambers measure only from 3 feet 8 inches to 5 feet across their straight inner ends, they gradually widen to about 6 feet at their outer curvilinear ends towards the west.

---

[1] In Chapter vi., under Duns or Pre-historic Forts. The similarity was so great that upon first acquaintance the writer believed this site to belong to the same class ; an inference definitely excluded, however, by the fact that the external or boundary wall at Machair Leathann proves to be a simple underground lining, not exceeding 18 inches in thickness, with a slight inward batter and set against a backing of mere sand. On the contrary, both Cnoc a' Comhdhalach and Eilean Maleit are enclosed by solid walls which stand above the surrounding surface.

[2] These straight inner walls are independent, not being bonded at either end to the radial divisions upon which they abut. Barely a foot in thickness, each has been capped by a single long and narrow slab, although that at chamber 8 was missing.

Each chamber in this section is provided with two doorways, situated between the outer extremities of the radial walls on either side and the inner face of the boundary wall. These doorways vary in width from 20 to 38 inches, with an average height of about 3 feet, and have in each case been spanned by a pair of slabs laid across in the form of a 'V'; the spreading ends being supported on the boundary wall, and the converging ends on the outer portion of the radial wall.

A general uniformity in height, at about 54 to 57 inches, was found to characterise the structure so far as here disclosed; this elevation applying equally to the curved boundary wall (upon which the doorway lintels rest) and to the radial partitions and the straight inner walls—the latter being coped with long slabs, and therefore presumably entire. The regularity of level thus displayed by all the four sides of each chamber, and the apparent completeness of these walls, may be taken as indicating that they remain at practically their original height; while the V-shaped lintels, and the presence of other slabs projecting in a few places horizontally near the tops of the radial walls, would lend support to the local statement that their roofs consisted of flat stones.

Thus far we have confined our attention to the group of four chambers first excavated, which are also shown in the accompanying photograph, taken at the time when their original plan lay fully exposed; an opportunity which did not recur, as very soon the whole space became filled with drifting sand, while fresh damage has unfortunately since taken place through the removal of the larger slabs. It is difficult enough to avoid doing harm in the actual process of excavation, and here we have a typical instance of another kind of injury which too often follows from an outside source; so that, if only for this reason, it becomes the more necessary to examine and record every detail at the time.

Encouraged by distinct indications that another chamber adjoined this group of four at each extremity, the writer persevered in gradually excavating the whole site, of which a sketch-plan, drawn approximately to scale, is here given. From this it will be seen that the structure comprises fourteen radial chambers, arranged side by side so as to form an irregular circle with an outer diameter ranging from 34 to 37 feet, and enclosing an interior area which measures from 22 to 25 feet across at different parts. There have been two entrances: one

EARTH-HOUSE, MACHAIR LEATHANN, FROM NORTH.

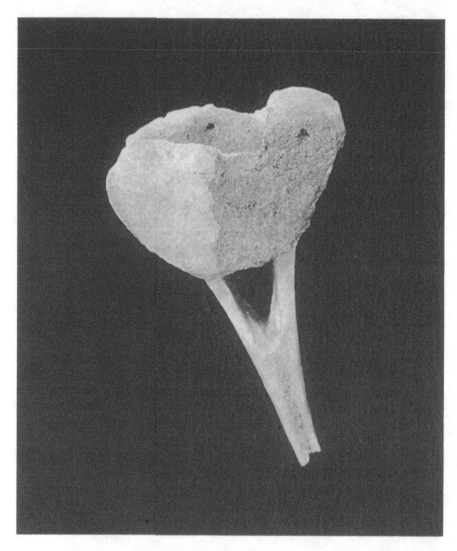

WHALE-BONE FROM EARTH-HOUSE AT MACHAIR LEATHANN. TO SCALE OF ONE IN TWO.

by a low and narrow access through a supplementary oval chamber on the east; and the other, of much larger dimensions, communicating directly with what seems to have been an outer courtyard on the south. For convenient reference the radial chambers are numbered 1 to 14 upon the plan (Nos. 7 to 10 being those excavated by the cattle-herd, and shown in the photograph), while the oval eastern chamber and the southern courtyard appear as A and B respectively.

The description already given of chambers 7 to 10 will apply in a general way to all the radial enclosures, which may be roughly averaged as each measuring about 6 feet in length by 5 feet in width. It must however be noted that only three of these additional chambers (making, with the four already described, exactly half of the whole fourteen) showed traces of having been walled across their inner ends; and also that the access from chamber to chamber, at their outer circumference, did not continue through the full circuit, being interrupted at two points (between chambers 3 and 4, and again between 6 and 7), where the radial partitions joined on to the boundary wall instead of leaving a gap; while of those twelve openings which once served as interior communications, four had been built up with rude masonry at some later period.

Taking the whole series of fourteen radial chambers individually, the following details may be noted as worthy of special remark.

Chamber 1 occupies a position at the mid-east, and is here given precedence from the fact of its having served as one of the two entrances to the Earth-House. Close to the north wall of this compartment a short passage (4 feet 3 inches in length, and still partly roofed by three cap-stones) led eastwards into the exterior chamber A, which is of entirely different character from the others, being oval in shape and of much greater dimensions. This passage was paved, and shows a height of 32 inches by a width of 28 inches where it leaves chamber 1, being narrowed however to 19 inches at its exit into chamber A by a block of stone set on end at that point. A doorway 19 inches wide, and capped as usual by two slabs placed in the form of the letter V, led into No. 2, which adjoins immediately on the south.

Near the centre of its curved outer wall, chamber 2 contains a bole or ambry, 6 inches high and 11 inches wide, but expanding within and recessed to a length of 31 inches. Here lay a concave fragment of pottery, chipped to a roughly circular shape about 7 inches in diameter—as if for use as a dish—and clearly recognisable as part of a large craggan which had been ornamented with a band of raised zig-zag pattern, representing a type not uncommonly found in pre-historic forts. A doorway, 37 inches high, and varying in width from 12 to 20 inches, once led into chamber 3, but had been latterly built up.

Chamber 3 is different in character from any of the others, extending southwards through the outer wall to double the ordinary length, and there terminating in a doorway 43 inches wide and 5 feet 6 inches in height. This door opened inwards, and had been secured by a transverse bar fixed into niches built on either side, that to the east measuring 10 by 7 inches with a recess of 22 inches. A little within, at a somewhat higher level and not exactly opposite each other, were also found two small rectangular boles, about 8 inches square and penetrating the wall to the extent of 16 inches. There has been no doorway between Nos. 3 and 4.

Chamber 4 is peculiar as having its inner end bridged by a lintel 4 feet 7 inches long, apparently without any wall beneath. A gap, 20 inches wide, leads into No. 5, but no cap-stones remain.

Chamber 5 is the narrowest of all, measuring only 39 inches across its inner end. A doorway, 25 inches wide and 41 inches high, gave access from it into No. 6.

Chamber 6 is notable as being paved with small flat stones, its outer wall standing in apparently complete condition to a height of 57 inches above the floor-level. There was no doorway from No. 6 to No. 7, its place being partly occupied by a rectangular bole 23 inches in length by 18 inches in height, with an inward capacity of 12 inches. Recessed into the curvilinear outer wall of this chamber are two other and larger boles. Of these the eastward is situated 27 inches above the floor, with an aperture 19 inches wide and 18 inches high, its straight sides ending in a curved back at an extreme length of 29 inches; while within the slab-sill which forms its front base, this bole was found to dip abruptly for 6 inches to a clay floor covered by a layer of limpet-shells intermixed with fragments of coarse pottery. The third bole enters the boundary wall 22 inches to the west of that just described, at about the same level, and is placed at the extreme west end of the chamber. This ambry was less regular in shape, with a height of 24 inches and a recess of 30 inches, but bulging inwards from a width of 18 to 24 inches and showing a floor laid with pebbles.

The inner end of chamber 6, measuring 5 feet 4 inches across, was blocked by a thin wall with a single cap-stone (as in the case of Nos. 7 to 10), so that access to this chamber could only have been obtained by passing through No. 5. Pavement was not found in any other chamber, and the fact of No. 6 being provided with three recessed ambries, of fairly large dimensions, would suggest that it may have served as the larder of the colony.

Chamber 7 was closed at its inner end by a wall and slab 60 inches in length, and communicated with No. 8 through a doorway 38 inches wide.

Chamber 8, of very similar appearance, had a wall 55 inches long across its inner end, although without any slab above. Its doorway into No. 9 measured 20 inches in width by 34 inches in height, this latter dimension being proved by the existence of a floor-slab lying imbedded within its base.

Chamber 9 had an inner wall and slab 44 inches in length, with a doorway 24 inches wide leading to No. 10.

Chamber 10 was also of the same character, having a wall and slab 55 inches long across its inner end, and a 22-inch doorway into No. 11.

Chamber 11 showed slight indications of a wall having at one time closed its inner end—a width of 53 inches. There was a doorway 24 inches wide to No. 12.

Chamber 12 has no trace of an inner wall, the gap of 54 inches being fully open. A doorway of 22 inches once led into No. 13, but had been built up at some later period.

Chamber 13. Here the roof seems to have been raised at least a foot above the general average, as the curvilinear boundary wall of this chamber showed a height of 6 feet, gradually falling to 5 feet at the inner ends of its radial walls. From the obvious fact that these remain in a practically complete state of preservation, some dependence may be placed upon their relative heights. The inner end of No. 13 measured about 5 feet across, this space being still partially closed by what seems the lower portion of an original wall, now varying from 18 to 24 inches in height. In this connection it is to be remarked that an 18-inch doorway once led from No. 13 to No. 14, but, like the analogous gap between Nos. 12 and 13, had been afterwards built up. Under these secondary conditions, chamber 13 must have possessed an access of some kind, and the only reasonable solution seems to be that this chamber, during its latter occupation, was reached by stepping over the low wall to which reference has just been made.

Chamber 14 lay open at its inner end, there showing a width of 55 inches; while a doorway, 21 inches wide, though closed with rough masonry, seems once to have led to chamber 1.

Here it may be noted, with regard to the radial walls which separate the chambers, that these vary from 17 to 25 inches in width at their inner ends, usually broadening towards the outer circumference, and this in some cases to a marked extent. Generally speaking, it was further observed that the lintel-slabs (already described as resting in V-shaped pairs across the interior doorways) were more substantial in the eastern half of the structure, there showing also at several places in the form of two or three tiers, one lying above another in vertical succession. To a small extent clay was found adhering to the lateral walls in at least four or five of the chambers, but this seemed to be merely a superficial layer, representing a plaster rather than a cement.

The central area — or, in other words, the interior space surrounded by the fourteen radial chambers — is almost circular in shape, having a diameter of 22 feet north and south by 25 feet east and west. Although the writer did not excavate the whole of this large court, a sufficient portion was laid bare to prove with some certainty that it contained no traces of any structural walls. It was interesting however to find that the enclosure had been furnished with a well-constructed hearth, not exactly in its centre, but 2 feet south of that position. Of a generally oval shape, although partly angular on the north and east, this fire-place measured 49 by 42 inches, with its longer axis from north to south, and had a border of thin slabs, 2 or 3 inches in width, set on edge and raised about 3 inches above the clay floor which remained in good preservation both inside the hearth itself and for some distance around, at a level corresponding with that shown by the wall-bases throughout the entire fabric.

Having thus dealt with the central erection at Machair Leathann, we must now give some description of its two annexes, each of which served as an entrance to the main structure.

Reference has been already made to chamber A as lying within the same sand-mound, due east of the radial chamber 1, and joined to it by a short and narrow passage. Oval in shape, and measuring nearly 18 feet north and south by 12 feet east and west, chamber A is enclosed by a wall little over a foot in thickness, with a greatest present height of 40 inches, this latter showing at the north end, where a single slab still projects inwards and upwards as if starting to form the roof. Recessed into the wall of this chamber are no fewer than thirteen small structural niches, including three groups of three, chiefly near the floor level and some at the very base. Its outer entrance was at the south-eastern extremity, through a passage 44 inches in length and gradually increasing outwards from 23 to 34 inches in width. The inner end of this doorway was obstructed to the height of about a foot by a long slab or sill set across it on edge, and here, placed on end just inside the north verge of the sill, was found part of a large vertebra of the whale, showing a cup ($2\frac{1}{2}$ inches in diameter) hollowed out in the centre of its thicker end, and also distinct marks of its sides having been artificially shaped by some sharp instrument. Within the short passage lay a considerable quantity of ashes intermixed with limpet-shells, bones, and fragments of pottery, these kitchen-midden remains extending beneath not only the sill but also both of the side walls.

The annexe B adjoins the south end of chamber 3, communicating with it through a doorway 43 inches wide, of which the jambs are still complete to an apparently original height of 5 feet 6 inches. Measuring 25 feet in length, and edged by slender walls on the east and west but open on the south to a width of 15 feet, this approach shows no indication of any roof, nor indeed of having been walled across its outer end, and ought probably to be classed as a courtyard.

The whole site yielded very few relics of its former occupation, even the ordinary kitchen-midden remains of ashes, with shells, bones, and fragments of pottery, being generally scarce. Several hammer-stones and lumps of slag were obtained, and four pieces of cetacean bone, three of them cut-marked, as was also part of an antler. In addition to these we secured by purchase two articles, both of them understood to have been found in the chambers first excavated towards the west. One of these was a slender bronze pin; the other consisting of a smoothly rounded and knob-like portion of bone, about an inch and a half in diameter, and regularly incised upon one of its curved sides with five small circles, each containing a dot in its centre, while the opposite surface (now partly defective) shows a cluster of ten dots,

with another pair of these upon the extreme edge. There still remains
to be noted a fragment of what seems to have been the upper stone of
a quern, specially interesting because of its being marked on the lower
face by a rude Latin cross about an inch in length.

A descriptive account contained in an Admiralty publication[1] bears
so closely upon the present subject that it must here be quoted at
length :—' Of the dwellings of the ancient inhabitants, the remains of a
whole village may be seen about two miles south of Ushinish lighthouse, South Uist; and the following are the details of the best specimen
which the destructive hand of man has allowed to remain. The building
is circular, 26 feet in diameter, and the interior face of the wall about 4
feet high. Inside and around the circle are nine or ten rectangular
blocks of masonry 2 feet thick, from 4 to 6 feet long, and as high as
the inner wall; these blocks radiate like the spokes of a wheel, and
leave a clear space of 10 or 12 feet in the centre. Enough of the
roofing remains to show its plan; overlapping stones roofed the space
between the outer wall and the interior supports, and from the latter
the continued projection of overlapping stones formed a dome over the
middle space; several small square recesses were distinctly traced in
the inner wall. A most interesting feature is the presence of a sub-
terraneous passage and chamber, the entrance to which is only 21
inches square, so that a large man could scarcely pass through it:
other houses partake of this character, but are not so perfect as the
one described.'

The above notice evidently refers to a site in Glen Ushinish,[2]
marked ' Erd Houses' upon the Ordnance map; and, apart from the
suggestion of a central dome, it might almost literally apply to the
arrangements disclosed in the Earth-House at Machair Leathann,
although the central court there measures from 23 to 25 feet in
diameter as compared with the 10 to 12 (or 15) feet at Ushinish. To
the present writer, however, it seems out of the question that even this
lesser area could have been roofed by a series of overlapping stones,

---

[1] *Sailing Directions for the West Coast of Scotland*, 1885, part i. pp. 7-8.
[2] Clearly identical with that described by Captain F. W. L. Thomas in *Proc. Soc. Antiq.
Scot.*, vol. vii. pp. 165-167, and figured upon plates xxxiv. and xxxv. of the same volume ; though
according to this paper (read at a meeting of the society in March 1867) only five of the radial
piers then remained. The measurements also show a slight difference, giving a total diameter of
28 feet and an inner span of 15 feet, as against 26 feet and 10 or 12 feet respectively. Captain
Thomas further mentions an Earth-House on Boreray, St. Kilda, known as Tigh an Stallair and
evidently bearing a close resemblance to that at Ushinish, *Ibid.*, pp. 173-175. See also Macaulay's
History of St. Kilda, 1764, pp. 54-55.

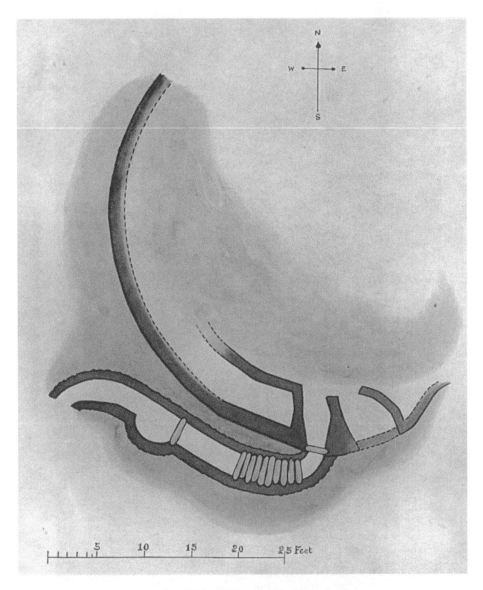

EARTH-HOUSE AT UDAL, GROUND PLAN.

EARTH-HOUSE AT UDAL, FROM EAST.

while the existence of such a dome covering a span of 25 feet must clearly be regarded as impossible. No doubt, both at Machair Leathann and Ushinish, the outer radial compartments were roofed with stone slabs, but if the interior courtyards were also covered, it could only have been by means of wooden poles.[1]

On the north end of the same hillock at Machair Leathann, 100 yards north-west from the Earth-House already described, some kitchen-midden remains show upon the surface, and we were informed that an underground passage had been there discovered. Partial excavation confirmed this statement, revealing a subterranean gallery which evidently had its entrance from the south, first taking a north-easterly direction and then turning abruptly to the east. The outer portion was so much ruined as to afford no data for measurement, but that lying west and east showed a length of about 9 feet by a width of 18 inches, with a single cap-stone still in position at a height of 5 feet 4 inches above a paved floor. This passage led directly into a chamber of irregular shape—averaging about 7 by 5 feet in dimensions—with, at its north-east corner, a slab-covered doorway 36 inches wide, entering what seemed to be a second chamber. The structural arrangement (so far as here disclosed) suggests that of an Earth-House of ordinary type, with a narrow gallery giving access to a group of two or more consecutive chambers.

We were further told of another underground gallery (presumably of similar type) in a sand-hill now under cultivation, some 300 yards to the east, and situated almost midway between this site and Skellor graveyard, but to the north-west of the latter.

At Udal, two miles to the north-east, is a group of four conspicuous sand-hills, afterwards more particularly described when treating of that special class in Chapter VII. Meantime,—as bearing upon the present subject of Earth-Houses,—it may be noted that, well up the steep-sides of the larger mounds, yet distinctly below their summits, the remains of three separate curved walls were traceable, two of

---

[1] There was no sign of the beginning of a roof over the main chamber or court at Machair Leathann; and, while excavating this structure, it was also noted as a significant fact that the interior contained very few loose stones, whether large or small. We are informed that this site has furnished the building material for many cottages, which may well be the case; and yet it is hard to conceive how a substantial dome could have vanished so completely, leaving not a trace behind. Moreover, a dome of the necessary elevation to provide stability would have been too conspicuous for this class of structure.

them showing to the extent of semi-circles, but the third merely in a short arc.

(1) The best defined of these sites—about 15 feet up the southern face of the south-west hillock—was sufficiently excavated to disclose a narrow passage about 10 yards in length and somewhat in the form of the letter S, which had its entrance from the south, leading first towards the north-east, then taking an easterly direction and finally an abrupt turn to the north, where it emerged into an underground structure of pre-historic type. This winding access varied from 19 to 30 inches in width, apart from the fact of its passing (3 yards within the outer doorway) through a circular cell 45 inches in diameter, the north wall being here (as usual) perpendicular, but the south wall coved inwards so as clearly to have formed a guard-chamber, while at this point the outer wall was also strengthened to double its general thickness of about twelve inches. The roof of this passage still remained intact for a continuous stretch of 7 feet near its east end, though elsewhere only two isolated lintels were found in original position, all the roof-slabs showing at a very uniform height of 32 to 34 inches.

The boundary wall of the main structure was traceable on the south and west throughout an arc 70 feet in length, apparently representing half of a complete circle about 50 feet in diameter, of which the northern portion may still lie hidden beneath the summit of the mound. This enclosing wall (bedded, like all the others, upon mere sand), showed a thickness of about 2 feet, with a height varying from 28 to 46 inches; while an inner concentric wall was also found extending for several yards on the south at an interval of 4 feet. From the passage, already described, access was had to the interior through a doorway 17 inches wide and 32 inches high (covered by a single slab) this entrance leading northwards for 6 feet between walls about 30 inches apart.

No attempt was here made at a complete excavation, and the writer must content himself by giving a rough plan of the portion actually laid bare. Very few relics were disclosed, these including some bones and fragments of pottery, together with a number of large coarse shells—*Buccinum undatum*—a kind rarely found at other ancient sites in North Uist.

(2) Upon the same sand-hill, towards its south-east end and at a

lower elevation (about 10 feet above the base), is another semi-circular wall of very similar appearance. This could be followed for 62 feet, showing at the east to a height of 32 inches, and at the west to 50 inches in seven courses of flat stones.

(3) On the west face of the other large sand-hill at Udal—that towards the north-east—a curved wall was also visible, though in this case only for a length of 20 feet.

CHAPTER VI

DUNS, OR PRE-HISTORIC FORTS

FROM still existing traces it is evident that North Uist must have contained about a hundred ancient forts, erected no doubt at widely different times, and ranging, both as to origin and use, from some very remote period until well into the sixteenth century. Eighty-six of these strongholds are here enumerated and their positions marked upon the accompanying map as certified either by tangible remains, or in a few cases merely by local tradition;[1] while incidental reference is also made to many other sites, of which several no doubt belong to the same class although less sufficiently vouched as regards their structural character.

Of those to which separate numbers are here affixed, no fewer than seventy have been island-forts—chiefly of small dimensions[2] and situated in fresh-water lochs—but including ten built upon rocky islets within sheltered arms of the sea, and all of them near the coast-line, from which indeed five or six are easily accessible over the strand at ebb-tide, being insulated only at high-water.

Upon the landward portion of North Uist, the writer has been unable, with any certainty, to identify the sites of more than sixteen ancient forts standing either on promontories or knolls, while perhaps only one of these—Dun Caragarry—can be regarded as occupying a position of much natural strength.

By far the commonest type of fort in North Uist is that of an islet surrounded at the water's edge by a comparatively slender rampart, and apparently having held, within the area thus enclosed, several

---

[1] Only thirty-nine of the eighty-six are marked 'Dun' or 'Caisteal' upon the Ordnance map. It is true that 'Dun na Carnaich' is shown at Kirkibost, but clearly in error, this site undoubtedly representing a burial-cairn of the 'Long cist' type. On the other hand, two 'Tumuli,' marked upon the west slope of Beinn na Coille, are here included as ancient forts.

[2] To all appearance, several of the minor island-forts have been built upon foundations at least partly artificial, though it seems obvious that in each case the site was chosen so as to take advantage of natural conditions already existing.

small erections of even less substantial character. With few exceptions, each of these island-forts has been connected with the nearest shore by an artificial causeway, the top of which does not in many cases reach within about 12 inches of the normal water-level; while the fact that these causeways usually remain in almost original completeness would infer their submergence to have been arranged of set purpose, presumably by way of affording an additional safeguard. Here it must be noted that, throughout this whole district, so many islets have been furnished with causeways that the provision of such an access cannot of itself be relied upon as definitely significant; for which reason no site is included in the following list as an island-fort upon this ground alone, chief importance being attached to the discovery of traces, however scanty, of a former defensive wall.

While at least fifty of the forts here noted belong to the simple type above described, it is unfortunately now impossible to classify the remainder with like precision, owing to the fact that many have long since fallen into a state of hopeless dilapidation, some indeed to the extent of being totally erased.

Of the whole number, hardly more than twenty can be looked upon as even moderately well-preserved, although amongst these it is interesting to find several distinct varieties, supplemented in a few cases by individual features which do not seem to have been recorded in other localities.

Three island-forts—Dun an Sticir, Dun Torcuill, and another in Loch Hunder—are undoubtedly to be classed as Brochs, a character amply certified to them by the presence of galleries at various elevations within the thickness of their walls, which still partially remain to a height of from 6 to 10 feet. It seems noteworthy that both of the first mentioned are exactly uniform in size, showing an exterior diameter of 60 feet and an interior of 40 feet, while the third specimen measures little more than half of these dimensions. Two promontory-forts—Rudh' an Duin (Vallay) and Cnoc a' Comhdhalach (Griminish)—have also evidently been brochs, though now in very ruinous condition. Both sites have been carefully excavated, with the result that Rudh' an Duin shows an interior diameter of 44 feet, surrounded by a massive wall ranging from 9 to 18 feet in width, but unfortunately nowhere exceeding 40 inches in present height; while Cnoc a' Comhdhalach has yielded many relics of its former occupation, these including two small quartzite pebbles (symmetrically oval in shape and marked with peculiar indentations) of a type often found in brochs, and presumably used as whetstones or perhaps for striking fire with a piece of flint.

In all probability several other forts in North Uist may yet be revealed as brochs in the event of their thorough excavation. One indeed—Dun Ban, in Loch Hornary, Grimsay—was thus treated nearly fifty years ago by Captain Thomas, who contributed a description and ground-plan of this structure to *Archæologia Scotica* (vol. v., pp. 399-402), from which it would seem to possess some of the characteristics of a broch, although these have again become hidden under a dense growth of vegetation.

Among the numerous island-forts, three deserve separate notice as presenting features which are certainly rare, or possibly even unique, since but a solitary example of each type is now recognisable.

First, and most outstanding in character, is Dun Ban, Loch Caravat (near Carinish), which shows distinct evidence of lime-mortar having been freely used in its construction, thus radically differing from every other pre-historic fort examined by the writer, whether in the Hebrides or elsewhere.

Upon a larger island in Loch Huna are the ruins of another Dun Ban, still showing as a group of rectangular foundations enclosed at the water's edge by a strong defensive rampart. Here is to be noted the peculiar feature that this outer wall has apparently contained, within its thickness, several cup-shaped cells from 3 to 4 feet in present upper diameter but narrowing downwards to half that width; while the excavation of two specimens seemed to confirm their structural origin.

The fort in Loch na Caiginn (Portain) is remarkable as having its *clachan* or causeway flanked at the island end by walls which extend on either side for a considerable distance into the loch, facing the shore at angles of about forty-five degrees. These must clearly be looked upon as breastworks, erected to provide shelter for the occupants while guarding the landward approach in case of attack.

Attention has already been drawn to the fact that, with rare exceptions, each of the sixty loch-forts in North Uist was provided with an access to the neighbouring shore over a substantial causeway. Only in two cases—near the centre of Loch Hunder, and at the south end of Loch Obisary—does the existence of such a feature seem absolutely negatived, while in six or eight others the point may be regarded as doubtful.

Throughout the whole district these causeways show great irregularity as to their dimensions, which vary between extreme limits of about 11 to 120 yards in length and 3 to 10 feet in width; although 30 or 40 yards by 5 feet would represent a fair and very typical average. It is noticeable that the usual line of direction followed by this approach is not straight but more or less curved, while double curves (shaped like the letter ' S ') and zig-zags are also found, each of these more elaborate forms being attested by two examples.

Although, at the present day, twelve or fourteen causeways stand somewhat above the water-level, it must be taken into account that several, if not most, of this class are situated in lochs which show clear evidence of having latterly become reduced alike in area and depth, whether from artificial or other causes. There is reason however to believe that in a few of these cases—especially at Dun an Sticir and Dun Torcuill [1]—the causeway still occupies the same relative position to the water-level as when it was originally erected, having always stood slightly higher than the normal surface of the loch.

On the other hand, it would seem that the prevailing type of causeway in North Uist has been that of a submerged access, built up to within 12 or 18 inches of the ordinary water-level; a conclusion thoroughly supported in many localities by still existing circumstances, which moreover give no sign of having undergone any change.

Seven causeways must here receive particular notice on account of their being interrupted by one or more gaps, each of them clearly structural in character and evidently arranged for the definite purpose of serving as a pitfall in the way of any intruder.[2] The following list shows some variety of detail among those specimens observed by the writer.

[1] Both of these are situated in lochs which are to some extent affected by the tide. It is thus the more instructive to note that Loch an Duin (with its branches, Loch a' Mheirbh and Loch Bru) contains four island-duns, all approached by causeways, of which two are distinctly submerged, while another stands level with the present surface, and the fourth (at Dun Torcuill) shows an elevation of several inches.

[2] The existence of such gaps, as also the eccentricity of outline shown in many of the causeways, appear to be specially significant as bearing upon the original relative position of the latter. It is obvious that neither of these peculiarities would confer much advantage if exposed above the surface, whereas their value would be indefinitely increased if they stood under water, with hidden features thoroughly familiar to the occupants of the fort itself and yet presenting a serious obstacle against all outsiders.

Loch an Duin (east of Trumisgarry); two gaps of 3 feet near the shore; causeway of zig-zag outline and submerged.

Broch in Loch Hunder; two shallow gaps near the island end, 2 and 3 feet wide: causeway curved, and now standing above the water-level.

Loch a' Gheadais; gap of 2 feet in width and a foot in depth, half-way out; the causeway curved and submerged.

Dun Ban, Loch Hornary; five gaps, each about 4 feet wide, one descending 30 inches, but the others only 12 inches; causeway curved and submerged.

Loch nan Gealag; gap of 6 or 7 yards in deep water near the island; causeway slightly submerged.

Loch nan Clachan; gap of 6 feet, more than half-way out; the causeway partly submerged.

Dun Thomaidh; tidal causeway; gap of 16 feet at the island end, visible at low water.

There is little doubt that gaps of the same type exist in other submerged causeways, and might still be verified were it practicable to make a thorough investigation by means of a sounding-rod, during calm weather.

In connection with the broch near the east shore of Loch Hunder may be noted an interesting and elaborate system of three causeways, two of these having furnished an additional circuitous access over an intermediate island; while there is also the appearance of a somewhat similar network of causeways at Dun Scor, in the north end of Loch Caravat.

Upon comparing the general arrangements of those island-forts in which the outer wall is still fairly well preserved, it would seem that, as a rule, the main entrance stood not exactly opposite, but somewhat to one side of, the point where the causeway landed; this access having often been supplemented by one or two others clearly distinguishable as boat-entrances or water-gates, several of these leading into small harbours within the fortified area. Attention must be drawn to the fact that five of the lochs which contain island-forts are also provided with harbours of a larger and more conventional type; each of them enclosed by breakwaters built out into the loch and now showing at about the surface level, either in the form of a semi-circular annexe to the island itself, or standing near the shore across the mouth of a bay within easy distance.

It is further to be remarked that in three cases distinct evidence was found of small structural enclosures upon the bank nearly opposite the landward end of the causeway, these having presumably served as shelters for cattle belonging to the occupants of the neighbouring forts.

Among the landward forts, Dun Caragarry may be instanced as now displaying most individuality in character. This stands in a wild and inaccessible district upon an isolated crag, of which each weaker portion has been reinforced by solid masonry, and contains within its centre a small detached dwelling of bee-hive form in a state of good preservation. Here also, under the slope of a huge boulder, is a natural recess walled into a chamber of oblong shape, its floor still showing a thick layer of kitchen-midden shells together with fragments of pottery, and evidently remaining in much the same condition as when abandoned by its former tenants.

Upon the recent excavation of several ancient forts in the north-west corner of North Uist, it was found that two of these contained central hearths, and others have been provided with drains emerging through or near the outer doorways. In the same locality, three forts are noticeable as accompanied by straggling annexes, each represented by a group of small cells or chambers which show no regularity as to form or arrangement and are clearly due to a later occupation; while a secondary origin may also be suggested for the radial walls still visible within Cnoc a' Comhdhalach and Eilean Maleit, so closely duplicating the structural type revealed in an Earth-House at Machair Laitheann.

Having further regard to the fact that lime was used in the walls of Dun Ban (Caravat), and also to the presence of inserted rectangular erections upon other sites, it would appear that several of the North Uist forts were either built or re-adapted for secondary purposes within a distinctly later period than can be assigned to most of those still traceable throughout the Western Isles. There seems indeed every reason for attributing both of the last-mentioned features to the period of Clan rule, which, in the Hebrides at least, can hardly have commenced until after the final abandonment of the Norse supremacy in A.D. 1266.

S

It may be safely asserted that no part of Scotland has been more self-contained and difficult of approach than the island of North Uist, with the natural consequence that even beyond mediæval times —which for the Outer Hebrides may well include the sixteenth century—antiquated systems of household defence would there persist long after having become obsolete in more accessible localities through the progress of civilisation. This statement is confirmed by the written and oral traditions of Clan MacDonald which refer to Dun Steingarry, Dun Scolpaig, and Dun Aonghuis, as being inhabited about the years 1505-1520, and also record a comparatively modern —if but temporary—occupation of Dun an Sticir, ca. 1601-1602; the incidents themselves fully agreeing with historical facts, from which the dates can be approximately fixed.

A large proportion of the ancient forts in North Uist stood near the comparatively fertile and better populated western and northern shores; and yet, by a reaction of the very causes which led to their origin, these are the most ruinous, having evidently served as convenient quarries during a long course of years. It is thus chiefly in the more remote and untenanted districts, towards the east and south, that examples of this class have suffered least interference with their original plan, although, after all, no very particular account can be given of even the best-preserved fort, unless as the result of systematic excavation.

One experience of the present writer seems here worth recording. He selected four unbroken mounds in the Airidh Mhic Ruaridh neighbourhood as somewhat promising, either in position or general appearance, although none of them was certified by any suggestive local name, still less by tradition. Out of these four it must be confessed that the first—upon the island of Torogay—proved a complete failure. When however the others were excavated in turn, each disclosed itself in the character of a fort, yielding an ample reward in details of ground-plan, besides numerous specimens of patterned pottery together with hammer-stones and other implements used by the former inhabitants.

Throughout the following list a strictly geographical sequence is adopted, commencing at the north-east corner of North Uist, and thence proceeding sun-wise by the east and south to the west and mid-north.

Upon an island in Loch an Sticir at Newton is DUN AN STICIR, or   • 1
'fort of the skulker,' approached by a wide and well-preserved causeway through shallow water from the south-west shore of the loch,
which is to some extent tidal and consequently brackish.   Here indeed
is a series of causeways, one subsidiary branch extending completely
across the west end of the loch and there traversing two flat islets,
of which the southern and larger is marked upon the Ordnance
map as *Eilean na Mi-Chomhairle*,[1] a name clearly to be associated
with the 'Dunamich' shown for Dun an Sticir in Blaeu's atlas of
1654.   From the east side of this islet, the main causeway, $3\frac{1}{2}$ yards
wide and 50 yards in length, leads in a slight curve towards the
north-east, there joining a third and larger island,[2] in the centre of
which stands the ruined Dun an Sticir, one of the most important
and interesting structures of its class in North Uist.

This fort is circular and of considerable size, covering an area
60 feet in diameter, and still shows a continuous exterior outline
except where broken by a wide gap on the north.   Its interior
was originally also circular, consisting of a courtyard which
measured 40 feet across, though the effect of a secondary adaptation has been to contract this space into a rectangular shape by
the insertion of four straight walls at a later and comparatively
modern period.

The massive outer wall, ranging from about 9 to 12 feet in
thickness, together with distinct evidence at various points that this
contained a gallery raised 6 feet above the floor level, clearly attests
for Dun an Sticir the character of a broch, other details yielding
further proof in the same direction.

Dealing first with Dun an Sticir in regard to its original plan,
this is well shown upon the east, at which side the main wall has a
total thickness of 8 feet 9 inches, and also upon the south where its
width extends to 12 feet; in each case containing a central gallery
about 24 inches wide, outlined with special clearness for some
distance on the east, at which part both gallery and wall are best
preserved, the latter standing with a slight inward batter to the
height of $9\frac{1}{2}$ feet above the present outside level of the soil.   At the

---

[1] Gaelic for 'island of bad counsel.'
[2] This islet is reported to have shown, within living memory, a wall around its edge where now
merely a ring of loose stones is traceable.

west are traces of a gallery about 3 feet in width, while on the north side most of the original wall has entirely disappeared through changes made in connection with a secondary occupation.

It may be added that, where still measurable, both the outer and inner divisions of the main wall show a thickness varying from 3 to 5 feet at different points; and that the intervening gallery seems to have had its access from the west side of the original court-yard, where a regularly shaped opening, 45 inches wide, still exists through the inner half of the main wall. Upon the ground, immedi-ately outside the fort near this point, lies one large stone more than 7 feet in length, which possibly served as a roof-slab across the passage.

On the south-west side of Dun an Sticir, at a point where the wall shows a total width of 11 feet, its outer division has been broken through so as to leave a wide gap immediately above the present exterior base. This breach discloses, within the very centre of the main wall, a cell in the shape of a flattened oval measuring about 10 by 5 feet in greatest length and breadth, of which the floor has evidently been at the natural ground-level, although now covered by so much accumulated rubbish[1] that its original roof-height can merely be estimated at somewhat over 5 feet. The access to this chamber still distinctly shows as entering its west end through a low rectangular doorway 24 inches wide, from which point the first portion of the roof is composed of five long slabs rising step by step in succession eastwards, and clearly representing the under side of a staircase to the gallery immediately overhead.[2]

Another interesting feature is found close to the east end of the oval cell, where, at about 7 feet above its present base, the inner por-tion of the wall is pierced by a rectangular aperture 29 inches wide and 16 inches in height, this having evidently served to supply the gallery with light and air. The typical broch would indeed be furnished with a vertical row of such openings, all communicating from successive tiers of gallery to the central courtyard, which, in its earliest stage, would be free from interior walls or other large obstructions.

[1] Here was found a hammer-stone bearing marks of use.
[2] Three yards to the east, within the centre of the main wall at its mid-south and about 6 feet above the outer base, was observed a short portion of gallery, its floor composed of three slabs still in position, and evidently forming part of the roof of a second cell with a coved west end, and presumably entered from its east.

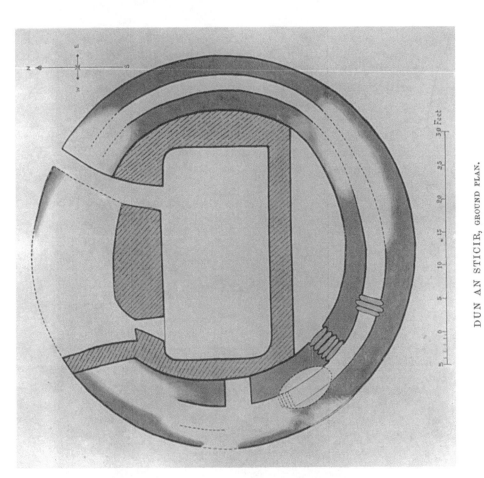

DUN AN S'TICIR, GROUND PLAN.

DUN AN STICIR, FROM WEST.

The outer access to this former broch—as also to its secondary adaptation—was from the north-east, where a passage intersects the original main wall in its whole thickness of 10 feet, having thence been afterwards continued for other 7 feet through the added structure so as to emerge directly into the secondary interior space yet to be noticed. This entrance was apparently reached by a step of 18 inches above the exterior surface level, and the passage itself seems to have measured a width of from 32 to 40 inches in its outer division, increased to 42 inches where it traverses the inner and later portion of the wall.

Some description now falls to be given of the secondary structure which has been erected within Dun an Sticir, so as wholly to alter its original aspect by converting the circular courtyard into a single large chamber, oblong in shape although slightly rounded at three of its corners.[1] Measuring a length of 33 feet east and west, by a breadth of 16½ feet north and south, this chamber has been formed by the insertion of parallel dry-stone walls within the circular courtyard ; that on the south with a clearly defined thickness of 42 inches, so as to leave (between its own straight outer edge and the curved inner face of the original main wall) a vacant arc showing a maximum width of 8½ feet. The corresponding vacancies left at both the east and west ends of the rectangular enclosure were of but slight extent, and seem to have been made up with loose stones. These three walls are mere insertions, practically not disturbing the original plan ; but it is quite otherwise with the north wall, which, though also straight as to its interior line, is pierced by two openings (a doorway towards the east and a splayed window near its west end), with a curved outer face extending between these points so as to give it a thickness varying from 5 to 7½ feet. This doorway has already been described as 42 inches wide, and apparently forming a continuation of the original entrance. The window is a more prominent feature, with its deep splay, almost 5 feet in length, widening from only 7 inches outside to 37 inches across its inner sill. It is evidently in connection with this window that the secondary construction of Dun an Sticir has involved most damage to the primary, the whole upper portion of the original north wall having here been demolished across its full width and for a space of about

---

[1] This secondary structure may be conjectured as dating from some period not earlier than the sixteenth century.

20 feet in length,—and this clearly of set purpose as interfering with the later requirements.

The present base of the interior is raised 2 or 3 feet above the natural outer level, part of this elevation being certainly due to soil accumulated upon its original floor. Outside the main fort, a few yards to its east, are the foundations of two separate buildings, both of them small and apparently rectangular.

Among the ruins of Dun an Sticir were recently observed some kitchen-midden remains of bones and shells, while the east edge of the island also contains ashes, together with fragments of ancient pottery.

A local tradition is still preserved in the original Gaelic as to one temporary occupant of Dun an Sticir. This was Hugh, son of Archibald the Clerk (*Gilleasbuig Chléirich*), a younger son of Donald Gruamach,[1] whose father, Donald Gallach, had been treacherously murdered *ca.* 1506 by his own brother, the earlier Gilleasbuig Dubh.

Archibald the Clerk[2] was thus lineally descended from Hugh MacDonald of Sleat, the founder of Clan Huistein, and we find him acting as 'captain' of that clan for at least six years during the minority of his nephew, Donald Gormson, whose father—Donald Gorm —had been killed at the siege of Eilean Donan in 1539.[3]

As locally narrated, the story runs that Hugh, son of Archibald the

---

[1] *The Clan Donald*, vol. iii. pp. 468-469. Another version makes him a son of Donald Gallach and, in that case, grand-uncle of Donald Gormson.

[2] So unclerkly that he could not sign his name ; *Ibid.*, vol. iii. p. 20.

[3] *Ibid.*, pp. 20-21. See also Gregory's *History of the Western Highlands and Isles of Scotland*, pp. 146, 170. In *Reg. Sec. Sig.* (MS. vol. xv. folio 47) appears, under date 22nd March 1540-1541, ' Preceptum Remissionis Archibaldi Ilis alias Archibald the Clerk,' with others, for the burning of Eilean Donan Castle. The *Exchequer Rolls*, vol. xvii., contain two further references to the same individual, viz. (p. 557, 3rd August 1542) :—' Compotum Archibaldi McConnell, alias Archibald Clerk, receptoris firmarum insule de Ewist, redditum per eundem,'—£135, for ' three terms' from 1st May 1541 ; and on 31st July 1542 (p. 649) the following entry—' North Ile off Oyest, extendens ad xlv mark land, preter terras ecclesiasticas ejusdem. Assedatur Archibaldo McConnell alias Gillaspe Cleroch pro spatio quinque annorum, et introitus ad festum Penthecostes ultimo elapsum, solvendo annuatim pro eisdem lxvi li. xiijs. iiijd.' It will be observed that the surname is here given as McConnell, this however being quite in accordance with other arbitrary forms taken by ' MacDonald ' in documents of the sixteenth and seventeenth centuries. A marked instance may be quoted from *Collectanea* (pp. 9-12), where an ' Obligation' of 1576 commences as being granted by ' James McDonill growemych,' although it bears the signature of 'James McConill growmeicht, with my hand at the pen led,' etc. This was undoubtedly James MacDonald of Castle Camus in Sleat, a younger son of Donald Gruamach, and guardian to his grand-nephew Donald Gorm Mor. In *Reg. Mag. Sig.* ' McConeill' is given as the surname of the heir apparent to MacDonald of Glengarry (17th March 1606), and Sir Donald ' McConnald de Slait' for Sir Donald Gorm Og MacDonald (12th March 1617) ; while the normal spelling of MacDonald of Dunnyveg and the Glens is ' McConnell,' or ' McConnyll ' over a space of many years. While, in a sense to be regarded as the slips of successive notaries, these are explained by the initial ' D ' of Donald becoming aspirated into ' Dh ' in the genitive case.

Clerk, laid claim to some portion of North Uist,[1] and, accompanied by his step-mother, took refuge in Dun an Sticir with the purpose of there fortifying himself against his relative — evidently a second cousin—Donald Gorm Mor (then chief of Clan Huistein), who sent a strong party to apprehend the usurper. Hugh, seeing that it was hopeless to resist a siege, swam from the fort to a neighbouring islet, and might have escaped had he not been betrayed by his step-mother.[2] Even then, being a strong and desperate man, his capture was by no means easy; but, this effected, and his arms bound, he was conveyed to Duntulm Castle in Skye, and there cast into a dungeon.

The same account adds that Hugh was fed upon salt beef containing large and strong bones, with the aid of which latter he nearly succeeded in breaking through the wall of his prison at a part still shown as 'the hole made with beef-bones by Hugh, son of Archibald the Clerk,' who was left in this dungeon to perish from thirst.

Further details are contained in the *New Statistical Account*, under the parishes of Kilmuir and Snizort in Skye,[3] where it is told that Hugh built a fort at Penduin, on the east shore of Loch Snizort, still named *Caisteal Uisdein* but apparently never completed. While this fort was in course of erection, Donald Gorm Mor discovered, from a

[1] From the 'Letter of Obligation' of 17th March 1575-6 (already quoted, *Collectanea*, pp. 9-12), it would appear that during the minority of Donald Gorm Mor (son of Donald Gormson, who died in 1573) the descendants of Archibald the Clerk held some substantial footing in North Uist. James MacDonald of Castle Camus (the granter of this obligation, and guardian to the heir) here refers to 'the partising and deuisioun maid betwix me and Clane-alespik clerych of the said Donill McDonill gormes rowmes and boundis.'

[2] This tradition is found with several variants, one account stating that Hugh's sister was the wife of MacLean of Boreray, and visited her brother at Dun an Sticir under pretence of friendship, although taking six men with her to secure his capture.

According to another and still more circumstantial version, Hugh at one time possessed the confidence of his kinsman and chief, Donald Gorm Mor, who gave him the factorship of North Uist. It would however seem that he soon abused this position by putting to death (? *ca.* 1580-1585) four brothers of the MacVicar family (*Clann a' Phiocair Mhóir*; see under Carinish, in Chapter IX., *postea*), each of whom possessed a dun and a farm in North Uist. As to Dun an Sticir, this authority adds that Hugh occupied the fort alone, being 'maintained there by the kindness of a lady, who went once a day to the Dun with food. The Dun is in the middle of a lake and is reached by stepping-stones. Hugh was polite enough to see the lady over the stepping-stones when she visited him, and it was while in this act that his pursuers succeeded in securing him':— (*The History and Traditions of the Isle of Skye*, by Alex. Cameron, Inverness, 1871, p. 55). Hugh's death from the agonies of thirst in Duntulm Castle has no variant, although the above would absolve his stepmother (or other lady) from any act of treachery. It is at least certain that Hugh, son of Archibald, was 'ballivus' of North Uist in 1588 (*Reg. Sec. Sig.*, MS. vol. lvii. folio 75), and, considering what is known of his character, all the rest might well follow.

[3] Inverness-shire, pp. 258-260 and pp. 289-290. See also *The Clan Donald*, vol. iii. pp. 46-48. Yet another version is quoted by Dr. Johnson (*A Journey to the Western Islands of Scotland*, edition of 1817, pp. 110-111) as referring to the chief of Clan Donald and to Hugh, his 'next heir.'

mis-addressed letter, that his relative was plotting against him, and promptly sent orders to his faithful kinsman and ally, *Domhnull MacIain 'ic Sheumais* (hero of the fight at Carinish in 1601) to seize the traitor and bring him from Uist to Duntulm Castle. This narrative states that Hugh attempted to escape by dressing himself in female attire and starting to grind with a quern, although the disguise proved useless on account of his stature and masculine appearance.

In any case it would seem that this tragedy occurred *ca.* 1601-1602, since we find 'Hucheoùn McGillaspeik in Watternes' alive in April 1600, being apparently identical with the 'Hucheoun McKgillespy of Trauternes' mentioned in November 1586.[1]

Near the east side of North Uist, distant a mile and a half from Dun an Sticir, is a ruined fort in LOCH IOSAL AN DUIN[2] or 'loch of the lower fort,'—a brackish loch close to the south shore of the Sound of Harris, whence it is invaded by the tide at high water.

 • 2

This island-fort stands in the south-west corner of the loch, and has been surrounded at its outer edge by a wall, of which the foundations still remain, while within its centre are distinct traces of a circular erection enclosing an area about 11 feet in diameter. The whole surface of this islet is thickly overgrown by brambles and nettles, together with the red-currant in special profusion, this latter possibly representing a garden-escape from Newton, two miles on the west. Wild angelica was also observed here.

This dun has been approached from the west shore of the loch by a well-defined causeway, first running straight out in an easterly direction and then curving southwards to join the island in a total length of about 25 yards.

 • 3

DUN MHIC LAITHEANN[3] stood upon a small precipitous rock

[1] *Reg. Privy Council*, vol. iv. p. 122, and vol. vi. p. 169. A 'Remission' was granted, 7th Dec. 1562, to Donald Gormson, his uncle James MacDonald of Castle Camus, and (his cousins) Donald and Angus, sons of Archibald the Clerk, for depredation and homicide committed in Mull, Tiree, and Coll ; *Reg. Sec. Sig.*, MS. vol. xxxi. folio 48. Hugh's brother, Donald, died before 26th July 1581, when an escheat was granted to John, Bishop of the Isles, 'of all guidis movabill and unmovabill . . . quhilkis pertenit to umquhile Donald McGillespic clereischt, baillie of Trouternes, Hucheoun McGillaspie his brother, . . . and James McDonald Gromiche of Castell Cames,' all of whom had been previously put to the horn 'for non payment of thair fermes maillis teindis and dowteis' ; *Reg. Sec. Sig.*, MS. vol. xlviii. folio 29 ; also *Collectanea*, pp. 13-14, 18-19.

[2] A hundred yards to the south, and upon considerably higher ground, is *Loch Àrd an Dùin*, containing a rocky islet apparently never occupied by a fort. It would seem that both of these place-names are attributable to a common origin—that is, to the island-dun in the lower loch, the only example of its class which could be verified in the neighbourhood.

[3] According to Captain Thomas (*Archæologia Scotica*, vol. v. p. 399), 'Dun Mac Laithairn, *i.e.*, the castle of the son of Loarn,' although this suggested derivation seems quite untenable.

ISLAND DUN IN LOCH IOSAL AN DUIN, FROM WEST.

DUN NIGHEAN RIGH LOCHLAINN, PORTAIN.

close to the south of Groatay island, which is situated just within the east entrance to the Sound of Harris and less than 400 yards from Crogary na Hoe, the nearest point on the main portion of North Uist. This rocky islet is indeed normally joined on to Groatay at low water, although the connecting strip of shingle (100 yards in length) must often be impassable in bad weather. The writer may add that when — not without difficulty — he visited Dun Mhic Laitheann in July 1906, the sea was breaking roughly against its east base, which lies fully exposed to the Minch, while the inner waters towards Cheese Bay were quite calm, thus presenting a very marked contrast.

Owing to the steepness of its sides, this rock has afforded a position of some natural strength, being practically inaccessible except from the west, where traces of the entrance still appear. Its grassy summit may be described as oval in outline, measuring at least 50 yards east and west by 30 yards north and south, and was evidently further protected by a wall around its edge, portions of this rampart showing a thickness of 10 feet 6 inches on the north (in four courses to a height of 42 inches) and of 9 feet on the west.

The north-east corner of Dun Mhic Laitheann has been occupied by an oblong erection of peculiar type, 50 feet in length but only 10 to 12 feet in width, its west end now standing entirely open, although once no doubt contracted into a doorway. Two sides of this construction are formed by the outer rampart itself, the third consisting of a parallel wall inserted on the south.

Within the east end of this fort, at its highest point, are the foundations of a massive rectangular building with walls 6 feet thick and an interior which measures about 23 by 15 feet. The lowest part of the whole area is near its centre, and here was observed the most interesting feature in connection with this site—a walled tank or reservoir, 11 feet in diameter and still containing water.

Little importance need perhaps be attached to the local statement that, under Cromwell's rule, a company of forty or fifty men was temporarily quartered in Dun Mhic Laitheann ; a tradition which may refer to the year 1653 when garrisons were placed in Lewis and also in other parts of the Hebrides.[1] It is worth noting, however, that

---

[1] *Scotland and the Commonwealth* (Scot. Hist. Soc.), p. 221.

T

during the reign of King Charles I. (evidently *ca.* 1633-1640) a store-house, for the purposes of the herring-fishery, had been erected on the island of Hermetray[1] in the Sound of Harris, only half a mile to the north-east of Groatay, so that it seems not improbable that this fort may have been occupied for a short period in the seventeenth century, an event which would naturally lead to some structural alterations.

4   Dun nighean righ Lochlainn, or 'fort of the daughter of the king of Norway,'[2] is the very interesting—even if erroneous—name locally given to a small island dun of striking appearance, situated two miles south-west from Groatay.

This fort stands in the north end of Loch an Duin[3] near the centre of the Portain district, a wide peninsula which lies between the sea-inlets of Loch Maddy on the south and Loch Aulasary and Cheese Bay to the north.

Dun nighean righ Lochlainn is of very regular cylindrical form, rising so abruptly from the water's edge as to leave practically no outer margin. In total diameter it measures $29\frac{1}{2}$ feet over its exterior wall, which remains to an average height of about 5 feet, reaching a maximum of 5 feet 9 inches at the north, and varying in thickness from 4 to $4\frac{1}{2}$ feet. The islet itself—very possibly of artificial origin—has been approached from the shore on its north-east by a slightly curved causeway about 30 yards in length, still continuously traceable some-what below the present water-level and joining the fort near the centre of its east side. A yard to the south of this point are clear traces of the inner entrance, 2 feet in width, and raised 12 inches above the outer base by a single step, thence seeming to have directly traversed the main wall with a supplementary inward extension for about 2 yards through a flag-covered passage barely 4 feet high. Apart from this latter feature, the interior of the fort (measuring 21 feet in diameter) is now so entirely choked with loose stones and an overgrowth of brambles as to afford little clue to its original arrangements. Towards

---

[1] Martin's *Description, etc.*, p. 51.

[2] The same title is also verbally applied to an island-fort of similar type contained in another 'Loch an Duin' at Breinish on the north side of Loch Eford, although this coincidence would tend to weaken rather than to confirm any real association in either case with the daughter of a Norse chieftain. *Lochlann* is the Gaelic equivalent for 'Norway,' probably meaning 'fjord-land'; MacBain's *Etymological Dictionary of the Gaelic Language*, p. 362.

[3] In widely separated parts of North Uist there are at least three lochs bearing this too generic name.

the mid-north, however, leaving an open space of 2 feet between its northern end and the surrounding rampart, there still remains an independent radial wall, 52 inches long and 21 inches thick, evidently complete in itself as always unattached at both ends, and perhaps having formed a barrier to guard the inner doorway of the entrance passage.

Within the southern arc, the interior face of the main wall contains three small boles, each about 15 inches high, but varying in width from 16 to 21 inches and recessed for 18 to 24 inches; these all uniformly placed at an elevation of 3 feet above the original floor.

Near the landward end of the causeway, and half-way up the somewhat steep face of the bank which here forms the northern shore of Loch an Duin, are the remains of two semi-circular stone erections each enclosing a space which measures at its extremes about 5 by 3 feet, with an opening southwards so as directly to overlook the island-fort. From their small dimensions these would almost seem to have been shelters for watchmen to guard the approach.

A little below this pair of chambers or cells is some appearance of a narrow underground passage, already tentatively noted in Chapter v.

The northern shore of Loch an Duin mainly consists of a long and elevated neck of land partially separating that sheet of water from Loch na Dubhcha on its farther side, although these lochs are united to the east of the fort and causeway by a short channel 20 yards in width, still passable over a series of stepping-stones.

Within the south margin of the same promontory, 50 yards west from the causeway, is a small triangular bay which has evidently served as a boat-harbour in connection with the island-fort nearly opposite. The mouth of this creek, about 15 yards wide, is blocked by a row of very large stones set in line almost to the present water-surface, but pierced towards its west side by a clear opening or entrance two yards in width.

In the local designation 'Dun nighean righ Lochlainn,' the title 'king of Norway' is one which is vaguely applied throughout the Hebrides, and especially so in oral tradition. 'Norse chieftain' would doubtless be nearer the mark, or the descriptive term may simply refer to some leading man of mixed Norse and Celtic blood, if indeed it contains this modicum of historic truth.

• 5   In LOCH NA CAIGINN are the remains of another island-fort, 500
yards to the south of that last described, but representing a quite
different type.

Situated in the north end of the loch, this islet lies near a
promontory on the west shore, from which it is easily accessible over
a substantial and somewhat curved causeway, 30 yards in length
by 5 feet in width, and now standing 2 feet above the ordinary level
the water.   In its outer portion the causeway is interrupted by several
large stones which protrude across its surface, having evidently been
there placed to serve as obstacles against the approach of a stranger.[1]
The most prominent characteristic of this causeway is, however,
that its island end has been flanked, at angles of about 45 degrees, by
two lateral walls or breastworks, built out from the fort into the
water and there projecting to a very marked extent.   While both of
these wings are obviously strategic in design, and resemble each other
in general appearance, they differ considerably as to size ; the northward spur having a length of 28 feet and a thickness of only 24 inches,
while that to the south is of much larger dimensions, with a length of
45 feet by a thickness which varies from 66 inches at the island to 38
inches half-way out, and a height of 42 inches.   The whole arrangement thus shows a somewhat elaborate system of defence, and we are
not aware of a similar plan having been adopted in connection with
any other fort.

The island itself may be described as oval in shape, with a greatest
length of 50 or 60 yards from east to west, and evident indications of
having been at one time completely surrounded by a wall close to the
water's edge.   The entrance to this enclosed area is still traceable
in a width of 28 inches near the point where the causeway joins the
island, and a little to the east has stood the main fort, apparently
measuring about 45 feet in diameter over its walls, although these
latter are very indistinct and nowhere exceed three feet in present
height.

In the north-west corner of Loch na Caiginn, within 150 yards of
the island-fort, is a small bay which shows clear indications of having

---

[1] On the occasion of the writer's first visit, he found a large 'clattering stone' upon the
surface of this causeway, though little importance can now be attached to a feature so peculiarly
liable to lose its poise.   Further reference is made, at p. 150, to a local belief that flat slabs were
purposely thus laid to give warning of any intrusion ; see also *Archæologia Scotica*, vol. v.
p. 400.

ISLAND DUN IN LOCH NA CAIGINN, PORTAIN.

DUN TORCUILL, FROM NORTH.

been formed into a boat-harbour by means of artificially constructed breakwaters, and this no doubt for use by the occupants of the neighbouring dun.

We were locally told of another island-fort in a large loch on the Portain peninsula, 'high up, near Crogary na Hoe.' This description apparently points to Loch na Cointich, which, with its two islets, the writer has viewed from a short distance without finding any sign of a dun, though it seems quite probable that one formerly existed.

Four miles north-west from Loch na Caiginn, but distant only 2 miles due south from Dun an Sticir, is DUNAN DUBH, 'the little black fort,' upon an islet in Loch a' Mheirbh or 'loch of the dead man.' Although separately named, this latter is merely a branch of the Loch an Duin next to be mentioned as containing Dun Torcuill, being connected with it by a long and narrow channel.

    ● 6

Situated near the centre of Loch a' Mheirbh, Dunan Dubh has been approached from the north bank through shallow water by a still practicable causeway 40 yards in length, its outline taking the form of a double curve somewhat in the shape of an 'S.' The islet is thickly covered with heather, but shows at various points an outcrop of natural rock to an elevation of about 15 feet. Along its base, nearly a yard from the water's edge, traces of a surrounding wall are still visible on the north and south; while the central mound is so completely overgrown, that, under present conditions, no data are available with regard to the interior structure which certainly existed there.

In the main division of Loch an Duin [1] stands an island-fort known as DUN TORCUILL, one of the three brochs which can be definitely recorded in North Uist, and perhaps the finest example there recognisable as belonging to this particular class.

    ● 7

Dun Torcuill is connected with the shore by a massive causeway or *clachan*, which extends southwards in a slight curve from a promontory on the west side of the loch. This approach, midway in its total length of thirty-five yards, crosses a flat rock just above the water-

---

[1] 'Loch Mearral' in *Archæologia Scotica*, vol. v. p. 402 ; but there evidently confused either with Loch a' Mheirbh—the north-westerly branch of Loch an Duin—or possibly with Loch a' Vearal, near Teilem, 2 miles to the north-east.

Loch an Duin is distinctly tidal, the sea entering it at high-water from a remote and very tortuous branch of Loch Maddy.

level, and is locally said to have one or more 'clattering stones' still resting upon it in original position.

The island is completely walled around its edge, the southern and larger portion being occupied by the broch proper, while the remaining space—that next to the causeway and covering almost one-fourth of the whole area—forms an annexe enclosed within a separate rampart which abuts against the main fort at both east and west. This annexe is subdivided into three minor enclosures of irregular shape, the causeway approach leading directly into the central of these through a gateway (still measurable as 4 feet wide) in the outer wall, thence taking an abrupt turn to the right and traversing the western court so as to reach the entrance of the main structure. At the east edge of the island, in the smallest enclosure, is a rectangular erection with an oblong vertical opening towards the loch, 33 inches high and 17 inches wide, its base precisely at the water's level. This is obviously a latrine, and attributable to a secondary origin as may also be the case with other features shown by Dun Torcuill and its annexe.

Dun Torcuill is a massive circular fort, with a total diameter of 60 feet, its dry-built wall showing a width of 7 to 12 feet at different points, but nowhere exceeding about 10 feet in present height. The central area thus enclosed is also of circular form, measuring 40 feet in diameter, with its entrance at the north-west, now filled with loose stones but still traceable as 45 inches wide and evidently passing straight through the main wall, which is there 12 feet thick.

Reference has already been made to Dun Torcuill as belonging to the broch type, a fact which is clearly proved by the existence of chambers and galleries within the thickness of its rampart.[1]

At a point in the centre of this wall towards the west, near its top and about 20 feet distant from the outer edge of the doorway, may still be seen a ruined chamber or cell, 36 inches wide and coved at its south end; while, just beyond this chamber and somewhat higher up, are the remains of a gallery traceable as about 33 inches wide for a length of 6 feet.[1] After a short interval, another portion of gallery—

---

[1] With reference to Dun Torcuill, Captain Thomas states in *Archæologia Scotica*, vol. v. p. 402, —'There is an appearance of a gallery or passage about 2½ feet wide in the thickness of the wall, interrupted at two points, at least, by stairs.'

DUN TORCUILL, ALONG SOUTH EDGE.

DUN TORCUILL, GALLERY AT NORTH.

no doubt a continuation of the same—shows for 10 feet at a slightly lower level, narrowing gradually from 42 to 29 inches in width until it vanishes at a much damaged part of the wall, but only to reappear farther on as descending abruptly towards the base, where it seems to terminate in a chamber with a coved roof, of which several vaulted tiers still remain in position at the south.

In the opposite or north-east wall of Dun Torcuill, 33 feet from the outer end of the doorway and at an elevation of nearly 6 feet above the base, another stretch of gallery lies disclosed through the removal of one or more of its roof-slabs. This section still remains intact for about 12 feet towards the north and to a less extent on the south, measuring 24 to 32 inches in width by 43 inches in height; while the wall of the fort is here at its weakest, showing a total thickness of from 6 feet 9 inches to 7 feet 7 inches. There are further indications that the roof of this gallery formed the floor of another immediately above, a point which is very significant in its bearing upon the type represented by the original structure.

Within its central area, Dun Torcuill has evidently contained a secondary erection of oblong shape, somewhat resembling that already described at Dun an Sticir, but upon a smaller scale. This construction seems to have measured about 20 feet east and west by 14 feet 4 inches north and south, its west wall showing a thickness of 39 inches, although that on the east is very indistinct.

Here it may be added that the whole site is thickly strewn with fallen stones, this remark applying alike to the circular interior and to the galleries and chambers in the wall. No attempt was made to clear out the débris, but it is certain that a week's judicious labour would be well rewarded by the disclosure of further details.

It would seem that the personal name associated with Dun Torcuill most probably refers to some chieftain of Clan MacLeod. According to its own tradition, this clan was founded by *Ljótr* or *Leod* —a son of Olaf the Black, who died in 1237—Leod being succeeded in Lewis and Harris respectively by his two sons Torquil and Tormod,[1] whose names persist among the MacLeods to the present day. It is

---

[1] Torquil is the Norse Þorkell or Þorketill, in Gaelic *Torcull*; Tormod being the Norse Þormóðr, apparently represented by the Gaelic *Diarmad*, as also by *Dermot* and *Norman* in modern usage.

further noticeable that the MacLeods of Dunvegan and Harris disputed the ownership of North Uist with the MacDonalds from 1542 until 1618,[1] a period to which the secondary occupation of Dun Torcuill might reasonably be assigned.

• 8   Towards the north end of Loch an Duin has stood another but evidently much less substantial Island-Fort, its site now showing merely as a flat oval islet (composed of small stones and elevated little above the water's surface) with extreme measurements of about 32 by 48 feet, and some appearance of a former boundary wall 4 feet in thickness. Here the chief feature is a causeway, about 60 yards in length and of eccentric outline, which has served as a communication between this island and the opposite shore of the loch at the south-east. In its outer half, this causeway takes a zig-zag form,[2] consisting of three successive portions which run almost at right angles to each other, the access then following a straight course towards the bank, where it emerges to the surface[3] over two large flat stones about 4 feet long and placed nearly a yard apart, and—after another interval of a yard—joins on to a massive and gradually rising pier, 14 feet in length, which rests upon the neighbouring bank at an elevation considerably above the normal water-level.

It is evident that the two gaps just mentioned are structural in character, and have been contrived so as to give additional protection at the shore end of the causeway; although, where similar arrangements are observable in connection with other island-forts in North Uist, these openings usually occur either midway in the approach or towards its outer extremity.

Four hundred yards to the south-east, another island fort has stood near the centre of Loch Bru, an eastern and very weedy branch of Loch an Duin, with which it is connected by a narrow channel. For • 9   convenience this is here noted as DUN BRU, since we could find no specific name attached to the site—a green-capped rocky islet with a greatest elevation of about 10 feet, the fort itself occupying only

---

[1] See p. 33, *antea.*

[2] Another causeway of this zig-zag type is also to be found at Dun an t-Siamain in the Eaval district.

[3] Having regard to the tidal character of Loch an Duin, there is every ground for believing that this causeway was originally (as now) submerged throughout more than five-sixths of its total length ; a point indeed which can hardly be doubted, since, under other circumstances, little or no advantage could have been gained either by its eccentricity of outline or by the provision of two gaps close to the shore.

part of the whole area and measuring from 30 to 33 feet in diameter over its walls.   There is also some appearance of an outer rampart on the south-east, evidently erected to guard the entrance at the end of a now ruinous causeway, about 60 yards in length, which formed the shore approach.

It has thus been shown that at least four island forts were contained within Loch an Duin and its two branches.   These latter—Loch a' Mheirbh and Loch Bru—must necessarily have shared the tidal character of the main loch, although in a less degree as being situated farther away from the sea-inlet.

Upon a hillock near the west shore of Loch an Duin is a standing-stone with a height of 39 inches above the surface, while a second slab, 4 feet in length, lies at a short distance to the north.

Half a mile from Dun Torcuill, in the mouth of a muddy bay between Siginish and Alioter, is the smallest of the seven islands in North Uist which bear the name of Oransay.   This islet is accessible at low water from a neighbouring promontory to the south, upon the extremity of which can still be traced the remains of a circular erection measuring about 28 feet in diameter over walls 42 inches thick, and bordered by the shore throughout the greater part of its circumference.

A mile south-east from Dun Torcuill, and about 20 yards off the northern extremity of BAC A' STOC, lies a rocky sea-islet in one of the devious branches of Loch Maddy, here contracted into a narrow channel through which the tide sets in rapid stream.

According to local tradition, this rock was occupied as an ancient fort,[1] a character which is also borne out by still existing evidence.   That portion of its area which stands above the reach of spring-tides may be taken as measuring approximately 6 yards in width by 12 yards in length, with a maximum elevation of about 5 feet.   Here detached fragments of a wall are traceable along the south edge, while less distinct remains of some interior erection also show near the summit.   Facing south, under the slope of a massive boulder which forms its roof, is a small recess built up at each side and of sufficient capacity to hold a man in sitting posture.

---

[1] Until within quite recent times known under a specific name, although most unfortunately this seems now to be lost.

We were assured that, even at low-water, this islet cannot now be reached from the neighbouring shore, although there are some indications that an access formerly existed over a group of intervening rocks.

● 11   Loch Fada contains many islands, two of which have been walled and evidently come into the present class. The larger of these measures about 120 yards in length by 50 yards in breadth, and is situated at the east end of the loch, occupying almost its whole width.   The remains of an enclosing wall are traceable at many points within the face of a steep bank of peat which forms the outer edge of this comparatively flat island. Part of the west side, however, shows a line of vertical rock about 5 feet in height along its margin, and here no artificial wall appears except by way of supplementing gaps in this natural barrier.

There is evidence that this island was provided with built entrances at its north and south extremities, as also with causeways from both these points to the neighbouring shores, although the supposed northward access could not be traced beyond a small intermediate islet.

At the south end, a second wall stands a little within the general enclosure, and in the same direction, near the water's edge, a narrow paved way extends for some distance along the beach. The whole interior area is so densely covered with peat as to show no traces of its having contained any separate buildings except one just within the northern boundary wall, near which also lie three oblong slabs between this outer wall and the water's edge. Portions of two querns were found at the east shore of this island. Here the fox-glove was abundant, together with numerous specimens of a white-flowered *Pinguicula*.

● 12   Half a mile to the west and close to the north of Eilean Mossam, is the other site in Loch Fada which shows indications of having been fortified. The entire surface of this islet was evidently occupied by a circular enclosure, measuring about 40 feet in diameter over its wall, which is still traceable at many points and shows a boat-entrance, 4 feet in width, on its north-east. A single flake of flint was noticed here.

In a hollow near the centre of a narrow islet in the west end of Loch Fada, and completely hidden amidst the heather, is a small oval erection unaccompanied by the slightest trace of any defensive work, and therefore most probably a mere dwelling or hiding-place. The interior of this cell or chamber, at a level apparently half-way up its original height, measures about 54 by 36 inches, distinctly contracting upwards with the rise of the wall into a domed or bee-hive form, although its upper half is now lost. The entrance seems to have been through a narrow passage leading from the south.

Another similar erection is reported as standing near the edge of a larger island to the west of Eilean Mossam, and not far from the north shore of Loch Fada.

A mile and a half north-west from Lochmaddy village, within the angle formed by the roads which lead to Trumisgarry and to Sponish, is LOCH NA BUAILE, containing near its west end a high wooded island, said to have been occupied by an ancient fort. According to good authority, the walls of some erection could here be traced about forty years ago, at a time when the summit lay bare. Under present conditions, however, its surface is so completely overgrown by the mountain-ash (to a height of fully 6 feet) and the honeysuckle, that no structural remains are visible,—the whole island showing as a mere hillock with steep edges and a comparatively flat top covered by luxuriant vegetation.

The traditional character given to this site is supported by the existence of a causeway under water in a marked curve from the south-east edge of the island to a small rock, across which it is continued to the south shore of the loch, although a recent artificial increase of 2 feet in the level of Loch na Buaile renders the line of this causeway all the more difficult to follow.

Upon a promontory at the south-east corner of this loch, close to the ruins of a modern dwelling, is a mound which possibly represents another pre-historic site, fragments of rude pottery having been recently disclosed there.

A little to the south is *Loch an Aastrom*, a tidal sheet of water fully a mile in length and containing about twenty islets. Some of these may have been occupied by ancient forts, though the writer was unable to find any remains worthy of special notice.

It seems probable that a fort stood near *Stròm Mór* upon the summit of *Rudh' an t-Sruith Bhig*, a small but well-marked promontory 400 yards east of the bridge beneath which the tidal current from Loch an Aastrom rushes seawards at the ebb.   This site is very indistinct, showing only a few irregular groups of stones, with doubtful traces of an enclosure about 30 feet in diameter.   From the north edge of the same promontory a massive causeway extends across the narrowest part of Strom Mor, while immediately to the east lies *Loch Houram*, another of the many inner recesses of Lochmaddy Bay.

● 14   Near the centre of OB NAN STEARNAIN,[1] a tidal and very shallow loch at the roadside half a mile north-west of Lochmaddy, is a rocky islet evidently once surrounded by a wall except perhaps at its south-east edge which consists of steep rock.   This enclosing wall shows at various points along the base, especially on the north, where three or four courses remain in a width of seven feet; while the elevated central portion of the islet also contains traces of some former building.

In all likelihood this island was connected with the shore by a causeway, although no indication could be found of any such approach, which may now lie hidden under the thick accumulation of mud at the bottom of the loch.

In Loch Skealtar, fully a mile to the west of Lochmaddy village,
● 15 is EILEAN BUIDHE or 'yellow island,' which has been occupied as a fort and still shows the remains of a protecting wall around its edge. A causeway of unusual length is also traceable as running, somewhat below the present water-level, from a slight promontory on the south shore of the loch to join the west end of this island—a distance of about 120 yards.   The main gateway, 42 inches in width, is clearly defined at the island end of the causeway, and has been supplemented by two boat-entrances, one of them on the south-west and the other towards the north-east.   Of these, the first-mentioned seems to have been specially wide and with a flat base throughout, a point which may in some degree indicate the character of the boats then in use.   The other access, on the north side of the island, measures 48 inches in width, leading into a shallow basin or harbour protected by a wall and even now filled with water.

Eilean Buidhe is a large grassy island, about 100 yards in extreme length but of very irregular shape.   It has contained at least four

[1] Meaning literally 'bay of the terns.'

DUN TORCUILL, GALLERY AT SOUTH.

EILEAN LIERAVAY, FROM SOUTH-WEST.

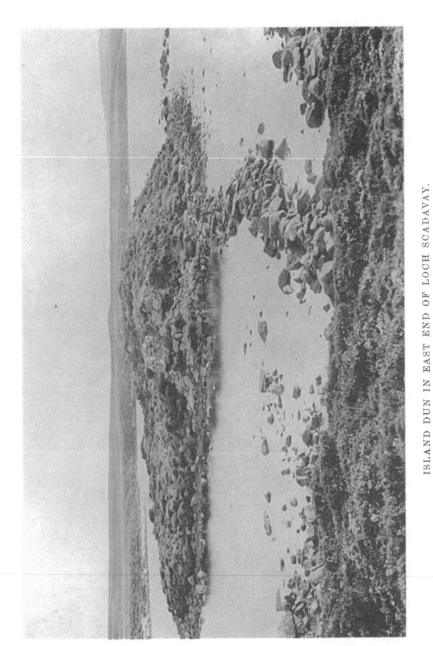

ISLAND DUN IN EAST END OF LOCH SCADAVAY.

circular erections of 6 to 8 yards in diameter, as also a considerable and perhaps natural mound near the centre of its north side. The enclosing wall shows a thickness of about 4 feet, with a greatest present height of 45 inches.

On the south bank of Loch Skealtar, near the landward end of the causeway, stand the ruins of several small enclosures, these being locally explained as 'cruives' (Gaelic, *crùban*) erected to provide shelter for cattle belonging to the former inhabitants of this fort.

In the north-east corner of *Loch nan Geireann* (half a mile east of Loch Skealtar, and not to be confused with the much larger *Geireann Mill Loch*) is a flat and somewhat circular island which possibly represents the site of another fort, though it was considered best to leave this in the category of doubtful identifications. There are slight traces of a wall at its south edge, while between this island and the east shore of the loch—an interval of more than 100 yards—stands an irregular row of large stones sufficiently near each other to serve even now as a practicable access or causeway. Near the centre of the same loch is a smaller island, very rough as to its surface and with indications of a surrounding wall, though a still more significant feature is the existence of a causeway leading under water to a promontory on the north.

At *Cnoc nan Cuigeal*, a little to the north of Loch nan Geireann (between it and Loch an Aastrom, already mentioned) are two conspicuous hillocks, each of them containing loose stones upon its summit. The northmost of these knolls is comparatively regular in shape, resembling a flattened cone upon which there seem to be traces of a former erection, apparently measuring about 32 feet in diameter over its walls.

To the south of Loch Skealtar, four other sites may be noted in passing. Two of those are upon *Scaalan*, a rugged point which separates *Stròm Dearg* from *Stròm Bàn*, half a mile to the west of Lochmaddy pier. The more elevated position is scantily marked, with only two erect stones at its western edge; but 150 yards to the east, there still stands an irregularly built enclosure measuring about 50 by 30 feet. Here were found some fragments of crude pottery, as also a lozenge-shaped iron rivet-head 2 inches in length and apparently of Viking origin. Upon a northern spur of Stromban, the next point to the south-west, seems to be the site of an ancient structure now represented by a slight mound with some very large stones lying upon its surface. Midway between the east end of Stromban and Eilean Lieravay is an islet which dries off at half-tide, showing the remains of some erection with an interior diameter of about 16 feet.

Fully a mile to the west is LOCH SCADAVAY, noteworthy as the largest of the many lochs in North Uist, and also for its eccentricity of outline, consisting of a tangled series of devious and comparatively narrow arms which straggle in all directions, over a range of 4 miles north and south by 2½ miles east and west.

● 16   Within an eastern bay, between the promontories marked *Rudh' a' Chlachain* and *Àrd Smeilish*, is an islet connected with the shore on its north by a causeway showing well above the summer level of the loch in a double curve, somewhat resembling the letter 'S,' in a length of 22 yards by a width of 4 feet. This island has clearly been walled around, except perhaps at its west side which rises abruptly to some height, and there are indications of a gateway with an ascent by three or four steps a little east from the landing-point of the causeway. Here the entrance passes through a guard-chamber built against the inner side of the fort wall and projecting into the interior area, with walls ranging in thickness from 2 to 3 feet and still partly remaining to a height of 4 feet. In general shape rectangular, though with rounded corners, this chamber shows an interior of fully 6 by 8 feet, its northern doorway being hardly measurable, but that on the south varying in width from 13 inches at the base to 17 inches above. Within its east wall is a bole 12 inches square and recessed to the extent of 18 inches.

Scattered over the island are three other small erections (one of them upon the west summit), round or oval in shape and measuring 6 to 7 feet across their interiors. These closely approach the shieling type and are of slender construction, but near the centre of the island, upon level ground, are the ruins of another and more important building, with a wall 2 feet thick, which encloses an area 11 or 12 feet in diameter.

From the west side of this island a semi-circle of large stones has been arranged in the loch, so as to form a boat-harbour with two gaps—small on the south, but larger on the north—left near the boundary of the fort.

Within a short radius to the north are four other islets, each supplemented by a causeway from the same narrow peninsula which leads to the fort already described; but upon none of these were we able to trace any structural remains.[1]

Two miles farther west, near the opposite extremity of Loch Scadavay, is a pair of green islands, both of them locally said to have been approached by causeways, though in neither case was it found possible to verify this statement as a fact. It is certain, however, that the westmost of these two—a long narrow island with steep sides, and a flattish top measuring about 8 yards across and 15 feet in height—has been walled all round upon its scanty margin close to the water's edge. This wall shows a thickness of 5 feet and is pierced by three boat-entrances, two of them at the north (one evidently leading into a small boat-harbour) and the other at the south, all showing a very uniform width of about 56 inches.

• 17

The road from Lochmaddy to Clachan-a-gluip bisects Loch Scadavay at a very narrow part which is bridged across. Both divisions of the loch are studded with innumerable islets, and it can hardly be doubted that others of these might also be classed as ancient forts, were it practicable to examine the whole area in detail—a task which would involve a lengthened period of close investigation under many difficulties.

A little east from the southern half of Loch Scadavay is *Loch Deoravat*, half a mile in length and containing fourteen islands, of which two have been provided with causeways to the neighbouring shore on the west. Both of these are unnamed upon the Ordnance map, though the larger—a dark island of some elevation and about 120 yards long—is locally known as *Eilean Dubh*. This we were unable to reach, its causeway being entirely submerged. The other, situated 100 yards to the south, is a small narrow islet not exceeding 2 or 3 yards in present width, but showing some evidence of a wall along its north edge, and, still more significantly, indica-

---

[1] Here seems a fitting opportunity to impress the fact that while causeways exist in connection with many islands, the inference to be deduced is by no means equally obvious. In other words, though almost every island-fort in North Uist has been approached by a causeway, there are frequent instances where such an access is found without any further indication of the site having been occupied as a fort.

ISLAND DUN AND CAUSEWAYS IN LOCH HUNDER.

tions of a semi-circular enclosure extending under water on its south. Although not here definitely classed, this ought almost certainly to be regarded as an island-fort.

In *Loch a' Chonnachair*, a mile to the north-east of Loch Deoravat, is a small island connected with the shore on its west by a causeway, in this case evidently forked—so as to take the form of the letter Y—two branches converging into one, towards the island end.

LOCH HUNDER lies two miles south of Lochmaddy village, at the west base of North and South Lee, and contains two island-forts. Of these the larger stands near the centre of the loch, and is known as Dun Ban or 'white fort' (a very common descriptive term, no doubt acquired within modern times from its general appearance), while the other is situated fully 200 yards to the south-east, and does not seem to bear any distinctive name.

• 18   DUN BAN has occupied the entire surface of an islet about 30 yards in diameter, which consists of solid rock and rises to a height ranging from 5 to 10 feet above the water-level. This site is equidistant about 250 yards between the east and west shores of Loch Hunder, and hardly appears to have had an artificial access from either, though a short portion of causeway is still visible as projecting towards it from the neighbouring fort on the east. The summit of Dun Ban has been surrounded at its edge by a slight outer wall 3 feet thick, further supplemented by a more substantial inner rampart which shows best on the north and west to a width of 5½ feet, enclosing an area about 55 feet in diameter.

At the mid-east of this islet is a clearly marked boat-entrance, 1·1 feet wide at its exterior, but thence narrowing inwards and also sloping gradually upwards over the rock. The north side of this water-gate consists of natural rock, while that on the south is formed by a separate wall, nearly 9 feet in length.

In addition to the concentric enclosures already mentioned, there has been a third and inner circular erection towards the east summit, measuring nearly 20 feet over its walls of about 30 inches in thickness and 3 feet in present height, with a doorway 34 inches wide on the east, facing the boat-entrance.

Dun Ban is completely covered by a rank growth of herbage, including the bramble, honeysuckle, and foxglove. It is now frequented by deer, and serves also as a nesting-place for herons, being evidently regarded as a secure retreat, free from any intrusion.

The other fort in Loch Hunder is noteworthy in several respects, ● 19 both as presenting a miniature example of the island-broch—with a marked resemblance to Dun Torcuill—and also in connection with its elaborate net-work of causeways.

This island is approached from the east bank of the loch by a curved causeway 40 yards in length, for the most part showing a width of 3 or 4 feet, though broadened to about 7 feet in one portion not far from the shore. Near its island end, this causeway is interrupted by two successive gaps measuring 2 and 3 feet across, both of them regularly paved in the now shallow bottom of the loch, and evidently constructed to serve as traps or obstacles in the line of approach. Here it may be incidentally noted that the water-level of Loch Hunder seems to have fallen at least 2 feet as compared with the conditions which formerly prevailed, the main access now standing to that height above the present surface.

Some description must be given of two or three additional causeways which also exist in connection with this site. From the opposite edge of the island-fort a causeway extends out into the loch towards the north-west for a distance of about 20 yards to a point where it divides; one branch continuing for several yards in a westerly direction (as if to join Dun Ban), and the other at first curving abruptly to the south and then taking a straight course towards a long island which lies about 50 yards to the south-west. But even this does not exhaust the whole arrangement, the last-mentioned island being in turn connected at its south end with the west shore of the loch by still another causeway which is built in the form of a zig-zag.[1] It was not found possible to determine how far the extension continues towards Dun Ban, as the loch here shows a rapidly increasing depth, though it may be remarked that wherever the bottom was visible to the north and west of the island-broch, it was almost literally paved with large slabs of stone, and this over so wide an area that the fact must be attributed to natural rather than to artificial causes.

---

[1] On the writer's first visit to this interesting site, a friend walked over the entire net-work of three causeways and two intermediate islands ; thus affording a very practical test of the excellent condition in which the whole circuit still remains.

This island-broch is distinctly circular in form, measuring 33½ feet from north to south over its walls, which there show a thickness of 6 feet to 6½ feet, thus leaving an interior area about 21 feet in diameter. The entrance was evidently at a point a little north of the junction with the landward causeway, although the wall is unfortunately here so ruinous that the original arrangement cannot be followed, nor indeed could the fort be accurately measured from east to west. On the south-east the wall seems to reach its greatest width at 9½ feet, while exactly opposite the causeway, and again on the mid-west, a thickness of 8½ feet is clearly shown. The interior area is filled with loose stones, covered by heather to an apparent height of nearly 5 feet above the original base, while the surrounding wall still remains to a fairly regular elevation of about 6 feet.

For short intervals within the thickness of the wall, both on the north and on the south-east, traces exist of what must either have been chambers or (less probably) a passage 27 inches wide, showing roof-slabs still in position so as to indicate a height of about 5 feet; while above these is some appearance of an upper gallery as in Dun Torcuill. It may be added that the chamber within the south wall seems to terminate towards the west with a coved end, and does not occupy a central position in the rampart, being situated distinctly towards its inner face.

In a hollow on the east bank of Loch Hunder, opposite the zig-zag causeway already mentioned, are the remains of an oval enclosure with its wall built of large stones to a present greatest height of 42 inches and showing an interior which measures about 20 by 16 feet. It is evident that this has served some purpose in connection with the neighbouring fort, not improbably as a shelter for cattle.

Half a mile to the south, at *Tota Hunder*, near the shore of Loch Eford, is a small promontory known as *Ard Bheag* and capped by a conical green mound with a number of stones embedded upon its summit. If these represent the foundations of a building, it would seem that we have here the site of another dun.

At Caragarry, 1½ miles south-east from Loch Hunder, is a rock-fort [1] situated in one of the least trodden portions of North

---

[1] So little is this site distinguishable from other neighbouring crags, that the writer had great difficulty in identifying the fort, although positively assured of its existence and given general directions as to the locality.

DUN CARAGARRY, FROM WEST.

DOMED CELL, DUN CARAGARRY.

Uist, commanding a wide view across the Minch towards Skye, and immediately overlooking the entrance to Loch Eford, beyond which the district to the east of Eaval lies clearly mapped out on the south.

DUN CARAGARRY stands at a considerable elevation half-way up the shoulder of South Lee, occupying a narrow isolated ridge of great natural strength, bordered on the north by a precipitous gully and on the south by a cliff hardly less steep, while its west end mainly consists of a single huge boulder fallen at some remote period from the hill-side of which this rocky spur is a semi-detached portion. The former entrance has evidently been by the more gradual slope towards the east, although no remains of the actual doorway could be verified. Double walls are traceable both here and at the south, in the latter position about 2 yards apart, but with a much greater interval on the east, where the outer wall has a thickness of 5 feet and shows at one point in no fewer than ten courses of thin stones resting against the edge of a rock. It is however along this east end that the defensive wall is now least conspicuous, the comparatively flat summit being elsewhere thoroughly protected either by the cliff itself or by masonry of small stones built into each natural fissure which had thus to be supplemented. While artificial work is apparent at every gap, notably in six courses at the north, the most continuous portions of wall adjoin the north and south edges of the boulder (a cube measuring about 15 feet across), which forms the middle half of the west boundary.

Within the centre of Dun Caragarry, amidst a vigorous growth of heather, was found a domed cell in nearly perfect condition, so closely preserving its original character that a couple of slabs laid across its top would suffice to complete the fabric. Formed by a wall 2 to 3 feet in thickness, this cell is mainly circular although extended northwards by a coved end, with the result that the interior assumes an oval shape measuring at its base [1] a length of 6½ feet by a width (east and west) of nearly 5 feet, the wall gradually tapering inwards and upwards to an opening about 36 inches in diameter at a present roof height of 4 feet. The doorway is on the west, and shows a width varying from 17 to 21 inches, its lintel consisting of a flat stone which still remains in original position.

[1] The original floor of this cell seems to have stood quite 12 inches below the outside level.

• 20

The massive boulder already noted as in itself supplying half of the west defence of Dun Caragarry, slopes up at an acute angle towards the east, thus producing a cave-like recess which has been enclosed by low walls so as to form an oblong chamber 10 feet long by 6 feet wide, its roof slanting upwards from the rock base at the west to a height of 4 feet on the east. At the inmost part of this cavity it was interesting to find a surface layer of kitchen-midden remains, evidently lying undisturbed in the same condition as when the fort was abandoned by its inhabitants at some remote period. This deposit consists of limpet-shells to a depth of several inches, while above these lay two fragments of pottery and several bones, although, apart from the combination, less significance would attach to the latter. In the ruined exterior wall on the south of the fort were also found shells, bones, and ashes of the ordinary kitchen-midden type, together with a hammer-stone and three fragments of patterned pottery.

The whole enclosure at Dun Caragarry seems to have measured about 35 by 48 feet within its outer barrier, although limited to a width of 26 feet by an inner wall on the south.

Immediately outside the east end of this fort, under a rock in the edge of the cliff, is a shelter (perhaps once a guard-chamber) made up in front by a rude wall so as to enclose a space of 10 by 4 feet, with a height of 27 to 30 inches. In still lower positions, close to the west and the north, are three or four other recesses of similar character, each showing distinct signs of artificial work, and one of them (at the mid-north) containing many limpet-shells strewn upon its floor.

At a distance of 20 or 30 yards down the slope to the south-east, are the remains of a substantial erection built against the side of a boulder and forming a chamber 6 feet long by $3\frac{1}{2}$ feet wide, its walls still fairly complete and almost 5 feet high. This structure occupies the west end of an oval enclosure, which measures about 12 by 24 feet and contains some very large stones in its wall, having in all probability served as a cattle-pen in connection with the fort.

Dun Caragarry stands amid surroundings wild in the extreme, at a spot affording no landward access save by a tedious climb and equally difficult descent over the shoulder of South Lee, though with much greater facilities of approach from the Minch, which a thousand

DUN BREINISH, FROM WEST.

ISLAND DUN IN SOUTH END OF LOCH OBISARY, FROM EAST.

years ago no doubt provided the main thoroughfare among the Outer Hebrides.

The occupants of this fort would here possess a naturally guarded reserve furnishing pasturage for their cattle, with some patches of soil suitable for producing grain, in addition to a convenient hunting-ground—these probably satisfying all their very modest needs.

Upon the peninsula of Breinish,[1] four miles to the west of Caragarry, in a small fresh‑water loch distant little more than 50 yards from the north shore of Loch Eford, stands a very symmetrical island-fort, here for convenience noted as DUN BREINISH.[2]   ● 21

Rising in circular form sheer out of the water, this fort bears a marked resemblance to another already described at Portain, near the north side of Loch Maddy.   The fact that each of these very similar island-forts is locally known under the name of *Dùn nighean righ Lochlainn* must be regarded as a somewhat unsatisfactory coincidence, tending rather to lessen the value of any implied tradition that either of them was actually occupied by a ' daughter of the king of Norway.' It must be added that the alternative title of *Dùn Eideann* was also found associated with the Breinish fort, this possibly conveying some reference to the occupant of *Uamh Creag Eideann*, a small cave already noted in the south face of Beinn Bhreac.

Dun Breinish has been approached from the north-west by a causeway 25 yards in length, and thence through an entrance which pierces the main wall about four feet to the north in an apparent width of 28 inches, there raised by a single step to an elevation of 27 inches above the outer base.

Over its exterior, this fort measures 28 feet north and south by 32 feet east and west, the wall having an average thickness of 54 inches with a present greatest height of 6 feet.   The inner area is completely filled with loose stones, covered by a rank growth of herbage, together with the mountain-ash and honeysuckle, thus showing few traces of its original arrangement.   Within the south-east side, however, still remains part of another and slighter concentric wall, there leaving a space of nearly 3 feet, this interval probably representing the passage to a small cell or chamber which seems to have stood inside the main wall at its mid-south.

---

[1] Norse, *breiðr-nes* or 'broad point,' here separating Loch Eford from Loch Langass.
[2] The loch itself bears the too common title of *Loch an Dùin*.

Loch Eford, the long and narrow sea-inlet which lies immediately to the south, contains numerous small islands, six or eight of them showing traces of former stone erections, presumably more or less adapted for defensive purposes. Although perhaps not one of these sites can be considered quite satisfactory in point of distinctness, several are here noted as the best defined.

Three-quarters of a mile west from Dun Breinish is the island of *Steisay*, coupled on its farther end to a small annexe—'Trefick Island' of the Admiralty chart—by a massive causeway which remains uncovered till nearly high-water. Upon this minor islet are the ruins of an erection measuring about 13 feet in diameter over its walls, but here, in common with all the other sites in Loch Eford, no tradition was forthcoming.

Half a mile still westwards lies a flat islet at the south-east extremity of Orasay, to which it is united at low-water. Here we are indebted to the Admiralty chart for the interesting place-name 'Ft. Orasay,' perhaps suggestive of an occupation in the seventeenth century (as at Dun Mhic Laitheann), especially since traces of old buildings exist both upon this and a smaller rock joined on to its south,—rectangular in the first case, but apparently circular in the second,—the latter being covered by spring tides, and locally known as *Sgeir nan Sgarbh*.

Again, to the mid-south of Orasay and not far from the kelp-works, is *Redcalf Island*, upon the east end of which are the foundations of a ruined enclosure measuring 22 feet in diameter over walls 4 feet thick.

On the opposite side of Loch Eford, a mile to the south of Dun Breinish, is LOCH NA CEITHIR-EILEANA,[1] or 'loch of the four islands,' all of these partly covered by saplings. The largest of the four lies in the south-west corner of the loch, about 40 yards north from a jutting promontory with which this island has been connected by a causeway joining its west end.

• 22

Close to the water's edge, the whole island has been surrounded by a wall, still generally traceable and showing a maximum height of about 5 feet at various parts, especially where it is pierced on the south and south-west by three separate boat-entrances. Of these latter the central and largest has a width of 5 feet, and is flanked

---

[1] There is another loch of this name, close to the road between Lochmaddy and Langass.

by massive side walls, the other two entrances being 4 feet
wide.

Nothing can be added as to the buildings which have certainly
existed within this enclosure, the somewhat elevated and irregular
summit being densely covered by a soft vegetation which effectually
conceals what may lie beneath. Here are numerous rowan-trees,
none exceeding 6 feet in height, and the honeysuckle is also very
abundant.

Near the east shore of *Loch Crogavat*, in the Burrival district
immediately south of the entrance to Loch Eford, is a heather-covered
island, connected by a series of stepping-stones with a small promontory to its north. Here, however, no traces of ancient occupation
could be observed.

Immediately to the west of Eaval and Burrival is LOCH OBISARY, a
large sheet of water, very irregular in shape and measuring a length
and breadth of two miles at its extremities, with a greatest depth of
151 feet in one part near its outlet to Loch Eford.

In the north end of Loch Obisary are two small islands which
seem to have been occupied as forts. One, nearest the north shore, is   ● 23
about 15 feet in height, with steep rocky sides, its surface covered by
vegetation such as the mountain-ash, juniper, and crowberry.[1] On the
south side of this island, close to the water's edge, are traces of a surrounding wall 5 feet in width; while on its north side, commencing
5 feet above the water-level and founded upon a base of perpendicular
rock, is another portion of wall about 3 feet thick, showing continuously for a length of several yards.

The next islet to the south-east shows as little more than a   ● 24
scattered group of stones slightly exposed above the surface of the
water. Here are traces of a circular wall, for the most part indistinct,
although on the east clearly defined in a width of 27 inches and a
present height of 3 feet, having evidently enclosed an interior space
about 12 feet in diameter.

In the south end of Loch Obisary are the scanty ruins of an
island-fort, its circular wall rising sheer out of the water so as to   ● 25
present the appearance, when viewed from the shore, of a large and

---

[1] Upon an island within the east extremity of Loch Obisary, near Burrival, is a group of
birch saplings ; a fact which calls for special notice, this being the only spot in North Uist where
a natural growth of the birch was observed.

almost unbroken ring of stones. Upon closer inspection this was found to measure a diameter of 60 feet over the surrounding wall, which is traceable at various points in a width varying from 45 to 57 inches and a greatest height of 4 feet on the north-east. The western half of its circumference shows however as a mere shell, being in parts submerged and elsewhere but slightly raised above the loch's surface.[1] Nearly half of the interior area is also under water, while no portion of the remainder is elevated more than 3 feet, although traces of two minor erections were here observed.

The most interesting features of this dun are disclosed in its east wall, through which, at a distance of 16 feet apart, are two clearly defined boat-entrances, each showing a width of 4 feet and remaining in a state of fair preservation. Both of these would appear to have led into small enclosed harbours, an arrangement merely indicated at the access nearest the south end of the island, but distinctly proved in the other case, where the doorway, across its base at the present water-level, still contains a sill over which a boat could be drawn into the shelter afforded by a walled depression of rectangular shape and measuring 6 feet in width by $9\frac{1}{2}$ feet in length. Within this obviously structural enclosure was found a saddle-quern lying in shallow water.

The central area of this fort, at about the normal water-level, contains an outcrop of natural rock, evidently existing in a considerable mass which would appear to be completely isolated, as the loch, around and close up to the island's edge, shows an abruptly increasing depth. Being thus situated in deep water near the middle of the loch, it would seem that this island-fort was not provided with any causeway. Elsewhere in North Uist are several fortified islets which had double accesses—both by land and water—but the site under present notice appears to have been wholly dependent upon the use of boats for its means of communication with the shore.

Here must be noticed another islet which lies between the 'ring fort' (just described) and the east shore of Loch Obisary, but much nearer the latter.

Ten or twelve feet in height, with comparatively steep sides and its top thickly covered by peat, this island shows at various parts of

---

[1] At the cost of a slight wetting, it was possible to make the entire circuit of this island, keeping close to its outer margin.

its edge the remains of a wall which probably once continued all the way round. Towards the east, a narrow causeway 20 yards in length leads from that shore of the loch, and precisely at the island end of this approach stand the fairly complete remains of a small rectangular structure measuring about 4½ by 5 feet, which has clearly served as a guard-chamber. Immediately south of the causeway is traceable the complete outline of a harbour sufficiently large to contain a number of boats, its protecting wall running outwards at a right angle on the south, and thence recurving on the east, where it is pierced by a well-defined entrance.

Upon the opposite or north-west edge of this island are traces of another and less clearly marked erection, the whole of these arrangements pointing to the fact that this intermediate island served as an appanage to the neighbouring dun, for which, under ordinary conditions, it would afford a convenient landing-place.

Half a mile south from this 'ring fort' in Loch Obisary is DUN AN   ● 26 T-SIAMAIN, or 'fort of the rope of twisted heather,'[1] upon an island in a small loch which takes its name from the dun. Lying within 25 yards of the east shore, this island is thence approached through shallow water by a causeway which extends to nearly double that length, owing to the fact of its running in an irregular zig-zag at four distinct angles. This access remains in a state of good preservation, chiefly in a width of from 3 to 4 feet, but broadened midway to 6 feet, and showing almost 2 feet above the present level of the water, although it is evident that the loch was formerly much deeper. At its inner end, the causeway is blocked by a massive and disfiguring piece of wall, no doubt erected in recent times for the purpose of keeping cattle out of the island.

Dun an t-Siamain is somewhat circular in shape, measuring about 44 feet north and south by 52 feet east and west over its outer wall, which shows all the way round in a thickness varying from 52 to 75 inches, with a greatest present height of 6 feet at the south-east. There is some appearance of a doorway, 33 inches wide, at a point slightly south from the island end of the causeway ; while the wall on the mid-south is pierced by a boat-entrance distinctly shown in an

---

[1] 'A rope of twisted straw or heath,' here certainly 'heather-rope'; and curiously enough, the writer when approaching this fort from the north shore of Ronay Sound, saw many fragments of heather-ropes strewn upon the surface.

exterior width of 7 feet 3 inches, narrowing inwards to the extent of 6 inches.

The interior is filled with loose stones covered by a profuse growth of brambles, so as greatly to obscure its original arrangements, although close to the east edge there seem to be traces of a circular cell measuring 51 inches across. At the north, partly within the thickness of the outer wall, are the remains of another cell which has apparently been dome-shaped, with a base diameter of about 4 feet, contracted to 3½ feet at its present top.

Upon the shore, nearly opposite the causeway but a little to the north, is a walled recess in the bank measuring about 13 feet in length by 6½ feet in width, probably having served as a cattle shelter. The wild-rose is so rare in North Uist that the occurrence of one small bush near the east side of this loch may be noted.

• 27   In Loch a' Gheadais or 'loch of the pike,' two miles east from Dun an t-Siamain, is an island-fort, its causeway leading northwards to a broad point which projects into the east side of the loch.

This is a rocky islet of irregular shape, with a mound rising in its centre to an elevation of about 15 feet, and enclosed along the water's edge by a wall, still in a remarkable state of preservation, and at the north showing nine courses to a height of fully 6 feet; perpendicular rock however supplying the place of this wall for a short distance on the south side. Upon the northern and lower end of this island are the ruins of a small circular building, apparently just within the former main entrance, which seems to have been close to the end of the causeway. This latter is slightly curved at both ends, and has a length of about 30 yards by 5 feet in width. It stands barely a foot below the level of the water and is still practicable by wading, while near its centre is a gap 2 feet wide and a foot deep, evidently left for defensive purposes.

At the base of Beinn na h-Aire on the northern shore of the sound which separates Eaval from Ronay, is a promontory locally known as
• 28   Rudh' an Duin, this place-name clearly indicating some association with a fort. From the fact of the point itself showing no trace of any such erection, this must presumably have been situated in the immediate neighbourhood; and here, barely 400 yards apart east and west, are two tidal islets, both of them evidently once walled around at high-water mark. The island to the east shows a green top covered

ISLAND DUN IN LOCH NA SRUTHAN BEAG, RONAY, FROM WEST.

DUN BAN, LOCH HORNARY, GRIMSAY, FROM WEST.

by luxuriant vegetation, with the remains of a curved wall along its south edge. The other island, towards the west, is still better defined as presenting a circular enclosure which has measured about 30 feet over its walls, the outer circumference being distinctly traceable at various parts, especially on the north and south.

Above the shore at Eaval, upon a smaller promontory 150 yards north-west from this last-mentioned site, is a flat-topped mound about 12 feet high which receives the local name of *An Dùnan*. In its west face is some appearance of a wall, but, apart from the significant title, no other special feature can be recorded.

Half a mile south from Rudh' an Duin, near the opposite shore of Ronay Sound, is a high rocky island conspicuous by its dark covering of heather, and fully an acre in extent. This is known as SEANNA   • 29 CHAISTEAL or 'old castle,' traditionally once occupied by a fort, of which however no traces remain. Close to its west, and joined on to the main island at half-tide, is a lower green-capped rock, with steep sides and a comparatively flat top which measures about 24 by 40 feet. This annexe locally bears the name of the 'the fort's kitchen,' but here again no confirmation was available, although both titles have probably been justified by formerly existing traces of occupation.

Seanna Chaisteal is separated from Ronay Beg[1] on its south by a narrow channel of about 30 yards, said to be fordable at the ebb of spring-tides.

Upon the island of Ronay, a mile and a half to the south of Seanna Chaisteal and a mile due east from Kallin in Grimsay, is LOCH NA   • 30 SRUTHAN BEAG, containing two islets. The southern and smaller of these is 5 or 6 feet in height, consisting of solid rock thickly covered with vegetation, and has been accessible over a curved causeway from the neighbouring shore, a distance of nearly 20 yards. This clearly represents the site of a former dun, of which some remains would no doubt be revealed by excavation.

At the east side of Ronay, immediately north from *Bàgh na Caiplich*, is a knoll showing upon its flat summit the foundations of a circular erection about 34 feet in total diameter. The rocky and almost precipitous west side of this hillock presents some appearance of steps leading downwards to a plateau adjoining its base.

---

[1] Ronay Beg is not a distinct island as its name would imply, but merely represents the northern peninsula of Ronay proper, a considerable island separated by a deep sound from the still larger Grimsay upon its west.

● 31　　　　Dun Ban is the name of a fort upon a wooded rock in the east end of Loch Hornary, towards the north-east corner of Grimsay, the large island which lies between the main portion of North Uist and Benbecula.

Captain Thomas[1] gives a detailed notice of this fort, which he excavated at considerable pains, and it seems necessary to quote his interesting account at nearly full length, more especially since this rock (after an interval of about fifty years) has again become so much overgrown by herbage and saplings as to show few characteristics of the dun, even when examined at close quarters. The present writer can only add that in 1907 he found the west wall to show a total thickness of nearly 11 feet, and its outer half, at the south-west, a width of 45 inches; while a doorway 32 inches wide was traceable as leading from the interior to a space between the walls.

This islet is described by Captain Thomas as 'about 50 feet in diameter, rising to a little peak about 12 feet high towards the centre. . . . The rugged rock, on which Dun Ban is built, is 16 fathoms from the shore, and there is 9 feet of water in the channel. A causeway has been formed by throwing stones into the water, and then placing stepping-stones, about 1½ feet apart, upon the causeway—originally, no doubt, they were above the surface of the water, but now, as in many other instances, they are overflowed.[2] . . . The causeway, in this instance,[3] shows some ingenuity in its contrivance, for instead of advancing straight from shore to shore, the line of direction would, if continued, pass clear of the island, but when near the island it turns sharply towards it, by which means the approach is well flanked. Dun Ban is unique in its construction, and may be called a fortified "Picts-house"—using that term in a technical sense—and may be described as an agglomeration of beehive cells embedded in a circular tower. The foundation is very uneven, and there has been no attempt to level it. The peaked rock rises and protrudes in the

---

[1] *Archæologia Scotica*, vol. v. pp. 399-402, with a ground-plan (to scale) on Plate LII.

[2] On p. 400 Captain Thomas refers to a local belief that one of the stepping-stones 'called the Monitor, or Warning Stone, was so balanced as to make a clatter when trod upon'; a tradition to which reference has already been made. We have been unable to verify the detached stepping-stones noticed by Captain Thomas, finding instead a series of five gaps left at wide intervals in this access. We would further judge that the top of this causeway has always, as now, been distinctly under the normal water-level of the loch.

[3] Here again the present writer cannot agree with this general conclusion, having found the typical causeway to an island-fort almost invariably curved rather than straight.

central area of the dun, and slopes in one of the chambers at a steep gradient. The entrance passage is opposite to the causeway, and was no doubt roofed with flags. . . . From the landing to the doorway of the dun the rock is clear for 13½ feet; from the doorway the passage rises gently for some feet.

'The entrance passage (a)[1] to Dun Ban has been at least 3 feet high, is 3 feet broad, and straight for 11 feet, where, on the east side, is a recess (b), which was apparently the usual guard-cell. The passage then curves to the left for 8 feet, and narrows to 1½ feet at what was the inner door, where there is a step (c) down into the court or area of the dun. The area is of a very irregular figure, with a breadth of about 11 feet; and is largely occupied by a protruding peak of rock which rises 4 or 5 feet above the floor of the area.

'Around the court are four beehive cells in the thickness of the wall. They are extremely rude, and when complete were roofed by overlapping stones. In a few places yet remaining the walls begin to come in to form the dome. The height of the centre from the floor was probably 8 feet. Of course a hole was left in the apex for the escape of smoke if the area was not roofed over. The cells were entered by doorways about 2½ feet square; the first (d) with a floor of about 24 square feet; the remaining wall is still 4 feet high. The second (e) is quadrangular, 11 × 4 feet, but instead of having a flat floor it is little better than a large hole 3 feet deep. The natural rock here slopes rapidly towards the water, and accidental ledges form a sort of steps down into the cell. The cell (f) on the north side is nearly quadrangular, and contains about 16 square feet. Opposite the main entrance, across the court or central chamber, is the entrance to a steep descending passage (g), 13 feet long, one of the sides being still 5 feet high; at its termination on the south side is a cell (h) of the same size and figure as some of those in use in Lewis at the present day. Opposite to its doorway, part of a rude staircase (i) yet remains, which leads to the battlements or roof of this strange castle. An inspection of the ground-plan will show, that while for about ⅞ of its circumference the enclosing wall is from 10 to 14 feet in thickness, yet for about 9 feet the wall is extremely weak, being, in fact, hardly 2 feet thick; but it is to be observed that this side is furthest

[1] These italic letters refer to Plan LII. in *Archæologia Scotica*, vol. v. This plan shows a very irregular and by no means circular interior for Dun Ban, Hornary.

removed from possible attack, and that there is not room for more than two or three men to stand in front of the wall without falling into the water.

'No relics of importance were found in this dun; there were broken craggans, as rude as those still made in the west of Lewis, . . . which were probably in common use throughout the islands a century ago. . . . Ashes—some of sticks—the remains of cooking fires, were observed in two places, as noted on the plan[1]; and water-worn stones—were all that remained to indicate inhabitation or defence.

'Such is Dun Ban, Loch Horneray, as excavation revealed it; but when inhabited the solid wall was probably 15 feet high above the lake, and on this a parapet, say 5 or 6 feet high, sheltered the defenders from missiles from the shore.'

From personal observation it may be added that the causeway is about 4 feet wide, and leads in a curve from a jutting point on the southern and nearest margin of Loch Hornary to join the islet at its east end. Although completely submerged to the extent of about 18 inches, this causeway was clearly traceable throughout its whole course of 30 yards when viewed from the bank of the loch on a calm day. Under these circumstances there seemed, at a distance of 8 yards out, to be a line of five large stones laid across its breadth, these no doubt representing the stepping-stones described by Captain Thomas. Upon a second visit and a closer examination with the aid of a boat, this appearance, however, proved to have been deceptive, as none of the eighteen-inch spaces were found, but in place of these the equally significant presence at intervals of five clearly defined gaps, all of them plainly structural and averaging a width of 4 feet.

The central of these interruptions descends abruptly to a depth of nearly 4 feet below the surface,[2] the others dipping to not more than 30 inches. The purpose of this rather elaborate system is obvious as presenting a serious impediment to any stranger, and further involves the evident condition that five hundred or even a thousand years ago this causeway was submerged to much the same extent as now.

Loch Hornary is a long narrow sheet of water, trending from

---

[1] But not so noted. Presumably the 'water-worn stones' represent hammer-stones, and indeed these and fragments of rude pottery are almost the only relics which reward the excavation of ancient forts.

[2] Locally exaggerated as dipping suddenly to the bottom of the loch. A like statement is also made with regard to a supposed causeway at Dun Ban, in Loch Caravat near Carinish.

ISLAND DUN IN LOCH A' MHUILINN, GRIMSAY, FROM SOUTH.

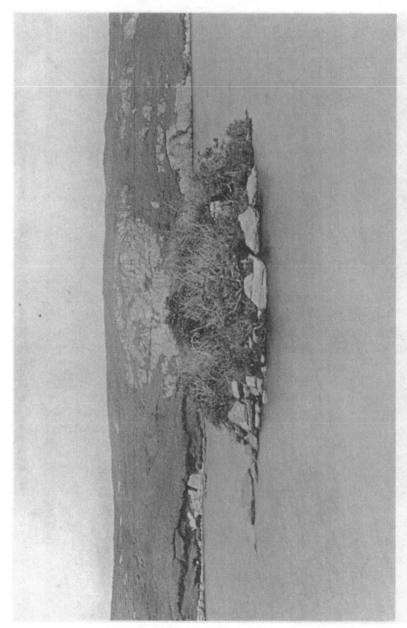

DUN BAN, LOCH CARAVAT (GRIMSAY), FROM SOUTH-WEST.

north-west to south-east and hidden in a deep cup among rounded hillocks, but also with precipitous sides at parts.

Near its west end are two small and very green islets, each showing solid rock in its base and now covered by a profuse growth of ferns and mountain-ash. We were locally informed that a causeway exists from the north-west shore to the outer of these islands—a distance of 30 or 40 yards—and could see the commencement of this near the water's edge. It is probable therefore that Loch Hornary thus contained a second dun, especially as this island shows some appearance of having been surrounded by a wall along its margin, while near its west end and at a higher elevation, four stones were found set in line and resting upon the natural rock.

In LOCH A' MHUILINN, near the south-east corner of Grimsay, is a ●32 small oval island evidently once occupied as a fort. About 9 feet in greatest elevation, its surface is so thickly covered by the blaeberry, crowberry, honeysuckle, and mountain-ash, as to yield no indications of its former character, except that the whole island has been enclosed at the water's edge by a wall between 2 and 3 feet in thickness and composed of small stones, while there is some further appearance at the south of a second wall two feet within, perhaps representing that of the main erection.

Although this islet stands in deep water, it is even now accessible from the north side of the loch over two other intermediate islands; the nearest of these practically forming an eastern annexe of the dun, being also joined by a causeway, 10 yards in length, to its larger neighbour on the north, which is in turn approached by a short causeway from the shore.

DUN BAN is the name of an islet in the east end of Loch Caravat, ●33 Grimsay, nearly a mile west from the Dun Ban already noticed in Loch Hornary.

This island is about 10 feet in height, with steep rocky sides lined at their base by a luxuriant growth of royal fern, while the summit itself presents a tangle of brambles and mountain-ash very difficult to penetrate.

From the fact that in several parts of the outer margin, gaps in the natural rock have been made up with small portions of dry-stone masonry, it is evident that the whole island was encircled by a wall;

and it would further seem that a squarely built pier existed at the west end, where the loch descends abruptly to a considerable depth.

This island is said to have been connected with the north shore of Loch Caravat by a causeway, the existence of which we were unable to verify.

Having thus noted three ancient forts in Grimsay, we now return to the mainland portion of North Uist. Here, at *Claddach-Carinish*, close to the west of *Bolltravagh*[1] and immediately opposite *Seana-baily*, stood DUN CHEIREIN, of which no traces are to be found, the traditional name alone remaining to certify its former existence. We were told however that this fort occupied the summit of the promontory, where a cottage now stands upon its actual site.

● 34

A mile north-east from Bolltravagh is an island-fort in LOCH NAN GEALAG, or 'loch of the sea-trout,' with a causeway of 30 yards leading towards it from a long and narrow promontory on the east shore. This causeway was locally said to end at a group of stones slightly above the surface, a statement apparently verified upon examination with the aid of a boat, as there seems to be a gap of 6 or 7 yards in deep water between that point and a pier which extends for 3 yards from the island at its south-west. If such was the case, it must have involved the use of either a short ferry or a drawbridge to render the fort accessible from the shore.

● 35

About 6 feet in height and measuring 25 by 30 feet, this island has evidently been surrounded by a wall which still remains in three or four courses of small stones along its southern edge. There is also the appearance of a small boat-harbour standing out into the loch at the north-east.

Near Knock-Cuien, half a mile to the north-west, is DUN BAN HACKLETT, upon a rocky islet in *Loch nan Garbh Chlachan* of the Ordnance map, locally known however as *Loch Hacklett*. This fort has been approached from the north shore of the loch by a curved causeway about 25 yards in length, over which the writer was recently able to wade at a very dry season, although even then it was in parts covered by water to a depth of 2 feet, besides presenting a more serious difficulty from the fact of its being coated with slimy moss.

● 36

[1] Bolltravagh is a large shallow bay, connected with the sea by a very narrow opening. It may evidently be translated as Gaelic for 'stinking bay,' in allusion to the stagnant mud there uncovered by the receding tide.

DUN BAN HACKLETT, FROM NORTH.

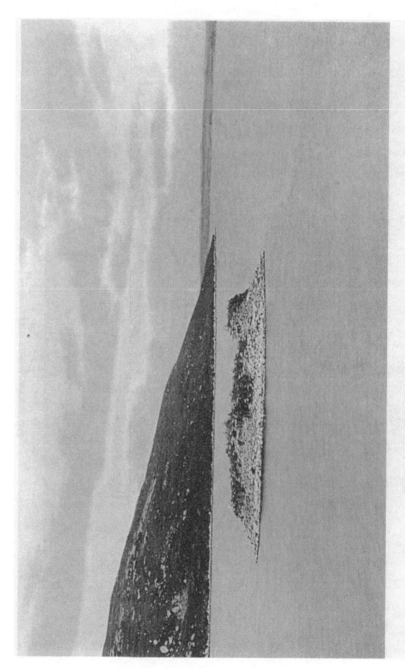

DUN BAN, LOCH CARAVAT (CARINISH), FROM SOUTH.

Around the edge of this island are still to be seen the almost continuous remains of a boundary wall about 3 feet thick, with a present height of nearly 6 feet on the west and also showing elsewhere in several courses. The whole enclosure is 60 feet across, and within its north end stand the ruins of an erection 27 feet in diameter when measured over its 3-foot wall, thus containing a circular interior of about 20 feet. This building has had its access from the north, where, almost opposite the causeway, the wall thickens to 54 inches and is pierced by an entrance passage distinctly traceable as 21 inches wide, and evidently once roofed with slabs at the level shown by its very regular top, a pair of these covering-stones still remaining towards its inner end. Immediately within the entrance is some appearance of a coved recess close to its west side; and a drain seems to have led from the interior area, emerging at a point about a yard west of the outer doorway.

The entrance passage to this fort is so complete and well-defined as to suggest a tempting subject for excavation, although the remoteness of the locality would render this task most tedious. The island is covered by brambles and honeysuckle, together with the mountainash, and lichens were found to be specially abundant in fine specimens of at least four distinct varieties.

Fully 100 yards south of Dun Ban is a high rocky island, connected by short causeways with two flat islets on its west and north. In line with this group, and near the west shore of Loch Hacklett, is yet another island, joined by a curved and still available causeway to a neighbouring point on the north. None of these lastmentioned sites afford any definite trace of former occupation apart from their connecting causeways, to which much significance can hardly be attached.

The name 'Hacklett' is evidently derived from the Norse *háklettr* or 'high rock,' although not here seeming to be very applicable. Another Loch Hacklett at Portain in North Uist has already been noted in association with an Earth-House, and it may be added that in Benbecula two places are known as *Hacklett* and a third as *Haka*.

Half a mile north-east from Loch Hacklett is LOCH 'IC COLLA, or • 37 'loch of the son of Coll,' a sheet of water most irregular in outline and situated immediately to the east of Loch Caravat, with which it is connected by a short stream.

In the south-east corner of Loch Mhic Colla is a flat island about 40 yards long, traditionally reputed as the site of an ancient fort, and further said to have been provided with a causeway towards the shore on its north. No trace of this latter feature could be verified, but it is evident that the whole island has been walled around its edge, and there is also the appearance of a boat-entrance in its south side, now almost hidden by overhanging alder bushes. This shrub is here very plentiful, and with a rank growth of brambles and nettles so thickly covers the surface as to conceal any traces of former buildings if their ruins still exist.

Captain Thomas mentions 'Dun Loch Mhic Coile, the door of which is still entire,'[1] a statement leading to disappointment in the case of the present writer. It seems probable however that this quotation may form a hearsay reference to Dun Ban, Loch Caravat, which is next described.

A mile and a half due west from the last is Dun Ban, covering the whole surface of an islet distant 100 yards from the south shore of Loch Caravat, an extensive sheet of water fully two miles north from its smaller namesake in the island of Grimsay. Here the titles both of fort and loch are duplicated in separate localities, tending to an awkward confusion which it becomes necessary to avoid by distinguishing these two sites as Dun Ban, Caravat (Grimsay) and DUN BAN, CARAVAT (CARINISH) respectively, the latter forming our present subject.

● 38

We have been definitely assured that a submerged causeway exists between this island and the south shore of the loch, complete as to both ends but interrupted midway by a gap where a 25-foot sounding line could find no bottom. This would be most interesting if substantiated as a fact, and may indeed simply convey an exaggeration of the truth, instances of such an arrangement upon a much smaller scale being clearly shown at Dun Ban, Hornary (Grimsay) and at Dun Thomaidh, as also with less prominence elsewhere in North Uist.

The writer could find no indication of this reported causeway, although very probably it does exist, and might (were the matter sufficiently important) even yet be traced beneath the surface; with, however, the all but certain result that the dimensions of its gap would prove to have been greatly over-stated.

[1] *Archæologia Scotica*, vol. v. p. 403.

In any case, Dun Ban, Caravat (Carinish) otherwise possesses a thoroughly individual character, as having its walls built with a tenacious lime freely applied, and consisting of calcined shells of the cockle and mussel.   So peculiar is this feature as to render the structure apparently unique,[1] not only among the ancient Hebridean forts, but also throughout a much wider mainland area ; while on the other hand it must be taken as pointing to a comparatively modern origin, perhaps so recent as the fourteenth or fifteenth century, a period classed in more accessible parts as late mediæval, though in the Outer Hebrides to be relatively treated as almost pre-historic.   In shape also, this island-fort shows a distinct variation from the normal type, being partly rectangular in form, except at the south-east where its sides curve symmetrically towards each other, but instead of joining, leave a wide triangular recess in the centre of that end, so as to give to the whole erection an outline somewhat resembling that of a heart.   This massive opening at the south has evidently served as a boat-entrance, still almost intact and measuring 15 feet across its mouth, but narrowed gradually to half that width at a point 12 feet within ; being thence abruptly contracted between parallel walls 4 feet apart into the doorway proper, which stands nearly 3 feet above the water-level.   A bar-hole here passes completely through the west jamb, and is matched by a corresponding recess on the east side.   It has been stated that an iron ring was recently to be seen fixed in the outer wall, but of this no trace could now be found.

The main wall of this fort still exists in its original and very uniform thickness of 6 feet, with a present height of 8 feet at the boat-entrance and about 5 feet in other parts, having suffered most damage towards the north and east.   The enclosed area shows dimensions of somewhat over 50 feet in extreme length and breadth, and has evidently contained several minor buildings within its northern half, the largest of these measuring 20 feet in width and stretching entirely across the fort.   This chamber (perhaps once sub-divided lengthwise) is rectangular except as to its north-east corner, which is rounded off in a distinct curve both outside and within.   Here were

---

[1] It is true that Captain Thomas (*Archæologia Scotica*, vol. v. pp. 385-386) in describing Dun Carloway—a broch situated near the west shore of Lewis—mentions that 'mortar of shell-lime . . . was used about the doorway, and for several feet on each side,' although considering this to mark a secondary occupation.

observed traces of two windows, both of them showing inward splays, one through the main wall at the east, and the other piercing the slighter partition on the south; while the west and north walls each contain a small bole or ambry.

Several small pieces of bone and a single fragment of ancient pottery were found near the surface. According to excellent authority this fort had a roof of flat stones supported by wooden beams, of which part still remained until about the year 1850; these slabs however being found so suitable for hearth-stones that all have since disappeared.[1] Another and quite independent account fully agrees with the above, adding that the roof-slabs rested upon posts of Scotch fir grown at Knock-Cuien near the south shore of Loch Caravat; a statement which seems too precise, although it may be founded on local tradition.

In the same loch, three-quarters of a mile to the north, is another small island known as DUN SCOR, hardly to be identified as the site of a fort from its surface appearance, although no doubt once surrounded by a wall at the water's edge.

This islet stands comparatively high, and is rankly overgrown by heather, brambles, and honeysuckle, together with a number of small rowan-trees. Eighty yards to its south-west, and said to be connected with Dun Scor by a causeway, is *Eilean Dubh Dùn Scor*, an oval and less elevated, though much larger island. Here are distinct traces of several erections, including one of rectangular shape near the south end and others upon the central summit, while the whole island has been enclosed by a wall which still measures in parts a height of from 2 to 6 feet, also containing three boat-entrances, two on the west and one towards the north.

Sixty yards farther west is a much larger but unnamed island, united to Eilean Dubh Dun Scor by a substantial causeway, which, although hidden under water, is sufficiently near the surface to impede the passage of a boat. This island lies close to the north side of Loch Caravat in the mouth of a long narrow bay which stretches westwards, and is furnished with two separate causeways, one of them short and clearly visible as leading to the north edge of the loch, while the

---

[1] In 1897 the writer noted part of one slab projecting inwards near the top of the wall which forms the east side of the main entrance.

DUN ON BEINN NA COILLE.

DUN NA DISE, BALESHARE FORD, FROM WEST.

other, joining a promontory on the south of this bay, is submerged and of considerable length.

We thus seem to have a net-work of four causeways connecting three islands not only with each other but also with opposite shores of the loch, so as to provide a double access, equally available both from the north and from the south.

At a distance of half a mile, on the west edge of BEINN NA COILLE, are two sites marked 'Tumuli' upon the Ordnance map, although both have evidently been forts.

The larger of these stands on the moor exactly at the base of Beinn na Coille, so that its comparatively flat top shows an elevation of almost 10 feet towards the low ground at the west, though only of 6 feet at the east, where it abuts upon the hill-slope. The whole structure[1] is too ruinous to be easily measurable, but it seems to have had an exterior diameter of about 39 feet with a wall 8 feet thick, thus leaving an interior of about 23 feet. No excavation was attempted, and the only relic found was a large stone with a deep flat hollow in its face—clearly to be identified as a saddle-quern.

● 40

The other and very similar site is on the slope of the hill, 120 yards to the east. This mound shows a present height of 6 to 8 feet, with traces on the south and west, near its summit, of an outer rampart indicating a total diameter of approximately 37 feet and an interior area which has measured about 21 feet across.

● 41

A mile north-west from Beinn na Coille are the remains of an island-dun in LOCH AN IASGAICH, connected with a neighbouring point on the west shore by a curved causeway 20 yards in length. This fort seems to have occupied only the south-west corner of the island, measuring a diameter of about 28 feet over its walls, which have been greatly damaged, no doubt through the removal of stones for the construction of shielings.

● 42

In the tidal sound (fully a mile wide) which separates Carinish from Baleshare island, is EILEAN SCALASTER[2] at the northern extremity of Eilean Mor, and practically annexed to it unless at high-water. Upon the north end of this islet are the ruins of a circular

● 43

---

[1] This is locally known as a 'Barp,' although clearly in error. Etymologically *barpa* meant 'a heap of stones,' a term which would fairly apply to both sites in their ruined condition. But it is manifest that each of these represents a fortified structure and not a burial-cairn.

[2] This place-name is perhaps of Norse derivation, although we are told that it is locally pronounced 'Shallastar.'

fort showing a present height of 4 feet and an interior area about 26 feet in diameter, enclosed by a wall nearly 5 feet thick. Its entrance seems to have been from the east, running straight inwards for a length of 10 feet between parallel walls 30 inches apart. Here were observed some fragments of pottery.

On level ground near the centre of Eilean Mor are traces of a circular erection with an interior diameter of 29 feet, its outer wall represented on the west by two courses in a thickness of about 5 feet. This site is locally known as *Tota Sgroilleig*, with evident reference to a female occupant. Half a mile to the south is the island of *Horray*, with some indications of a former building upon its central summit.

• 44　　Nearly half a mile north of Eilean Scalaster stood DUN NA DISE,[1] upon a rock at the north-east end of Eilean nan Carnan, to which it is joined at half-tide.

This rocky islet has a flat grassy summit, with naturally scarped sides which rise abruptly to a height of 12 or 15 feet above the strand. Along its edge, in an arc of 10 yards from south-west to west, the outer rampart of the fort remains in its original thickness of 8½ to about 12 feet, pierced on the west by the entrance passage, which had a width of 46 inches. At this part the wall shows in regular line, with two courses of large stones still in position, although elsewhere its outer face is greatly damaged, to the extent indeed of being entirely absent on the north and east.

Dun na Dise apparently measured about 45 feet across its interior north and south, by 60 feet from east to west, and may possibly have been a broch, now however so much ruined that excavation might even fail to settle this point. In the broken east edge several fragments of rude pottery were disclosed, one of them showing a raised pattern; and within the wall itself was found a small portion of shaped pumice—a material noted at nine different sites in North Uist, seven of these being ancient forts.

LOCH MOR, by far the largest loch in Baleshare island, has evidently contained four island-duns, two of them situated off a promontory on the north-east, while the others lie at some distance to the south. Taking these in order, and commencing at the north end

• 45　of Loch Mor, the first has stood upon a large and somewhat circular

---

[1] Perhaps *Dùn na dìth-sìthe*, signifying 'peaceless fort'; or less probably *Dùn a' Deas* or 'fort of the south.'

green island, surrounded at the water's edge by a rough and evidently modern wall, which may owe its existence to the fact that this enclosure now serves as a drying-green in use by the neighbouring crofters. A little within, and at a higher level, are traces of another wall about 4 feet thick, presumably the original outer rampart of the main fort which seems to have stood near the east side of the island, showing the remains of an inner wall perhaps 11 feet in thickness, while other ruins extend westwards over a further space of nearly 8 yards. It is to be remarked that the west half of this island bears no indications of any former buildings. The causeway runs from the east shore of the loch and is still in fair condition, measuring over 30 yards in length by 5 feet in width, and containing some very large stones.

The second of these islands, a little to the south-east, is both ● 46 lower and smaller, measuring about 35 by 56 feet over its surrounding wall, and with some traces of a building near the centre of this enclosure. Here the causeway has a length of 11 yards, running southwards from the promontory already mentioned.

In the southern half of Loch Mor the two remaining sites show as bare heaps of stones lying respectively near the east and west shores, little above the water-level, and not otherwise remarkable except that each has a causeway over which it can still be approached, both islets being evidently of artificial origin.

The islet nearest the south-east shore of the loch measures at ● 47 least 40 feet in diameter, and stands at its highest point barely 3 feet above the water; its causeway having a length of 17 yards by a width which varies from 4 to 5½ feet.

The fourth island, near the west side of Loch Mor, is now so much ● 48 destroyed (almost certainly through being used as a quarry) that the group of stones is too indistinct for measurement. On the other hand, the causeway is a most substantial piece of work, 42 yards long by 5 feet in width.

It may be added that Loch Mor is said to contain no fish of any kind, so that these causeways can hardly have been built as fishing-piers such as the writer has found elsewhere in North Uist, though never approaching the dimensions here recorded.

DUN NA H-OLA is marked on the Ordnance map half a mile south- ● 49 west of Loch Mor, but this site shows no traces of its original character, and can only be identified as a slight mound near the centre of the 'machair' which here stretches across the whole width of Baleshare Island. Local tradition states that *Loch na Pàisg*—now distant about 150 yards on the north—formerly extended southwards so as to include Dun na h-Ola as an islet within its area, until this end of the loch became filled by drifting sand at a comparatively recent period.

● 50   DUN MOR, Baleshare, is situated half a mile to the north-west of Dun na h-Ola, and was also evidently once an island, having been surrounded by the waters of *Loch an Dùin Mhóir*, close to the south end of which it now stands high and dry. Part of this site has been utilised as a cattle-fold, with the loch as its northern boundary and enclosed on the south by a wall crossing the middle of the fort.

The original outline of Dun Mor is now barely traceable in an apparent diameter of about 44 feet. Its entrance, however, still shows in a width of 28 inches at the north-east, with a distinctly elevated causeway, 4 feet wide, leading towards it from the former east shore of the loch.

Some kitchen-midden remains are disclosed upon the surface, but the chief feature at this site is a luxuriant growth of the Elecampane (*Inula Helenium*), which does not seem to occur elsewhere in North Uist.[1]

At Bal-Illeray, half a mile north of Dun Mor and within the cattle-fold used by the crofters of Illeray township, is a considerable mound capped by the ruins of several cottages, but also displaying some massive stones which must be assigned to an earlier and more interesting origin. Upon the south-west summit lie two symmetrical slabs of peculiar ogival shape, each having one flat end and two curvilinear sides which converge to a point at the other extremity. Both of these stones measure 57 inches in greatest width and length, by a very uniform thickness of about 7 inches.

On the west edge of the same mound are traces of a substantial curved wall, 4 feet thick, no doubt representing the ruins of some ancient structure which might be further revealed by careful excavation. This site does not seem to be identified by any special name or legend.

---

[1] It may be noted that at several localities in Tiree—particularly upon one fort, *Dùn Beag a' Chaolais*—the writer had previously found this herb, which was in olden times cultivated for the sake of the medicinal virtue possessed by its roots.

DUNAN MOR[1] stood upon the outer extremity of Rosamul in   ● 51
Illeray, at the north end of Baleshare Island.   This site is still marked
by a conspicuous mound, although no surface indications of its former
character are traceable, whether by way of structural or other
remains.

The summit of Dunan Mor is crossed by a dry-stone wall which
forms the northern boundary of a now disused cattle-fold; the existence of this fold obviously accounting for a local tradition which tells
how the farm-tenant suffered annually the loss of his best cow, a
calamity attributed to revenge on the part of 'the fairies' as the out-
raged denizens of Dunan Mor.

Returning from Baleshare to the mainland of North Uist, we find   ● 52
in LOCH NAN STRUBAN, near Clachan-a-gluip, the remains of an island-
fort, connected with the south shore of the loch by a causeway 35
yards in length.

The dimensions of this dun have evidently been about 33 by 37
feet, measuring over its outer wall, which shows a thickness of 4 feet
on the west though at other points so much ruined as to be hardly
traceable.

Upon a prominent knoll, 100 yards to the south, has stood a large
oval enclosure nearly 60 yards in length, north and south, by a width
of 45 yards east and west.   Notwithstanding the presence of some
stones of considerable size, it would be hazardous to claim for this
site any definite association with the neighbouring fort which it
overlooks.

LOCH HUNA, situated a mile north of Loch nan Struban, contains   ● 53
a large island-fort[2] towards its northern end.   This has occupied the
whole of an oval islet 70 yards in length, with a causeway connecting
it to a point on the north-west shore of the loch, a distance of about
30 yards.   The causeway[3]—4 to 5 feet in width, and remarkable for
the many large blocks of stone used in its construction—runs at first
straight out from the shore, and then curves slightly westwards to
join the island.   This latter is still surrounded at the water's edge by

[1] Literally 'Big little fort,' a curious mixture of adjectives evidently applied for the purpose
of distinguishing it from 'Dun Mor,' which has just been noted a mile to the south.
[2] Noted in *Archæologia Scotica*, vol. v. p. 402, as 'Dun Ban, on Loch Una, near Clachan-a-
Guilp.'
[3] During the very dry summer of 1905, this causeway was found to be passable without much
difficulty.

a wall showing a general width of about $4\frac{1}{2}$ feet, but thickened to 7 and even 9 feet on the north, where the main entrance passes through it in a clearly defined width of 42 inches at a point 5 yards west from the island end of the causeway.

Near the middle of its west side the island-wall has been pierced by a minor access measuring 27 inches across its outer opening, which however is contracted by a slab set on end so as to leave a free space of only 12 inches. This entrance is splayed for 5 feet inwards to a maximum width of 54 inches, from which point (presumably representing the inner face of the wall) it seems to have narrowed in a counter-splay, although the mass of fallen stones prevented any detailed examination.

The extreme south end of the island shows a wide boat-entrance, measuring $8\frac{1}{2}$ feet across at its exterior but slightly narrowing inwards, where it has been continued for a length of at least 6 yards.

A peculiar feature of the general enclosing wall—nowhere remaining to a height of over 5 feet—is that it seems to have contained within its thickness several small cup-shaped cells, to all appearance structural, especially since at two separate places on the north-east the presence of a cell coincides with a slight inward bulge of the main wall, as if to provide additional room for this insertion.[1] Three such cells (all in the northern half of the east wall, and including the two just mentioned) were cleared of the loose stones which they contained, then disclosing upper diameters of from 3 to 4 feet and basal measurements of between 2 and 3 feet, with a depth of nearly 5 feet descending to the surface level of the loch; while inside the northern and largest was found a hammer-stone. Elsewhere, especially within the boundary wall at the south-west, other similar cells may have existed, but no excavation was attempted in that quarter.

The interior arrangements of this fortified island would suggest for it a distinctly secondary occupation which has here almost wholly effaced the ruins of an earlier structure,—the original Dun Ban. Within its centre, upon a steep mound raised 10 or 12 feet above the

[1] The Rev. Canon J. A. MacCulloch, D.D. (in *The Misty Isle of Skye*, Edin., 1905, p. 262) mentions 'a dun, west of Dunvegan,' where an oval building, 4 yards in length, has 'a smaller chamber opening out of it. This chamber is not built on to the other, but is formed by the bulging out of the enclosing wall. . . . At this dun, and also below Dun Beag, near Struan, are small circular or oval structures 3 to 4 feet in diameter, and, as they remain, no more than 4 feet in height. Their purpose is an enigma. The one at Struan stands within the walls of an oblong building.'

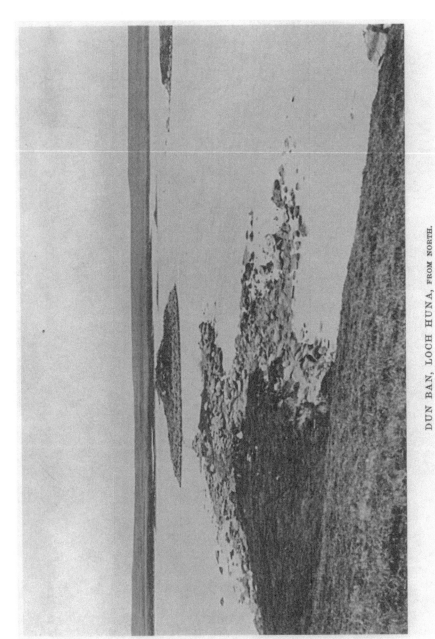

DUN BAN, LOCH HUNA, FROM NORTH.

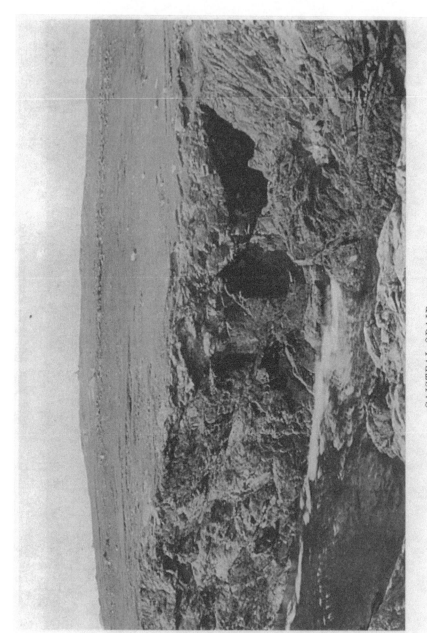

CAISTEAL ODAIR, FROM SOUTH.

outer grassy level, are the remains of a large rectangular erection standing north and south, with walls between 4 and 5 feet in thickness enclosing an interior which measures 54 by 19 feet; this oblong structure being supplemented by a semi-circular annexe at its north end.

The entrance to the main building was on its east side, through a doorway splayed inwards from 42 to 36 inches; while in the same wall, a little to the south, is another opening—evidently a window—splayed in the reverse direction, from 30 inches outside to 42 inches at the interior. Near the centre of the west side, and at a lower level, is the appearance of a small drain-hole. At the base of the mound are the remains of four other rectangular buildings, three on the west and one on the east, this latter measuring (as to its interior) $24\frac{1}{2}$ by $13\frac{1}{2}$ feet and having its doorway on the north.

From general indications, and especially the presence of some very large stones in the steep face of the mound towards the north and north-west, this large rectangular building has evidently been superimposed, in late mediæval times, upon the ruins of a pre-historic fort which might yet be traceable underneath.

A hundred yards north from Dun Ban is a round lumpy islet, 12 to 15 feet in height, with natural rock showing in its abruptly scarped sides. This is doubtfully supposed to have also been occupied as a fort, but the writer did not find first impressions bettered upon a later visit. If a dun existed here—and the site could hardly be more appropriate—the access to its summit was apparently from the north-west, and a sandy spit projecting landwards in shallow water might well suggest the position of a causeway, although it is stated that the depth increases nearer the shore.

It may be added that three or four green-capped islets in the southern half of Loch Huna appear to have been inhabited in former times.

In connection with the murder of Donald Herrach at Dun Scolpaig, incidental reference is made to DUN STEINGARRY 'on Loch Paible at Balranald' [1] as an occasional resort of 'Paul of the Thong,' who had been the active agent in that matter, and received in reward certain lands at Balmore from Gilleasbuig Dubh, brother of Donald Herrach

• 54

---

[1] Mackenzie's *History of the Macdonalds and Lords of the Isles*, p. 255.

and chief instigator of the crime.   This murder took place *ca.* 1506,[1]
and after his patron's death (evidently *ca.* 1516) Paul went in continual terror of his life from the sons of Donald Herrach,—a fear
justified by the event, as he was slain by Aonghas Fionn while endeavouring to reach the sanctuary of Kilmuir Church.

Loch Paible was at that period a sheet of fresh water, and covered
a much larger area than now, when it has become a mere branch of
the sea, drying off at ebb-tide.   This change was effected before the
year 1793 by an artificial cutting made through its narrow outlet—*Dig
Mhór*, or literally 'big ditch'—so that the loch must present a total
contrast to its former character and general aspect.

Dun Steingarry stood at the south-west corner of Loch Paible, its
site being traceable, close to the loch, as a symmetrical flat knoll
showing practically no remains of walls, though these might yet be
found by excavation.   From the contour of this slight knoll, a diameter
of about 44 feet is indicated for that of the fort itself, which, before
the loch was drained, evidently occupied an islet in shallow water.
Near *Hanglam*, a little to the west and immediately north of *Dig
Mhór*, is a well still known as *Tobar Steinagarry.*[2]

Three-quarters of a mile to the north, in a marsh near Balranald
steading and no doubt once included within Loch Paible, is a hillock
known as *Eilean Dubh*, the probable site of another island-fort, which
indeed may perhaps claim the title of 'the little Inch' associated with
Donald Herrach's capture.   Stones are visible in the edges and top of
this mound, and its measurement of some 43 feet in diameter would
also favour the suggestion here ventured, although, in the absence of
any local tradition, much stronger proof is required to justify its
definite inclusion as a fort.

In a marshy loch close to the west of *Eilean Dubh* is a low grass-
covered island of considerable size and bearing the name of *Rosamol*.
This however is very difficult of approach, and offers no special attrac-
tion as viewed from the nearest shore.

On the east side of Loch Paible, half a mile north-east of Dun

---

[1] See under Dun Scolpaig, *postea*, where are quoted several versions of this tragedy.   One
of these, given in vol. iv. of the MS. *Gregory Collections*, states that Donald Herrach lay sick
of a fever 'on the little Inch of Loch Pabill,' which would seem to be another and somewhat earlier
reference to Dun Steingarry.
[2] Also locally known as *Tobar Steilligarry*, and the site of the fort as *Cuithe Steilligarry*.

Steingarry, is a large enclosure known as *Cuithe Lianaclett*.[1] Within its upper portion is some appearance of a circular erection measuring about 35 feet in diameter over walls which are now very ruinous, especially as regards their exterior. Here perhaps stood a fort, although under present conditions this site must be classed as quite hypothetical. At least one fragment of ancient pottery was found at the mouth of a rabbit-hole, and it seems likely that additional evidence might be obtained by excavation.

Loch Sandary, half a mile east of Cuithe Lianaclett, has probably contained an island-fort, to be identified with the 'Dun Loch Shanndaidh' of *Archæologia Scotica* (vol. v. p. 403)—'the stones all taken away for building.' This site is also, however, too insufficiently vouched for definite inclusion ; though Dun Sandary perhaps stood upon a rounded point at the north-west corner of the loch, a promontory which has clearly once formed an island, and now shows a flattish top with rock protruding and a few loose stones on its surface.

In LOCH VAUSARY, two miles east of Balranald House, formerly ● 55 stood an island-fort which was approached from a slight promontory on the north shore by a causeway at least sixty yards in length. This islet is covered by a growth of ferns, brambles, and heather, together with the *Salix repens*, and now shows as a simple mound about 6 feet high at its centre and 50 feet in diameter.

Half way up the slope of Toroghas, a mile still farther to the east, are two green mounds about 20 yards apart and each measuring from 35 to 40 feet across. Although capped by modern shielings, both of these contain numerous large stones and in other respects show some appearance of having been occupied by massive circular erections of much earlier origin. Here were found fragments of coarse pottery and pieces of wood-charcoal.

Lower down, on a small rounded point at the east edge of Loch Steaphain, is another knoll covered by the ruins of several shielings, with further indications perhaps suggesting for this site also a more important character than that in which it has latterly served.

Upon the shoulder of SOUTH CLETTRAVAL, nearly a mile to the ● 56 north of Loch Vausary, are the ruins of a dun evidently built from

---

[1] *Cuithe* is a Gaelic word borrowed from the Norse *kví*, and signifies a cattle-fold. *Cuithe Lianaclett* might thus be translated as 'fold of the flax rock' (Norse, *lín-klettr*).

the stones of a neighbouring cairn which covered a long sepulchral chamber, elsewhere described under Pagan Burials in Chapter VIII. This fort stands within 3 or 4 yards from the west end of the now completely stripped burial-chamber, and shows an interior diameter of 26 feet, with a surrounding wall 8 or 9 feet thick, composed of large stones which remain in several courses. On the west side of the fort can still be traced its entrance, which seems to have traversed a circular chamber 54 inches in diameter, contained within the interior half of the main wall. The doorways at each end of this cell are only 27 inches wide, and the inner access has apparently been prolonged for about 2 yards into the central area through a covered way.

Sithean Tuath,[1] or 'north fairy-knoll,' a quarter of a mile north of Balranald House, is a small hillock rising abruptly in a marsh at the south end of Loch Scarie, and was doubtless once an islet in that loch, which flows into Loch Grogary, and, like it, has evidently been reduced in level through drainage operations. This mound measures about 50 feet across by 7 or 8 feet in present height, with steep edges and a flattened summit 26 feet in diameter. Its base has apparently been surrounded by a wall, and general indications would point to this as the former site of a dun.

• 57   DUN SCARIE,[2] 400 yards to the north of Sithean Tuath, stands upon an island near the west side of Loch Scarie, and is connected with the shore by a slightly curved causeway 6 feet wide and 34 yards in length. When the writer first visited this site in 1897, he found a neighbouring cottage newly erected with stones quarried out of Dun Scarie, and was also informed that Balranald House had been partly built with materials taken from the same source. A single fragment of ancient pottery, with some bones, periwinkle shells, and hammer-stones, were the sole relics observed here. The main structure seems to have been rectangular in general outline, but with rounded corners and its interior divided into three compartments. This site is now however so indistinct as not to afford data for precise measurements.

---

[1] Inferentially, a '*Sithean Deas*' or 'south fairy-knoll' ought also to exist. It seems possible that this may be represented by *Dùn na Dìse* on Baleshare Strand, or even by *Càrn na Dìse* near the shore at Claddach-Baleshare; but see p. 182, *antea*.

[2] Scarie is said to represent Zachary, a common name in the Macaulay sept.

The next fort to be noted is AN CAISTEAL (or 'the castle') at Ard • 58
an Runair, the westmost point of North Uist.

This is marked upon the Ordnance map at the north-west corner
of a large shallow bay (*Tràigh nam Faoghailean*) which separates Ard
an Runair from Hougary. The site of An Caisteal is just traceable
as a small flattish knob elevated about 15 feet above high-water
mark. Some large stones lie in its east face, where two fragments
of crude pottery were found. A little to the south are the remains
of a substantial dyke of turf and stones, extending westwards for some
distance across the promontory, although it is very doubtful whether
this had any association with the fort.

In the bank above the west shore of Traigh nam Faoghailean and
about 600 yards south of An Caisteal, a kitchen-midden was disclosed,
containing many fragments of ancient pottery, together with a few bones
and shells. No traces of any structural erection were apparent, so that
these remains may indicate a merely temporary or casual occupation.

A mile to the east of An Caisteal, the site of DUN GROGARY can • 59
still be traced upon marshy ground, at the west edge of Loch Grogary
which certainly extended farther in that direction at a period
when the slight mound occupied by this fort must have been a
separate island. That such was the case is manifest from the existence of a causeway, about 20 yards in length and 10 to 12 feet in
width, which connected Dun Grogary with the original shore of the
loch on the west. It is moreover evident that, within modern times,
the level of Loch Grogary has been artificially reduced to the extent of at least 5 feet by means of a deep cutting towards Hoglan
Bay on the north-west, at one point reaching a depth of nearly
20 feet below the natural surface.

In common with practically all the other forts situated in the
more frequented districts of North Uist, Dun Grogary has suffered
so much by being quarried that it now shows but slight indications of
its former character. There are, however, traces of both outer and
inner fortifications, the latter apparently measuring about 48 feet in
total diameter, with an exterior wall at an interval varying from 5
yards on the east to 8 or 10 yards in other directions.

Only two fragments of old pottery were observed, although we are
informed that many similar remains have here been found within recent
years.

At Tighary, close to the west of the public road and 300 yards north from Hough Mill, an island-dun once stood near the centre of ● 60 Loch Cnoc nan Uan. Both loch and fort, however, have long since disappeared, the former being now represented by a marsh, and the islet showing as a slight elevation contained therein.

The walls of this island-fort have been so completely removed as to leave hardly any trace of its original outline—perhaps about 50 feet in diameter,—although remains are visible of a curved causeway, 9 feet wide, which served as an access from the former west shore of the loch, a distance of 40 yards. The site has yielded at least one still available relic,—a peculiar block of water-worn stone, rudely triangular in shape and perforated by an irregular hole near its apex. This stone weighs 14 pounds and measures fully 10 by 6 inches over its extremes, with an almost uniform thickness of 4 inches. The only suggestion we can offer is that it may have been used either as an anchor or possibly for securing the end of a tether.

Half a mile to the east, upon an island in Loch Eaval, are the ● 61 ruins of a fort marked on the Ordnance map as Dun Mhic Raouill— 'fort of the son of Reginald (or Ranald),' from the Norse *Rögnvaldr*, represented by *Raonull* in Gaelic.

This island, measuring nearly 35 yards in diameter, is connected with the shore on the north-east by a submerged causeway about 50 yards in length, and still shows traces of a wall, 5 feet thick, surrounding it at the water's edge.

The interior arrangements evidently included a central structure 24 feet in diameter, with ramparts 9 feet wide; this being supplemented by an additional wall, 5 feet in thickness, situated at an interval of 10 feet and leaving a space of about 12 feet between it and the general enclosing wall. The first noted interval—that of 10 feet—has been sub-divided into at least eight segments by a series of transverse or radial walls varying from 2 to 4 feet in breadth.

At the west side of this island is a boat-harbour, artificially walled in a width of 5 yards and recessed to the extent of about 6 yards, with a shallow inner bend towards the south.

Of the interior walls at Dun Mhic Raouill, little more than the foundations remain. We were informed that stones have been systematically removed from this site by means of rafts, to serve for the erection of cottages in the vicinity.

Dun Scolpaig stood upon a low islet in a loch of the same name, • 62
near the north-west corner of North Uist. This loch is very shallow
and evidently much reduced in both depth and area as compared with
its condition at the period when the fort was built, having been partially drained away (in 1829) through *Allt a' Mhuilinn* which runs from
its west end into the sea at Port na Caipe.

Dun Scolpaig has now entirely disappeared, its site being occupied
by a small octagonal tower in the centre of the islet, which is surrounded
by a low wall near the water's edge. Both of these constructions are
of modern origin, lime-built and composed of stones from the fort itself,
having been erected about the year 1830 by Dr. Alexander MacLeod,
then resident at Balelone.

The *New Statistical Account* [1] devotes special attention to Dun
Scolpaig, stating that 'Donald Herroch (so called from his having
been born in Harris), a descendant of one of the Lords of the Isles,
and himself a very powerful individual, occupied this dun as a place
of residence.' A lengthy footnote tells how some jealous relatives
compassed the murder of Donald Herrach [2] under pretence of a leap-
ing-match, on which occasion Donald was strangled, within his own
fort, by means of a leather noose at the hands of an accomplice named
Paul, afterwards known as 'Paul of the Thong.' The same story
adds that a few weeks later, Aonghas Fionn (or 'Angus the Fair') son
of Donald Herrach, avenged his father's death by killing Paul with
an arrow at a spot a hundred yards south of Kilmuir Church, the
place being ever since known as '*Shead Phoil*, or *Paul's Field*.' [3] This
tradition incidentally refers to three ancient customs as still existing
at the commencement of the sixteenth century ; namely, the occupa-

---

[1] Inverness-shire, p. 170-171.
[2] Hugh MacDonald of Sleat (the founder of Clan Huistein) had at least six sons, of whom
John, his immediate successor, was perhaps the only one of strictly legitimate birth. The other
five (all by different mothers and all suffering violent deaths) were Donald Gallach, Donald
Herrach, Gilleasbuig Dubh, Aonghas Collach, and Aonghas Dubh. Donald Gallach and Donald
Herrach (whose mother was a MacLeod of Harris) were both killed *ca.* 1506 by their half-brother
Gilleasbuig Dubh,—the first actually, and the second by his orders. Within ten years (certainly
before 10th March 1516-1517, *Reg. Mag. Sig.*), Archibald or Gilleasbuig Dubh (who lived at
Oransay, North Uist) was in turn slain by his nephews, the sons of Donald Gallach and Donald
Herrach. This revenge was effected at a knoll in the glen between North and South Lee, to the
south of Loch Maddy, on the occasion of a deer-hunt, the actual spot being still known as *Cnoc
Ghilleasbuig Dhuibh* in the pass marked *Bealach a' Sgail* upon the Ordnance map : Mackenzie's
History of the Macdonalds and Lords of the Isles, pp. 253-255 ; also *The Clan Donald*, vol. i. pp.
312-314, vol. iii., pp. 11-16. In April 1508, Gilleasbuig Dubh had received a 'Remission' for the
murder of his brother, Donald Gallach (*Reg. Sec. Sig.*, MS. vol. iii. folio 161).
[3] We are told that the correct form is *Leathad Phàil*, or 'Paul's slope.'

tion of a dun as a dwelling, the use of the bow and arrow, and the privilege of Church-sanctuary. Without taking these points too literally, they are at least interesting on account of the conditions suggested.

Another version of the same affair, while differing as to details, confirms the story above quoted; stating however that Donald Herrach was resident at Balranald, being enticed thence to Dun Scolpaig; while the slaying of 'Paul of the Thong' (*Pàl na h-éille*) by Aonghas Fionn is deferred to a time shortly after the death of Paul's patron, Gilleasbuig Dubh,[1] and therefore *ca.* 1516-1517. So far as tradition may serve, this latter statement would appear to be sufficiently vouched, but we have the embarrassing complication of yet a third and quite independent narrative as to the murder of Donald Herrach, which, though agreeing that the ringleaders were his halfbrothers, Gilleasbuig Dubh, Aonghas Collach, and Aonghas Dubh, varies somewhat in other particulars.

This account runs to the effect that Archibald (or Gilleasbuig) Dubh was the main instigator, and having persuaded two of his brothers to join in the matter, all three went to (North) Uist,—'Donald Herrach being at the time sick of a Fever on the little Inch of Loch Pabill,[1] and married then to a daughter of Allan MacRuari, Laird of Moydart. They entered the Island to see him, but he suspecting their design called a servant whom he ordered to go for South Uist and desire Ranald Ban, Laird of Moydart, his brother-in-law, to send him 60 Ells fine Linnen and 60 Ells coarse Linnen. But they apprehended the man and forced him to reveal his errand to them, who judged that their brother wished Ranald Ban to send him 60 Gentlemen and 60 common soldiers. They carried their brother off to the Inch of Loch Skolpig where they bored two holes thro' the partition and drawing a Thong thro' the holes with a noose at the end of it, in this they put their brother's neck, when a fellow of the name of Paul was desired to pull hard at the cord until it broke. Donald said to his brethren, if they meant to take away his life, they should do it cleanly. With this, they made a spit red-hot in the fire, where-

---

[1] *The Clan Donald*, vol. iii. pp. 480-481 ; also Mackenzie's *History of the Macdonalds, etc.*, pp. 253-255.

[2] Evidently Dun Steingarry ; see pp. 187-188, *antea*. Ranald Ban, son of Allan MacRuari and chief of Clanranald, died in 1509, (*The Clan Donald*, vol. ii. p. 242, vol. iii. p. 229).

with they pierced his body,' etc.[1]   For this crime (soon followed by the murder of Donald Gallach upon the mainland at Loch Kishorn) it is said that Gilleasbuig Dubh was chased out of North Uist by Ranald Ban, brother-in-law to Donald Herrach, betaking himself for three years (that is, until after Ranald's death in 1509) to piracy in the Southern Hebrides.

CAISTEAL ODAIR, upon an elevated promontory at the north-western corner of North Uist, ought perhaps in strictness to be noted as a 'fortification' rather than a dun.   This is bounded on the south by *Geo a' Chaisteil*, and on the north by a smaller gully, being guarded by lofty precipices at every part with the exception of its south-east or landward side.   The defensive structure here takes the form of a stone rampart, about 120 yards in length and varying from 7 to 9 feet in thickness, which cuts off the outer and higher portion of the headland so as to enclose an area of considerable extent.   This wall can still be traced along its exterior base, and is pierced towards the south by an entrance passage 14 feet long and 5 feet wide, partly blocked by a slab 6 inches thick and measuring 56 by 50 inches across its extremes.   Immediately within is a group of four large stones, two of them standing on end, the others having evidently fallen from that position ; while, north of these and close to the outer rampart, are the shapeless ruins of several ancient erections.

The summit of this promontory is quite bare, being often swept by spray and no doubt even by breakers during stormy weather, notwithstanding its elevation above the sea-level.   In all probability the inhabitants of Caisteal Odair occupied only its eastern and more sheltered portion, especially the south-east corner near the entrance already described.

The name of Caisteal Odair [2] offers some difficulty in regard to its derivation, although perhaps the Gaelic *Caisteal odhar* or 'dun-coloured castle' may be accepted as both a simple and probable explanation.   Local opinion seems to favour a Norse origin, such as *Kastali-Óðar*, with some reference to the mythical *Óðr*, husband of

• 63

---

[1] This is quoted verbatim from vol. iv. of the MS. *Gregory Collections*, being an unpublished continuation of the narrative which breaks off at p. 324 of *Collectanea de Rebus Albanicis*. It would further appear that Donald Herrach's brothers were abetted by members of Siol Gorrie, a sept then prominent in North Uist.

[2] The 'Row Chastelorre' of Blaeu's map of 1654.   This name is certainly now pronounced 'Odarr' or 'Ottarr,' so that it may perhaps represent the personal name *Ottar*, as in Otternish ; see p. 90.

Freyja. To this is added the circumstantial statement that at Griminish Point (not half a mile south of Caisteal Odair) are yet to be seen the marks of Odr's heels upon the spot where he landed after a leap of ten miles from Heisker, taken for the purpose of defending his wife. The adjoining gully to the north is still known as *Geo Braodaig,* said to represent the Gaelic form of *Freyja.* On the farm of Griminish, a mile to the east of Caisteal Odair, is another site associated with it under the name of *Ceann Odair* [1] or *Penmore* ('Odr's head' or 'the great head') where, according to tradition, the giant's head was buried, this fact conferring upon the tenant of Griminish a right to club seals upon the Haskeir rocks! The place-name is now applied to a field immediately west of the farm-steading.

At Griminish, a mile to the east and at the opposite side of Beinn Scolpaig, is *Loch an Eilein* which contains not one but two islands, each apparently once occupied as a fort. The loch is comparatively shallow and now almost filled with reeds and a strong growth of other aquatic plants, the latter forming a matted crust over which it is possible in a dry summer to wade from the south shore to both islets, at the risk however of sinking through this treacherous and quivering mass to a further depth of several feet.

● 64   The westmost and larger island is marked Dun a' Ghallain [2] upon the Ordnance map, and has probably been connected by a causeway with the other islet (70 yards to the south-east) which is there unnamed. Dun a' Ghallain shows natural rock in its base, and seems to have been surrounded by a protecting wall near the water's edge. Its summit reaches a height of 8 or 9 feet above the loch, and when partially excavated, the foundations were disclosed of an irregularly shaped building with five or six sides running at various angles so as to form an enclosure which averages about 36 feet across in each direction. With walls now not exceeding 30 inches in height, but apparently 9 or 10 feet thick, the interior floor stands at an elevation of about 6 feet above the water-level, and seems to have been paved throughout,—generally with flat stones, but in parts with small pebbles covered by a thin layer of white sand.

The doorway of this structure was in its north-east corner,

---

[1] See also *Uist Bards*—'The Poems and Songs of John MacCodrum, etc.,' edited by the Rev. Archibald Macdonald; Glasgow, 1894, p. v.

[2] Near Daliburgh, on the west side of South Uist, are *Loch Hallan* and *Cladh Hallan*; the latter, as its name implies, being an old burial-ground.

GEO BRAODAIG.

LOCH AN EILEIN, FROM EAST.

entering from a passage 7 yards in length, which at first leads due south but mid-way bends abruptly to the west at a considerable angle. This passage has also been paved, and shows a width of about 30 inches in its outer portion, reduced to 24 inches at the inner door-way. A drain is traceable for several yards under the floor of the main erection, thence passing outwards through the base of its north wall.

From the irregularity, both in regard to plan and style of masonry, shown by the interior wall of Dun a' Ghallain as revealed through partial excavation, it seems probable that this represents a secondary lining inserted within an older and more substantial structure. Kitchen-midden remains were here scarce, comprising bones and un-patterned pottery, together with a single flint; while, on the other hand, articles in much corroded iron proved to be comparatively numerous, these including an ornamented dirk, a curved knife, and several lozenge-shaped rivet-heads of the Viking type. Portions of whale vertebræ, and half of either a mill-stone or a very large quern, are also to be noted.

The second and smaller island in the same loch does not bear the traditional character of a fort, although well known to possess a causeway still traceable as connecting it with the east shore of *Loch an Eilein*, a distance of about 40 yards. This islet receives the local name of EILEAN A' GHALLAIN,[1] no doubt derived from the strong growth of 'butter-bur' upon its surface, which stands to a height of about 4 feet. Here are distinct remains of a circular building with a diameter of 42 feet, this measurement including its outer wall in a thickness of from 7 to 10 feet. A paved entrance was found on the east side, opposite the causeway, and the interior area seems to have contained several minor erections.

Like its larger neighbour, this island was disappointing in results, yielding merely a few fragments of pottery and bones, together with one or two hammer-stones, some rounded quartz pebbles, and a broken whet-stone.

In LOCH OLAVAT, half a mile to the south, is the site of another island-fort with a causeway which still remains in good preservation. This islet is locally known as *Eilean Domhnuill a'*

• 65

• 66

---

[1] Four hundred yards to the north-east, near Vallay Sound, is a hollow known as *Lag a' Ghallain*.

spionnaidh (or 'island of Donald of strength') and has evidently been walled around; its central portion rising to a height of 5 or 6 feet above the present water-level, although there are distinct indications that the loch was formerly three feet deeper. Partial excavation of the summit yielded little result beyond confirming the statement that this island was at one time occupied by a fort, apparently measuring about 43 feet in diameter over its main wall, but now obscured by the foundations of two secondary buildings placed side by side. The existence of an earlier structure is further proved by the fact of these secondary walls standing upon a thick deposit of kitchen-midden ashes; while similar remains, intermixed with small fragments of ancient pottery, were also found near the centre of the island at a depth of from 12 to 17 inches beneath the later floor. Here were unearthed specimens of patterned pottery, together with a saddle-quern and a stone pounder.

The causeway runs north and south, having a length of over 40 yards and an average width of about 54 inches. Only its middle portion is now submerged, both ends showing high and dry upon the banks of the island and the shore; especially at the latter, where the causeway commences 20 yards from the south edge of the loch, with an elevation of nearly 4 feet above its present ordinary summer-level.

In LOCH NAN GEARRACHAN, fully a mile south-east from Loch Olavat, are two small islands both of them evidently artificial whether in whole or in part, and once approached by causeways from the shore. These islets lie towards the north and east sides of the loch and are very similar in general appearance, with flat grassy tops rising little more than 2 feet above the water, and (so far as visible) being entirely composed of small stones.

Each clearly represents the site of an island-fort, having been enclosed by a slender wall, of which the remains are traceable in not more than three courses, partly along its edge and elsewhere in shallow water at an interval of from 1 to 3 yards, the loch showing a marked increase in depth immediately beyond this outer limit.

● 67 The smaller islet is connected with the north shore of Loch nan Gearrachan by a causeway 35 yards in length and partly visible above the surface. This fort has been of circular form, with a diameter of about 32 feet over an outer wall which can be traced throughout most of its circumference, although standing under water

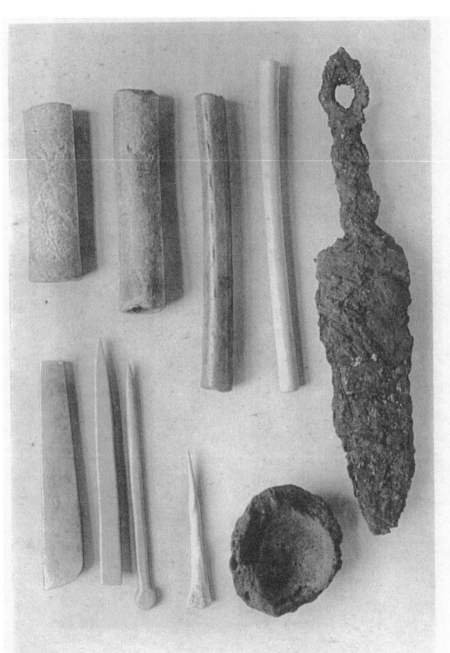

DUN A' GHALLAIN, POTTERY AND DIRK.   SKELLOR, SHAPED BONES.   ACTUAL SIZE.

DUN OLAVAT, FROM SOUTH-WEST.

on the south at a distance of 2 yards from the present margin of the island.

The second islet has evidently been oval in shape, measuring about 29 by 41 feet over a wall of which some remains still exist along the north and east edges, as also under water on the south and west.[1] The causeway is completely submerged, with a length of about 25 yards and joining the end of a narrow grassy point at the east, which rises little above the normal surface of the loch. Upon this islet was found an abundant growth of *Salix repens*, a plant observed at only one other locality in North Uist. • 68

LOCH NAN CLACHAN, a tidal loch 300 yards to the south-east, has contained a much larger island-fort, otherwise in its present condition closely resembling the two which have just been described. • 69

The island measures 83 feet east and west by 92 feet north and south, standing not more than 3 feet above the ordinary water-level, while surface indications point to its being at least partly if not altogether of artificial origin. It has been enclosed round the edge by a wall which is still traceable in a thickness of 5 or 6 feet, especially at the north and east, the whole interior area being strewn with many loose stones beneath the turf, now however so densely covered by reeds and rank grass as to afford no clue to the shape or size of the various separate buildings which it almost certainly once contained.

The main entrance, 3 feet wide, pierces the outer wall exactly opposite the island-end of a straight causeway, about 50 yards in length and 4 or 5 feet in width, which has served as an access from the north shore of the loch and is still visible above water throughout more than half of its course. At a point about 20 yards from the island this causeway shows a gap of nearly 2 yards, a feature to which reference has been already made as occurring in connection with several other island-forts in North Uist. It may be noted that, at its landward end, the causeway finishes with a curiously marked block of stone, measuring about 3 by 2 feet, of which at least three faces are covered by slight concave depressions nearly an inch in diameter. Although probably of natural origin, these symmetrical

---

[1] At the south shore of the loch, exactly opposite this island and curving in its direction, is a substantial pier which ends abruptly at a length of 15 yards, for the most part standing one or two feet under water.

pits or cups are so peculiar as to be of some interest. This
site is marked upon Blaeu's atlas of 1654 as 'Ylen Dunikrannil,'
no doubt representing the Gaelic '*Eilean Dùin 'ic Raonuill*' or
'island of the fort of Ranald's son'; a form which corresponds with
the *Dùn Mhic Raouill*, already described as existing in Loch
Eaval.

• 70   CNOC A' COMHDHALACH, or 'knoll of meeting,' is the name locally
given to a mound 400 yards north of Loch nan Clachan and within
30 yards from the west shore of Vallay Strand. Before its recent
excavation (in the summers of 1905 to 1907) this showed as a mere
grassy hillock of irregularly oval shape, measuring about 56 feet east
and west by 39 feet north and south, with a height of 5 or 6 feet
and steep sides which were suggestive of an artificial origin; a few
large stones also appearing upon its surface, although only at intervals
and not affording any evidence of structural form. Ten yards to the
east stood another mound of much smaller dimensions.

        The north and south edges of the principal hillock were first
slightly tested, yielding some typical kitchen-midden remains which
included wood-ashes, periwinkle-shells, and fragments of ancient
pottery, with a hammer-stone and a single flint chip—the latter
material being rare in North Uist. These finds encouraged systematic
excavation with the result of disclosing a large structure which was
found to possess various special features, some of them clearly attributable to secondary occupations at widely separated periods. Practically
all the larger stones had already been removed from the exterior
portion of the wall, so that its full original width is hardly traceable
except at one point on the south-west.

        When thus laid bare, the site at Cnoc a' Comhdhalach may be
generally described as consisting of a massive wall with a very
uniform present height of about 4½ feet at its interior face, enclosing an almost circular courtyard which measures 22½ feet in diameter
north and south by 24 feet east and west; this surrounding wall
further showing a clearly defined thickness of 9½ feet at the south-
west, and of apparently not less than 7 feet on the opposite side.
The walls of an entrance passage, 20 feet in length, are still distinctly
traceable to a height of 3 or 4 feet, this access leading from its outer
doorway (35 inches wide) at the mid-east, first in a sharp curve for
10 feet to the south-west and thence westwards in a comparatively

DUN IN LOCH NAN CLACHAN.

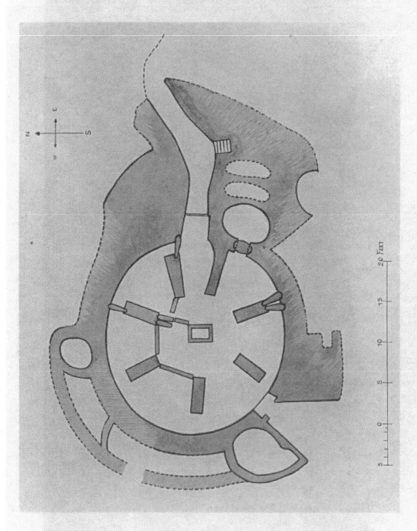

CNOC A' COMHDHALACH, GROUND PLAN.

straight line until it reaches the central enclosure. This passage shows a marked irregularity as to its width, which varies between extremes of 26 and 50 inches. At the widest part, midway in its course, a staircase rises from the passage floor into the south wall in a width of 21 inches by five narrow and rudely built steps now forming an ascent of 27 inches, although probably at one time continued to a higher level.

The passage itself seems to have been roughly paved from its outer doorway to a point 7 feet west of the staircase, where its floor is interrupted by a slab set on edge so as to present a sill 8 inches high, accompanied on the west by substantial stone jambs, evidently the cheeks of a former door which opened inwards.

The existence of this long eastward passage, containing a staircase situated 7 feet outside a former doorway, would suggest both these features as belonging to a secondary construction, a theory also supported by the fact that another and evidently more ancient entrance shows in the opposite side of Cnoc a' Comhdhalach. Here, to the south-west and raised a foot above the floor of the enclosed circular area, was found an opening which measures 32 inches across its inner end, though so carefully walled up as only to reveal itself upon close scrutiny. This old entrance first slightly expands outwards, but at a distance of less than 2 feet is abruptly contracted by a pair of jambs to a width of 23 inches, an aperture clearly once guarded by a door opening from within. The wall forming the north side of this access continues straight through the enclosing wall of the main structure in a length of $9\frac{1}{2}$ feet, while its southern boundary has a considerable outward splay so as to leave an exterior opening fully 8 feet in width, a feature which would seem attributable to a secondary even if remote origin. It may be added that there are indications of the whole gateway having been roughly paved at an elevation of about 12 inches above the natural surface.

Within the thickness of the main wall, close to the north side of this entrance, there still remains the complete outline of what was perhaps a guard-chamber. This shows as an irregular oval measuring 5 feet 3 inches north and south by 6 feet east and west, with walls which vary from 12 to 18 inches in thickness. At its east end this cell is distinctly coved or domed, a character which it still retains to a present roof-height of 17 inches in a broken arch consisting of thin stones in five courses.[1]

The outer portion of the circular wall which has formed the main structure at Cnoc a' Comhdhalach is now so imperfect as to yield few data as to its original dimensions. It certainly however had a thickness of from 9 to 9½ feet at both sides of the older south-west entrance; while, throughout an arc of 8 yards immediately north of the supposed guard-chamber, there are indications of a double wall with an intervening passage 24 inches wide. At this point the inner division of the wall measures from 32 to 42 inches across, and a like feature seems also traceable in a length of several yards at the mid-south. Hence we would class Cnoc a' Comhdhalach as originally 'a broch-like structure,' furnished at least in parts with a passage between double walls, although no satisfactory evidence of raised galleries could be found. On the north-east, at a distance of about 8 feet outside the central courtyard, are traces of a drain running for 4 yards in an easterly direction.

Some account must now be given of the peculiar arrangements disclosed within the interior court, which has been already noted as a circular area measuring nearly 24 feet in diameter. In the time of its original builders and occupants this court probably remained an almost if not entirely clear space, so far at least as concerned stone erections other than hearths, one of which indeed still exists at its centre. To secondary adaptations must be attributed a series of six detached radial walls which run at approximately equal intervals from near the inner circumference towards the centre of the court, leaving there an open space about 11 feet in diameter. These radial walls vary in length from 4 to 5 feet by a width of 15 to 30 inches, and have a uniform—as also apparently complete—height of 4 feet, this nearly agreeing with the present (although evidently not original) height of the surrounding main wall.[2] Further, these secondary walls leave gaps of from 20 to 33 inches between their

---

[1] Here may be noted the evident former existence of another oval cell, at least 5 feet in length, its northern half being still traceable at the south-east edge of Cnoc a' Comhdhalach, about 4 yards south of the staircase in the long east passage.

[2] Similar arrangements were also found within the fortified structure upon Eilean Maleit, and still more prominently in the Earth-House at Machair Leathann. It would thus seem that the central enclosures at both Cnoc a' Comhdhalach and Eilean Maleit have undergone a secondary adaptation into chambers of precisely the same type as those contained in a subterranean dwelling, so as to present examples of identity of modification in fort and Earth-House.

CNOC A' COMHDHALACH, INTERIOR, FROM NORTH-EAST.

CNOC A' COMHDHALACH, PASSAGE, FROM WEST.

ends and the inner face of the wall which encloses the court, thus affording a narrow access all the way round and close to the circumference, except where interrupted at the south-east by an additional unbroken wall which prolongs the eastern entrance passage for 6 feet inwards at its south side. Each of these gaps has almost certainly been bridged at about 4 feet above the floor level by two narrow slabs joining on to the boundary wall; one such pair still remaining at the mid-south, and two single slabs (each, from its position, evidently one of a former pair) covering other gaps in the northern arc.

The outer section of the courtyard, representing more than half of its total diameter, is thus divided by the radial walls into six separate chambers, each forming the segment of an arc with average dimensions of 6 feet in length and breadth, and each opening to the other at its outer end through a narrow continuous passage, while closed towards the centre by a thin wall. Two of these inner linings and part of a third still show to some extent, but the remainder are not now traceable.

The centre of the courtyard was thus a hexagonal space measuring nearly 11 feet across, which was entered directly from the inner extension of the long eastward passage and had its sides formed by the backs of the six radial chambers. On the floor, in the middle of this small area, still remains a rectangular hearth, measuring 34 by 19 inches and edged around by flat stones to a depth of 3 inches.

From the south-eastern chamber, close to the wall which there forms a continuation of the east entrance passage, is a doorway, 18 inches wide and 32 inches high, leading from the interior base into a supplementary cell about 5 feet in diameter.

Two if not three successive stages of construction have thus far been shown as here existent, while these by no means exhaust the distinctly separate periods at which Cnoc a' Comhdhalach was utilised for habitation, traces of several more recent occupations being abundantly disclosed. Proofs of these were laid bare within the central hexagonal space, where was revealed in section a mass of débris 5 feet in depth and containing successive strata of ashes and natural soil. For example, in its lower half, and within three feet above the original floor level, were two six-inch layers of red ashes together with a less pronounced third layer, all separated by equally thick accumulations of black earth.

Again, at a height of 5 feet from the base, in the centre of the area and immediately below the recent surface, were found three small slabs arranged in the form of a hearth 20 inches wide.

We have thus at Cnoc a' Comhdhalach distinct evidence of at least five successive periods of occupation, represented by the two central hearths and the three strata of ashes, all divided by layers of slowly accumulating soil, these latter betokening long intervals of rest; while earliest in date comes the original structure as it existed before the radial walls were introduced within its central area.

From close to the outer doorway of the long eastern passage, and extending farther in that direction for a distance of over 20 yards, was also excavated a straggling annexe which has consisted of numerous small cells or chambers, most irregular as to shape and size, and their slender walls nowhere exceeding 2 feet in present height. Only six of these cells show in complete outline, with dimensions varying from 24 by 30 inches to 5 by 7 feet; but traces of others are also visible, and it is evident that a continuous rambling passage once connected the whole series with the main structure. This annexe no doubt represents an outgrowth at a comparatively recent stage of occupation. Between it and the main building a heap of rubbish disclosed kitchen-midden shells in abundance, but it is noteworthy that the annexe itself yielded very few traces left by its former occupants, nothing indeed beyond three or four hammerstones and some fragments of unpatterned pottery. In connection with Eilean Maleit and Buaile Risary we have afterwards occasion to describe other annexes of very similar character.

During the excavation of Cnoc a' Comhdhalach several classes of relics were obtained in fair quantity. These included many hammerstones varying in material from a soft schist to the rarer quartz. A couple of thin flat rounded stones, 7 to 8 inches in diameter by about half an inch thick, had apparently served as covers for craggans. The upper and lower halves of a quern were also unearthed, differing greatly as to material and yet, from their equal diameter ($13\frac{1}{2}$ inches), both seeming to form part of the same contrivance,—the broken upper stone, thin and of hard close grain, but the lower of a coarse and much decayed schist. In the same category was a

CNOC A' COMHDHALACH, STAIRCASE IN WALL.

CNOC A' COMHDHALACH, HEARTH.

pounder, its outer edge showing marks of much use around the whole of its circumference. A flat oval piece of granitic schist, 7 inches in length, shows near the centre of each face a symmetrical cup 2 inches in diameter and three-quarters of an inch deep, although these hollows are not precisely opposite.

Three small flat pebbles, all somewhat oval in shape and averaging about 2½ inches in length by a thickness of half an inch, are so peculiar as to require individual notice. The largest of these is smooth upon one side, but with its reverse deeply marked by seven roughly parallel incisions running obliquely across the whole centre of that face and evidently caused by use in the sharpening of tools. The other two are water-worn quartzite pebbles, each bearing a short but well-marked oblique indentation near the centre of both of its flattish sides. These have probably served as a separate class of sharpening-stones,[1] and although their particular use is unknown, the type is recognised as of frequent occurrence in brochs. One of these specimens, more circular than oval in shape, is peculiar as having its outer edge artificially and very smoothly worn all round; whereas the second, with marks of use upon both ends, is otherwise a counterpart of examples from Kintradwell Broch (Sutherland) and Dun Add, a large hill-fort in Argyllshire.

Of very similar form, three other pebbles were found, although only one of them showed distinct signs of use; while to these may be added a number of small water-worn pebbles, significant only through the fact of their presence, evidently to serve some definite purpose. Here may be noted several whorls—three shaped from stone and one of pottery—as also nine sharpening or polishing stones, mostly very thin but including two of larger size, both of them trapezoidal in form and about an inch thick. A slender disc of schist, measuring fully an inch in diameter, had evidently been artificially chipped to circular shape. Only ten specimens of flint were here found, one apparently representing a leaf-shaped arrow-head. A much abraded piece of pumice, and a small moulded lump of red pigment were also discovered, though this latter may possibly not belong to pre-historic times.

Fragments of pottery were most abundant of all, many distinct

---

[1] An alternative suggestion is made that these may have served for striking fire with a piece of flint.

patterns, both raised and incised, being represented,—one of the latter in exceptionally coarse material nearly an inch thick and rudely marked with short parallel grooves. In baked clay three other curious articles were found; one very fragile and evidently the broken half of a shallow flat receptacle, an inch in diameter by not more than a quarter of an inch deep, perhaps analogous to a complete but thicker example afterwards to be described in connection with the structure at Buaile Risary. Both of the remaining pair are nearly flat on one side and slightly convex on the other, the smaller of oval and button-like form, slightly exceeding an inch in length; while the other is of almost rectangular shape measuring about 2 inches across, with all four edges regularly abraded. Lumps of unwrought clay were also found within the central area.

Specimens in bone or metal were rare, the former class including part of a stag's antler, and a small pin, noteworthy as closely resembling the modern article of commerce, having a flat thin head with sharp edges, in contrast to the knobbed head of early normal type. In bronze we can chronicle only two items, each complete when found, although unfortunately damaged forthwith. Both have evidently been pins, the shorter measuring little over an inch in length, with a stem of thick wire abruptly cut across at the point, and its head hammered into a spatulate oval. The other and larger pin of the same metal has a length of $3\frac{1}{2}$ inches, its head consisting of a half-inch ring folded over so as to lie flat upon the shaft.

Upon the centre of *Geirisclett*,[1] a promontory less than a mile to the north, is a mound, which, although evidently not belonging to the same class, afforded several specimens much resembling those found within Cnoc a' Comhdhalach. Excavation to a depth of 3 or 4 feet here disclosed traces of at least two comparatively modern buildings superimposed upon a site of much earlier date. This lower and more ancient erection shows as a large central chamber of irregular shape, bordered both on its east and west by groups of small cells, the whole extending for about 63 feet in greatest width. The main chamber contains within its centre an oblong hearth with rounded corners, edged by small stones and measuring nearly 7 by 6 feet. From the east side of this hearth are two drains, one especially prominent and leading right out towards the north-east boundary,

_____
[1] In South Uist is a *Geirnish*, at the south end of Loch Bee.

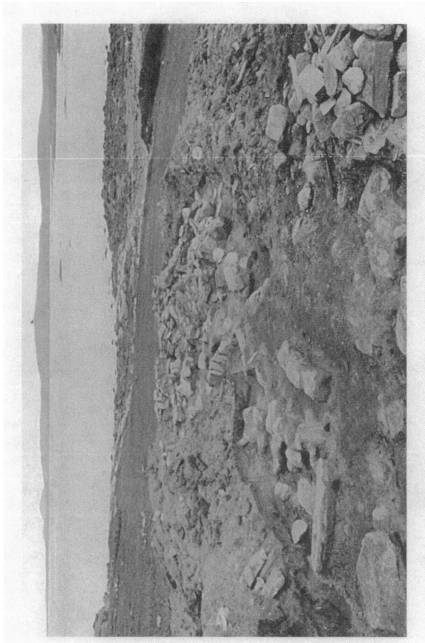

CNOC A' COMHDHALACH, ANNEXE, FROM WEST.

CNOC A' COMHDHALACH, POTTERY.   ACTUAL SIZE.

while the other is less distinctly traceable a little to the south. Upon the east, immediately below the turf, is a solid layer of kitchen-midden shells, from 12 to 20 inches in depth and chiefly composed of periwinkles.

From Geirisclett were obtained several roughly flaked pieces of flint, as also a few hammer-stones and polishers or sharpening stones; amongst these latter a flat oval quartzite pebble marked by an oblique indentation near the centre of each face, and thus bearing a close resemblance to other specimens found in Cnoc a' Comhdhalach. A small and much abraded lump of pumice is to be noted, while many fragments of pottery were found, showing various raised and incised patterns of similar type to those often occurring in pre-historic forts.

It was, however, in articles of bone that this site proved especially fruitful. These included two pins with peculiarly carved heads, five plain pins or bodkins, and two needles, in addition to twenty other pins of ruder form but all artificially pointed. The handle of a large knife (presumably mediæval in date) consists of two slips of bone enclosing a flat tang, all fixed together by much corroded iron rivets. A flat portion of cetacean bone also shows at one end a row of teeth, having probably served as a comb. In horn is to be noted a shaped fragment with flattened sides, bearing a deep incision near its tip and also containing a regularly formed slot pierced by an iron rivet at its broken lower end. Three portions of antlers were found, two of them merely cut-marked, and the third showing as a segment less than 2 inches in length, cut across at one end and pierced by a longitudinal hole through its centre.

EILEAN MALEIT,[1] a narrow rocky islet about 100 yards in length, is situated a quarter of a mile east from Cnoc a' Comhdhalach, near the south edge of Vallay Strand. Though always accessible up to more than half-tide, this island has been provided with a causeway, 5 feet in width, connecting it to the neighbouring shore, a distance of less than 30 yards.

Eilean Maleit has an elevation of about 12 feet, its steep northern face consisting of solid rock, while there is some appearance of a former wall along its south edge. Before the surface was disturbed,

• 71

[1] Or perhaps 'Maleec.' Its name is presumably of Norse origin, derived from the same root-word as *Malaclett*, the township a mile to the east.

traces of comparatively modern erections were visible both upon its centre (opposite the causeway) and towards its east and west extremities; these being evidently the remains of a dwelling and outbuildings erected by some crofter or cottar who had utilised older material which lay ready to his hand. We are informed that in like manner these modern erections—as also the causeway itself—have been quarried to serve in constructing the bridge which crosses the outlet of Loch nan Clachan.

Excavation of the summit of Eilean Maleit revealed a structure bearing some resemblance to that at Cnoc a' Comhdhalach as regards its interior arrangements. Here was disclosed a circular interior area measuring 24 feet in diameter, surrounded by a wall which varies from about 5 to 12 feet in width, but shows no indication of having contained a passage or gallery within its thickness. This circular court has been divided into 8 or 9 compartments, including an irregularly shaped central space which measures 12 feet in greatest length. Within its southern arc are four short walls radiating towards the circumference, although none of these joins the outer boundary,[1] the three segments thus formed lying also entirely open to the central chamber, without any trace of their inner ends having ever been closed. At the mid-west two parallel walls abut upon the circumference, there forming another pair of chambers more separate in character. Towards the north, at a level higher by about eighteen inches are two other chambers, their northern ends fully open to a passage which encircles the whole interior, keeping close to the boundary wall, except for a brief interval where the obstructing sides of the mid-west chambers cause it to deviate so as to pass through them at their inner instead of their outer extremities.

The main access to the whole structure clearly shows at the north-west corner, through a slightly curved passage fourteen feet long and about thirty-three inches wide. There have, however, been two other and more indirect entrances, these traversing annexes on the west

---

[1] These four radial walls vary in length from 32 to 72 inches, leaving gaps of 15 to 24 inches next the outer boundary. They present a very uniform height of 27 inches, a measurement not much exceeded by the surrounding wall, except on the north-east where it still reaches 45 inches. At Eilean Maleit there is no trace of narrow slabs bridging the gaps between the radials and the outer wall, as found both at Cnoc a' Comhdhalach and Machair Leathann.

CNOC A' COMHDHALACH; POTTERY, AND LUMP OF RED PIGMENT. ACTUAL SIZE.

CNOC A' COMHDHALACH; SHARPENING-STONES AND WHORLS. ACTUAL SIZE.

and north of the main building, and evidently to be considered as of secondary origin.

As already incidentally mentioned, Eilean Maleit has possessed two annexes, and it may be added that in both of these the outlines and dimensions of the component cells or chambers show much more clearly than at Cnoc a' Comhdhalach or Buaile Risary, the latter yet to be described. That on the west consists of seven irregularly shaped compartments, four of them small and measuring only about 3 to 4 feet across, but the others ranging in length from 6 to 12 feet, while it is noticeable that each of these latter is provided with a narrow doorway from the exterior of the structure. The northern annexe is threaded by a winding passage, 18 to 30 inches wide, which first traverses two small cells 3 to 4 feet in length, and then passes through an oblong chamber (recessed at both ends and measuring 12 by 6 feet over its extremes) to a separate northward exit 24 inches wide and 6 or 7 feet long. The existence here of two independent and somewhat parallel entrances would itself tend to prove the secondary character of this irregular annexe, as to which indeed there cannot be any doubt.

Hammer-stones were scarce at Eilean Maleit, but one deserves special notice. This is composed of hornblende, and, besides showing marks of considerable use upon its ends, has a symmetrical groove at the middle of each side, where it was evidently hafted. Many fragments of ancient pottery were found, several of them ornamented by various patterns, one piece being perforated near its rim by a small hole, clearly for the purpose of suspension. A lump of pumice is to be noted; as also a thin disc of schist, an inch and a quarter in diameter, which shows distinct evidence of its edges having been chipped to shape. Close to the west of Eilean Maleit is a much smaller islet with apparent traces of a former occupation.

BUAILE RISARY[1] is the local name of a large green mound half ● 72 way up the northern slope of Beinn Risary and a mile south from Cnoc a' Comhdhalach.

Over its extremes this hillock measures about 60 yards east and west by 50 yards north and south, with a height of 15 or

---

[1] *Buaile* is the Gaelic term for a 'cattle-fold,' a description hardly applying to this knoll, although, lower down and upon level ground, are the remains of a large modern fold which may have lent its name to this more ancient site.

20 feet on its north side where the surface slopes abruptly and discloses natural rock.[1] Upon the broad and comparatively flat summit were scattered several ruined shielings together with larger stones than could be referred to such an origin. It was clear that an earlier structure lay beneath, and excavation was therefore commenced at the south-east, with the result that an erection of peculiar type was there revealed. As at Cnoc a' Comhdhalach, the outer wall of Buaile Risary has been much quarried, though, on the other hand, this latter shows no present indication of having possessed any great strength, while its interior arrangements also afford a complete contrast to those at Cnoc a' Comhdhalach.

Measuring over its exterior wall, so far as this now stands in a width varying from 3 to 5½ feet, the main and apparently original structure at Buaile Risary seems to have been of circular form about 32 feet in diameter. Near its centre was disclosed a rectangular chamber measuring 10 by 8½ feet with additional squared recesses on the east, north, and south, into the last-mentioned of which (and much the largest of the three, its dimensions being 8 by 5 feet) has entered the main passage from a doorway still showing in a width of 30 inches through the outer wall.

Near the middle of this chamber was found an oblong hearth measuring 25 by 21 inches, edged at its back and sides by small stones for 2 or 3 inches above the floor level and containing reddish ashes to the depth of nearly a foot. Within a yard from the east side (or front) of this hearth may still be seen the inlet of a built drain (filled with small rubble and capped by thin slabs) which, for half of its course to the south-west, runs below the passage floor, afterwards penetrating several cross walls and finally emerging at the exterior a yard to the west of the main doorway.[2] From near the same starting-point are slighter traces of a second drain running towards the south-east.

This supposed original circular erection has also contained three other rectangular chambers, two at its west side being minor and apparently secondary, while the third, near the main entrance, shows massive walls extending for about 10 feet east to west and 8 feet north to south.

---

[1] A large stone upon this northern slope bears a group of several cup-marks.
[2] Within the exit of this drain was found a congealed mass of refuse, evidently consisting of fragments of coarse pottery long since dissolved in liquid waste.

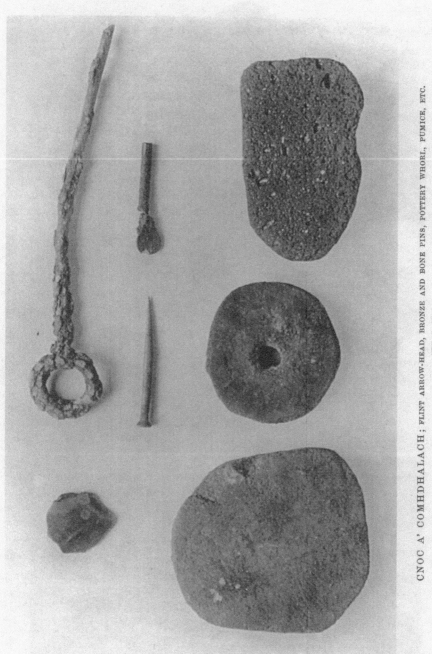

CNOC A' COMHDHALACH; FLINT ARROW-HEAD, BRONZE AND BONE PINS, POTTERY WHORL, PUMICE, ETC. ACTUAL SIZE.

GEIRISCLETT, POTTERY.   ACTUAL SIZE.

The remainder of the interior space has at one time been occupied by a number of small and very irregularly shaped cells, presumably all of secondary character.

Excavation disclosed the remains of an extensive annexe at the east side of Buaile Risary, measuring about 48 feet north and south by 25 feet east and west, and containing part of another but incomplete enclosure 24 feet in diameter with a wall from 36 to 42 inches thick. Near the centre of this area were found traces of a second hearth, consisting of a single slab edged by small stones. The annexe further included a group of nondescript cells varying from 30 inches to 7 feet in length, and connected by a short passage with the main structure to the south.

Outside this annexe, upon the northern summit of Buaile Risary, are the foundations of a well-built dry-stone house, more substantial than an ordinary shieling, although evidently of no great age. This erection contained fragments of pottery, some of modern date, together with others (both plain and patterned) similar to specimens dug out of the structure first described. Here also was unearthed a unique specimen, represented by a small oblong pebble with rounded ends, an inch and a half long by barely half an inch wide, bearing upon one flat side a series of eleven lines scratched across its face at equal intervals, all being roughly parallel and extending for the full width, except one which is oblique for part of its length, and another which shows only half-way across the surface. Almost throughout can be traced a stem-line, suggesting the character of an Ogam inscription, although any such theory seems untenable. It is certain however that these lines are not of natural origin, but have been deliberately made by human agency, the pebble most probably having served as an amulet.

Near the same spot was found a piece of sandstone, polygonal in form, and with four of its edges clearly shaped for the purpose of sharpening tools. Across its now incomplete extremes, this fragment measures about 4 by 3 inches.

As yet, less than half of Buaile Risary has been excavated, and the relics of its former occupation are not very abundant, though ancient pottery is represented in several ornamental designs, both raised and incised. Of this material was found half of the base of a very small vessel, measuring only 1½ inches across; and also a tiny bowl, little over an inch in diameter and half an inch thick, convex below, and its upper side cupped with a small recess such as might have been formed by the insertion of a finger tip to nearly the full depth while the clay was yet soft.[1]

Hammer-stones were not very abundant, but included one in the form of a ball 3 inches in diameter. A flat block of gneiss, measuring 8 inches square by a thickness of $2\frac{1}{2}$ inches, bore in the centre of one of its faces a slight circular depression, perhaps too shallow to have held a pivot, and therefore more probably indicating use as an anvil. There was also found a complete ring of granitic schist, although so much decomposed as to fall into several pieces. This was 5 inches in diameter and half as thick, perforated through its centre by a hole measuring 2 inches across at each face but bevelled inwards to a width of only $1\frac{1}{4}$ inches.

Several broken whet-stones are here to be recorded; as also a few small water-worn pebbles (chiefly of quartz, but none showing marks of use); seven flints, including a scraper; and five fragments of pumice, nearly all of them artificially shaped. The heads of two iron rivets, evidently of Viking type, are to be noted. In some parts of Buaile Risary, kitchen-midden remains of ashes, shells, and burnt bones were disclosed, and there can be little doubt that the unexplored portion of this mound would yield additional relics of its former occupation.

Upon the northern slope of North Clettraval, a mile west from Buaile Risary, is a group of three conspicuously green hillocks. Two of these adjoin each other, the westmost showing some traces of a wall along its north edge. This is noted as possibly the site of another fort, the whole measuring about 85 by 57 feet.

• 73   DUN THOMAIDH (' *Dùn Tomi* ' of the Ordnance map, and probably signifying ' the fort of Thomas ')[2] stood upon a small island in Vallay Sound, the narrow sea-inlet separating Vallay from Griminish, and across which there is a ferry exactly at this spot.

When the tide ebbs, Dun Thomaidh is accessible from Vallay

---

[1] In stone, a somewhat similar but larger vessel is recorded from a broch in Orkney; that specimen still containing a reddish substance which would apparently identify it as a receptacle for some pigment.

[2] Thomas is represented by the Gaelic *Tòmas* and the Norse *Tumi*. According to local tradition the 'Tomi' of this fort was a brother of 'Dunag,' their father having been 'a king of Norway.' *Tota Dùnaig*, on Vallay, is noted in Chapter VII.

GEIRISCLETT, SHARPENING-STONE AND SHAPED BONES.   ACTUAL SIZE.

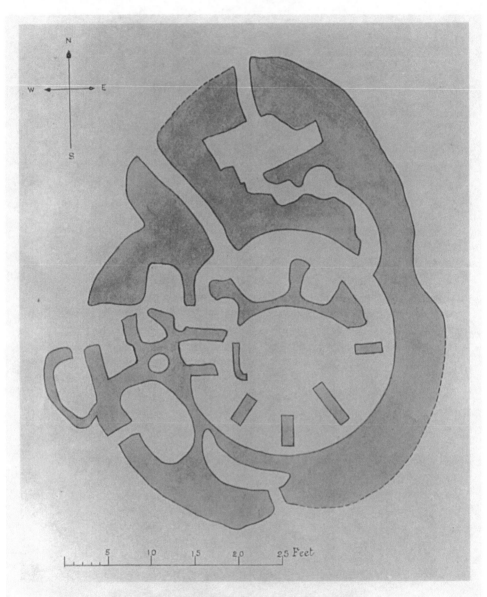

DUN ON EILEAN MALEIT, GROUND PLAN.

DUN ON EILEAN MALEIT, INTERIOR, FROM WEST.

DUN ON EILEAN MALEIT, POTTERY. ACTUAL SIZE.

island on the north over an unusually long causeway extending for no less than 87 yards.[1] This causeway has a width of 10 feet, and, although covered with sea-weed, its edges still show in line for intervals at about 6 feet above the level of low-water, resting upon a considerably wider mound of sand. Near the island end of this approach is a gap of about 12 feet, evidently thus arranged to serve as an impediment and suggesting the use of a draw-bridge over that short portion.

Dun Thomaidh has been defended by two concentric walls, nowhere however retaining more than four courses of stones in original position. Over its inner rampart, exactly at high-water mark, the fort has a diameter of 50 feet; and beyond this are the remains of an exterior sea-wall or breakwater at a distance which varies from 15 feet on the south to 19 feet on the east and as much as 30 feet on the west, in each case measuring between the outer faces. The landward entrance has evidently been upon the north side, a little east from the point at which the island is joined by its causeway. At the mid-east are indications of a boat-harbour 10 feet wide, its outer end showing nearly 6 feet below the base of the sea-wall.

So dilapidated is Dun Thomaidh as to offer little inducement for its excavation, and the writer can record only one relic from this site, namely, a broken hammer-stone found lying on the beach. Modern tradition states that many stones were removed from Dun Thomaidh upon rafts, for the erection of the farm-steading at Vallay.[2]

There is said to be a spring of fresh water upon a skerry (*Sgeir na Comh-strì*, or 'skerry of strife')[3] in Vallay Sound, 300 yards north-west of Dun Thomaidh and showing only about 2 feet above high-water mark at spring-tides. The writer has examined this skerry, and, although uncertain as to any individual spring, found several pools containing water which was brackish only to a slight extent.

---

[1] Strictly speaking, this causeway does not abut upon the island of Vallay proper, ceasing on the north at *Lingernish* which is sometimes an islet although at ordinary tides connected on the east with the promontory of *Morornish* on Vallay itself. From the north-west end of *Lingernish*, across the mouth of a small bay marked *Bàgh Clann Néill*, is a row of massive stones evidently there set in position, this barrier acting as a breakwater and keeping back the tide much in the same manner as a line of boulders afterwards described as stretching between Lombaidh-skerry and Rudha nan Corr.

[2] 'Dun Thornaidh . . . the stones of which were carried away to build a house at Valay,' *Archæologia Scotica*, vol. v. p. 402.

[3] In Loch Eford is *Eilean na Comh-strì*, showing only as a round green cap at high-water.

Lombaidh[1] is the local name (not however marked upon the map)
for a somewhat larger islet in Vallay Sound, 300 yards to the south-
east of Dun Thomaidh.   Before it was excavated, this island had a
dense covering of grass and other herbage, amongst which the prim-
rose flourished in quite abnormal dimensions, both flower and leaf
testifying to an extraneous enrichment of the soil.   Its rough surface
indicated the presence of many stones, and but little excavation was
necessary in order to reveal the fact that this island contained a group
of several ancient buildings.   The foundations of five or six separate
chambers were traceable ; one of them at the mid-south showing an
oblong interior of about 12 by 8 feet, with rounded angles ; while
another to the west measured 10 feet 8 inches by 10 feet and was curved
at its south-west corner.   None of the walls now exceed 18 inches in
height, their widths varying from about 30 to 45 inches.   Probably
the whole island was enclosed by a wall near its edge, but, as this
point is uncertain, Lombaidh has not been definitely classed as a fort.
No relics were here obtained except some fragments of rude unpatterned
pottery.

As the tide recedes, Lombaidh becomes greatly enlarged, being
then joined to a skerry on the north-east, with a considerable extent
of foreshore which is entirely covered at high-water.   Between Lombaidh-skerry and Rudha nan Corr (at Geirisclett on the east) is a row
of very large stones, evidently placed in line by human agency to form
a connection with the shore.   These blocks so closely adjoin each
other as to dam back the ebbing tide and thus cause a distinct
waterfall, below which the narrow channel is at that time easily fordable.

In Bagh an Acaire, the eastern bay of this branch of Vallay
Sound, a hundred yards south of Rudha nan Corr, is a tidal islet
known as *Eilean an Acaire*.   Even at high tides this is separated
by little depth of water from the Griminish shore on the south, and
indeed the remains of a dry-stone dyke—evidently the former march
between Griminish and Airidh Mhic Ruaridh—continue northwards
across the intervening beach and traverse the island itself near the
centre of its length.   Dating evidently from a still earlier period, and
perhaps the most notable feature of this site, is the fact that the western
half of Eilean an Acaire (and apparently that half alone) has been
enclosed by a semi-circular wall still distinctly traceable at a level

---

[1] Perhaps the Norse *lamb-ey,* or 'lamb island.'

BUAILE RISARY; HEARTH.

BUAILE RISARY; POTTERY AND MARKED PEBBLE. ACTUAL SIZE.

much below high-water mark.   This seems to indicate for Eilean an
Acaire a former occupation, concerning which, however, no further
suggestion offers itself.

The only fort to be noted upon the island of Vallay occupies a
small and low-lying point, known as RUDH' AN DUIN, towards the   • 74
east end of the island at its rocky shore 200 yards south from the
burial-ground at St. Mary's Chapel.

This site had rather an unpromising aspect, although in parts
showing traces of an exterior wall, and more particularly, at the
west, some appearance of a wide doorway; the latter inducing an
attempt at thorough excavation, with the result that it was revealed
as an access passing straight through a solid wall (only 3 feet in
present height) for fully 17 feet, in a width varying between 54 and 57
inches.   In the bottom of this passage was found a thin layer of
gravel with a built drain immediately underneath, shallow and capped
by small flagstones at the floor level.   The purpose here served by a
drain is sufficiently obvious, as allowing the sea-water which entered
the inner court of the dun to recede with the ebb.   Spring-tides rise
18 inches above the base level of the outer doorway, also flooding the
interior area to the depth of nearly a foot.

Before the accumulated rubbish was removed from this entrance,
there lay obliquely across its surface a flat block of stone 7½ feet in
length, most probably representing a cover-slab which formed part of
an original roof to the passage.   At a short distance within the main
enclosure was found a similar stone over 6 feet long, and two or three
others still lie outside the wall near the doorway.

When this entrance passage had been entirely cleared, the inner
face of the enclosing wall was plainly disclosed at each side and its
line followed throughout the whole circumference, leaving, however,
a gap of 25 feet on the south-east where this wall has totally disappeared, owing no doubt to the action of storms during many
centuries.

The interior court has thus a well-defined diameter of 44 feet, with
rock intruding at the north-east a little above the regular base.   Here
the main wall reaches its greatest present height of almost 5 feet,
which includes a layer of earth and small stones lying upon a boulder
within its centre, although the inner built face is nowhere more than
3 feet high.

The drain already mentioned as emerging through the entrance-passage was found to continue thither in a curve from a point 15 feet within the central area, where it has a covering of small flagstones, beneath which was disclosed a 3-inch layer of solid glutinous matter at least 16 inches wide and apparently representing an indurated mass of cow-dung, the accumulation of some remote period.

In marked contrast to the distinctness with which the inner face of the main wall still shows, its exterior (except on the west at each side of the entrance) is now so ruinous as to cause great hesitation in giving any details, apart from the general statement that it has been very massive, with a total thickness of from 17 to 18 feet, even slightly exceeded at one or two points. This difficulty is not diminished by finding the extreme outer portion of the wall in its southern half to consist of a series of large blocks of stone, many of them over 4 feet in length, arranged so as still to present a fairly regular exterior line practically without interruption except on the south-east, at the already noted gap of 25 feet. Situated upon the natural rock, and chiefly below high-water mark, this portion of wall has all the appearance of a separate rude outwork about 5 feet thick, composed of one or two blocks of stone as to its width, though hardly at any part now showing more than two courses in position to a height of 3 feet. On the east side of the fort are indeed traces of two separate concentric walls, standing (if we may so express it) somewhat parallel with each other, at an interval of from 9 to 13 feet between their outer faces.

From the above considerations the writer is strongly inclined to believe that on the south and east there existed two independent walls, separated by a space varying from about 4 to 7 feet in width; the outer defence taking the form of a breakwater or sea-wall which surrounded the fort in all except its landward or northern portion, merging into the principal wall both on the north-east and on the west, at the latter point precisely coinciding with the south edge of the entrance passage.

Regarded from either point of view, it is certain that the main wall at Rudh' an Duin has measured a thickness of 17 or 18 feet on the north and west, and not less than 9 feet on the south and east; these massive dimensions, together with the size and symmetrical form of the inner court, all suggesting for this fort the character of a

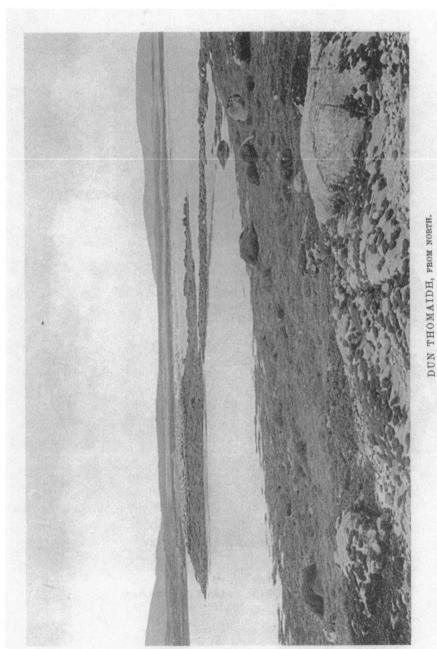

DUN THOMAIDH, FROM NORTH.

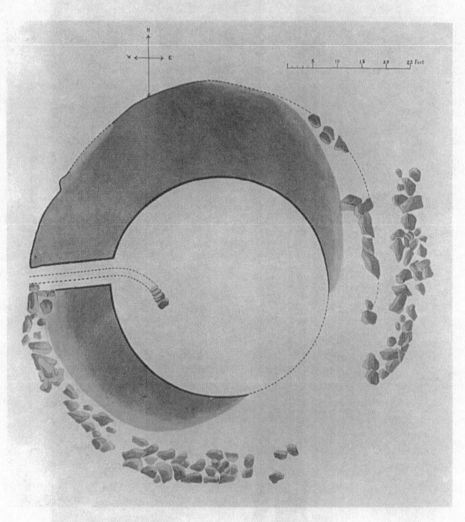

RUDH' AN DUIN, VALLAY; GROUND PLAN.

RUDH' AN DUIN, VALLAY; ENTRANCE PASSAGE.

RUDH' AN DUIN, VALLAY ; INTERIOR, FROM SOUTH-WEST.

broch, or at the least, of a broch-like structure. No sign could be found of any staircase ascending within the wall from the interior court, nor are there traces of galleries such as the thick wall might with equal probability be expected to contain. It seems very possible however that an access led upwards in the now vacant space on the south-east, while, if galleries once existed, these would naturally occupy a higher position than 3 feet above the general base.

Rudh' an Duin afforded few relics of special interest in regard to its former occupants, the débris chiefly consisting of earth and small stones, with a proportion of soil varying in different parts from about one-half to two-thirds of the whole material. Hammer-stones proved scarce, including however two of circular form very equally worn all round their edges, and a specimen of the rude ordinary type composed of quartz. In stone, two other items must be noted; one a perforated ball with flattened sides, about 2 inches in diameter by a thickness of $1\frac{1}{2}$ inches; the second being a comparatively thin piece of schist worked into the shape of a T and measuring $4\frac{1}{4}$ inches across each extremity, its purpose even more difficult to conjecture. Several small oval pebbles of somewhat peculiar form were also discovered.

Many fragments of pottery were unearthed, these chiefly plain and very small (some of a distinct and stony texture), but a few bearing various raised or incised patterns; together with the massive handle (4 inches long by three-quarters of an inch wide) of a once capacious jug, and part of a diminutive crucible.

The only specimen of bronze was a thin fragment about an inch and a half square, pierced by five small holes; while in iron, close to the northern wall of the interior, lay many fragments of a much corroded two-edged longsword, its mould left in portions of the wooden scabbard which had evidently preserved shape much longer than the metal before also completely decaying. Sufficient of its hilt still remains to indicate the greatest width of the blade as about $2\frac{1}{4}$ inches, with a 1-inch flat tang and a rounded guard or cross-piece half an inch in diameter. In addition may be noted a piece of bone bearing cut-marks and three small portions of cetacean bone, also one bit of pumice.

At various parts were disclosed kitchen-midden remains consisting of ashes, bones, and the shells of the limpet and periwinkle, but these

2 E

were nowhere plentiful, being chiefly confined to the entrance passage. From the fort itself only one small nodule of flint was obtained, another flake being found in the creek immediately to its west.

To the east of Rudh' an Duin the southern margin of Vallay island has evidently been bordered by a sea-wall of massive stones, traceable for a considerable distance along the beach towards the north-east at a little below high-water mark. Farther on, where the bank is more abrupt, are some appearances of a slighter wall upon the verge immediately above the shore.

At Malaclett, on the main portion of North Uist immediately opposite Rudh' an Duin, is a promontory named *Àrd a' Phuind*, the traditional site of some ancient building. Here remain the foundations of walls both curved and straight, but these can hardly be considered as of special importance.

Upon the 'garry' or hill-pasture of Middlequarter township, distant fully a mile to the south-east of Malaclett, is a wide upland valley containing several minor lochs, in the largest of which—Loch Eashader—is a flat island showing traces of a slight wall around its edge, and certainly in remote times occupied as a fort.

● 75 This we include as DUN EASHADER, perhaps an artificial (or at least partly artificial) island showing hardly more than 3 feet above the water-level, and measuring 52 feet in diameter over its boundary wall, which shows in parts as apparently only about 3 feet thick. Immediately within its south edge seems to have been a shallow enclosed basin or harbour, an oval of some 15 by 9 feet, and the whole islet evidently rises in somewhat conical form out of deep water, which was so much discoloured as not to allow any observation of the causeway which probably existed. At the north-east margin of Dun Eashader is indeed the semblance of a pier, a feature reproduced in more distinct character on the directly opposite end of a long and very narrow promontory 40 yards to the north. In all likelihood these piers represent the extremities of a submerged causeway, although it was unfortunately not found possible to verify this suggestion. The jutting point above-mentioned—150 yards in length, and averaging about 3 yards in width—extends from the east shore of Loch Eashader to a bare flat rock which faces the north side of the islet and deserves special notice as being itself provided with a massive and irregularly winding causeway which follows the natural outline, raised about

RUDH' AN DUIN, VALLAY; POTTERY, INCLUDING CRUCIBLE.   ACTUAL SIZE.

EILEAN AN TIGHE: STONE ADZE, FLINT SCRAPERS, AND POTTERY. ACTUAL SIZE.

a foot above the ordinary water-level and ceasing abruptly where it joins the more elevated east shore.

Dun Eashader thus seems to have possessed an approach consisting of two successive causeways, the first division normally upon land (represented in winter by shallows), and the second through water of considerable depth; while, alternatively, it is possible that this latter interval may have been served by a ferry instead of a causeway.

The site of DUN SKELLOR, at Sollas, a mile and a half due north of • 76 Loch Eashader, shows as a conspicuous mound about 10 feet in height, immediately north of the farm-house bearing the same name.   On its east edge, for a continuous length of 3 yards, the exterior face of a massive curved wall (suggesting that of a broch) is disclosed in at least three courses of large stones not far from the present summit. Outside this, and also at another broken part, were found some kitchen-midden remains, including pottery with many bones and shells.   In the north-west face, at about the same level as the portion of wall on the east, were also noticed three consecutive stones apparently in original position.   Taking a radius from these two portions of wall to the centre of the mound, this fort would seem to have had a diameter of from 50 to 60 feet, measuring across the wall at each side. Captain Thomas refers to Dun Skellor, 'from which it is said the materials for several farm-steadings have been taken—it had a well in it of considerable depth.' [1]   No trace of this well could now be found, although we are told that one existed a few yards east of the fort.

A mile south of Dun Skellor, the Ordnance map shows *Sgùrr an Dùin* as the westmost spur of *Beinn Dhubh Sollas*.   This place-name is merely noted in passing, since it doubtless bears some reference to the site just described, and does not indicate the existence of another fort.

Nearly a mile to the east of Dun Skellor, just within the boundary of Sollas township, are the remains of an island-fort, now locally known under the name of TOLOMAN.[1]   The island now shows as a • 77 mound towards the west end of a marsh which represents a former loch, distinctly shallow in character and drained off within perhaps comparatively recent times.

---

[1] *Archæologia Scotica*, vol. v. p. 402.

[2] 'Toloman' clearly represents the Gaelic *tolman*, or 'little round hillock,' borrowed from the Norse *holmr*.

This fort has suffered greatly through its convenient situation as a quarry for building purposes, so that all the larger stones have been removed, and the surface evidently often turned over. As a consequence, the interior, even where partly exposed, affords no clue to its original arrangements, consisting merely of heaps of loose stones interspersed by kitchen-midden remains, such as bones, shells of the mussel and periwinkle, and fragments of rude pottery.

In exterior dimensions Dun Toloman appears to have measured about 70 by 54 feet, the central portion being somewhat circular, supplemented both at its east and west by annexes of flattened oval shape. Outside this main structure are traces of three or four small separate buildings, and the whole island has evidently been protected by a boundary wall near its edge.

It seems certain that a causeway led between this fort and the higher ground either to the north or west, although no indication of a former access is now visible.

● 78   A mile east from Toloman, and close to the farther end of OBAN SKIBINISH, is a rock which has been occupied as a place of defence. Surrounded by the sea at half-tide, this island-fort has been provided with a causeway more than 40 yards in length and about 4 feet wide, curving southwards to the shore at *Rudha nan Cnamh* but now much damaged.

The main structure may be roughly taken as showing an inner diameter of about 27 feet enclosed by a wall 4 feet thick; portions of this latter being visible especially on the south and west, although hardly any traces are to be found near the other and more exposed edges, which now chiefly consist of bare rock. At the south this wall remains to a height of 3 feet, and here, directly opposite the island end of the causeway, has been the entrance through a passage only 20 inches wide and now about 3 feet high. Across the doorway still lies a large stone, which has certainly fallen from its original position, whether formerly serving as a lintel or otherwise. Part of the inner area shows a scanty covering of grass elevated barely a foot above the reach of spring-tides, and here were found some kitchen-midden ashes.

Joining the outside of this fort at the mid-south, a supplementary wall projects in an eastward curve, running parallel with the main structure at an interval of 9 feet, as if to guard the entrance.

EILEAN AN TIGHE; POTTERY. ACTUAL SIZE.

DUN AONGHUIS and CROGARY MORE, from WEST.

It was interesting to find that this rock is still known as *Eilean Holsta*, a place-name which evidently includes the Norse *staðr*, its form also bearing a close resemblance to that of *Tolsta* in Lewis.

Near the shore, a hundred yards to the south-east, is another and higher tidal islet evidently once walled around its edge. Upon the grassy summit of this rock, at the east side of a comparatively modern ruin, is a thick slab of stone imbedded on end, showing three cup-marks upon its irregular upper surface.

Three miles south of Oban Skibinish, in one of the least trodden portions of North Uist, is SRATH BEAG AN DUIN, a valley situated ● 79 between Loch Mousgrip and Beinn na h-Aire. This is here noted because of its significant place-name, which certainly indicates that a fort once existed in the immediate neighbourhood, even if local tradition is silent upon the subject.

Towards the east of this *srath*, a little to the north of *Allt nan Seilicheag*,[1] is a rocky mound with some traces of an old structure on its west end. This, although a most unsatisfactory site, seems to have been the fort in question, and a number of large blocks of stone, lying at irregular intervals, may suggest for it a diameter of 35 to 40 feet. There is also the appearance of an inner erection measuring about 9½ feet across its circular interior, with walls 40 inches thick and containing some very large stones, evidently far too massive to have been collected for a mere shieling, and indeed presenting a marked contrast to the slender ruins of two or three shielings of the ordinary type upon the same mound.

Half a mile to the north, at the southern edge of a rapid burn in *Bogach Mhic Fhearghuis*, stands a hillock about 15 feet in height and capped by the remains of no fewer than eight shielings. This mound is conspicuously green, and the adjoining burn quite picturesque with its waterfalls—most unusual features in the scenery of North Uist.

In the north end of Geireann Mill Loch, five hundred yards south from the recently dismantled mill, is a narrow and rocky islet known as EILEAN AN TIGHE,—grass-covered and with a profuse growth of ● 80 brambles, as also, to a less extent, of wild roses and royal fern.

Here can be traced the ruins of four or five old erections, one (to

---

[1] A mile to the south is another streamlet of identical name, which also flows into the west side of Loch Scadavay.

the south-west) rectangular in shape and perhaps the most modern, with interior measurements of 13½ by 11 feet, its walls 2 feet thick and still 30 inches high ; a doorway in its south-east corner clearly showing a width of 33 inches. Immediately to the north of this, at the highest part of the islet, are the remains of another building 12 feet in diameter with walls 30 inches thick ; while the centre of Eilean an Tighe (upon lower ground) has evidently been occupied by two adjoining circular erections of similar appearance, and towards its south-east are less distinct traces of still another small enclosure.

Considering its limited area, this island proved remarkably fruitful in relics of its former occupation. Fragments of pottery (nearly all of these showing patterns in great variety) were especially common around its edge, both above and below the present water-level ; while there were also found a well-polished and almost perfect miniature stone adze 2¼ inches in length, and half of a smoothly wrought stone axe. Hammer-stones included both the ordinary type and notably several of spherical shape measuring 3 to 4 inches in diameter ; while six flint scrapers are also to be noted, together with a dozen flaked portions of the same material.[1] Two small lumps of partially abraded pumice were found at this site.

A little to the south of Eilean an Tighe, and somewhat parallel therewith, extends a long jutting point marked *Àrd Reamhar* upon the Ordnance map—more strictly speaking, an island accessible by stepping-stones. From *Àrd Reamhar* a distinct pier or causeway runs northward for from 10 to 20 yards as if to join the south-east corner of Eilean an Tighe, although, even under the favouring circumstances of calm water, this could not be verified as a connecting link.

Half a mile down the east side of Geireann Mill Loch is a rocky peninsula[2] joined to the shore by a low sandy ridge 10 yards in length, which shows upon its surface the remains of a former causeway. Here can be traced the outline of a circular erection measuring about 24 feet in diameter over walls apparently 3 or 4 feet thick. At this site were found several fragments of unpatterned pottery and a single hammer-stone.

---

[1] Two of these closely resemble specimens in flint and chert recently received by the writer from a friend in Basutoland, there found in a 'donga' some fifteen feet below the adjacent surface.

[2] Although now a promontory, this showed as an island so recently as ten years ago, before the sluice near the old mill had been taken away, thus reducing the water-level by about two feet.

Upon a larger and very green island, near the centre of the loch, seem to be the foundations of an old building, but in this case no access by a causeway was traceable.

It is to be noted that the north end of Geireann Mill Loch lies within 200 yards of a sea-inlet which forms an almost land-locked branch of the Sound of Harris. The tide here recedes for a considerable distance, so as to leave a muddy strand containing a number of scattered rocks which become islands at high-water. One of these bears upon its flat summit, at an elevation of 6 or 8 feet, the foundations of a round or oval building with interior measurements of about 11 by 13 feet.

A mile to the north-east, facing the island of Oransay, is the peninsula of Clett, its summit perhaps once occupied by a fort, although the indications are too slight to justify more than this note in passing.

In Loch Aonghuis, less than a mile east of the now abandoned Geireann Mill and within about 100 yards from Ahmore Strand on the north, is DUN AONGHUIS or 'the fort of Angus,' occupying the whole • 81 area of the island upon which it stands. Of circular shape, this island measures about 34 yards in diameter over a fairly preserved wall which surrounds it close to the water's edge, showing both at east and west a present greatest height of 6 feet by a thickness of 7 feet 9 inches. On its north-west, Dun Aonghuis has been provided with a massive boat-entrance, gradually diminishing in width from 8 feet at its exterior to about 7 feet at the inner face of the enclosing wall which here reaches a thickness of 13 feet; this water-gate being further continued inwards for a distance of 15 feet between parallel walls 6½ feet apart, thus giving it a total length of 28 feet.

Upon its east side, Dun Aonghuis was approached from the nearest shore of the loch by a causeway 60 or 70 yards in length, now for the most part submerged but showing a width of about 11 feet at its island end. A few yards south of this point has been the landward entrance to the fort, through a doorway 44 inches wide, which tapers inwards and leads directly into the southmost[1] of three adjoining chambers, all somewhat rectangular in shape with rounded corners, and each having the island-wall as its east boundary.

[1] This measures about 13 feet 6 inches by 11 feet 9 inches, and contains a long thin slab set on edge near its west wall.

In the centre of Dun Aonghuis can be traced the foundations of what was evidently the principal building which it contained, a wall 4 feet in width here enclosing an interior of 38 feet north and south by 12 feet 9 inches east and west, entered near the north end of its east side through a doorway 27 inches wide. This erection has been sub-divided towards its south by a thick wall pierced by a narrow entrance of 16 inches. Near the island end of the causeway was found a small lump of pumice, and in the same locality a stray plant of the red-currant, like those which have been already noted as occurring in profusion at Loch Iosal an Duin.

Dun Aonghuis is said to have been occupied by Aonghas Fionn,[1] younger son of the Donald Herrach who was murdered in Dun Scolpaig about the year 1506. It would seem that this 'Angus the Fair' lived for a time in Skye, whence he came to North Uist in order to avenge his father's death upon 'Paul of the Thong,' the tool of his uncle Gilleasbuig Dubh. Whatever be the date of its original construction, this fort was not improbably used by Aonghas Fionn after the death of Gilleasbuig Dubh, which the writer would place *ca.* 1516 —certainly not earlier than the year 1510.

Upon the beach at the extreme northern point of Oransay, two miles north-west from Dun Aonghuis, is a jutting rock marked *Kelig*[2] on the Ordnance map, but locally known as *Dùnan Ruadh* or 'little red fort,' a place-name too significant to be passed without notice. An island at only the very highest tides, this rocky ledge bears no trace of any structural arrangement, unless indeed a few loose stones which rest upon its scanty covering of sand and grass may indicate the former presence of walls.

• 82   DUN NA MAIRBHE ('fort of stillness' or 'fort of the dead') stood upon a small tidal island close to the east side of Ahmore Strand at Trumisgarry. This islet practically consists of an elevated rock, and although tidal in a strict sense, its base lies well above the average high-water mark, never being separated from the shore on the north and east by more than a shallow ford of 15 or 20 yards.

The main fort is traceable as measuring about 62 feet in diameter over its walls, with an exterior rampart at an interval of 12 feet on

---

[1] Mackenzie's *History of the Macdonalds*, p. 255. See also under Dun Scolpaig, p. 193, *antea*.

[2] A name which is said to correctly apply to a skerry off Machair Robach, nearly a mile north-east from Oransay.

the east but approaching within 4 or 5 feet at the almost perpendicular west edge. This outer wall is clearly shown on the north-
west, but at the west has totally disappeared, so that its position can
only be inferred from the small available margin.

Adjoining the precipitous west side, and rising little above the
strand, is a flat semi-circular space also at one time protected by a
wall, perhaps as an annexe to the fort and communicating directly
with it by a steep path. The ordinary approach to Dun na Mairbhe
was evidently, however, up a gradual slope at the south-east.

Local tradition states that the name of this fort is derived from
the fact of a bloody battle having been fought there.

OBAN TRUMISGARRY, a small tidal loch 600 yards east of Trumis-   ● 83
garry Church and close to the road which leads to Newton and Port
nan Long, has contained an island-fort near its west end. This loch
is very shallow, and here, as also at Loch an Sticir, Loch an Duin
(Torcuill), and others of the same class, the ebb and flow are often so
slight as to be barely perceptible.

The islet measures about 40 feet in diameter, with an elevation
of from 3 to 4 feet above the water, and has had an access from the
northern shore of the loch over a causeway 30 yards in length. Towards the east side of this island lie a few very large stones, and it
would appear that the main structure was oval in shape, with exterior
dimensions of about 38 feet east and west by 30 feet north and
south.

Upon the bank at the shore end of the causeway is a small
circular mound, its surface now broken but still 6 feet in height and
evidently once occupied by a building which served in some association with the fort. To the north of the island, partly upon the shore
and partly within the loch, stand a dozen large stones set on end and
arranged in an arc, of which the concave side faces the islet towards
the south-east.

AN CAISTEAL stood close to the shore at Vallaquie, 600 yards   ● 84
north of Dun na Mairbhe and not far from an Earth-House which
has been already described. Its site is still pointed out upon the
summit of a small grassy point known as *Cnoc a' Chaisteil*, at the east
side of Vallaquie cattle-fold ; and although no traces of walls are
visible, some kitchen-midden shells and fragments of ancient pottery
have been recently disclosed at the mouths of rabbit-burrows.

Another and lower promontory, 200 yards to the west, is marked 'Site of Castle' upon the Ordnance map, but evidently in error, as this shows no sign of former occupation, consisting merely of rock covered by a scanty growth of turf.

● 85   DUN ROSAIL occupied the summit of a rocky hill a mile north from Oban Trumisgarry, and was no doubt of considerable importance, being certainly the most prominent and among the strongest in natural position of the few landward forts recorded in North Uist.

Unfortunately Dun Rosail is now so much dilapidated as to show little of its original arrangement apart from a mound of generally circular outline. In a gully below its steep south-west side are the ruins of several small buildings which may not improbably have been subsidiary annexes. Only a few bones and fragments of rude pottery could be observed at the fort itself, but near its south base were also found some kitchen-midden remains.

The name of Dun Rosail is probably to be derived from the Norse *hross-höll* or 'horse hill'; an explanation given by two independent authorities as representing *Rossal*[1] in Mull and *Rossol* in Lewis. In North Uist there occur the somewhat similar place-names, *Rosamol* at Balranald, and *Rosamul* at Illeray in Baleshare, perhaps signifying *hrossa-hólmr*, 'horse islet,' or *hrossa-múli*, 'horse-ridge.'

Dun Rosail is also locally known under the variant title of *Dùn Errachal*, although this form does not seem to be in common use.

● 86   CNOC A' CHAISTEIL, or 'hillock of the castle,' upon the island of Boreray about twenty yards from its south-west shore, seems to have been occupied by a promontory-fort of the simpler type so common throughout the western isles.

This site has evidently served as a quarry, with the result that no remains are traceable except the indistinct foundations of a wall apparently 4 feet thick, enclosing a somewhat circular space about 60 feet in diameter. Massive rock shows within its centre, slightly above the general surface.

---

[1] The *New Stat. Acc.*, Argyllshire, p. 306, quotes this Rossal as representing the Gaelic for 'judgment' or 'justice'; a translation which we have been unable to verify from the Scottish Gaelic, although O'Reilly's *Irish-English Dictionary* (Dublin, 1817) gives *rosal* as meaning 'judgment.'

ISLAND DUN IN OBAN TRUMISGARRY.

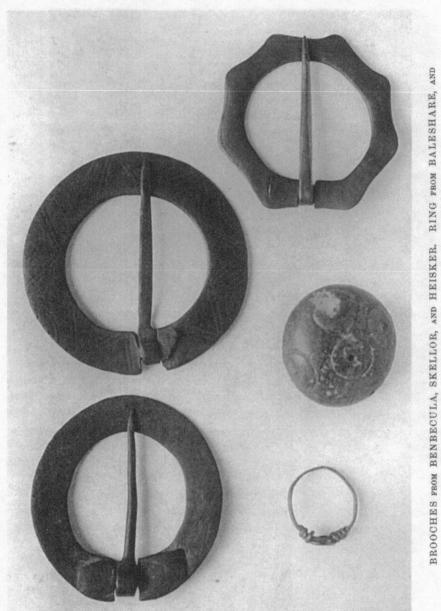

BROOCHES from BENBECULA, SKELLOR, and HEISKER. RING from BALESHARE, and ORNAMENTED BONE from MACHAIR LEATHANN. ACTUAL SIZE.

CHAPTER VII

SAND-HILL SITES

AT least twelve of this class (though few among them covering an area of any extent) are to be noted at the present day,—a qualification most necessary, since the blown sand-hills are subject to continual change; what was clearly visible half a century ago being perhaps now quite hidden by grass or bents, with all the possibilities of a reverse action taking effect fifty years hence, or long before that time. It is therefore impossible to deal with these mounds in any exhaustive or even definite manner, and we can only describe such as lay bare at a very recent period. In North Uist, these sites—nearly all of them showing indications of ancient dwellings—are confined to its west and north shores, the parts most open to the Atlantic and chiefly bordered by wide sandy 'machairs' interspersed with knolls, the surface being more or less overgrown with bent-grass.

Commencing—as with the forts—at the north-east corner of the main island, and thence proceeding sunwise, the first noticeable sand-hill is at RUDHA NA TRAGHAD, a shelving slope which faces southwards on the east side of Port nan Long. Here are disclosed various relics of human occupation, perhaps the earliest being represented by several small ruined Cists[1] evidently covering burnt burials; while close to these were found lumps of iron slag and red ashes, as if from a furnace.

Fragments of ancient pottery (some ornamented with lines) occurred in so great profusion as almost to suggest the locality as one where these semi-baked vessels had been manufactured. One rim (harder and containing less grit than usual) was decorated by a thin slip in the form of a slightly raised ring fully an inch in diameter, applied to the exterior (from which it afterwards fell apart), while there was also still visible the mark where another similar ring had

[1] Noted in Chapter VIII.

been attached. These ornamental rings were clearly supplementary, added when the vessel was otherwise complete.

We are informed that bone pins and bronze (or brass) brooches have occasionally been found at Rudha na Traghad, but, upon repeated visits at long intervals, none of these were observed, and only two pieces of flint. Part of a small clay crucible was found here, and fragments of iron are not uncommon, some of them apparently boat-rivets of Viking type.[1]

From Port nan Long to Baleshare Island is an abrupt transition— from the north-east to the south-west of North Uist—but it would seem that sand-hills have never existed at the more rugged east and south shores of the main island.

The southern half of Baleshare is known as *Eachkamish* and entirely consists of low sandy 'machair,' barren save for a few cultivated patches amid a scanty growth of bent. At the east side of Eachkamish, near its unnamed south point, is a small inlet which bears the local name of *Linne h-Earail*, with TOTA H-EARAIL[2] 300 yards to the north,—a sandy knoll showing traces of walls upon its summit, and also affording some kitchen-midden remains. Tradition states this to have been the home of a sea-faring man (presumably a pirate, Harald by name) who was accustomed to bring his vessel to anchor in the *linne* or pool, announcing his arrival by the discharge of a gun.

About midway on the west side of Baleshare is a group of sand-hills immediately above the shore. Perhaps the most interesting division lies at the north-west extremity of Eachkamish, 400 yards south-west from Teampull Chriosd and locally known as SLOC SABHAIDH or 'saw-pit.' Here is a series of distinct kitchen-middens containing ashes and shells of the periwinkle, limpet, and cockle, together with bones, some of these artificially shaped. A few hammer-stones were found, including several specimens in quartz, but as a rule much damaged by exposure. Pottery is scarce except in small fragments, upon which three simple patterns were noted. Bone pins have occasionally been found at this general site, one with a well-polished stem and squared head; while there are also to be recorded part of a small bone netting shuttle, and a thin bronze ring ornamented

[1] That is, with one head rounded, but the other squared or of lozenge-shape.
[2] Near Grenetote, ten miles to the north, is a rocky hillock marked *Cnoc Nic h-Earail* upon the Ordnance map.

with twisted wire, probably of the Viking time, not later than
A.D. 900–1000.

The southern portion of Sloc Sabhaidh was apparently devoted to
burials, of which notice is taken in Chapter VIII. Upon a small
separate knoll at the north lay several cut-marked bones of the
whale, as also a heavy and rudely fashioned saddle-quern. It is said
that some years ago two round flat stones with large holes through
their centres were here discovered. Above the beach was found a
cocoa-nut still retaining part of its husk, and we were told that
these are sometimes washed ashore in clusters as fallen from the trees.

At CEARDACH RUADH, or 'the red smithy,'[1] half a mile to the
north-west, is a second interesting site upon a lofty sand-mound
close to the sea. To judge from the quantity of slag and ashes still
remaining, this title seems well bestowed; but no special find was
made, apart from portions of an antler and three separate tines,
together with a few hammer-stones, broken flints, and fragments of
crude pottery. Here cists and bones are sometimes disclosed beneath
the blowing sands, and pins of bone and brass have been found.

Baleshare terminates at its extreme north-west in a very narrow
spit of sand, a mile in length and bearing the name of *Slugan*. As to
this promontory the writer cannot speak from personal examination,
but has been informed that it does not offer any interesting sites.

KIRKIBOST ISLAND may be mentioned in passing, on account of the
extensive sand-hills along its west margin, although in our experience
these proved wholly disappointing. Here are sometimes washed ashore
hollow and hermetically-sealed balls of green glass, about five inches
in diameter and understood to be floats from the nets of fishermen on
the Newfoundland banks. We have however seen one with the
name 'Aasnaes' moulded across its mouth, a fact clearly indicative
of Scandinavian origin.

Kirkibost Island now supplies most of the bent-grass locally used
for making horse-collars, mats, chairs, etc.

At PAIBLE, upon the large promontory north of Kirkibost Island,
are some broken sands to the south and west of Creag Hasten. This
latter is a group of curious rocks upon the top of a hillock, with the

---

[1] There is a *Geo na Ceàrdaich* on the north side of Vallay, and the place-name *Loch na
Ceàrdaich* occurs twice in North Uist,—to the east of Loch 'ic Colla and of Geireann Mill
Loch.

appearance—from a distance—of the ruins of an old castle. Very little of interest was to be noticed at this site.

In the HEISKER (or 'Monach') group, both Ceann Ear and Ceann Iar contain numerous sand-hills. Upon the writer's visit in July 1906, he found a kitchen-midden of shells and ashes near the north-west corner of Ceann Ear, close to a cist with human bones revealed by the shifting sands; and, towards the north-east of the same island, another large midden of limpet-shells. At Ceann Iar, where the surface is less broken, only two hammer-stones were observed. It seems certain, however, that this general site covers many relics of former inhabitation.

From a former resident on Heisker was acquired a copper brooch, measuring 2 inches across and of octagonal outer shape although circular within. This brooch, of late mediæval type, has its pin undamaged.

Heisker was until recently noted for its bent-grass, from which were fashioned various useful articles, including thick heavy baskets made expressly for the conveyance of grain to the mill.

BELLOCHBAN (Gaelic for 'white pass') lies near the shore immediately west from Loch Hosta, and consists of a range of grass-covered hillocks, many of these appearing as terraced plateaux. It is stated that not long since these sand-hills lay bare to a much greater extent than now, the turf having latterly obtained mastery. The best portion, as at present disclosed, is a scarped mound by the roadside with at least one kitchen-midden containing many shells and bones, together with fragments of ancient pottery,[1] some of them marked with patterns among which were distinguished six varieties of design. Other minor breaks show towards the north and west, but these yielded only a few hammer-stones and lumps of slag, with a single flint.

At Bellochban, within recent years, have been found several pieces of shaped bone about half an inch in diameter and apparently used as pivots; and of the same material, a netting shuttle, four pins, and a broken needle, as also a much decayed bone whorl with a diameter of two inches. In addition we figure a small vertebral segment

---

[1] It is noticeable that in the eastern half of this restricted site the remains consist chiefly of shells, ashes, and pottery, with very few bones; while, twenty yards to the west, bones are exceedingly numerous, with few shells and little or no pottery. Some of the bones show cut-marks, and others have been charred.

BELLOCHBAN, SHAPED BONES. ACTUAL SIZE.

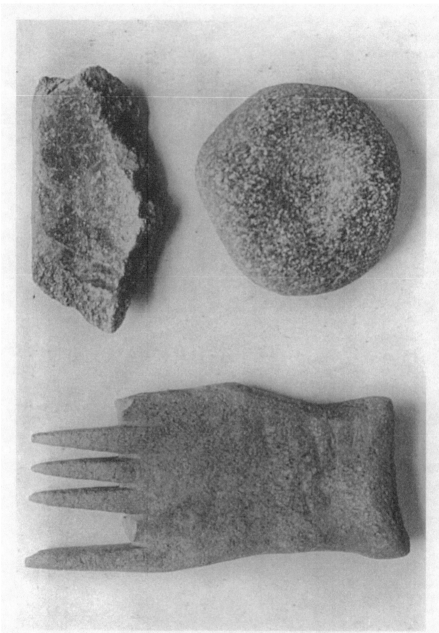

VALLAY CATTLEFOLD; BONE WEAVING-COMB, ETC.   ACTUAL SIZE.

(measuring 2 by 1¼ inches) shaped outside, and with flattened ends each pierced by a small round hole, while the interior has been hollowed into a smooth oval more than an inch long. Of very different character is a brass brooch in the form of a ribbon bow-knot, probably of late mediæval date.

Passing reference must here be made to SITHEAN MOR, an isolated sand-hillock close to the shore at Callernish. A description of this site is given in the next chapter when dealing with *Sithean* as a place-name in North Uist; although Sithean Mor itself, from another point of view, ought perhaps rather to be associated with pre-historic dwellings than with pagan burials.

On VALLAY ISLAND, near its south shore, is a large cattle-fold[1] where the drifting sand from time to time reveals slight traces of at least three ancient buildings together with more numerous layers of peat-ashes and kitchen-midden remains, including shells of the limpet and periwinkle as also bones of various animals, some of them cut-marked. This is practically the only bared expanse upon the island, and here have recently been found many relics which attest its occupation at a remote period.

From this site the best specimen in bone is a weaving-comb measuring about 4 by 2 inches and fashioned in the shape of a hand with six fingers, two of the latter unfortunately broken. Of the same material are six pins, three needles, and four borers; also some artificially pointed tines, and portions of several antlers, two of them bearing transverse cuts. A flat piece of bone, 3½ inches long, has been shaped to spatulate form and pierced by a small hole near one end. The bronze relics include a needle, the broken fastening of an ancient brooch, and two pins each nearly 4 inches long. One is plain with a conical ribbed top; the other being much more elaborate, its still complete perforated head enclosing a loose ring, three-quarters of an inch in diameter. The stem of this pin is decorated in front by fine lines and circles near its top, and, though rounded in the middle portion, is flattened towards both ends.[2] Several broken iron

---

[1] It was formerly the practice to remove turf from this fold to serve as top-dressing for neighbouring cultivated patches, but in recent years there is no appearance of the sand being again mastered by vegetation.

[2] In general form and ornament (though not in the attachment of its head) this pin bears a close resemblance to one from 'a burying ground' on Heisker, figured in *Proc. Soc. Antiq. Scot.*, vol. ii. p. 176. A small copper needle was also found in Vallay cattle-fold.

rivets (evidently of the Viking type) are to be noted, and also occasional lumps of slag.

Very few hammer-stones were found, these however including two specimens in white quartz, a rare material for this class, though similar examples were obtained at Baleshare and Udal as also else-where in North Uist. Other items are two stone whorls; a flat quartzite pebble, 2 inches in diameter, showing slight hollows at the centre of each face; a 2¾-inch disc of sandstone, ⅜ of an inch thick; and four fragments of steatite which must have formed part of at least two distinct vessels. Flint was represented only by two coarse nodules and a thin flake shaped as if for use upon a gun. Lumps of unwrought clay and many fragments of ancient pottery occur, two rudely incised patterns—one of large dots and the other of lines—being especially common some years ago, although now quite scarce. Other patterns had evidently been made by impression of the finger tip or nail, while a raised zig-zag was also noticeable.

Various other sites upon Vallay may here be noted, almost all of them within the middle portion of that island.

A slight elevation in the field immediately north of Vallay House is locally known as *Tota Dùnaig*,—'Dunag' being said to represent a woman's name, while 'Tota' signifies the 'roofless walls of a dwelling.'[1] At this place the surface—over an area of from 20 to 30 yards in diameter—is strewn with many shells of the limpet and periwinkle, in addition to a few bones and fragments of pottery. Tota Dunaig was partially excavated, with the result of disclosing the foundations of an ancient building, or more probably of two successive erections, one standing upon kitchen-midden débris attributable to a still earlier period. The structural remains are slight, their only special feature (apart from an adjoining oval cell, with a polished stone axe found close to its east side, as noted in Chapter VIII.) being a narrow recess within the west end, 5 feet in length by a greatest width of 16 inches diminishing to 11 inches at an interior doorway near the south-east corner. Excavation was not

---

[1] This site is here noted for convenience, although not strictly a sand-hill. According to local tradition, *Dùnag* was the daughter of a king of Norway and sister to *Tomi* whose name is associated with an island-fort in Vallay Sound. Within the neighbouring wall of this field, 20 yards to the west of Tota Dunaig, are several large stones with distinct marks of having been blasted, an appearance which agrees with the statement that the ruins of this pre-historic building were thus utilised.

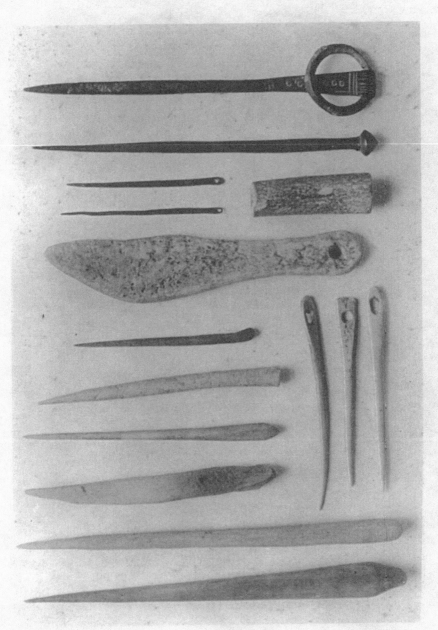

VALLAY CATTLEFOLD; PINS AND NEEDLES IN BRONZE AND BONE. ACTUAL SIZE.

VALLAY CATTLEFOLD; POTTERY.   ACTUAL SIZE.

carried beyond a depth of 2 or 3 feet, but here were found a quartz hammer-stone, several rims of pottery showing three distinct ornaments, fragments of two quern-stones, and part of a cetacean bone cut-marked at one of its ends.

In the field next adjoining on the west, are two large and shapeless boulders which locally bear the individual names of *Bochin* and *Bachin*,[1] although we could learn of no tradition or explanation.

To the east of the cup-marked rock in the same field, a few loose stones were found upon the surface, and slight excavation here revealed the foundations of an old dwelling and one hammer-stone lying near. Two hundred yards to the north, similar conditions led to the disclosure of a row of stones set on end, and a hearth covered by red ashes, together with two or three hammer-stones, several fragments of rude pottery, and part of a bone pin.

Cnoc Ailt, a hillock near the ferry to Griminish, has evidently been occupied, showing kitchen-remains of ashes and pottery.

On the north side of Vallay, at *Geo na Ceàrdaich*[2] midway between Traigh Himiligh and Traigh Hanivaig, occurs the place-name *Bùthag Lìr*,[3] said to represent 'the tent (or booth) of Lir.'

According to local tradition this refers to the temporary residence of a Norseman who was shipwrecked upon a neighbouring reef, himself escaping although his son and daughter were drowned and afterwards buried near this spot. Here, close to the shore, is a sand-heap about 3 feet high and 20 feet in diameter, surrounded by the ruins of a former walled enclosure, this also containing (towards its west end, and lying immediately above the beach) a megalithic slab which measures 11 feet 9 inches in length by a width of 53 inches and a thickness of 9 inches. A little to the west seem to be the remains of some old erection, where were found several flat pieces of much weathered sandstone, apparently brought from some far distant source, this rock being foreign to North Uist.

A hundred yards to the south is a more conspicuous mound between 3 and 4 feet in height and presenting some evidence of structural

---

[1] Also phonetically given as 'Bochal' and 'Bachal,' suggesting the Gaelic *buachaill* and *bachall*, or 'herdsman' and 'shepherd's crook.' Both stones have at some time been bored for blasting, although this operation was not carried into effect.

[2] 'Creek of the smithy.'

[3] Phonetically, this seemed to be 'Buag Lear.' *Liernish* is the name of a promontory at the south end of North Uist, although probably quite unrelated as to origin.

form. Upon partial excavation this proved to be another heap of sand, almost covered with loose stones and its outline indicated by the foundations of somewhat rectangular walls enclosing a space about 20 feet in length (north and south) by 16 feet in width. At each of its northern corners is a slab set on end, and close outside its north and south walls were found two hammer-stones well marked by use. Within the centre of this heap, 18 inches below its top, was disclosed a layer of fine black ashes in a thickness of 2 or 3 inches, and above this (towards the south) lay many fragments of slag, some adhering to stones and others to small portions of bone with which it had come in contact while in a molten state.

It was noticeable that, although the centre of this mound was tested to a depth of $5\frac{1}{2}$ feet (or 2 feet below the surrounding level) the whole consisted of pure sand, with the exception that in the very base lay a flat stone resting upon decomposed rock, while between these levels were slight traces of ashes, evidently filtered down from the upper stratum. On the west of this mound, exactly outside its walled edge and a foot below the surface, is a cist which contains a human skull and bones, representing an unburnt burial laid at full length, north and south.

Elsewhere upon Vallay, especially within half a mile west from the farm-steading, bone pins and fragments of ancient pottery bearing simple patterns are sometimes found. Five stone whorls may also be noted, with several pieces of flint and an occasional hammer-stone.

At SKELLOR, near Sollas and fully a mile east from Vallay, is another site of this class. Here the most prominent feature is an ancient graveyard upon the grassy summit of a sand-mound, now separated from the shore by an extensive 'machair' or plain, although it seems at one time to have been an island. This latter point is strongly suggested by the configuration of a long natural ridge or terrace which bounds the south side of the machair for nearly a mile east and west, evidently representing a former sea-beach when the present coast-line (that of Machair Leathann, bordering Traigh Iar) was under water, conditions of level which would also make islands of Ard a' Bhorain and Udal.

In the steep west edge of Skellor burying-ground is disclosed a thin but typical stratum of kitchen-midden débris, and here were

VALLAY; WHORLS AND SHAPED BONES. ACTUAL SIZE.

UDAL; BONE TALUS, NORTH-WEST SAND-HILL.

found fragments of rude pottery ornamented with various patterns. This layer shows at intervals for many yards to the north, while the talus is strewn with loose shells of the limpet and periwinkle, and just beyond its west base is a solid mass of those of the limpet almost exclusively.

Westwards from this graveyard, at the north base of the long natural terrace already described, were found three flints; a few hammer-stones; part of an antler; three bone pins; four short hollow segments of the same material, with flattened ends; and a rectangular piece of bone 2¼ inches long by three-eighths of an inch thick, its faces well squared and its ends cut off abruptly. Some iron rivets, evidently of the Viking time, were also noticed. To the east of Skellor graveyard no relics of interest could be observed.

Upon Machair Leathann, towards the north and north-west, are scattered numerous hillocks of sand, some of these disclosing kitchen-midden remains where the turf is broken,[1] ashes and limpet-shells predominating, together with some plain pottery. Perhaps the largest of these mounds is half a mile to the north-west, and here was seen at least one ancient hearth with bones, shells, the usual fragments of pottery, and several pieces of slag.[2]

UDAL is situated towards the outer end of the jutting point of which Ard a' Bhorain forms the northern extremity. It lies 2 miles north of Grenetote, and may be held to include an area of about half a mile in each direction, extending between Veilish and Oilish[3] from south to north, and in width traversing the peninsula from Traigh Iar to Traigh Ear. The entire promontory is held by the Grenetote crofters, who there find excellent pasturage for their cattle and also cultivate the sandy soil in numerous unenclosed patches of potatoes and grain.

That Udal formed a township in remote times can hardly be doubted. This is attested not only by tradition[4] but also by many traces of inhabitation even now apparent. Since the name does not occur in any of the old charters of North Uist, which are available from

---

[1] Since 1906, the hummocks immediately north of Skellor burying-ground have again been put under cultivation to some extent.
[2] Beneath was afterwards discovered a large Earth-House of peculiar type,—see pp. 121-128, antea.
[3] Upon the west side of Ard a' Bhorain, and both of them islands at spring-tides.
[4] See Chapter IV., under Hosta, for a traditional account of the burning of Udal.

early in the sixteenth century, the deduction naturally follows that its occupation antedates that period.

Here four extensive sand-hills, ranging from about 15 to 30 feet in height, form as it were the corners of a square, the east and west pairs separated by a narrow strip of arable soil, while the individual mounds lying towards the south-west and north-east are much the largest.

In the steep sides of each hillock are to be found slight ruined walls, usually more than half-way up from the base. These are apparently the remains of ancient structures, including three Earth-Houses already noted as such in Chapter v., two upon the mound to the south-west and one on that to the north-east. In connection with the two smaller sand-hills, traces of buildings are least distinct; but upon both of the larger mounds, in addition to the curved walls already noted, others exist which are straight, having evidently formed part of somewhat rectangular structures. There is especially to be noted a portion of wall about 15 feet up the north face of the south-west hillock, showing in eight courses of thin flat stones to a height of 3 feet. Again, on the west slope of the other large mound (that situated to the north-east) is part of a similar wall but consisting of larger stones.[1]

Where a stratum of kitchen-midden appears in the scarped edge, —this occurring at several points in each mound,—it usually lies at least 6 or 9 feet below the present summit. One such layer (on the south-west sand-hill) could be traced into the crevices of the wall distinctly above its base, thus sufficiently proving that (here at least) the wall existed before the refuse was deposited. The talus of each sand-hill shows a large intermixture of shells of the periwinkle and limpet. In some parts would also appear an undisturbed stratum of the former alone, and again, not far from the same spot, a separate layer of limpet-shells under similar conditions; while upon the north-west mound, bones of animals—these generally split—outnumbered the shells, almost covering the sand. Cockle-shells occur in occasional groups, but the mussel, oyster, and clam are quite rare.

Near the base of one mound were observed a human toe-bone and part of a skull, while elsewhere an almost complete and very massive

---

[1] At the west base of this sand-hill are to be seen the foundations of two other small rectangular erections.

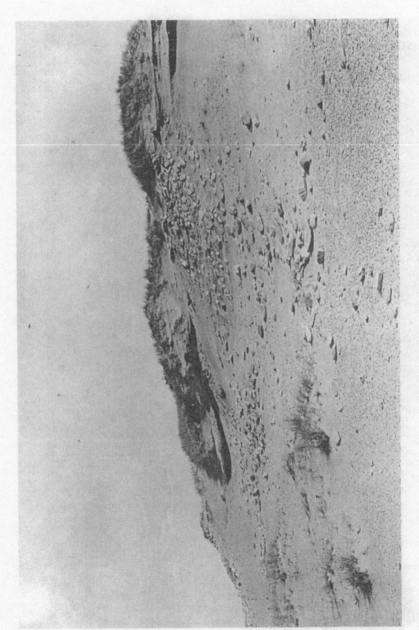

UDAL; NORTH-EAST SAND-HILL.

UDAL; SHELL TALUS, NORTH-EAST SAND-HILL.

UDAL; SOUTH-WEST SAND-HILL.

UDAL; KITCHEN-MIDDEN, SOUTH-EAST SAND-HILL.

skull was revealed, measuring three-eighths of an inch in thickness at its posterior base.

Fragments of rude pottery are often found, and yet the surface conditions so greatly vary that sometimes even these are scarce. No unbroken 'craggan' could be obtained, although the remains of what seemed to have formed two complete vessels were found crushed under an overlying mass of sand. The entire rim of another plain jar was pieced together, showing a diameter of 4 inches across its mouth. Specimens of patterned pottery are frequently disclosed in a variety of simple designs, these including rims with various arrangements of dots and short lines upon their upper edges, while another vessel shows the marks of finger tips set in like position. Incised lines and dots also appear upon lateral fragments, and part of a flat handle (fully an inch wide and nearly as thick) has a lozenge pattern on three of its sides. Two fragments are perforated by holes beneath their rims, evidently to allow the vessels to be suspended. In raised patterns were found a large zig-zag and a straight band. The narrow and very regularly shaped neck of a jar of grey smooth-surfaced material—quite different from any other specimen noted in North Uist — may probably be classed as late mediæval.

At this site artificially shaped bones are not uncommon, chiefly in the form of pins, although two needles and part of a netting shuttle were also obtained. By far the finest specimen in bone is a strong flat pin, $3\frac{3}{4}$ inches long by a width of half an inch at its rounded head, and tapering gradually to a sharp point. This is ornamented by five groups of parallel lines incised across its face, and is pierced through the head by a small hole. Of the same material, many rough fragments were found bearing deep transverse cut-marks, and several portions of horn, either similarly treated or showing upon their ends clear signs of much use, evidently as borers or perhaps in some cases as pivots. Remains of the deer are somewhat plentiful, these including tines, and the base of an antler carefully sawn across at three different angles; and the whale (or other large cetacean) is represented by several pieces of bone showing cuts from some sharp tool.

Hammer-stones are by no means numerous, but amongst them were noted a few in quartz, usually much weathered or even broken through the middle. Flint is decidedly scarce, and the writer can only record four fragments.

Other finds included lumps of slag; a single piece of pumice; some iron rivets (mostly imperfect, but apparently of Viking type); a thin whorl of sandstone; as also wood-charcoal and burnt bones, together with charred grain. Part of a vessel in steatite was obtained, and we are told that many such have been found at Udal. Although of comparatively modern date, notice may also be taken of an octagonal brass button with a circular pattern etched and gilt around its margin, the angles containing trefoils separated by groups of short curved lines.

Practically all the finer specimens from Udal were acquired from the neigbouring crofters, who recognise this site as fruitful in such relics.

To the west of Udal, in the steep north edge of Oilish, a little above high-water mark, is visible part of a rude wall in four courses, with a deposit of kitchen-midden shells outside its base.

ARD A' BHORAIN is the name of the outer portion of the long promontory upon which Udal is situated, and about half a mile to its north-east. Immediately south of Ard a' Bhorain proper, the main point is traversed by a narrow gully running approximately east and west, which tradition states to have been a ford at some remote period. We were further assured by an old inhabitant that even within living memory this hollow has been filled by the sea, although only at rare intervals and by abnormally high tides.

Here a rough cart-track leads outwards to an old burying-ground on the east edge of Ard a' Bhorain. This roadway passes between minor sand-hills, and at both of its sides are disclosed scanty kitchen-midden remains, including ancient pottery together with shells and bones. A single flint is also to be noted.

Among the sand-hills at the east side of the largest ORANSAY in North Uist,—a tidal island lying west of Vallaquie,—was found, ca. 1865-1870, a small hoard of gold ingots and finger-rings, the latter of a twisted pattern on one side, the other portion being plain.

In Dr. Joseph Anderson's *Scotland in Pagan Times: The Iron Age*, p. 107, are figured specimens of plain and plaited gold rings ' found somewhere in the Hebrides ' and now preserved in the National Museum of Antiquities, Edinburgh. It would seem very probable that these are from Oransay, but in any case certain that they are of similar type. The gold rings from this particular hoard include one plain solid and six plaited; the solid ring being penannular, while of

UDAL; POTTERY.   ACTUAL SIZE.

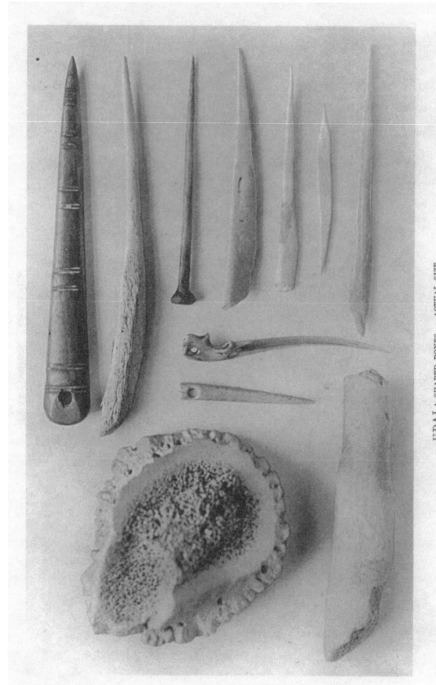

UDAL; SHAPED BONES. ACTUAL SIZE.

UDAL; SANDSTONE WHORL, ETC.   ACTUAL SIZE.

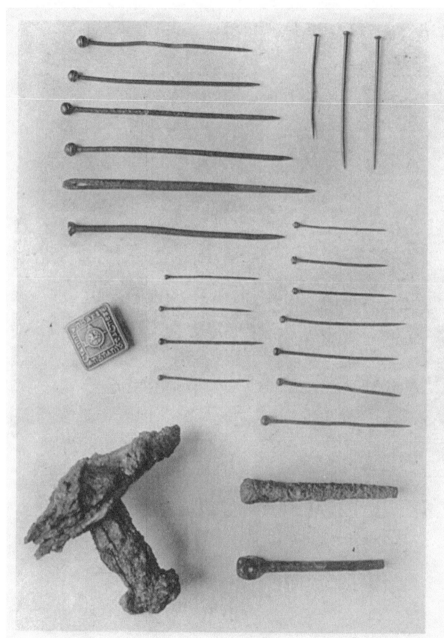

BORERAY; BRONZE AND BRASS PINS, ETC.   ACTUAL SIZE.

the plaited rings two are formed 'of three wires each, intertwisted, and the ends soldered together.' The other four are slightly larger and composed of eight wires, but finished by the hammer alone.

This site is not extensive, being also now so much covered with bents that no special characteristics are visible.

Near AN CORRAN, at the south-east corner of Boreray, is a stretch of broken sand-hills, 400 yards in length and situated well above the shore. The general character of this site is fully vouched by traces of five or six old dwellings, together with kitchen-midden remains in the form of shells, bones, and fragments of ancient pottery. Apart from these, two visits revealed little of special interest except a much corroded bronze pin, a few iron rivets (several of them distinctly of the Viking type), and a solitary flint with a semi-circular recess in one edge, probably a gun-flint.

It is said that many bronze pins were formerly found here, and of these we succeeded in purchasing a few specimens, but only two of earlier than mediæval type. One has a length of $2\frac{1}{4}$ inches, with a flat rounded head slightly ornamented by dots; while the other is only $1\frac{1}{2}$ inches long, consisting of a thick stem and polygonal head, the latter with dots in the centres of eight of its thirteen facets. Of more recent date were small pins of bronze or brass wire, some with heads formed by knobs and others by wire rolled around. We have also to note a large brass needle, a brass ring with embossed ornament, and a button of white metal lettered 'Clann nan gael.'

CHAPTER VIII

PAGAN MONUMENTS AND BURIALS

In any attempt to classify the various types of pre-historic burial which are known to exist in Scotland, it seems impossible to do otherwise than follow Dr. Joseph Anderson.[1] Premising that no traces of palæolithic man in North Britain have yet been substantiated, a brief summary of Dr. Anderson's conclusions would place the sequence somewhat as undernoted.

Neolithic Period. Burials in Chambered Cairns, the chambers being completely structural, with passages leading into them, and the whole covered by large mounds of stones. Some of these are 'Long Cairns,' although more commonly they approach a circular shape. The earlier burials are unburnt, while the later are cremated and the ashes accompanied by urns rounded at the base. Among the 'grave-goods' no object in metal is found, the material being limited to bone or stone, flint prevailing. These chambers were apparently used for many successive interments, and contain, in addition to human remains, bones of the common domestic animals, presumably the refuse of funeral feasts.

Bronze Age. (a) Burials associated with Megalithic Circles or separate monoliths; occasionally unburnt, but generally after cremation and accompanied by flat-bottomed urns. (b) Cairns, covering cists instead of chambers with passages. (c) Cists, formed by five (or more) stone slabs: either unburnt but contracted, the skeleton lying crouched upon one side; or cremated, and accompanied by urns. In the Later Bronze to Early Iron Ages, the cist is occasionally covered by a small cairn, but more often merely set in the ground. Throughout the Bronze Age, the implements or ornaments deposited with the burial are either of bronze or well-worked stone, such as flint arrow-heads. Gold ornaments sometimes occur, while amber beads

---

[1] The Rhind Lectures in Archæology for 1881-1882 ; *Scotland in Pagan Times*, Edinburgh, 1883-1886.

and necklaces of jet are not uncommon, although none of these can be chronicled from North Uist.

EARLY IRON AGE. Full length burials, unburnt, but of this class few have been identified.

The later period of the Iron Age is best known, as regards Scotland, in the burials of the Viking time, which have special features peculiar to themselves. These interments are either cremated or uncremated, and with them occur the iron rivets of boats, iron swords, shield bosses, and implements, as also ornaments in bronze, silver, and gold. During the Bronze and Iron Ages alike, the burials are generally characterised as being separate or individual, or at most in pairs. They often however closely adjoin others of their own type, so as to form family or tribal cemeteries.

MEGALITHIC BURIALS.

Under this heading we first take up the Chambered Cairns or 'Barps' in North Uist; and here, although involving a digression at some length, it becomes necessary to discuss the meaning and application of this word *Barpa*, a term which seems peculiar to the Outer Hebrides and Skye. Treating it as Gaelic, the dictionary translation is sufficiently expressive,—'A conical heap of stones, supposed to be memorials of the dead. Sometimes called *Barrows*.'[1] But, judging from its so locally restricted use, *Barpa* is evidently not of true Gaelic origin, being rather a loan-word from the Norse,[2] although the Barps are attributable to the Neolithic Age, having been erected long before the era of Scandinavian supremacy in the Hebrides. It would thus appear to be a name given by the Vikings to monuments which had already existed for many centuries. Little has been written regarding the Barps, but the name is evidently a Hebridean synonym for the Anglo-Saxon *beorg* or 'barrow, a mound raised over graves,' in this case a heap of stones; and it can hardly be doubted that *barpa* and *beorg* are attributable to a common origin. One thing is certain, that,

[1] MacLeod and Dewar's *Gaelic Dictionary*, 1893, p. 57. MacBain's *Dictionary* (1896, p. 26) gives 'barrow, cairn (H. S. D., a Skye word),' this local association being correct to a limited extent.

[2] Cleasby and Vigfusson's *Icelandic Dictionary*, 1874, p. 681, has '*varp*, a casting, throwing,' and '*varpa*, to throw, cast'; also, p. 698, '*verpa*, . . . to cast up a cairn or the like,' with five quotations from the Sagas. *Verpa* is here associated with the Anglo-Saxon *weorpan*, the English 'warp,' and the German *werfen*.

in all cases where they have been sufficiently examined, the Barps declare themselves as chambered cairns of a massive type,[1]—the most remarkable as also perhaps the most ancient of the burial-sites now to be observed throughout the Long Island from Lewis to Barra.

Lewis contains at least one Barp, situated about two miles northwest from Gress and near Loch a' Chairn. Martin[2] notes this as *Cairn-warp*, which is shown by Captain Thomas[3] to be an obvious pleonasm. The same writer quotes its name from the Ordnance map as Carn a Mhare, 'but it should be Carn a Bhairce (pro. " Vark-e "). . . . So completely is the meaning of this word forgotten in Lewis (although in common use in Uist) that Barp or Barc has been transformed into a son of the King of Lochlinn, who was killed on that spot while on a hunting expedition, and was buried there, hence called Carn Bharce Mhic Righ Lochlinn.'[4]

In North Uist there are only four Barps which bear that local designation,—two of them, near Maari and Loch Caravat, being ' Long Cairns,' while Langass Barp is of distinctly circular form, and the fourth at Knock-Cuien has been almost entirely removed. It must be added, however, that another large cairn upon the southern slope of Marrogh equally deserves this title, bearing much resemblance to Langass Barp, although known simply as a *Tigh Cloiche*, the Gaelic for 'stone-house.' All five (except Hacklett Barp at Knock-Cuien) remain in comparatively good preservation, so as to indicate their original features, and North Uist also contains at least eight other

---

[1] The old *Statistical Account*, vol. xiii. p. 320, says of the Barps :—'What makes these any way remarkable, is their great size, and their distance from any place where stones could be found. Some of the stones are so large, that it is inconceivable by what mode of conveyance they were carried up hill to the ground where they lie. They seem to be the tumuli of leaders of great influence, who have signalized themselves by their valour or accomplishments.'

The *New Statistical Account*, Inverness-shire, pp. 169-170, hardly betters the above description :— ' They are called *barps*, a word evidently not of Celtic origin. It may probably have been derived from barrow, a heap or mound. Be this as it may, the uses for which these immense piles were, with Herculean labour, put together, are unfortunately unknown ; and, in the absence of all authentic record and tradition, conjecture, at best uncertain, is all that can be substituted. Some, from their formation, suppose them to have been Druidical circles or Temples. Some, that they were towers forming places of defence and protection at a very early period, against the incursions of enemies, while they likewise served the purpose of beacons to give warning to the inhabitants of the approach of danger. . . . It is, however, more probable that they were the tumuli of eminent warriors.'

[2] *A Description*, etc., p. 8.

[3] *Archæologia Scotica*, vol. v. p. 377.

[4] The *New Statistical Account*, Inverness-shire, p. 170, mentions one 'above Roudh in Harris,' but this is a fort, and we have been unable to hear of any Barp in Harris. A fort on the west slope of Beinn na Coille in North Uist was locally described as a Barp ; and to further help matters, is marked 'tumulus' upon the Ordnance map.

sites which are recognisable as dilapidated Chambered Cairns, making a total of thirteen. Most of these are in somewhat elevated positions, although two—near the east base of Craonaval—are less prominently placed.

South Uist[1] has four Barps, situated at Lochboisdale, Frobost, Kildonan, and Howmore ; and near the centre of Barra the Ordnance map shows *Dùn Bharpa*.[2]

Near the head of Loch Caroy, in the parish of Duirinish, Skye, are two tumuli locally known as 'the *Barpunan*.'[3]

Dr. R. Angus Smith[4] figures and describes two large sepulchral cairns in Argyllshire, which, if in the Long Island, might fitly have been termed Barps. These stand near the shore of Loch Etive, and are known as Carn a' Bharan and Carn Ban (Achnacree). Carn Ban was excavated and found to contain a chamber of three compartments, in two of which were ancient urns with round bases, and pebbles of white quartz.

Apart from the Long Island, and the not very remote Loch Etive and the island of Arran,[5] perhaps the burial-cairns which come nearest to the Hebridean 'Barp' are two (of a group of four) near Skelpick in Sutherland ;[6] while at Fiscary (a few miles to the north, and in the same parish of Farr) the writer noted four others which struck him as being smaller examples of the same type. These are all shown upon the Ordnance map as 'tumuli.'

It is evident, indeed, that the Barp (and equally, the *Tigh Cloiche*) is closely related to (1) the English 'Long Barrow' of Yorkshire, Wiltshire, Gloucestershire, and Somerset ; (2) the 'Horned Cairn' of Caithness ; and (3) the normal Chambered Cairn which is to be found in Orkney, Caithness, Sutherland, Argyllshire, and elsewhere in Scotland.

The Barp has affinities with all three—in possessing a structural chamber—but most closely with the ordinary chambered cairn from

---

[1] In South Uist it is still remembered that there was a custom of walking three times sunwise round a Barp on Sunday ; see also Martin's *A Description, etc.*, p. 85.

[2] Noted in the *New Statistical Account*, Inverness-shire, p. 170, as a Barp 'but of less magnitude.'

[3] *Ibid.*, p. 335.

[4] *Loch Etive and the Sons of Uisneach*, edn. of 1885, pp. 57-58 and 216-227.

[5] Dr. Thomas H. Bryce, in two important papers contributed to the Scottish Society of Antiquaries, (*Proc. Soc. Antiq. Scot.*, vols. xxxvi. and xxxvii.), describes somewhat similar chambered cairns in Arran.

[6] Dr. Joseph Anderson's *Scotland in Pagan Times : The Bronze and Stone Ages*, pp. 260-263.

which it is little differentiated unless by its massive capstones and
larger general dimensions.[1] If really a separate type, it is perhaps
even more completely structural, being marked as to its outer
boundaries by large stone slabs placed on end at intervals, in this
respect approaching the Horned Cairn, which is also quite as large.

In fine, the Barp is a massive Chambered Cairn, and as such
attributable to the Neolithic Age. How many thousands of years
this takes us back, is a question not easily answered.

It would further seem that the Chambered Cairn was superseded :
first, by a smaller cairn (of somewhat similar character) within a
megalithic circle;[2] *secondly*, by the megalithic circle with no interior
cairn ; and *thirdly*, in the later Bronze Age degenerating into a simple
cist, either covered by a cairn or merely set in the ground without
any lasting outward indication or memorial.

Having thus to some extent discussed the general subject of Barps,
it now remains to describe those of North Uist in particular, premising
however that, surrounded as they are by grass or heather, it is most
remarkable to find little or no encroachment of herbage upon them,
the line of demarcation being more or less abrupt in all the seven or
eight better-preserved Barps which the writer has closely examined
in North and South Uist.   We now take up in detail the four Sepulchral Cairns in North Uist to which the title of Barp is locally attached,
and, after them, the other Chambered Cairns which are more or less
of the same character and have equally deserved the name, although
all except one (at Marrogh) have been greatly denuded of their
covering piles.

And first ; the two Barps which are ' Long Cairns,' in this respect
differing from all of those known under that title in North and South
Uist, as also from the isolated examples in Lewis and Barra, of which
the writer cannot speak from personal examination.

BARPA NAM FEANNAG (or ' cairn of the hooded-crows ') is situated
towards the northern extremity of North Uist upon a rocky hillock
in Bogach Maari, 400 yards east from Geireann Mill Loch.   This
Barp shows as a long irregular mound of loose stones lying approximately east and west, 160 feet in length by 47 feet in width   near   its

---

[1] The cairns of Caithness and Sutherland usually have their chambers divided into two or
three compartments, as against the normal and larger single chamber of North Uist.
[2] As at Clava, Inverness-shire ; *Scotland in Pagan Times : The Bronze and Stone Ages*, pp.
300-302.

BARPA NAM FEANNAG, FROM WEST.

BARPA NAM FEANNAG, ENTRANCE, FROM SOUTH-EAST

CARAVAT BARP, FROM EAST.

CARAVAT BARP, NORTH EDGE.

east end, though narrowing to 15 feet at the west. It is both widest and highest on the east, there reaching an elevation of 8 or 10 feet, while the other end does not exceed 2 feet in height above the adjacent surface level.

Barpa nam Feannag is specially noticeable as being pitted by many slight hollows, perhaps merely due to the displacement of stones, although these cavities are so numerous and so regular in size and shape as to suggest the possibility of their having been structural. No chamber is disclosed, but from analogy with the other large cairns of North Uist (whether known under the title of Barp or *Tigh Cloiche*) it seems certain that one existed within the massive east end. Here, covered by a large flat stone at the exterior base, is a rectangular opening which evidently formed part of the original entrance passage; while, at a short distance within the ruined cairn, another large slab (7½ feet long) stands upon edge, having no doubt served either as one side of the passage or as part of the chamber itself.

In any case this is obviously a sepulchral cairn of the neolithic period. Considering the fairly preserved outline of Barpa nam Feannag, it is the more remarkable that none of the upright boundary slabs could be noted which elsewhere seem characteristic of this general type.

Near the south end of North Uist, between Loch Caravat and the ford to Grimsay, is another very similar cairn, here for convenience named CARAVAT BARP. This is greatly dilapidated, especially towards its east end, where the cairn has been used for the erection of several shielings, in addition to having served throughout many years as a quarry for the neighbouring crofters. Caravat Barp measures 180 feet in length by a width which tapers from 50 feet on the east to 14 feet at the west, this latter portion still standing to a height of about 10 feet. No trace of any entrance passage could be found, but there are slight indications of a chamber towards the east, and some evidence of structural form is also apparent on the north edge, where five slabs remain in erect position at intervals in regular line.

As already stated, the writer is unaware of the existence of any but these two Barps of the 'Long Cairn' class, all the others examined being either rudely circular in form or so much destroyed as not to preserve their original outline.

Of the circular and apparently normal type, by far the best specimen is LANGASS BARP, situated in the central portion of North Uist about five miles south-west from Lochmaddy, upon a slope immediately south of the road which there crosses the island. This Barp measures about 72 feet in diameter by 18 feet in height. Upon its summit are two small oblong erections which however must be regarded as blemishes added in recent times. At irregular intervals in the outer edge of this cairn, stand thirteen large slabs, most of them showing at its north base.

Langass Barp is clearly recognisable as a chambered cairn of massive type, both the inner half of its entrance passage and a complete megalithic chamber being already revealed, while by the removal of a heap of fallen stones the outer portion of its access could no doubt also be traced. This entrance is from the east side and at equal level with that of the surrounding moor, thence leading straight into the doorway of a large chamber, a total distance of 22 feet. For 16 feet from its outer entrance the passage has been low-roofed, apparently not exceeding 39 inches in height by a width of 32 inches, these measurements still showing in a cleared portion, which seems also to have been paved with small stones. The shorter second division of the passage (barely 6 feet in length) still has its covering slab in original position, measuring 56 inches square by 7 inches thick, beneath which is a roof-height commencing at 49 inches (an abrupt rise of 10 inches as compared with that of the outer division of the passage) and thence gradually increasing to 6 feet at the point where it joins the chamber through its inner doorway. The south wall of this part of the passage consists of one very tall and wide slab set on edge, while the north side, being composed of smaller stones, presents a much less perfect condition.

The doorway into the megalithic chamber varies in width from 18 inches at its base to 26 inches above, its south side being formed by one of the chamber slabs and its north by a pillar-stone of somewhat triangular shape with a girth of 38 inches. Here the chamber is entered by its south-east corner and presents an impressive sight, the structure remaining practically complete as when originally erected. In dimensions it extends $9\frac{1}{2}$ feet east and west by 6 feet north and south, the roof sloping upwards from 6 feet at the narrow entrance to 7 feet 6 inches in the north-west corner. Its sides consist of

LANGASS BARP, from south-east.

LANGASS BARP, INTERIOR OF CHAMBER.

six massive slabs set on edge, the largest (at the west end of the north wall) measuring 5 feet 6 inches wide by at least 7 feet 6 inches in height above the original floor. The side slabs do not everywhere quite join each other, nor even do they in all cases meet the roof, the four larger gaps thus left (two in the west wall, one at the south, and another in the north-east corner) being filled with small flat stones carefully built upon their faces and evidently forming part of the original construction.

The roof consists of two immense slabs,[1] 10 to 12 inches thick, with a third superimposed so as to overlap a vacancy, about a foot wide, left between the first pair.

The floor has been partially cleared next the south and west ends, but upon more than half its area there still lies a heap of moist dark soil mixed with ashes and some small loose stones, to a maximum depth of about 2 feet. It is evident that here have been deposited many burnt burials, since thoroughly intermingled and also to some extent dispersed. Upon the surface of the cairn, immediately north of the entrance passage, recently lay a heap of débris removed from the interior, and in this were found several fragments of thin pottery—three of them patterned in lines—belonging apparently to at least three distinct urns, some wood-ashes, burnt bones, a barbed flint arrowhead (clearly showing signs of its subjection to fire), as also a scraper and five other flaked fragments of the same material, together with a curious piece of talc neatly chipped to circular shape, measuring $1\frac{1}{4}$ inches in diameter and pierced by two holes close together near one of its edges.

We have been assured upon the best authority that Langass Barp contains a second chamber with its separate access from the north side, our informant having entered this within the past thirty years;[2] while it is also stated that even a third chamber exists. Upon this subject we can add little, except that the east chamber already disclosed occupies but a small proportion of the whole structure, ample

[1] Their length and width are not measurable unless by removing the loose stones which form the summit of the cairn; although we find it definitely stated of Langass Barp in *Sailing Directions for the West Coast of Scotland*, London, 1885, p. 7, that 'The entire monument has a cyclopean look, and the roof-stone, which covers one-half of the sepulchral chamber, is $10\frac{1}{4}$ feet long by 7 feet broad.'

[2] A second eye-witness entirely confirms this statement, he having also entered the passage though not the chamber. According to this friend, the only entrance into the Barp shown at that time (about thirty years ago) was from its north side.

space remaining for at least two others. Repeated examination of the exterior would suggest that, if other chambers are yet to be found, these probably lie towards the south-west and mid-north sides of the cairn, where slight traces of additional entrance passages may at least be imagined, although admittedly no real proof, whether positive or negative, can be forthcoming unless by means of considerable excavation.

The amount of labour imposed by the erection of so massive a pile as Langass Barp must necessarily have been enormous, and such as could only be justified by a very rare and notable occasion. No doubt its purpose was to commemorate the death of some great chief, for whom it would serve alike as tomb and monument, afterwards probably forming the burial-place of his immediate descendants.

At Knock-Cuien, a mile east from Caravat Barp and a little to the south-west of *Loch nan Garbh Chlachan* of the Ordnance map (but locally known as *Loch Hacklett*) are the scanty ruins of BARP HACKLETT, the fourth[1] and last of the chambered cairns in North Uist to which the name of Barp is applied. So little remains of this erection that it can merely be described as an irregular mound, not over 6 to 9 feet in present height, with a suggested diameter of about 70 feet, taking its boundary as marked by some stones set on end at intervals, presumably in the edge of the original cairn, as in other cases. Many stones lie around, but no large slabs are visible, the site being thus certified by tradition alone.

In 1903 the nearest crofter built a cottage with stones from this ruined Barp, and two years later we were told that he had been seriously troubled during the winter nights by loud noises, understood to be caused by the offended original 'inhabitants' of the Barp itself, amongst them 'the first Druid who lived in the Hebrides'! Should these noises continue, it was the crofter's expressed intention to pull down his cottage and rebuild it with materials from a different source.[2]

Upon the southern slope of MARROGH (and situated 2½ miles north from Langass Barp, to which it bears a close resemblance)

[1] Still another Barp was doubtfully reported as in the Portain district on the north side of Lochmaddy Bay. Upon examination, this was found to consist merely of an irregular heap of stones at the east base of a cliff about midway between Camas Crubaig and Loch Grota. A few large stones seem to have been artificially placed, but this site is more probably that of a cist than of a chambered cairn.

[2] At a more recent visit we observed that the foundations of a new and larger cottage had been laid, although perhaps for reasons quite apart from the story above quoted.

LANGASS BARP; FLINTS, POTTERY, AND DISC OF TALC. ACTUAL SIZE.

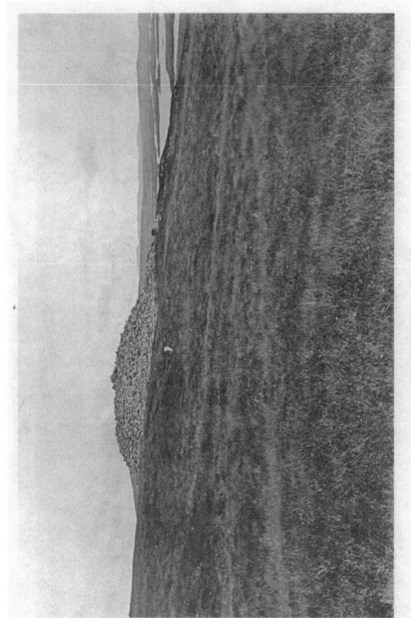

MARROGH BARP, FROM WEST.

MARROGH BARP, ENTRANCE, FROM SOUTH-EAST.

CHAMBERED CAIRN, AIRIDH NAN SEILICHEAG.

is another chambered cairn locally known under the name of *Tigh Cloiche* or 'stone-house,' although clearly deserving the title of Barp. This measures 60 feet in diameter, with a greatest height of about 16 feet, and a long entrance passage is traceable at the south-east as 31 inches wide and apparently 19 feet in length, nearly filled with small stones but still showing a roof-slab in original position. The floor of the main chamber stands about 6 feet above the natural level at the outer base, the passage thence gradually rising and evidently following the surface of the mound upon which the cairn was built. In shape this chamber is circular rather than square, with an irregular diameter of about 8½ feet. One of its two covering slabs remains in position near the present summit of the cairn, the other being slightly displaced. These stones measure respectively

8 feet 9 inches by 5 feet 6 inches, and

9 feet 7 inches by 5 feet 9 inches,

each with a greatest thickness of 15 inches, although averaging about 12 inches.

This chamber has evidently been ransacked, and only a fragment of wood-charcoal could be found. The base of the cairn is lined at intervals round its margin by ten large stones on edge, and some 200 yards to the west is an isolated standing-stone. Outside the base, especially on the east, are the ruins of numerous shielings, obviously constructed from the stones of this Barp. Here is a luxuriant growth of the foxglove, a plant not common in North Uist, although occurring upon several ancient sites at widely separated intervals.

Half a mile south of Marrogh, near the west extremity of Loch Scadavay, is a large green hillock known as AIRIDH NAN SEILICHEAG (literally 'shieling of the snails'). This undoubtedly represents another chambered cairn, although much ruined for the construction of shielings, five or six of these showing upon its summit and western slope. The whole mound is thinly covered with turf, an exceptional condition as regards the Barps in general.

The axis of this cairn lies from north-west to south-east, and has a total length of fully 30 yards, natural rock outcropping at the south base. Upon its north-west slope are scattered at least twenty conspicuous slabs, while, nearer the north end, portions of two separate megalithic chambers still remain. That these evidently formed part of more than one chamber is attested by the fact that the whole space thus occupied (in a length of 17 feet) varies in width from 4 feet at the north end to almost 9 feet at the south, besides which the floor level of these extremities appears to have differed to the extent of at least 3 feet—circumstances hardly applicable to a single chamber, however irregular might be its shape.

Under the above conditions, the northern and smaller chamber had a width of only 4 feet. Here two pillar-stones still support a pair of covering slabs in almost original position, while a third large slab, measuring 8 feet 6 inches long by 5 feet wide, has been completely dislodged so as to slant upwards and rest against the south end of this chamber.

At a somewhat higher level, and 2 or 3 yards farther south, is a separate group of four erect pillar-stones enclosing a still larger but fallen slab, which measures in length 9 feet 5 inches by a width of 4 feet 9 inches, with a thickness of about 14 inches. This evidently represents another chamber nearly 9 feet wide.

The contents of the smaller chamber have clearly been disturbed; within it was found a fragment of charred bone, and elsewhere part of the rim of a large thin urn.

Upon the extreme north slope of the mound lies a detached pillar-stone which measures 8 feet 4 inches long.

Four miles to the south, upon comparatively low ground to the east of CRAONAVAL, are to be noted two neighbouring chambered cairns of the same class. The westmost, and in most respects the finer of this pair,[1] stands about 400 yards west of Oban nam Fiadh, near another but much smaller loch which seems to have no name. The entrance passage clearly shows upon the south-east, and is noteworthy as having its sides practically intact, though only one covering stone remains—at the inner end. This passage measures 7 feet in length and 27 inches across the outer opening, but widens inwards to 42 inches. It is flanked outside by two slabs on edge, each about 36 inches long and showing for 30 inches above the surface, standing at an angle on either side of the opening. The chamber is much dilapidated, but one stone of the north-east side remains intact, 4 feet square above ground and 15 inches thick, with two much larger roof-slabs leaning against it. Another huge block of stone occupies its original position on the west side, but is so much

---

[1] Each is marked 'Stone Circle' upon the Ordnance map.

CHAMBERED CAIRN, OBAN NAM FIADH.

CHAMBERED CAIRN, NEAR EAST BASE OF CRAONAVAL.

imbedded as to be only measurable as 6 feet in width by 17 inches in thickness ; and three of the covering slabs are each about 7 feet long.

This chamber has evidently been dug to its floor, and part of the contents thrown out, including fragments of sepulchral pottery (one patterned), bits of wood-charcoal, and charred bones, together with kitchen-midden shells.

Close to the south-west of the main chamber is a group of five or six very large slabs and pillar-stones mostly lying in confusion, one measuring 64 by 50 inches with a thickness of 11 inches ; while the general appearance is such as almost to suggest that a second chamber has here existed. The whole mound now measures about 40 feet in diameter.

Six hundred yards to the south-east is the other and somewhat similar site. Here the entrance is no longer traceable, but five stones in the side walls of the chamber still stand erect, enclosing a nearly circular space 10½ feet in diameter. Two fallen roof-slabs measure respectively

10 feet by 6 feet 3 inches by 11 inches, and
7 feet by 6 feet by 11 inches.

Two miles to the north-west, upon the east summit of CRINGRAVAL (a small hill 129 feet in height, near Clachan-a-gluip) is one of the most dilapidated specimens of this class in North Uist. The Ordnance map marks it simply as 'Standing Stone,' and indeed there is an isolated standing-stone upon this hill, though near the other or western summit. Several of the thirteen Barps or chambered cairns of North Uist are locally associated with either standing-stones or stone circles in near proximity, and it may be that the presence of these is not accidental but in some connection with the cairn itself. At the south-east of this chambered cairn are two large parallel slabs set on edge, with all the appearance of having formed part of the entrance passage. Of these the eastmost is 76 inches long and 66 inches in height above the surface. Towards the centre all that is shown of the chamber itself are two or three pillars more or less erect, and two large flat slabs or cap-stones about 6 feet long by 15 and 12 inches thick respectively.

A mile and a half north of Cringraval, upon an elevated plateau half-way up the south-western shoulder of UNIVAL, is an ancient site marked upon the Ordnance map *Leacach an Tigh Chloiche*, meaning 'place of slabs of the stone-house.' The Gaelic name is thoroughly applicable, since here exists a stone circle (to be afterwards noted in detail), together with the remains of a small chambered cairn, now completely laid bare, within the south-east of its circumference. This chamber measures 10 feet 6 inches by 6 feet 9 inches, and is roughly oval in form, surrounded by seven upright pillar-stones. Of these latter, the innermost (namely that at the north-west end of the chamber) measures 5 feet 6 inches above ground, being considerably taller than any of the others.

Four miles north-west of Unival, upon the southern slope of South Clettraval looking down upon Lochs Vausary and Steaphain, is another *Tigh Cloiche* on the commonty known as GARRY HOUGARY. This is a circular mound, measuring about 57 by 52 feet and 8 feet high, and is readily to be identified as a chambered cairn with its entrance from the south-east. The passage shows two fallen cap-stones, while a third, somewhat within, occupies its original position. Still farther in, across the entrance to the chamber, lies a large roof-slab, also undisturbed but measuring 10 feet by 3 feet 4 inches with a thickness of 12 inches. Six erect slabs remain in the round of the chamber, and inside lies a large broken cap-stone, its two fragments together measuring 8 feet 7 inches by 6 feet 6 inches by 12 inches. Upon the floor of this chamber, as also in the passage, were found several fragments of pottery, evidently sepulchral, and it was clear that some excavation had been attempted. Towards the south-west edge of the mound is a group of smaller slabs lying on the surface.

At AIRIDHAN AN T-SRUTHAIN GHAIRBH, on *Guala na h-Imrich*, the east slope of Beinn a' Charra and half a mile north of Loch Feirma, is a mound evidently once encircled at its base by a number of standing-stones. Of these only four now stand erect, while a fifth lies dislodged, showing a length of 6 feet 6 inches. The mound itself is apparently the site of a former Barp or chambered cairn, afterwards occupied by shielings. Near its centre lies one large slab with a general thickness of 14 inches, split and bearing the marks of drills in eight round holes at its edges, and still retaining a length of 6 feet 5 inches. This, no doubt, represents part of a fallen cap-stone, and at its west end are two other large and symmetrical slabs imbedded

CHAMBERED CAIRN, CRINGRAVAL.

CHAMBERED CAIRN, UNIVAL.

CHAMBERED CAIRN, GARRY HOUGARY.

CAILLEACHA DUBHA, BORERAY.

upright within the soil. An entrance passage shows for 10 feet from the south-east base, with one roof-stone in position near its outer end and a large slab forming part of its south side. Water stood in this passage, which measures 33 inches wide and has an apparent height of 37 inches.

Near the north-east corner of Boreray Island the Ordnance map marks a row of three stones under the name of CAILLEACHA DUBHA. These stand upon the slope of a hill immediately north of the school-house, and examination showed not only three stones set on end in line, but also a still larger flat slab lying on the ground close to their north and locally known as 'the table.' The dimensions of this latter are 8 feet 7 inches by 7 feet 7 inches with a somewhat uniform thickness of 15 inches. Of the three erect slabs, that to the west measures 6 feet 10 inches in width and almost 7 feet above ground, while the others are each 5 feet 10 inches wide and 18 inches thick, but show only 4½ to 5 feet above the present surface level.

Almost parallel with these slabs, at a distance of from 1 to 2 yards on the south, is another row of seven smaller stones set on end or edge in a line extending for about 7 yards. To the writer it was evident that this megalithic site can only represent a sepulchral chamber of the Barp type, now completely stripped of its covering cairn.

Notice must here be taken of another and quite distinct variety of Sepulchral Cairns which is represented in North Uist by at least five specimens. Although only two or three of these show any remains of a covering cairn, there can be no doubt that all were originally surmounted by large heaps of stones, and come into the class of Long Megalithic Cists.

Perhaps the most characteristic is situated close to the west shore at Kirkibost, being marked upon the six-inch Ordnance map as DUN NA CARNAICH, nothwithstanding the fact that it is no dun but a Long Cist composed of megalithic slabs. The much ruined cairn shows a greatest diameter of about 60 feet with a height of 6 feet near the centre, but has evidently served as a quarry, a wide gap having been cleared through it from east to west. Immediately to the north of this opening is disclosed an incomplete cist still traceable to a length of 21 feet. Three large slabs stand on edge at each side in parallel lines from 3 to 4 feet apart, but no covering stones remain. The cist lies approximately north-east and south-west, and its largest slab (in the east side) measures 5 feet 6 inches in length by a height of 4 feet 6 inches above ground. Eighteen yards north of this site is a tall monolith known as *Clach Mhór a' Chè*, and to be individually described among other standing-stones.

At the east side of Unival, upon a flat of the slope and a quarter of a mile north-west from the island-fort in Loch Huna, is a shieling-mound known as UAMH AIRIDH NAM FAOCH, literally 'cave of the shieling of the periwinkles.' At the north base of this artificial hillock is a Long Cist with five covering slabs lying almost in their original positions and showing a total length, east and west, of 18½ feet. These rest at the present level of the soil upon a series of much imbedded side-slabs set on edge, and the width of the chamber is thus distinctly measurable as from 66 to 70 inches, so that it would apparently be still possible to ascertain both the original length and height by means of excavation. The two largest slabs are 7 feet 4 inches and 6 feet 6 inches in length, each having a width of 45 inches.

Four hundred yards north-west from the *Tigh Cloiche* already noted at Garry Hougary, and upon the adjoining hill-pasture of GARRY TIGHARY, are the remains of what appears to have been a Long Megalithic Cist or chambered cairn of the Arran type, without any trace of an entrance passage. This is quite destitute of covering, a fact readily explained by the existence of a pre-historic fort within a few yards to the west, and evidently built from the stones of the missing cairn. The chamber itself lies north-west and south-east in the form of a long parallelogram, with interior dimensions of 32 feet by 4 feet 6 inches. The end stones and part of the north and south walls still show in somewhat original position, consisting of seven large slabs placed on edge, more than half of them fallen inwards. The slab which forms the north-west end is 4 feet 6 inches long, while that adjoining it on the south (the two forming a corner) is much more massive, with a length of 8 feet and a height of 4 feet 4 inches above ground. Fifty yards to the west is a solitary standing-stone—58 inches high, 78 inches wide, and averaging a thickness of about 24 inches—while upon the hill-side, midway between this Long Cist and the neighbouring *Tigh Cloiche* upon the same hill of South

LONG CIST (DUN NA CARNAICH), KIRKIBOST.

LONG CIST (UAMH AIRIDH NAM FAOCH), UNIVAL.

LONG CIST, GARRY TIGHARY.

LONG CIST, GEIRISCLETT.

Clettraval, is another monolith which stands nearly 5 feet above ground and measures 45 inches wide by 31 inches thick.

The point at the north-east corner of Baleshare Island is known as CARNAN NAN LONG, and here was probably a Long Cist of the general type just described. Immediately above the shore is a mound about 40 feet in diameter and 10 feet high, strewn with stones lying in the turf, the whole site bearing some resemblance to Dun na Carnaich, with indications of a chamber which has measured about 15 by 4 feet. On the west of its summit lie two large slabs, measuring respectively 58 inches in length and breadth by 11 inches thick, and 46 by 33 by 9 inches, the smaller showing a recent fracture at one end.

Upon GEIRISCLETT, almost exactly at high-water mark, on the extremity of a small point which projects eastwards into Vallay Strand, are the ruins of another Long Cist lying approximately north-west and south-east. Three of its sides appear to be intact, consisting of five slabs still in upright position (one of them 5 feet 6 inches wide and standing quite 5 feet above the base), while part of a fallen cap-stone was found within the west end. From present appearances this chamber has measured 10 feet 3 inches in length, while its breadth varies from 3 to 4½ feet, the north side being angled outwards from near its centre. The east end is now entirely lost, but at that part are slight outer indications of a narrow passage bending towards the south. At a distance of three yards down the beach, and covered by high tides, is a conspicuous slab, 12 feet 9 inches long by 4 feet wide and 10 inches thick, no doubt having served as the main cap-stone. A second slab, nearly 6 feet in length, also lies upon the shore immediately to the north. When cleared of the accumulated rubbish this chamber was found to be paved throughout, the inner half standing at a slightly lower level. Inside were discovered several fragments of patterned pottery—evidently portions of two different vessels—together with a flint scraper and a broken hammer-stone. Around the east end of this Long Cist can still be traced, for several yards both on the north and south, the edging-stones of a former large cairn, the inner portion of which has clearly been utilised for some comparatively modern buildings close at hand.

Imbedded within the grassy surface, 30 yards to the west, lie two large slabs which probably formed part of the neighbouring cist, especially as no trace could be found of any structure beneath. These measure in length 10 feet 3 inches and 5 feet respectively, with a thickness of about 12 inches, their ends slightly overlapping.

On the summit of Craonaval, about a yard apart, are two recumbent slabs, the larger measuring 11 feet 10 inches in length by a width of 50 inches and a thickness of 11 inches. This rests upon at least four small stones, two of them at the west and two at the north, while under its south edge is a vacant space more than a foot deep and recessed inwards to the extent of about 2 feet. Close to its north lies the second and smaller slab, imbedded in heather at both ends, but not less than 8 feet long by 62 inches wide and 10 inches thick ; also showing a similar cavity beneath its southern edge and supported on the west by two small stones, as no doubt elsewhere by others. This site evidently marks an ancient burial, and bears the local name of LEAC A' MHIOSACHAN or 'slab of the month-old little one.'[1]

Half a mile to the south, upon the slope of Craonaval which overlooks Loch Caravat, is a still more imposing relic in the form of a huge slab 23 feet 1 inch in length by a greatest width of 6 feet 6 inches and a minimum thickness of about 16 inches.[2] Known as ULTACH FHINN—literally 'Fingal's armful' but translated to us 'Fingal's lift'—this megalith lies approximately north and south, elevated little above the surrounding moor, although obviously set in position by human agency, since it rests upon half a dozen comparatively small stones which are in turn supported by an underlying cairn. Beneath this slab, towards its south end, is a cavity 2 feet in height ; but still more significant is the fact that along its outer edges, and roughly parallel therewith, are visible the tops of slender enclosing walls exactly at the present surface level. These stand close to the

---

[1] Martin writes : 'There is a stone of 24 foot long and 4 in breadth in the hill *Criniveal*, the Natives say a Giant of a month old was buried under it'; *A Description, etc*, p. 59. It may be that Martin here confuses *Leac a' Mhiosachan* with *Ultach Fhinn*, but perhaps in his time the former consisted of a single slab which has since been broken into two.

We are informed that the same title of *Leac a' Mhiosachan* is locally given to two other megalithic sites in North Uist. At one of these a flat oblong stone rests upon the ground at exactly high-water mark on the north edge of a narrow promontory at the west end of Loch Langass. This slab measures 9 feet 8 inches long and 3 feet wide, by a thickness varying from 4 to 12 inches as it bulges considerably at the centre. The second is reported as lying near the south base of Flisaval, between Loch Scadavay and Loch Skeltar, although, after careful search, the writer was unable to verify this site.

[2] Its whole upper face is comparatively flat, whereas the under side projects irregularly, having a thickness of at least 30 inches at its north end. According to tradition, Fingal lifted this enormous block of stone,—a fact proved beyond dispute by the mark of his thumb showing as an indentation of 12 by 4 inches on its east edge !

LONG CIST, GEIRISCLETT; POTTERY. ACTUAL SIZE.

LEAC A' MHIOSACHAN, CRAONAVAL.

ULTACH FHINN, CRAONAVAL.

POBULL FHINN, LANGASS.

megalith on the south and west, but on the east at a very regular distance of about a foot, while on the north there is a wider interval varying from 3 to 4 feet. Careful scrutiny of the whole site leaves no doubt as to its artificial character.

Three yards west from Ultach Fhinn are the ruins of another and apparently quite separate cairn. This seems to have measured about 20 feet east and west by 15 feet north and south, containing within its north-east corner a small rectangular chamber 6 feet long and 43 inches wide. No very large stones are here disclosed, apart from five slabs imbedded on end, two in the north margin and three at the west.

The eighteen or twenty examples of Chambered Cairns and Long Megalithic Cists already enumerated are clearly referable to interments during the later Stone or early Bronze Ages, and there is every reason to believe that the list by no means includes all of this general type yet to be discovered in North Uist.

Upon the east slope of Beinn Langass, not far from its summit, are two megalithic sites which hardly lend themselves to definite classification. Of these, one is marked upon Wm. Johnson's map of 1822 [1] under the name (so far as decipherable) of ' Baishunes Grave.' Here is a group of three slabs, the larger pair lying one above the other, but separated towards the west by a smaller stone fixed between,[2] while the third slab lies close to the east at a somewhat lower level. The upper slab measures 8 feet 4 inches by 4 feet, with a thickness of $4\frac{1}{2}$ inches, that upon which it rests having a length of 7 feet 6 inches by a width of 6 feet 6 inches and a thickness of about 15 inches. Beneath is a distinct hollow, with some evidence of lesser stones serving as supports at both ends. The name ' Baishune' has given some difficulty, but we are told that *Baistain* represents a still common Uist form of Archibald.

The second group, lower down the slope and only 5 yards to the east, seems to be known as *Leac Alasdair.* Here, at an angle of about 45 degrees and presumably in natural position, is a large boulder measuring about 12 feet in length and breadth, with a thickness of from 30 to 34 inches. Close to the south base of this rock lies a slab 7 feet 8 inches long and 5 feet 5 inches broad, faced at its west side

---

[1] Edinburgh, published by John Thomson & Co.
[2] It is noticeable that each of these three stones is cup-marked, one of them doubly.

by a row of three stones set on edge or end; while immediately to the east is a second and larger slab, 10 feet in length by 5 feet in breadth and 12 inches thick, showing a hollow beneath. Near *Leac Alasdair* is said to be a well named *Tobar Alasdair*, this no doubt being represented by a pool which forms the source of a small burn within 20 yards to the south-east.

Scattered over various parts of North Uist are many green hillocks, generally showing signs of former occupation and almost invariably capped by ruined shielings; although upon these mounds it is not uncommon to find pillar-stones and large flat slabs which have evidently been taken thither to serve a more important use. Several examples may here be individually noticed.

BUAILE MAARI, upon the south shoulder of Maari hill and half a mile north from Barpa nam Feannag, consists of three distinct hillocks, each bearing the ruins of abandoned shielings. Near the summit of one of these mounds may still be seen a huge slab which measures 12 feet 7 inches by 5 feet 11 inches, with a thickness of 16 inches, to all appearance representing the cap-stone of an ancient burial-chamber. Near the south base of this mound lies another slab 9 feet 3 inches long by 4 feet wide and 10 inches thick; while towards the south-east a third slab is slightly imbedded on edge, measuring 8 feet 3 inches in length by 3 feet in breadth (so far as it is visible above the surface), with a thickness of 12 inches.

Upon BEINN A' CHAOLAIS, half a mile east of Port nan Long and amidst the ruins of several shielings, is a large slab which measures 7 feet 3 inches by 5 feet, with a thickness varying from 10 to 20 inches; and near it lies another flat stone more than 5 feet in length.

East of the 'Committee Road,' near the southern base of TREACKLETT is a conspicuously green mound about 12 feet high, with a ruined shieling on its top and several others close to the west. This hillock shows some indications of a wall along its east base, and in its north edge lies one slab measuring 6 feet 8 inches by 2 feet 5 inches, accompanied by other stones of considerable size. Here indeed may perhaps have been an entrance passage from the north side, indicated (though without any certainty) as 28 inches wide and about 3 yards long.

At GUALA MHOR, close to the north-east of Loch Hunder, is a

small rocky hillock upon the top of which lies a flat slab 8 feet 2 inches long by 4 feet 2 inches broad and 11 inches thick, partly resting on solid rock but elsewhere supported by two stones of no great size. A smaller slab lies immediately to the north, and at the south stands an erect stone marked upon one face by a number of slight bosses, although these are probably due to natural agency.

Upon the west slope of EAVAL, facing Loch Obisary, are two mounds about 200 yards apart. The Ordnance map marks these as 'Tumuli,' a description which may be quite accurate, though each is now capped by the remains of several shielings.

It would be easy to enumerate other sites which present a somewhat similar appearance, but the foregoing may suffice to draw attention to a few instances where an ancient burial-cairn probably lies hidden beneath the ruins of comparatively modern erections.

STONE CIRCLES.

This class of megalithic monuments is still represented in North Uist by at least four examples; three of them being of normal type, while another is not only much smaller in dimensions but also contains a chambered cairn within its boundary, and a fifth is tentatively recorded in the absence of full knowledge as to its actual character.

POBULL FHINN [1] claims precedence as the most conspicuous stone circle in the island. This is situated upon a natural plateau in the southern slope of Beinn Langass, about 100 yards north of Loch

---

[1] Also locally known as *Sornach Coir' Fhinn*, although the Ordnance map incorrectly transfers this name to the stone circle which is here next described. The identity of *Sornach Coir' Fhinn* with *Pobull Fhinn* is confirmed by the following reference in *Sailing Directions for the West Coast of Scotland*, 1885, part i. p. 6 :—'On the north side of Loch Eport, is an elliptical ring, called Fingal's Furnace, 118 feet long by 98 feet broad. This ring is curiously placed, occupying the whole area of a small level terrace on the steep side of the hill ; and has sixteen stones in position, the largest being seven feet high.'

Pobull Fhinn is Gaelic for 'Fingal's people' or 'the white people' ; *fionn-gall* (in the nominative) representing 'fair foreigner,' or 'Norseman.' *Sornach Coir' Fhinn* gives more difficulty, although *sorn* means 'a kiln, oven, or furnace,'—whence *sornach* 'place of the furnace'—while *coire* signifies 'a kettle,' or sometimes 'a ring, a girdle.' Thus a literal translation might be 'the ring of Fingal's furnace.'

It is interesting to find the word *Fhinn* repeated in the names of no fewer than three separate megalithic sites at Langass and Craonaval, prefixed by *Pobull*, *Sornach*, and *Ultach*, all within a mile from the west extremity of Loch Eford. *Pobull* further appears in connection with both of the stone circles in this locality—*Pobull Fhinn* and *Sornach a' Phobuill*—as also in *Loch a' Phobuill*, 200 yards west from the latter.

Langass, an inner recess of Loch Eford. Of oval rather than circular form, Pobull Fhinn measures about 120 feet in length, east and west, by 93 feet, north and south, this area being further marked by a slight and evidently artificial mound, upon the outer edge of which stand eight large pillar-stones in upright position. Ten or twelve fallen slabs also remain in line with those still erect, and along the north margin (where it joins the sloping face of the hill) are traces of a slender wall. Supplementary to the regular outline of this enclosure, and 4 feet within its east end, stands a tall independent stone; while 7 feet beyond the west boundary lie two fallen slabs, the larger of these exceeding 9 feet in length.

A mile and a half to the south-west of Pobull Fhinn is another stone circle which locally bears the name of SORNACH A' PHOBUILL, although shown upon the Ordnance map as *Sornach Coir' Fhinn*. This stands upon the moor between Craonaval and the shallow *Loch a' Phobuill*, and is represented by a very regular circle 130 feet in diameter. Upon careful examination thirteen stones were here counted as still remaining erect in the circumference, eight of them towards the west. Only three pillar-stones are noticeable from a distance, the rest being almost hidden by an accumulated growth of peat,[1] beneath which others no doubt still remain. The tallest slab measures 5 feet in height above the broken surface, and there are many wide blanks where no stones appear; while, on the other hand, two pairs of erect slabs show intervening spaces of not more than 7 feet, thus suggesting the existence of an unusually large number of pillars when the whole circumference was complete.

Near Carinish, half a mile to the west of Caravat Barp, is another stone circle. Like *Pobull Fhinn*, this occupies a slightly elevated plateau and is oval in shape, measuring about 120 feet east and west by 90 feet north and south. Fourteen stones—five of them still erect, and mostly of no great size—now remain in its circuit. Perhaps the tallest, measuring 8 feet 4 inches in length, lay flat at the east edge; while outside the west end were two other fallen slabs, one of them recently broken through its middle as if for the purpose of being removed.

---

[1] Thus presenting very similar conditions to those which must have been shown by the stone circle and avenues at Callernish, Lewis, before the encroaching peat was there removed to a depth of 5½ feet; see Captain Thomas's description, quoted at p. 6, *antea*.

STONE CIRCLE, UNIVAL.

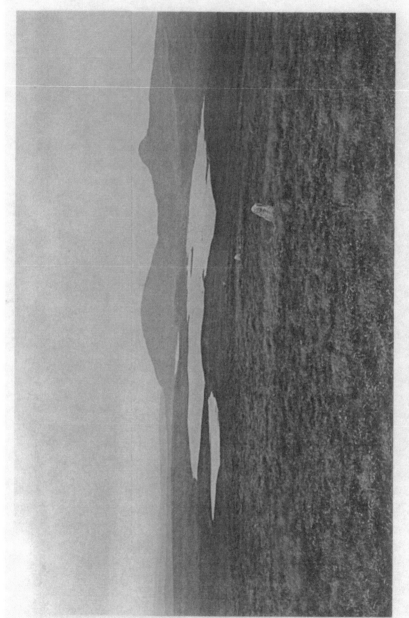

NA FIR BHREIGE, BLASHAVAL.

LEAC NAN CAILLEACHAN DUBHA, VALLAY.

CLACH MHOR A' CHE, KIRKIBOST.

The fourth stone circle is at *Leacach an Tigh Chloiche*, on the south-west shoulder of Unival, half a mile west from Loch Huna. This is much smaller than those already described, having a diameter of only 50 feet with nine stones still in erect position; while, outside the circle and 11 yards to the west, is another monolith, 8 feet high, 5 feet 2 inches wide, and 12 inches thick. This circle is of special interest as containing a small chambered cairn within its south-east edge.[1]

The remaining site cannot be definitely classed as a 'stone circle,' though bearing some resemblance to that type. Upon Bogach Maari, midway between Barpa nam Feannag and Buaile Maari, this shows as a mound about 60 feet long and 35 feet wide, by 6 feet in height. Five large stones lie in or near the base, and three in line along its centre; but no more can be stated beyond the fact that here is an oval mound (its axis from north-west to south-east), possibly artificial and certainly occupied by a group of eight large and somewhat shapeless blocks of stone.

STANDING-STONES.

Among these monoliths is a row of three stones set almost in line upon a ridge which forms the west spur of Blashaval, three miles to the north-west of Lochmaddy. These are locally known as *Na Fir Bhreige* or 'the false men,' tradition adding that they represent three men who had deserted their wives in Skye and suffered the penalty of being turned into stones by a witch. None of them now stands more than three feet above the soil, within which all are so much imbedded as to give no indication of their actual length. That in the middle seems to be the largest, measuring 39 inches in width by a thickness of from 4 to 6 inches; while the others stand at intervals of 25 yards on the east and 39 yards on the west.

Martin, evidently writing of quite a different locality, makes the following statement :—' There are three Stones erected about five foot high, at the distance of a quarter of a mile from one another, on Eminences about a mile from Loch-Maddy, to amuse Invaders, for which reason they are still called false sentinels.'[2] This may probably

---

[1] Already noted at p. 252.
[2] *A Description*, etc., pp. 58-59.

refer to a series of mounds two miles west from Lochmaddy and a little north of *Garbh abhuinn Àrd*, the burn which connects Loch Scadavay with Loch Skealtar. An endeavour was made to verify a reported line of hillocks each capped by an erect slab. This, however, proved fruitless so far as regards any standing-stones, although a group of mounds certainly exists.

Upon the hill-side at *Toroghas*, 500 yards north of *Loch Mhic Gille-Bhride*, are two standing-stones about 40 yards apart. That to the west is in the centre of a small boggy pool, the stone measuring 44 inches above water and at least 30 inches below. The other slab is 44 inches wide and stands only 30 inches above the surface, although evidently much imbedded. There is no trace of any circle, and the two stones are known as *Fir Bhreige*, presumably in default of a better explanation.

On the south edge of Vallay, immediately above the shore a little to the east of St. Mary's chapel, are two large erect stones standing side by side, north and south, known as *Leac nan Cailleachan Dubha*. The taller of this pair of slabs, after having been cleared from an accumulation of soil on its east, measures about 6 feet in height above ground, by a width of 4 feet 3 inches. These stones are at the east end of a slight mound and undoubtedly represent a pre-historic burial-site.[1] The local story is not without interest, telling how two women caught in the act of milking cows 'which did not belong to themselves' were put to death and here buried; the stones being placed to commemorate the event and warn others against this particular crime.[2]

Upon *Druim Àiridh Iomhair*, at the east side of Geireann Mill Loch, lie two large slabs which very possibly represent fallen monoliths. Each of these is somewhat pointed at one extremity; the larger of the pair measuring 14 feet 8 inches in length by fully 7 feet in width, and the other 13½ feet by 4 feet 7 inches, their thickness varying from 9 to 16 inches. Near the edge of a small loch immediately to the east, was found in August 1899 a hoard of six carefully wrought stone-axes or 'celts'; these lying close together, imbedded within the peat, above which the end of one axe was partly exposed.

---

[1] A much-worn hammer-stone was found here.
[2] According to a North Uist tradition, this form of theft—*faobh-bhleoghainn*—was in early times punished by the offender being buried alive; a penalty afterwards commuted to the loss of an arm or a hand.

Among the isolated pillar-stones in North Uist, perhaps the most important is *Clach Mhór a' Chè*, which has been already noted as standing 18 yards north of the so-called Dun na Carnaich close to the shore at Kirkibost. This measures 8 feet 9 inches in height by a width of 3 feet 9 inches and a thickness of 6 to 12 inches, and is mentioned by Martin[1] as a standing-stone 'at the Key opposite to *Kirkibast* 12 foot high, the Natives say that delinquenrs were tyed to this Stone in time of Divine Service.' *Clach Mhór a' Chè* is a puzzle as to the latter portion of its name, a literal translation reading, 'great stone of the world.'[2] It is supposed to mark the site of battle, in which case *Cè* may represent a proper name.[3]

On the summit of Beinn a' Charra, near the Committee Road, is a tall monolith sloping so much towards the south as to stand about a yard off the perpendicular, with a height of 9 feet 3 inches above the soil at its north and fully 11 feet from the bottom of a small pool which lies at its south. This is an immense slab measuring 6 feet 9 inches in width at its base and a foot less at a yard from its top, with a varying thickness of 21 to 30 inches.

Martin notes 'a very conspicuous Stone in the face of the Hill above *St. Peters* Village, aboue 8 foot high.'[4] This situation would apply to the hill at Balelone, where, immediately behind the house is a broken monolith; one half standing erect to a height of about 5 feet above the ground, and the other half, 4 feet 9 inches long, lying close beside it.

Near the north side of *Loch na Buaile Iochdrach*[5] is a small

---

[1] *A Description*, etc., p. 59.

[2] The Highland Society's *Gaelic Dictionary* (1828), under 'Cé, earth (the planet),' notes, 'Clach mhòr a' Ché, in the island of North Uist, supposed to be a monument dedicated to a Pagan deity named Cé.'

Writing of Taransay in Harris, Captain Thomas (*Archæologia Scotica*, vol. v. p. 398) refers to the ruined *Teampull Cè* in that island,—'the saint here being, undoubtedly, a lady; for if any male was buried in her cemetery, he was found above ground on the next day.' Strangely enough, Martin (p. 49) notes this *Teampull Cè* as a chapel dedicated to St. Keith, making a directly contrary statement as to the burials there allowed.

[3] It seems barely possible that this may refer to Cé, one of the seven sons of the traditional Cruithne (reputed ancestor of the Scottish Picts), the others being Cait, Cerig, Fib, Fidach, Fotla, and Fortrenn, of whom Cait and Fib are supposed to have given their names to Caithness and Fife.

The suggestion is made that Keith, Dalkeith, and Inch-Keith are also derived from this Che or Cé (*Place-Names of Scotland*, second edn., 1903, by Rev. James B. Johnston, pp. 96, 162, 170).

[4] *A Description*, etc., p. 59. It is evidently this stone to which reference is made in the *New Stat. Acc.*, Inverness-shire, p. 169, as 'Caracrom,' at Balamartin.

[5] Unnamed upon the Ordnance map, but lying at the south base of Unival a little to the west of Loch Huna.

standing-stone about 3 feet in height, 100 yards to the south-east of a group of four shieling mounds.

Incidental notice has already been taken of various separate standing-stones, one of them near Dun Torcuill, and others which are found in obvious association with the stone circle upon Unival, the chambered cairns at Marrogh, Cringraval, and Garry Hougary, as also with the Long Cist at Garry Tighary.

UNCHAMBERED CAIRNS.

These apparently belong to a somewhat later period than that with which the megalithic burials are to be associated. The writer must here content himself by enumerating the ten or twelve which he has observed in North Uist, these averaging 15 or 20 feet in diameter and each of them no doubt originally erected to cover one or more cists.

Close to the south-east edge of the smaller Lingay, near the centre of Ahmore Strand, is an evidently artificial mound about 20 feet in diameter and 6 feet high, with a westward spur 11 feet in length by a width of fully 3 feet.

At Stromban, near Lochmaddy (30 yards west of another site which has been noted on p. 158) is a very similar mound covered by turf and loose stones, about 20 feet in diameter and 5 feet in height.

Garbh Eilean Beag, a tidal island immediately north of the Carinish chapels, contains two grass-covered cairns, one of them large.

At *Rudha na Dise*, upon Claddach-Baleshare opposite Dun na Dise, the Ordnance map shows two significant place-names—*Càrn na Dise*[1] and *Rudha Chàrnain dithich*. We could make nothing of these sites, apart from being locally informed that a cairn once stood at the shore a little east of the neighbouring cottage.

At Carnach, fully a mile to the north-west, on the end of a small peninsula, is a large conical mound known as *Càrnan Buidhe* or 'little yellow cairn,' and showing many loose stones in its grass-covered surface.

Upon the south slope of Craonaval has evidently been a large

[1] Possibly thus named in some association with *Sithean Tuath* at Balranald, seven miles to the north-west.

STANDING-STONE ON BEINN A' CHARRA.

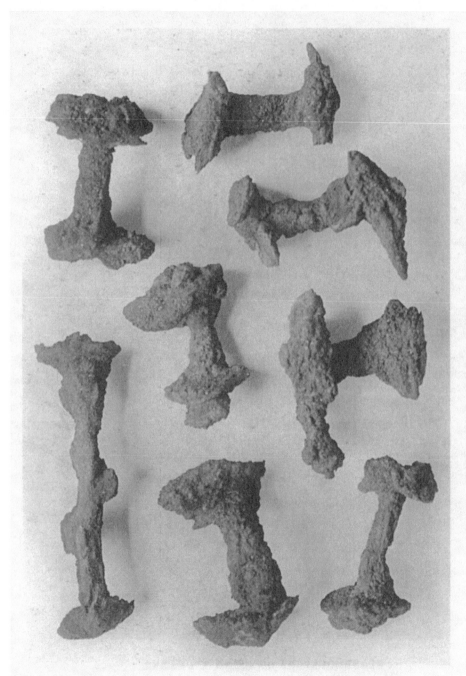

VIKING RIVETS FROM CARNAN MOR, OTTERNISH.   ACTUAL SIZE.

cairn, already described in connection with *Ultach Fhinn* which lies close to its east.

North of *Loch a' Phobuill* are the ruins of a cairn at least 13 feet in diameter and containing some stones which measure about 5 feet long. Here again is the appearance of a narrow spur, projecting for several yards towards the south-west.

At the end of Ard an Runair, opposite Hougary, are two grassy mounds which seem to come into this class, the larger measuring a diameter of 18 feet across its base.

Of somewhat different type, perhaps rather approaching that of the Long Cist, are two other sites which must also be recorded. One is a small rocky islet near the north-west corner of Loch Fada, which contains two large boulders at its south end, the summit of this islet having apparently been occupied by a cairn about 18 feet in length and 6 feet in width, built upon solid rock at an elevation of 6 feet above the water. The other stands upon Eilean nan Gillean, a rocky point close to the north of Caisteal Odair at Griminish and surrounded by the sea at spring-tides. This is an evidently artificial structure of rectangular shape, measuring about 39 by 16 feet over its ruinous boundary walls, which consist of large blocks of stone.

Cairns of smaller size than those described above are much more numerous, although from their nature so apt to escape notice that any attempt at an exhaustive list is out of the question. If fuller evidence were available as to their original character, it is also probable that several of the sites here noted might be found to exhibit special features which would definitely refer them to their respective periods.

At *Scaalan* near Lochmaddy, upon the slope facing the island of Lieravay, is a group of six small cairns.

Near the middle of Ronay is *Beinn a' Chàrnain*, a place-name which would indicate the existence of a cairn of this class.

The same remark applies to *Eilean a' Chàrnain*, a small island immediately to the west of Eilean a' Ghiorr in the North Ford, near Grimsay.

Off the south-west extremity of North Uist proper, in the ford between it and Baleshare, are no fewer than three tidal islets each known as *Eilean nan Càrnan* (in the plural) and therefore having

2 L

once contained two or more cairns. The southern and smallest of
these islands lies a little west of Carinish and shows no ancient
remains. The next (opposite Claddach-Baleshare, and with Dun na
Dise upon a rock adjoining its north-east extremity) is half a mile in
length, with traces of several cairns, none of them very conspicuous;
while the most northerly of the three, close to the shore at Illeray,
seems to have been enclosed by a wall along its edge, two small cairns
also showing upon mounds near its north and south ends.

Eilean Mór, which is also in the Baleshare Ford, north of Horray,
contains a cairn upon an elevation towards its south extremity.

At *Sloc Sàbhaidh*, on the west side of Baleshare, within the base
of its southern sand-hill, was observed a circle of small stones laid
so as to enclose a space about 3 feet in diameter. Near this spot
were found many flakes of flint (a material comparatively rare in
North Uist) together with small fragments of ancient pottery and
some charred bones, probably indicating the site of a burnt burial.

Upon the promontory of Ard an Runair, opposite Hougary, two
cairns have been already noted, one of them large. Farther south,
near the centre of the same point, are scattered numerous cairns, most
of them within two adjoining walled enclosures, each of considerable
area. The larger of these is to the south, containing an isolated
boulder (*Sgeir na Circe*[1]) surrounded by about fifty cairns; while
nearly thirty may be counted in the northern enclosure, which is
smaller and more irregular in shape. Outside these, towards the west
side of Ard an Runair, are other cairns, one having apparently been
confined within a structural wall of large stones.

The most extensive of the seven tidal islands in North Uist which
bear the name Oransay has been noted at pp. 238-239 in connection
with a hoard of gold ingots and rings found in a sand-hill. This site
seems to have been at the north-east end of the island, where
the sand is now unbroken, being thoroughly knit together by bent-
grass. Here, upon a stony slope immediately to the north-west, is a
group of about twenty small and much ruined cairns, although many
others have no doubt existed. These were evidently once enclosed
within a dry-stone dyke which is still traceable on the north and west,
while very few cairns are to be seen outside this boundary. Upon
two visits there were found on the surface a dozen flaked flints includ-

---

[1] *Uist Bards*—'The Poems and Songs of John MacCodrum, etc.,' p. viii.

ing three scrapers, as also many fragments of rude pottery, chiefly lying near the largest cairn. The summit and northern portion of this site consist of little more than bare rock, its lower end towards the south being thinly clothed by turf. If we may hazard a suggestion, the whole area was formerly covered with sand (still visible at several parts) in which had been set a number of burnt burials resting upon the solid rock and protected by heaps of small stones. Such a theory would readily account for the dispersion of the cairns and their contents. Slight excavation was attempted, with the result of disclosing sand and clay both above and within the rock-crevices.

Nearly half a mile to the west, on the opposite side of this promontory, is a rocky slope showing the apparent remains of another group of similar cairns, together with two yard-wide circles outlined by fragments of white quartz, although flint seemed here to be absent.

A separate division of small cairns, distinctively of the Iron Age, may be noticed as containing Norse burials, recognisable from their association with iron rivets of the Viking type, already described on p. 228.

The most prominent of these is at *Rudh' a' Chàrnain Mhóir* upon the extreme point of Otternish, overlooking the Sound of Harris and directly opposite Berneray Island. This, from partial examination, was vouched by the remains of a skeleton and typical iron rivets to be the unburnt burial of a Norseman with his boat. Even his name may be conjectured, and with some probability of correctness, as Ottar; while his death certainly took place before the eleventh century. Fifty yards to the south is a smaller cairn, which, from the occurrence of at least one similar rivet, would seem to represent another Viking burial. This latter site is known under the name of *Càrnan Beag*, to distinguish it from *Càrnan Mór*, already noted as standing close to the edge of the cliff. At *Càrnan Beag* (without however giving any place-name), the Ordnance map marks ' + Human Remains found A.D. 1870,' and both cairns no doubt contained burials of the same type and period. Portions of similar rivets have also been noted at Rudha na Traghad, half a mile to the south, thus indicating another Viking burial within a short distance.

In a rabbit-hole at Scaalan, near Lochmaddy, upon a hillock to the north of a group of small cairns, was found the lozenge-shaped head of a rivet, measuring two inches across. We are informed that, after a severe storm some years ago, a quantity of 'large rusty nails' was disclosed at a spot on the west side of Baleshare Island. But such traces are indeed not uncommon upon any bared sand-hills throughout North Uist—as at Vallay, Skellor, Udal, and Boreray—it being almost certain that numerous Viking burials existed (and may even yet remain) at various parts near the shore.

STONE CISTS.

This is a class of burials impossible to enumerate, even as regards those which have already been discovered and examined more or less thoroughly. In the first place, cists rarely afford any surface clue to their presence, being often disclosed in a very casual way. And further, the typical cist is so small, that, when once laid bare and probably rifled of any contents, its re-discovery is neither easy nor very instructive as to result.

Upon the sandy slope at Rudha na Traghad, a little to the east of Port nan Long, the writer found a small cist apparently not exceeding two feet in length. This contained an inverted urn of coarse pottery, six inches in height, and with a diameter widening from $4\frac{1}{2}$ to $5\frac{1}{4}$ inches. Although showing traces of disturbance, this vessel still held some dark viscous matter, probably indicating a cremated burial; and upon its flat base (this however in upper position as already explained) is crudely incised an ornamental design. Close to the urn lay a small circular flat stone which would exactly fit the inverted mouth.

A little south of Port nan Long, upon the tidal beach named *Faodhail a' Chaolais*, are four regular blocks of stone apparently placed by human agency so as to form a massive rectangular erection which perhaps comes into the same category; although, if this be the case, its dimensions present a striking contrast to those of the burial-site last described.

Farther to the south-west, the Ordnance map shows 'Stone Cist found A.D. 1840,' and again (west of Newton House) 'Stone Cists found A.D. 1845,' these dates however being somewhat too remote for practical purposes. It is also stated that human remains have been recently found near the south base of Dun Rosail, and that, west of

POLISHED STONE AXE, TOTA DUNAIG, VALLAY. ACTUAL SIZE.

CISTS EXCAVATED AT SITHEAN AN ALTAIR, VALLAY.

this at Clachan Iosal, a cist was disclosed in a small hillock bearing the local name of Cnoc na h-Atha.

In connection with a cave in the south-east face of Beinn Bhreac, a small plateau has been noted as situated immediately in front of it and at the same level. Here, at a distance of four yards from the cave, is a group of stones set in position; five slabs still remaining erect on end (the tallest to a height of 45 inches above ground); while two others rest on edge, the longer measuring 51 inches. These form a cist with dimensions of about 43 by 24 inches, evidently once covered by a cairn ten feet in diameter across its base. A semi-circular wall abuts against the slight cliff, and seems to have enclosed both cave and cairn.

The largest islet in Loch Veiragvat, near its west shore, was examined in the hope of finding a dun said to exist there. No such traces were discovered, but on the other hand there seemed to be the indistinct remains of one or two cists.

As a doubtfully reported Barp, although without any apparent claim to the title, a site in the Portain district has been noted as more probably that of a cist. At the east base of a cliff, amidst many fallen rocks, is one slab which bears a row of four cup-marks along its edge and is supported by other stones which seem to have been artificially placed.

Martin,[1] writing of the Heisker islands in 1703, states—'There was a Stone Chest lately discovered here, having an earthen Pitcher in it which was full of Bones, and assoon as touched they turned to Dust.' The present writer found one cist containing human bones, near the north-west corner of Ceann Ear; and has been informed of a group of six upon the same island, as also that, both in Ceann Ear and Ceann Iar, sites of this class are often disclosed by the shifting sand.

While some excavation was being made at *Tota Dùnaig*, in the field behind Vallay House, an oval cell was discovered two feet below the surface. This was built of comparatively small stones resting either upon edge or end, and its interior measured about $5\frac{1}{2}$ by 3 feet. Although evidently representing an ancient burial, no definite confirmation appeared, unless perhaps from the fact that close outside its east edge lay a finely polished stone-axe, $6\frac{1}{2}$ inches in length and with distinct marks of a former hafting near one end.

[1] *A Description, etc.*, p. 60.

Elsewhere upon Valley Island two small cists have been already noted close to a ruined Earth-House, and another at Geo na Ceardaich.[1]

Near the centre of Valley, surrounded by arable land, is *Sithean an Altair*, a small mound of sand measuring about 30 by 18 feet, with a height of 5 feet and its axis from south-west to north-east. This knoll was thoroughly explored during the summer of 1904, the soil being afterwards replaced in deference to the numerous interments which had been laid bare.

A first and merely superficial examination of the summit revealed three long stones placed on end close to each other, their tops being level with the surface of the mound. About a foot beneath their lower ends were several other stones set on edge, but irregularly placed, the whole presenting no definite structural form.[2] On this occasion the most striking feature was a scattered layer of small water-rolled pebbles of white quartz at about a foot below the summit. Two flints had been previously found upon the cultivated area a little to the east.

Later and more complete excavation of Sithean an Altair was begun at its centre and thence followed out to both ends. Within the central base were disclosed two small stones, each about a foot in height and standing on end, with indications of a cremated burial lying between, although fragments of the skull showed no marks of having been subjected to fire. To the west of this, and also near the base, was the appearance of another cist measuring 36 by 27 inches and partly enclosed by four flat slabs each about 18 inches square and standing on edge. Here were some fragments of burnt bones. East from these, but 18 inches above the natural base, was evidently another cremated burial within a cist 4 feet long and formed by not fewer than ten comparatively small and rough stones set on edge or end. Ashes were also found here. The three (if not five) cists which have been thus far enumerated were unfortunately, and perhaps almost unavoidably, destroyed in the process of excavation; but the few bones and ashes were carefully laid beneath a cairn composed of the edging stones of these cists

[1] See pp. 118 and 234, *antea*.
[2] And yet, to judge from analogy with the burnt burials afterwards discovered lower down, these probably also represented the remains of cists.

and of similar loose stones found either upon the surface or lower down.

Within the northern half of Sithean an Altair, and situated not more than 2 to 3 yards from its centre, is a series of five or six cists, some of them upon the base, and others 6 inches higher up. Two of these, at the base to the west, each measured about a yard long, one of them being complete as to outline. Another group to the east apparently included portions of at least three cists, one with its border stones laid upon their flat sides 6 inches up ; another showing similarly but at the base ; and the third with stones on edge or end 6 inches above the normal level. Upon the base, midway between these groups and 2 yards north from the centre of the mound, stands a cist composed of five stones set on end, enclosing a cremated burial, without any cover-slab but containing bone-ashes and a single white pebble. This cist measured at its top a diameter of about 17 inches across the interior and 24 inches over the uprights, being the only one in the northern half which showed distinct traces of cremation, all the others having evidently been long since emptied of their contents.

The southern part of Sithean an Altair (shown upon the accompanying plate) yielded more definite results in a series of four cists, varying as to size and shape, but each affording clear proof of its character as the site of a burnt burial. Immediately south of the centre is a pair of cists, one formed of stones resting upon their faces almost at the base of the mound, with interior dimensions of about 33 by 18 inches. The skeleton must have been very imperfectly cremated, although bearing some marks of fire and accompanied by calcined oyster-shells. The femora, with portions of the vertebræ and ribs, were but slightly charred. Directly above, and indeed resting upon the west wall of this cist, at about a foot higher than the base, stands another built of stones set on edge and measuring about 14 inches square inside. Farther east are two other cists, one bordered by stones on edge, raised about 6 inches above the natural level, in size 24 by 17 inches and plugged by a slab of poor quality, evidently its original cap-stone. The outer cist towards the east is nearly 30 inches in length, also built of stones set on edge, but situated at the base and enclosing, among its contents of ashes, a pebble of white quartz.

The ancient remains covered by Sithean an Altair thus comprise at least twelve or fourteen cists, all indicating cremated burials, and therefore attributable to the late Bronze Age ; eight of this number yielding further proof of their character by the burnt bones or ashes which they contain. In two examples the cremation has been very incomplete, and two other cists contained single specimens of the rounded quartz pebbles so common in this mound. Indeed the total number of water-rolled stones (from 1 to 4 inches in length, and quite half of them consisting of white quartz) disclosed during the excavation of Sithean an Altair was at least two hundred and sixty. In addition, though not associated with individual inter-ments, were found a portion of deer's horn and several hammer-stones, none of these latter bearing marks of much use.

The fact that cists were here found at four different levels—upon the natural base, and at elevations of about 6, 12, and 18 inches —would infer successive burials at various periods perhaps widely apart; while their mutilated condition proves that this mound had been previously disturbed, also explaining the absence of pottery and other relics.

MISCELLANEOUS.

Less prominent as to definiteness of character, are several other mounds in North Uist which bear the significant place-name of *sithean* or 'fairy knoll,'[1] a title probably implying some local tradition as formerly existent with regard to each, although in not a single case does it now appear to be recoverable.

The most prominent of these sites is *Sithean Mór*, upon the outer extremity of Callernish and close to the shore at the west entrance of Vallay Sound. This grass-covered heap of sand, measuring fully 30 yards in length by 20 yards in width and 12 to 15 feet in height, is a very conspicuous object even when viewed from a distance. Thanks to investigations made by a colony of rabbits, Sithean Mor clearly showed itself as having been associated of old with human inhabitation, whether or not also covering burials of a still earlier period. In its south-east face was already disclosed an extensive kitchen-midden, yielding in parts a vertical section of from 6 to 12 inches, and

---

[1] It would seem that, as a general rule, the term of *Sithean* or 'fairy-knoll' indicates a pagan burial-mound.

consisting chiefly of shells of the periwinkle and limpet, with occasional split bones and fragments of rude craggans. This pottery was ornamented with patterns in eight distinct varieties, including crescents, lines, dots, and the impressions of finger tips. A few hammer-stones were found, one so small and thin as perhaps to have been a limpet-striker; also a sharpening-stone and a portion of horn bearing two sliced opposite faces.

A cutting was driven completely through Sithean Mor from north to south, a distance of 66 feet. This revealed the kitchen-midden as a mere superficial layer, about a foot below the grassy surface and reaching a maximum thickness of less than two feet, apparently confined entirely to the east end of the mound. Underneath was a solid mass of fine sand, no doubt drifted thither by the wind, and remarkable as the only such heap in the vicinity. In all probability its existence is due to some original cairn which has served as a nucleus, but unfortunately the area covered by Sithean Mor is too great to warrant a thorough search at its base for what, after all, may not exist.

Upon the level and cultivated ground immediately south of Sithean Mor are further kitchen-midden traces, and here a fragment of patterned pottery and a solitary flint were recently found; while we are also informed that ancient burials have been disclosed at this south edge.

Near Tighary, at the north end of Loch Eaval and situated upon a slight elevation at Cnoc Eaval, is a small and very green mound now measuring about 8 by 6 yards across its base and 5 feet in height. This is known as *Sithean Eaval* and stands in the midst of arable ground, being composed of sand with gravel and small stones, in other respects also bearing a strong outward resemblance to *Sithean an Altair* on Vallay, already described.

At Middlequarter, a little north of the road between Sollas and Malaclett, is a pair of adjoining mounds, each about 6 yards in diameter, and 4 or 5 feet in height, that to the west consisting of sand and the other of dark soil. These are locally named *Dà Shithean*, being evidently artificial, and it is said that burnt stones have there been found.

Upon Knock-Cuien, at the southern extremity of North Uist and close to the eastmost cottage of this township, is *Sithean Hacklett,* a hillock showing a semi-circular line of stones within its west face.

Each of the sites just mentioned seems to deserve its distinguishing name, although, in the case of four others, the title *sìthean* may have been erroneously acquired. One of these is upon Machair Robach at Vallaquie, its special designation being perhaps of quite modern origin, due to the existence of a prominent knoll, to all appearance simply a large natural sand-hill covered with grass. Sithean Dubh, a shapeless and very rocky hillock by the roadside at Alioter, seems hardly worth noting, since this is understood to be a fancy name recently invented for Cnoc Alioter. At Roisinish, on the north side of Loch Eford, one of several islets in Loch Mhic Gille-chroig is known under the title of Sithean Mhic Gille a' Gheig, but this also appears to have no special interest. Cnoc an t-Sithein, east of the smithy at Malaclett, is certainly vouched by good authority, being thus marked upon the Ordnance map. This, however, is believed to be an error for Cnoc Sitheil or 'peaceful hillock,' a name which correctly occurs as that of another irregular rocky knoll near the south-east corner of Ahmore Strand. To none of these can any importance be attached, though *sìthean* as a genuine place-name always deserves careful attention.

Cup-marked rocks and stones ought perhaps to have been wholly included among pagan remains, though it is found convenient to describe the two more important groups under Ecclesiastical Sites in the next chapter, these being closely associated with the Holy Well at Ard 'a Bhorain and the graveyard on Boreray Island.

In North Uist we are able to chronicle specimens of this much debated class at six different localities in addition to those just mentioned. In each case, both as regards position and arrangement, their occurrence can hardly be ascribed to natural causes.

At Portain, upon the covering slab of a supposed cist west of Loch Grota, are four cup-marks, three of them in a row near its edge, the other being smaller and out of line.

At 'Baishune's Grave,' near the summit of Beinn Langass, are three stones marked with similar hollows. Here the thin upper slab shows a cup upon each of its west corners, a groove leading from that at the south for a distance of 3 feet to nearly the opposite edge of this slab,—an inch deep at its commencement, but gradually tailing off. The lower slab, and also an intermediate stone, bear each a single cup-mark upon one corner.

About 20 yards north of Teampull Clann a' Phiocair at Carinish, a flat boulder shows upon its upper surface a pair of cup-marks about 3 inches wide by an inch in depth.

Three or four similar marks were found upon a large stone lying in the north edge of Buaile Risary.

On a tidal islet near Oban Skibinish are three cups recessed within the upper end of an erect stone.

At Vallay, in the westmost walled field, is a group of fifteen cup-marks on a flat rock showing just above the surface. These include four which are especially distinct, the largest measuring $3\frac{1}{2}$ inches across its top by a depth of $1\frac{1}{2}$ inches, very regularly worked in conical form. A few inches to the west appear three smaller cups arranged in an arc, these being also well shaped but only 2 inches in diameter and correspondingly shallow. Again, placed irregularly to the south, may be counted eight other less clearly marked indentations. The rock thus distinguished lies 100 yards from the shore, and can therefore bear no relation to another and quite separate type of 'shell-bait basins' afterwards noticed in Chapter x.

North Uist contains various other sites, which, while perhaps referable to pagan times, do not lend themselves to classification, being even possibly of natural origin. Among these the most prominent is a group of large stones, chiefly mere shapeless boulders, lying above Traigh Himiligh at the north shore of Vallay. Here, surrounded by other large blocks, is a conspicuous oblong cube of stone which measures fully 8 by 4 by 3 feet. Underneath this block are several much smaller stones, though it may never have been actually poised upon them.[1] The remarkable feature is that at least two of its six sides are almost mathematically squared, while the others present a somewhat rougher condition. It seems hard to believe that this mass of granitic gneiss could have acquired its right angles and comparatively smoothed faces (even across the grain) through natural and fortuitous agency.

---

[1] In a recess underneath this massive block was found a hammer-stone, and two flat pieces of sandstone were also noted as evidently not belonging to the locality but carried thither from a considerable distance.

OBLONG CUBE OF STONE AT TRAIGH HIMILIGH, VALLAY.

GRAVEYARD AT SAND, FROM EAST.

CHAPTER IX

PRE-REFORMATION CHAPELS, AND OTHER ANCIENT ECCLESIASTICAL REMAINS

THIS important class of antiquities is taken in geographical order, commencing, as with the forts, at the north-east corner of North Uist, and thence working sunwise to the mid-north.

Great assistance has been derived from the two volumes of *Origines Parochiales Scotiæ*,[1] a most valuable work, unfortunately never completed as to the Scottish mainland, and yet happily (for our purpose) covering the entire Hebridean area. Upon an outline map of 'Part of the Diocese of the Isles,' appended to the *Origines* (vol. ii. part 2) are marked two parish churches and no fewer than ten chapels in North Uist and its several annexes.

Practically all the twenty-one sites enumerated in the present chapter lie close to the shore; the central portion of this parish not containing a single locality known to be associated with early Christian remains.

* I.   First in order we take SAND, a mile north of the modern *quoad sacra* church at Trumisgarry and 'undoubtedly one of the two parish churches of North Uist mentioned by Monro in 1549.'[2] This was dedicated to St. Columba, and is shown upon Blaeu's map of 1654 as 'Kilchalmkil,' in 1561 pertaining to the Abbot of Iona. An 'Obligation,' dated 17th March 1575-1576, enjoins a payment to 'Johne Bischop of the Ilis . . . for the kirklandis and teyndis of Sandey, tuentie bollis beir, of the mett and mesour of Vyest.'[3]

---

[1] Compiled and edited by Cosmo Innes and James B. Brichan ; Bannatyne Club, 1850-1855.
[2] *Origines*, vol. ii. p. 376. The district of Sand has latterly reassumed something of its former importance, the northern section of North Uist having been erected into a *quoad sacra* parish in the year 1833. Hugh MacDonald of Sleat, who gave his name to Clan Huistein or 'Clan Donald north,' is said to have been buried at Sand in 1498 ; see *antea*, pp. 32, 91-92.
[3] *Collectanea*, pp. 3 and 10.

CROIS MHIC JAMAIN.

CROIS AN T-SAGAIRT.

Indistinct traces of the south wall of St. Columba's Chapel[1] still remain, much imbedded in sand, at the west side of its burying-ground, which is one of the two in North Uist most frequently used for interments. This graveyard occupies the whole of a large mound, and is remarkably well kept, considering the fact of its being entirely unenclosed. Only two memorial stones were noticeable as at all peculiar; one of them apparently the broken socket of a cross, of which the shaft had measured 3 or 4 inches wide; and the other an erect slab standing about 33 inches above ground, 22 inches in width and pierced by a 3-inch circular hole through its centre at about 2 feet from the top. Fifty yards to the south, kitchen-midden remains are distinctly visible upon the 'machair' in parts where turf has been removed.

A hundred yards north of Sand burying-ground the Ordnance map shows *Druim na Croise*, evidently to be identified with a rocky grass-covered hillock upon which no doubt once stood a cross. A little west of this, and not far from the shore at *Hornish*, is the traditionary site of a still earlier chapel than that to which reference has been already made.

A mile and a half to the north-east, near Port nan Long, is a site marked Crois Mhic Jamain,[2] tradition agreeing as to its ecclesiastical character although the specific name seems hardly known. Now showing merely as a slight oval hillock 54 feet long by 32 feet wide, and apparently once walled around its base, this is subdivided into two lesser mounds, each capped by a small erect slab. These stones are both quite plain and stand about 18 feet apart, the taller measuring 3 feet in height by 2 feet in breadth—presumably the cross itself —while the other is smaller and less regular in shape.

Half a mile to the south-east of St. Columba's graveyard and 100 yards north of Dun Rosail, is a huge block of gneiss, rough upon its north face but smooth on the south, and measuring 8 feet 8 inches in height by 11 feet in width and from 3 to 4 feet in thickness.[3] On the

---

[1] Mr. T. S. Muir, in his *Characteristics of Old Church Architecture, etc.*, Edinburgh, 1861, p. 225, remarks, 'The west end of a chapel is standing, the rest of it greatly reduced, and partly buried under a huge sand-heap.' It is said that, so recently as about the year 1800, this chapel was still in use. According to the *Old Stat. Acc.* (vol. xiii. p. 314, published in 1794), 'There is no church at present in this place, the house in which divine service used to be performed having lately fallen to ruin.'

[2] 'Human Remains found A.D. 1862.'—Ordnance map. We are told that a very large skull was discovered at this site.

[3] Noted in Martin's *Description, etc.* (p. 59) as a stone 'about 8 foot high at Down-rossel which the natives call a Cross.'

✳ south face is incised a Latin cross, ornamented by terminal knobs upon its top and arms, and with a 2-inch spike shown as descending from its broadened base, the extreme measurements being 15½ by 11¼ inches—a 'cross fitché.' This stone is variously known as *Clach an t-Sagairt, Clach na h-Ulaidh, Crois an t-Sagairt*, and *Crois Aona'ain*[1] or *An'adhan*, all except the first name being quoted from the *Scottish Geographical Magazine*, vol. iii. p. 243. The crosses above mentioned may have had some connection with St. Columba's Chapel— the parish church of Sand—perhaps as marking its sanctuary limits. Fully half a mile to the south is an old well, now disused but still bearing the title of *Tobar Chaluim Chille*; while, 400 yards east of this, is another ancient site at *Creag Laiaval*, close to the south base of that cliff and consisting of a green mound, with some evidence of a building on its summit, besides traces of a wall which formed a semi-circular enclosure abutting against the rock at both ends. This is in a dry position with a pleasant southern aspect, and it was locally suggested that here stood a chapel and perhaps a burial-ground.

Throughout the east border of North Uist ancient ecclesiastical sites are most rare, although several not very definite exceptions may be noted.

On the north side of Portain, near Loch Aulasary, occurs a group of three place-names—*Cnoc Mór an t-Sagairt, Cnoc Beag an t-Sagairt*, and *Loch an t-Sagairt*—all obviously referring to a priest, and at least suggestive that a chapel formerly stood in that vicinity.

Two miles north-west of Lochmaddy, between the sea-lochs known as Loch Minish and Loch Blashaval, is an islet bearing the significant
✳ II. name of EILEAN AN TEAMPUILL. This lies in the narrows which separate Collastrome from Minish Island, being accessible over a good causeway at low water, and even for the whole day at neap tides. Here are some remains of a structural erection within an enclosure, the latter oval in shape but the former stated to have been rectangular.

✳ III.   From Minish to the island of RONAY, situated at the south-eastern extremity of North Uist, is a stretch of eight miles. Martin notes 'a little Chappel in the Island *Rona*,[2] called the *Low-landers*

---

[1] Evidently the 'Crois Adhamhnain' of *Carmina Gadelica*, vol. ii. p. 222, commemorating St. Adamnan, who died A.D. 704.

[2] *A Description*, etc., p. 56. This 'Rona' certainly represents the Ronay of North Uist, its situation being specified as about two miles south of Loch Eford ; *Ibid.*

Chappel, because Seamen who dye in time of Fishing, are buried in that place.' This would apparently infer the existence of a pre-Reformation chapel, and a rocky knoll near the west side of Ronay, north of the only dwelling which that island contains, is known as *Cnoc nan Gall*, thus to a certain extent verifying the 'Lowlanders' of Martin. Upon Ronay are also found the place-names *Rudh' an t-Sagairt* and *Beinn an t-Sagairt*, much in the same way as those already recorded in the Portain district.

GRIMSAY, the large island immediately west of Ronay, contained two ancient chapels, both situated near Kallin, which is understood to derive its name from these,—*Na Ceallan*, or 'the cells.' The more important was dedicated to St. Michael and stands upon a hillock ✻ IV. near the extremity of St. Michael's Point, at the south-east corner of Grimsay. Its foundation is attributed to Amie Mac Ruari (wife of John, first Lord of the Isles), which would give it a date of about 1350-1390. This chapel is noted by Captain Thomas as 'Teampull Mhichael,' with interior dimensions of 23½ by 14 feet and walls 30 inches thick. Writing of St. Michael's chapel in 1871, he describes it as then much ruined, 'the east wall being quite gone, and the south side, in which was the door, is but 3 feet high. There is 9 feet of the west wall left, in which is a splayed, straight-lined window, and it is nearer to the north than the south side. In the north wall, which is 9 feet high, are two windows; the eastmost is destroyed; but the western is rectangular, 1¼ foot wide on the outside, with parallel sides (4½ feet high) for ¾ foot, then splayed to 3 feet on the inside.' [1]

In May 1905 the present writer noted much the same conditions, except that the west and north walls had been still further ruined, while the east wall was in parts about 18 inches high. The west gable then stood to a height of 8½ feet at its centre, although so much broken towards each side that the former window could hardly be traced. The north wall showed recent damage and was nowhere more than 3 feet high, without any appearance of the two windows mentioned by Captain Thomas.

[1] *Archæologia Scotica*, vol. v. p. 244, where a ground plan is also given. Captain F. W. L. Thomas believed St. Michael's, Grimsay, to represent the 'Lowlanders' Chapel,' located by Martin upon the island of Ronay; but the latter authority was probably correct.
We read that St. Michael the Archangel was 'the favourite saint with the Norse settlers, and especially associated with the horse.'

Around this chapel are the remains of a rectangular enclosure which measured about 63 by 54 feet, evidently once serving as a graveyard but disused for many years.

* v.

Dr. Alexander Carmichael[1] notes the site of a second chapel, with its graveyard, upon low ground about 150 yards north from St. Michael's. Of this no traces now remain, and even its dedication has been forgotten, although the former existence of two chapels is still attested by the local name *Teampull nan Ceall*—in the plural. Upon Grimsay, within a mile to the north-west of Kallin, is also found *Loch an Aba* or 'loch of the abbot.'

In the 'North Ford,' between Grimsay and the main portion of North Uist, are numerous tidal islands, some of them inhabited. Near the centre of one is a prominent conical mound locally known as

* *Crois Eilein Ghiorr*, with many stones in the surface near its flattened top, where probably once stood a cross. Towards the east end of the same island is another and smaller mound, but as to neither of these could any definite information be obtained.

A mile farther west, immediately beyond Eilean Leathann, is *Eilean na Mnà Mairbhe* or 'island of the dead woman,' a place-name erroneously shown on the Ordnance map as nearly a mile to the south and half-way across the ford to Benbecula. This is a small narrow islet, with a central mound upon which are traceable the walls of an enclosure about 30 feet in diameter; three slabs set on end perhaps marking old burials. Here may have possibly stood a former chapel within its graveyard.

Near the south-west corner of the Orasay which lies at the inner end of Loch Eford, opposite Langass, is a somewhat similar site containing the foundations of a rectangular structure placed east and west, with interior measurements of about 20 by 12 feet. Within stand three small slabs in erect position, and some fragments of rude pottery were found at a rabbit-hole in the north edge.

Five miles north-west from St. Michael's, Grimsay, upon the peninsula of Carinish, are two adjoining chapels known as TEAMPULL NA TRIONAID and TEAMPULL CLANN A' PHIOCAIR, or the Churches of the Trinity and of Clan MacVicar.[2] So far as regards present appear-

---

[1] *Proc. Soc. Antiq. Scot.*, vol. viii. p. 276.

[2] Strangely enough, the Carinish 'Temples' are entirely ignored both by Monro in 1549 (at best always brief), and by Martin in 1703—a traveller who described North Uist from personal observation and usually with much detail.

ST. MICHAEL'S CHAPEL, KALLIN.

TEAMPULL NA TRIONAID, AND TEAMPULL CLANN A' PHIOCAIR.

ance, and especially the style of architecture, Teampull Clann a' Phiocair might seem to antedate its larger neighbour by several centuries. On the other hand, tradition is probably correct in assigning to Teampull na Trionaid the earlier origin ; any architectural difficulty being explained by the theory of this ' Temple' having been at least once completely and once partially rebuilt, whereas the other may remain as it was first erected, with little or no change. As a result we would have in the smaller and apparently older chapel its original Celtic characteristics, but in the really more ancient Teampull na Trionaid, no special feature earlier than its round-headed doorway, together with various secondary alterations perhaps ranging in date almost up to the close of the sixteenth century.

It is elsewhere noted that in pre-Reformation times North Uist was provided with two parish churches, one at Kilmuir (St. Mary's) and the other at Clachan Sand (St. Columba's) ; and it seems certain that neither of the twin ' Temples' at Carinish ever held this distinction.

The name *Teampull* is itself uncommon, evidently implying some distinctive character explained by Professor Donald MacKinnon as denoting a stone church in contrast to one built of wood and wattles.[1] As already suggested, the solution of an apparent difficulty with regard to the comparative ages of the Carinish 'Temples' might thus lie in the rebuilding of Teampull na Trionaid at three distinct periods ; first, from the wood of Columban times into primitive stone ; again, from Celtic to Gothic style (perhaps by Amie MacRuari, *ca.* 1350-1390, accounting for the pointed north window) ; and finally, a reconstruction during the sixteenth century into its latter form.

Here is by far the most interesting ecclesiastical site in North Uist, these twin chapels being much better preserved and also displaying greater individuality than is elsewhere to be found in this class throughout the whole island.

The interior of TEAMPULL NA TRIONAID measures 61 feet 8 inches VI. by 21 feet 6 inches, with walls averaging a thickness of about 40 inches, increased to 48 inches in the east gable.[2] Three of its sides

---

[1] In *The Scotsman*, 8th December 1887 ; one of a valuable series of articles contributed to that newspaper during the years 1887-1890.

[2] In precise thickness the other walls were measured as :—south, 39 inches ; west, 43 inches ; and north, 38 inches. Captain Thomas, in *Archæologia Scotica*, vol. v. p. 242, gives the external dimensions of this chapel as 68½ by 27¾ feet.

are carefully built of flat undressed stones laid in rude courses, while the masonry of the west gable presents a complete contrast,[1] with no attempt at the same regularity and containing neither door nor window. The south wall, which has suffered most damage, was pierced by at least one window as perhaps also by the original doorway, now represented by a gap towards the west end. The east gable stands complete up to the sill of a former large window,[2] with indications that this measured about 7½ feet in width, though no clue remains as to its shape.

The lofty north wall of Teampull na Trionaid, when viewed from its exterior, seems to represent at successive levels two or three distinct stages (if not periods) of construction, as evidenced by differences in the style of masonry. The north-west outer angle of this chapel is now in a perilous condition, having lost many of its cornerstones and being also very imperfect near its base. In a lesser degree, the same remarks apply to the north-east angle.

It is in the north wall of this 'Temple' that are to be found the only definite architectural features bearing upon its date or dates. Of these, what appears to be the most ancient is a plain round-headed doorway, through which a vaulted passage (afterwards noticed in detail) leads into the adjoining Teampull Clann a' Phiocair. East of this doorway, and evidently within a former chancel, is a Gothic window splayed deeply inwards both at its top and sides; the original form of its base not now showing, as the sill has been completely destroyed. In external height, this window seems to have measured about 54 inches, and interiorly its roof arch is splayed considerably upwards. As to width, the cross splay has apparently been from about 8 inches at the outer opening to as much as 66 inches inside. There is an ambry 24 inches wide beneath the east edge of this window, and one of smaller dimensions is to be noted within the east gable close to the north-east corner at an evident height of at least 10 feet above the original floor, almost proving the existence of a

---

[1] It is locally stated that the upper portion of the west gable fell, and had to be rebuilt. See also *Archæologia Scotica*, vol. v. p. 227 (foot-note).

[2] Mr. T. S. Muir in *Characteristics of Old Church Architecture, etc.*, p. 226, suggests that 'the unusual height of the walls and size of the east window, indicate a foundation of importance, though probably of no great age.' The latter remark may well apply to the north-west door and to the east window, although hardly to the original structure. Below this window has been a well-executed base-moulding across the exterior of the east gable. The bevel course has, however, been partly removed, leaving unsightly gaps.

PORCH CONNECTING THE CARINISH TEMPLES.

KILPHEDER CROSS.

second story, no doubt a priest's house. The east gable also contains another ambry below the former large window. This shows as a recess of 21 inches, generally squared although its roof is slightly curved ; the interior being so choked with rubbish that its width and height could not be accurately measured.

In the north wall, near its west end, there existed so recently as 1897 a second doorway with an obtusely angled head, then serving as the regular access, though from its nondescript style this could hardly represent an original feature. Seven years later this entrance was found walled across, its pointed top having then entirely disappeared.

The windows (as also, according to report, the south doorway), were faced with hewn sandstone, but their sills and jambs have suffered greatly by removal for various purposes. The north wall still remains in its evidently complete height of 18 or 20 feet; the west gable and small portions of the east and south walls also standing to about the same elevation.

The west and south walls are characterised by a most unusual feature—each of these containing two horizontal rows of upright rectangular opes or 'oillets' which measure from 8 by 7 inches to 12 by 9 inches, running straight through the walls and being undoubtedly structural. The north wall also shows a single row of oillets at a somewhat lower level.

The west wall is pierced by three of these loop-holes or oillets below, and by four above, at respective elevations of nearly 6 and 11 feet as compared with the outer base. The south wall, so far as now existing, shows four lower oillets and one upper; while the north wall contains five similar opes, all of them below.

It is, however, interesting to note that, taking the two rows in the west gable as a standard, the levels of the oillets in the other walls by no means coincide ; the inferior series, both in the north and south walls, occupying a distinctly lower position as compared with those which pierce the west gable. On the other hand, the single upper oillet still shown in the south wall is slightly above the level of the corresponding tier in the west gable.

These facts would apparently agree with a very simple explanation that the oillets were left as rafter-holes, and that Teampull na Trionaid (in its later form, though not originally) had a sloping 'loft' or gallery at its west end, and was further provided with an upper story; this latter suggestion having been already made with special reference to the ambry situated high up in the east gable.

An alternative though quite unsatisfactory solution has been elsewhere offered, namely that these oillets were left for the purpose of holding beams to support scaffolds from which masons could work in building the upper portions of the walls.[1] Against this view may be urged the fact that these opes are thoroughly structural, and that no real attempt can have been made to close them after they had served a temporary purpose.

Mr. T. S. Muir,[2] writing of Teampull na Trionaid in 1867, states: 'It would appear that till about the beginning of the present century the interior of the greater church was decorated with sculptures similar to those still existing at Rodil, as I was told that one Macpherson, an octogenarian living at Cladach, Carinish, remembers of having seen, when a boy, stones in the walls figured with angels, armed men, animals, etc.' Captain Thomas[3] appends a note upon the same subject, supplied by Dr. Alex. Carmichael and giving a local tradition to the effect that there was formerly a pinnacle upon the east gable of Teampull na Trionaid with the figure of a three-headed giant on its top, presumably as representing the Trinity; although some say that this image occupied a niche within the gable. Dr. Carmichael adds:—'There were several pieces of sculpture, both inside and outside of the church, but these being of freestone were carried away for sharpening stones.'

Reference has been already made to a round-headed doorway in the north wall of Teampull na Trionaid, and some description must be given of the short passage which leads through it into Teampull Clann a' Phiocair. The parallel exterior walls of the twin temples are barely 5 feet apart, and this connecting porch or passage shows as an entirely independent structure, abutting upon (though not bonded to) the walls at either end, which fact proves it to be a secondary

[1] This is the theory adopted by Captain Thomas in *Archæologia Scotica*, vol. v. p. 227. The same writer adds (*Ibid.*, pp. 237-238) :—'I have noted the occurrence of holes in the gable of St. Kenneth, Loch Laggan, Badenoch'; and also mentions another chapel (St. Helen's, Aldcamus, Berwickshire) as having its west gable 'copiously pierced with rows of diminutive square holes.' MacGibbon and Ross in *The Ecclesiastical Architecture of Scotland*, vol. i. p. 325, mention this west gable of St. Helen's as 'rebuilt in the fourteenth or fifteenth century. It is without opening of any kind, save the numerous putlog holes used for the masons' scaffolding when erecting the building.'

[2] In *Barra Head. A Sketch*, p. 41; privately printed, Leith, 1867.

[3] *Archæologia Scotica*, vol. v. p. 226.

insertion. With a greatest interior height of about 6½ feet, the passage is now so much choked by rubbish as not to afford exact measurements. Although entering by a rounded arch on the south, it emerges into the northern chapel through a flat-headed doorway which has inclined jambs widening from about 30 inches across the top to 36 inches at the floor level.[1] It narrows from south to north, passing through the wall of Teampull na Trionaid in a width of 54 inches and thereafter becoming contracted to 45 inches. In each of the side walls of this passage is a small rectangular window, laterally splayed from 6 inches at the exterior to 24 inches within, but flat both at top and bottom, showing a height of 15 inches. It has a saddle-roof which slopes to east and west, and is covered by thin overlapping slabs of stone.

TEAMPULL CLANN A' PHIOCAIR is built of rude water-worn stones ⁎ VII. interspersed with numerous thin and very small slabs, the whole being so irregularly laid as to present a quaintly antique appearance. Its gables and south wall are fairly complete, though little of the north wall remains; while the roof is understood to have consisted of flat overlapping stones, a point which however cannot be now verified. The upper portion of the east gable is distinctly thinner than its lower half.

The interior dimensions of this smaller chapel are 23 feet by 13 feet 4 inches, its exterior measuring about 28 by 19 feet, with walls which average a thickness of 30 inches. Apart from the north wall (of which no more can be said than that it seems never to have contained a doorway) this chapel has been lit by three narrow rectangular windows, all of them splayed. The most complete is in the east gable, splayed inwards in all four directions from an exterior approximately 6 inches wide and 26 inches high to about 37 by 46 inches at the inner face of the wall. On each side of this window is a small ambry, one measuring 16 by 17 inches and the other 16½ by 14½ inches. In the south wall, a little east of the passage which communicates with Teampull na Trionaid, is a window splayed laterally from 5 inches outside to 31 inches within, having also a downward splay from its outer sill, although no vertical measurement is available as the upper portion is broken away. The third window was in the west gable, not exactly at its centre but somewhat

---

[1] This feature would apparently indicate a Celtic origin.

towards the south,[1] and near it is another ambry measuring 24 by 12 inches a little to the north.

Since Teampull Clann a' Phiocair shows no indication of any other access, it would apparently follow that the south doorway, secondarily enclosed within the short connecting passage, was also its original entrance; this chapel, under such conditions, virtually becoming a mere annexe to Teampull na Trionaid, which would then form its sole means of approach.

The close proximity of these Temples is a noteworthy feature, while the position of their doorways so exactly opposite each other seems even more remarkable.

Both erections contain numerous burials within their walls, and immediately to the south is a semi-circular graveyard still in use. Here, adjoining the south-west corner of Teampull na Trionaid, stands a small rectangular and comparatively modern tomb. Thirty yards west from the smaller chapel is an oval knoll, its flattened top surrounded by the remains of a wall enclosing an area which measures about 50 by 40 feet.[2]

Tradition states that Teampull na Trionaid was built by Amie MacRuari,[3] wife of John, first Lord of the Isles, but although it seems highly probable that Amie may have repaired and enlarged this church, ca. 1350-1390, the theory of its foundation by her is quite untenable. This latter point is historically certain from a charter of Godfrey, lord of Uist, dated 7th July 1389 and confirming 'capellam sancte trinitatis in Wuyste et totam terram de karynche,' etc., to the monastery and convent of Inchaffray,—all as previously granted to them by Christina, daughter of Allan MacRuari and aunt of Amie, at a period which can hardly have been later than about the year 1320.[4]

---

[1] This now shows as a mere ragged gap, and it is to Captain Thomas (*Archæologia Scotica*, vol. v. p. 228) that we owe any definite notice of its character—'a small window, like others, with an ambry on one side. The window is considerably on one side of the centre of the wall—a deviation not often observed in other chapels.'

[2] As to this enclosure, local explanations are somewhat contradictory. One holds it to represent nothing more than a crofter's stackyard, which purpose it may indeed have latterly served. Another version is distinctly more picturesque, describing this as an ancient 'place of punishment,' around which offenders were compelled to walk seven times, against the sun,—a penalty which presumably had some moral effect.

[3] *Collectanea*, p. 298.

[4] *Charters of Inchaffray Abbey*, Scot. Hist. Soc., p. 136; the same being also confirmed, 6 Dec. 1410, by Donald, second Lord of the Isles (*Ibid.*, p. 137). As noted at p. 25 *antea*, this Christina was the mother of Isobel of Mar, first wife of King Robert the Bruce.

According to another and perhaps better authority,[1] ' *Teampall Chairinis*' was founded by Bethog, daughter of Somerled and first prioress of Iona from *ca.* 1203, a date which would come nearer the truth, although it is evidently to early post-Columban times that must be referred the original construction of Teampull na Trionaid.[2] This might well agree with a rebuilding or enlargement of the fabric by prioress Beatrice in the thirteenth century and by Amie MacRuari a hundred and fifty years later, to some extent justifying both of the statements already quoted.

Teampull Clann a' Phiocair must evidently also be assigned to some remote period, but here no records are available, and even the dedication of this chapel is locally unknown.[3]

The name Teampull Clann a' Phiocair would almost seem to have been acquired in post-Reformation times, and may perhaps be explained by the cumulative evidence of certain facts and traditions. It is credibly stated that, during the sixteenth century, Donald MacVicar (known as *Am Piocair Mór*) and his four sons[4] held a large portion of North Uist. Of these sons, Donald had Carinish and Claddach-Carinish; Angus (*Aonghas Mhánta*) the fifteen (?) penny-lands of Baleloch, Balamartin, and Balelone; Hector, the lands of Caolas Bernera, Baile Mhic Phail, and Baile Mhic Conain; while John, the youngest, lived with his father who held the whole island of Baleshare together with Eaval.

[1] 'The Book of Clanranald' in *Reliquiæ Celticæ*, vol. ii. p. 157. See also Skene's *Celtic Scotland*, quoted at p. 23, *antea*. The Rev. James MacDonald's *General View of the Agriculture of the Hebrides*, Edinburgh, 1811, p. 705, contains a description of the Nunnery Chapel of Iona as it existed a hundred years ago, with the statement that 'upon one monumental stone there is the following inscription : *Behag Niin Shorle vic Ilvrid Priorissa* ; *i.e.* Beatrice, daughter of Somer-led the son of Gilbert, prioress.' Although two of these authorities translate *Beathag* as Beatrice, it ought to be noted that the Gaelic Dictionaries edited by MacBain and by MacLeod and Dewar agree in giving *Beathag* as Sophia, the latter stating *Beitiris* to be the equivalent of Beatrice. In further complication we have the *Highland Society of Scotland's Dictionary* (Edinburgh, 1828) explaining *Beathag* as Rebecca. Such divergences are, to say the least, very confusing.

[2] *The Clan Donald*, vol. i. p. 465, says of Teampull na Trionaid :—'There are traces of a foundation older than the days of Somerled, going back to the time of the Celtic Church, shown by indications of one at least of those bee-hive cells characteristic of that early phase of church architecture.' The present writer has been unable to verify any trace of this bee-hive cell.

[3] It is true that the confirmation granted by Godfrey of the Isles in 1389 is prefaced as 'in honore sancte trinitatis et beate Marie virginis gloriose.' But since this charter proceeds to describe the subjects simply as 'capellam sancte trinitatis in Wuyste,' together with certain lands, and no mention is made of a second chapel, this reference to the Blessed Virgin Mary can hardly be founded upon as specially significant.

[4] In Chapter VI., under Dun an Sticir, p. 143, reference has already been made to the tradition that these four MacVicars were killed in cold blood by Hugh, son of Archibald the Clerk, *ca.* 1580-1585. It is further added that their father, Donald, was still alive, but happened to be from home at the time, thus escaping the fate of his sons.

In *Archæologia Scotica*, vol. v. p. 228, the modern title of this chapel is said to be derived ' from some families of the Macvicars who took possession of it for burying therein. An old man still living, John Macvicar, Balsher, told me lately that he saw this ruin roofed and thatched with heather.'[1]

In the immediate vicinity of the Carinish 'Temples' once stood two crosses, now only certified by the local names applied to their sites, these showing as knolls about 100 yards to the east and south of Teampull na Trionaid and respectively marked upon the Ordnance map as *Cnoc na Croise Mór*[2] and *Cnocan na Croise Beaga*.[3] Close to the east of the latter was *Loch na Trionaid*, with *Loch an Aba*[4] 300 yards on its south, both of these now drained off so as in summer to be recognisable as little more than marshes. Parts of *Loch an Aba* still indeed contain water to the depth of about a foot, and near its centre is an island which bears the name of *Eilean nan Tighean* and has been approached over a causeway from the south shore. This island shows traces of an enclosing wall, and towards its north end are the ruins of a large rectangular erection with interior measurements of about 40 by 20 feet, while to the south of this have also stood two or three minor buildings.

Two hundred and fifty yards south-west of the twin chapels is *Tobar na Trionaid* which in all probability served as the well in connection with them. This is lined with a wall, and although but recently disused is very shallow and of distinctly uninviting appearance. *Sruthan na Comraich* or 'stream of the sanctuary,' a mile to

---

[1] A communication from Dr. Alexander Carmichael, quoted by Captain Thomas in his valuable 'Notices of Three Churches,' etc., 1871. According to Captain Thomas (*Proc. Soc. Antiq. Scot.*, vol. xi. pp. 505-506) the population of North Uist in 1861 included ninety-eight persons bearing the surname of MacVicar. We are further informed that a Baleshare family of this name still use the chapel as a burying-place.

It may be noted, *quantum valeat*, that Hugh MacDonald,—the founder of Clan Huistein, who died in 1498,—had a son, *Aonghas Dubh*, by a daughter of 'Maurice Vicar of South Uist. Maurice's daughter was red-haired, ruddy-faced, lived by turns in Argyle and Oransay in North Uist, where she died and was buried in Collumkill in Sand,' Gregory's *Collections*, vol. iv. p. 180 of the MS.

[2] The base, or perhaps merely the socket, of this cross is reported as still existing within the summit of the knoll.

[3] 'Small hillock of the little cross' as we would translate it, although assured upon the spot, with much circumstantial argument, that *cnocan* is here the plural instead of a diminutive and refers to a group of three small mounds (standing approximately in line, north and south) each of them said to have once been surmounted by a 'little cross.' Within the same enclosed field is still another hillock, known as *Cnoc Pheadair*.

[4] There is also a *Loch an Aba* on the island of Grimsay.

the south and forming part of the ford to Benbecula, was no doubt the sanctuary limit in that direction, though perhaps never marked by the cross usually placed at such boundaries.

Close to the shore, 300 yards north-east from Teampull na Trionaid, is *Cnoc nan Aingeal* or ' knoll of the angels,'[1] whatever may be the origin of that name as applied to a rugged natural hillock of no particular shape, yet bearing the remains of a cairn upon its north summit. Immediately to the east of this, in the centre of what has certainly been a marsh if not a former shallow loch, is a symmetrical mound about 20 yards in diameter and 12 feet high, with traces of a wall encircling its base at a very uniform interval of 2 or 3 yards.

Some account of the Battle of Carinish, fought between the MacDonalds and MacLeods in May 1601, has been given in Chapter IV. under Carinish as a place-name.

It is said that there was a school or college at Carinish, and such may probably have been the case in mediæval times. An Act of Parliament, 13th June 1496, ordered ' that all barronis and frehaldaris, that ar of substance put thair eldest sonis and airis to the sculis fra thai be aucht or nyne yeiris of age, and till remane at the grammer sculis, quhill thai be competentlie foundit, and haue perfite latyne. And thaireftir to remane thre yeris at the sculis of art and Jure, sua that thai may haue knawlege and vnderstanding of the lawis,' etc., under a penalty of £20 (*Scots* being understood).[2] To judge from this specimen of official orthography, it would seem not very difficult then to pass an examination in ' perfite latyne,' and still less to ' be found able sufficientlie to speik, reid, and wryte Inglische,' as was enjoined upon the eldest son or daughter of ' everie gentilman or yeaman within the said Ilandis' by ' The Band and Statutes of Icolmkill,' 23 August 1609.[3]

At Carnach, near Clachan-a-gluip, two miles north-west of Carinish, stood *Crois Moireaig* or ' cross of little Mary,' the diminutive   *

---

[1] ' Colliculus Angelorum' is twice mentioned in Adamnan's *Life of St. Columba*, its locality being identified by Bishop Reeves (in his *Adamnan*, p. 428) with *Sithean Mór*, a large knoll near the centre of Iona. This phrase seems indeed to represent the Gaelic *sithean* or ' fairy-mound.'

[2] Thomson's *Acts of Parliament*, vol. ii. p. 238. As is remarked however in *The Clan Donald*, vol. iii. p. 145 (in special connection with the Carinish school and the *Act* of 1469) this law would be ' practically inoperative in the Highlands.'

[3] *Reg. Privy Council*, vol. ix. p. 29.

being used as a term of endearment. No trace seems to remain of the actual cross, although its traditional site is still pointed out. Five hundred yards farther to the north-west, in the neighbouring ✱ ford to Baleshare, *An Crois Eilean* is shown upon the Ordnance map, but as to this we can only note that a slight mound exists near its centre.

Towards the south end of Baleshare Island, about two miles ✱ VIII. west from Carinish, are the scanty ruins of TEAMPULL CHRIOSD,[1] with its adjoining graveyard still in occasional use and apparently once walled around, though now entirely open. This ‘Temple’ has been lime-built, and a small portion of its west gable remains to the extent of about 6 feet in width and 6½ feet in height, with a thickness of 32 inches. The foundations of its south wall are also traceable, especially towards the east where these measure 28 inches across, and its interior dimensions may be roughly taken as about 42 by 12 or 13 feet, formerly divided into two unequal parts, that to the west being slightly shorter than the other.

Teampull Chriosd is popularly held to be one of several chapels founded by Amie MacRuari.[2]

Three hundred yards north of Teampull Chriosd is a grassy hillock ✱ known as *Crois Mór*, while at an equal distance on the east is *Creag Thormaidh*, both of them supposed to have been sanctuary limits.

The place-name ‘Ballienakill’ or ‘Balnakelie’ (correctly *Baile na Cille*, ‘township of the chapel’) occurs in old documents[3] as situated

---

[1] A dedication not unknown elsewhere in Scotland, four ancient parishes bearing the same title under the varied forms of Kilchrist, Kirkchrist, and Christ's Kirk. There were two parish churches known as Kilchrist,—that of Strath at the south side of Skye, and another in the south-east of Ross-shire (now part of Urray) ‘where its ruins and cemetery still remain,’ *Origines Parochiales*, vol. ii. pp. 343-344, 523. Kirkchrist in Kirkcudbrightshire forms the southern district of Twynholm parish ; and Christ's Kirk (or Rathmuriel) has been united with the parish of Kennethmont, Aberdeenshire : the churchyards of both being still in use :—Groome's *Gazetteer*, pp. 976, 261. Besides these, Kilchrist chapel stood within the combined parish of Kilninian and Kilmore in Mull ; while the lands of ‘Killiecrist’ are mentioned at Kilkerran in Kintyre :—*Origines Parochiales*, vol. ii. pp. 320, 16. We also read of at least five other chapels of similar name in the counties of Wigtown, Lanark, Stirling, and Aberdeen. The largest of three former chapels in St. Kilda (that associated with the regular burial-ground there) is noted by Martin (*A Late Voyage to St. Kilda*, London, 1698, p. 83) as ‘*Christ Chappel*, near the Village ; it is covered and thatched after the same manner with their Houses,’ etc. The Rev. Kenneth Macaulay (*The History of St. Kilda*, London, 1764, pp. 70-71) describes this under the same dedication, also stating that it measures 24 by 14 feet, with uncemented walls.

[2] *Archæologia Scotica*, vol. v. p. 235.

[3] *Collectanea*, pp. 2, 10 ; see also Chapter IV. under Place-Names.

in 'Eillera' or 'Illera,'—according to local belief, in the immediate neighbourhood of this Temple.

Upon the smaller Kirkibost Island, a mile north of Baleshare, is said to have stood a chapel of which the dedication is now forgotten. Its site is doubtfully shown near the west side of the island, a few yards south of an old cattle-fold already noticed in Chapter v. as containing an Earth-House.

HEISKER, or the MONACH ISLES, played a distinct and perhaps *IX. even an important part among the ecclesiastical settlements of pre-Reformation times.

We are told that a small monastery[1] once stood upon the western islet of Shillay, occupying the site of the present lighthouse.

Ceann Iar—separated from Shillay by a strait of 600 yards—is partially identified by Dr. Alexander Carmichael with *Heisgeir nan Cailleach*[2] or 'of the nuns,' this writer stating that a community of these holy women 'lived there far into Reformation times, and only died out from natural decay,' as also that the site of their house had been pointed out to him by 'a lonely old woman who lived on the spot.'[3]

Upon Ceann Ear—the largest and most easterly of the main group—can still be seen faint traces of an ancient burial-ground near its north-east corner. This is marked *Cladh na Bleide* upon the Ordnance map and has been almost certainly associated with a former chapel, of which no tradition seems now to remain although a slight wall is visible at the west base of a sand-hill. It was evidently here, 'in a burying ground' on Heisker, that was found a bronze pin with an ornamented swivel-head.[4]

Three of the Heisker islands contain individual hillocks, to each of which is locally given the significant title of 'cross'—a feature no doubt once existing in actual form. These are *Crois Leandal* (taken * phonetically) west of the cottages on Ceann Ear; *Crois Shivinish*, a * conical mound near the centre of the island bearing that name; and *Crois na Cuaig* ('of the cuckoo') near Hakinish on Ceann Iar. *

---

[1] In Appendix A. to the *Crofters Commission Report* of 1884, p. 465. From this monastery is evidently derived the general name of the Monach group.

[2] In Chapter IV. pp. 72-74, *antea*, are quoted various documents referring to Heisker from the ecclesiastical point of view.

[3] *Crofters Commission Report*, as noted above.

[4] Now in the National Museum of Antiquities, Edinburgh; *Proc. Soc. Antiq. Scot.*, vol. ii. p. 176.

Outside a cottage at Ceann Ear we noticed a symmetrical fragment of stone, measuring 13 by 7 inches and 5 inches thick, with a rectangular boss about 3 inches wide extending completely across its centre, and a slight hollow (2¾ inches in diameter) at one end. This had been brought from Ceann Iar, and evidently once formed part of a cross.

The *New Stat. Acc.* of North Uist[1] mentions 'several crosses rudely cut on stone' as existing 'in some of the burying-grounds, particularly in the island of Husker.'

Returning to the main island of North Uist, we next come to CLADH CHOTHAIN near the east side of Ard an Runair, where has been an ancient burying-ground, though the writer is unable to identify its site—apart from a walled enclosure containing a group of small cairns, noted in Chapter VIII.—and could find no satisfactory tradition as to the former existence of a chapel.

Cladh Chothain seems to be merely a variant of Kilchoan, which name occurs in connection with several old chapels in Lochalsh, Knoydart, Ardnamurchan, and Skye, as also in other parts of Scotland; there commemorating St. Comgan, brother of St. Kentigerna.[2]

At the north end of Ard an Runair is a tidal islet known as *Eilean Trostain*, said to be named after St. Drostan, a nephew and companion of St. Columba.

Martin writes,[3]—'There is a Stone in form of a Cross in the Row,[4] opposite to *St. Maries* Church about 5 foot high, the Natives call it the water Cross, for the antient Inhabitants had a Custom of erecting this sort of Cross to procure rain, and when they had got enough they laid it flat on the ground, but this custom is now disused.'

Three-quarters of a mile due east from *Cladh Chòthain*, and a little to the south of Hougary village, is the graveyard of KILMUIR— *Cill Mhoire*, or St. Mary's Church—from which the united parish of North Uist takes its name. This burying-ground covers the summit of a knoll and is of considerable area, having been somewhat enlarged

---

[1] Inverness-shire, p. 169.

[2] Bishop Forbes' *Kalendars of Scottish Saints*, Edin., 1872, pp. 310, 373. St. Kentigerna was mother of St. Fillan and died A.D. 733.

[3] *A Description*, etc., p. 59.

[4] 'Row' is clearly the Gaelic *rudha* 'or point,' referring to Ard an Runair where Cladh Chothain was situated exactly opposite Kilmuir churchyard and nearly a mile to its west.

about the year 1900, when its boundary wall was rebuilt and extended so as to form a rectangle in place of a circle as before. Upon lower ground, close to the west, is the shell of a barn-like structure which served as the parish church from the year 1764 until it was replaced in 1894 by a modern building a mile farther east.

Within the graveyard, which is still in regular use, are four family tombs consisting of square enclosures surrounded by high walls. Of these, the Balranald tomb (dated 1768) is the largest and occupies a central position, in all probability standing upon the site of the original church.

In 1866 Mr. T. S. Muir here noted 'two cruciform pillars, ... each 4 feet in height, one of peculiar shape, the other of the ordinary Latin form. The last, I was sorry to see, has been injured considerably since my visit in 1855, the north arm, then entire, being now nearly away.'[1] Of Muir's 'cruciform pillars' the second has since disappeared, but the other 'of peculiar type' still remains in the same condition as figured by him at p. 38, except that it now stands only 36 instead of 46 inches above ground. The head of this cross bears a circular boss in the centre of its west side, and although both arms have been broken off close to the shaft, 'round hollow angles'[2] are prominently shown at the four points of intersection, and a small hole has been pierced in its back, halfway through the stone.[3]

What was evidently the base of a much smaller cross also exists in the form of a socket-stone measuring about 12 inches square by 6 inches thick, and bearing in its top an oblong hole of 3 by 2½ inches with a small circular recess at each corner.

Kilmuir churchyard contains three other erect grave-stones which must be regarded as quasi-crosses of somewhat nondescript type. These are of mediæval if not even comparatively modern date, and two of them may be dismissed as having heads which represent a trefoil, and a trefoil without its upper lobe—this latter stone being, in other words, bifoliate. The third is still more peculiar, in general outline following that of the cross figured by Muir, but with short rounded

---

[1] *Barra Head. A Sketch*; pp. 38-39, Leith, 1867—a thin quarto, of which only fifteen copies were issued for private circulation.

[2] The name given to this type of ornament by Mr. J. Romilly Allen in *The Early Christian Monuments of Scotland*, Edin., 1903, p. 51.

[3] In its complete state this must have borne a marked resemblance to the Kilpheder cross, afterwards described.

arms and its head divided into twin lobes separated by an additional 'round hollow angle,' making in this case five in all, four at the arms and one at the top.

Of quite another class, a thin oblong stone has been faintly incised with a Latin cross, while another rough slab is noteworthy as bearing, in considerable relief, a cross-potent supplemented near its base by an extra (or fifth) bar, a type for which we can find no technical name.

In addition to the above are two large slabs, one measuring 54 by 26 inches with the raised but much worn figure of a man holding in front of him a broad-sword, its point depressed. The other, nearly 7 feet long by 4 feet wide, is a table-stone supported upon pillars and bears various devices in relief, the most important of these being a shield charged with the arms of MacDonald of Sleat—quarterly : 1, a lion rampant ; 2, a hand in armour, holding a cross-crosslet fitchée ; 3, a lymphad (or galley) sails unfurled and oars in action ; 4, a salmon naiant ;—while lower down is a group of conventional emblems including a coffin and skull, an hour-glass, cross-bones, shovels, and scythes. Round the edge of this table-stone, and also immediately below the shield, are traces of an incised inscription, now undecipherable but said to have been in memory of Hugh MacDonald of Baleshare who died in 1769 at the age of 63.[1]

Kilmuir church had a sanctuary attached, though this was evidently of small extent, perhaps corresponding with the glebe, since it appears that the Goular Burn, in the close vicinity, formed the southern boundary of both. Part of the glebe, adjoining this rivulet, is named *Leathad Phàil* or 'Paul's slope' from an incident elsewhere recorded in connection with Dun Scolpaig.[2]

It is interesting to find that the immediate neighbourhood of Kilmuir churchyard is locally known by the still earlier title of *Colasaidh*. As bearing upon this point a legend may here be quoted to the effect that it had been at first proposed to build the church on Hosta, but this plan was changed in obedience to the command given by a voice from the sky,—'*Seachain Hough agus Hosta, agus dèan Cill-Mhoire an Colasaidh,*'—that is, 'Avoid Hough and Hosta, and build St. Mary's church in Colasay.'[3]

---

[1] *The Clan Donald*, vol. iii. pp. 538-539.
[2] In Chapter vi. p. 193, *antea*.
[3] *Colasaidh* is said to be a stone near the centre of Kilmuir churchyard, so large that at one

At Balranald, three-quarters of a mile to the south-east, is *Loch na Cille*, although, in default of further evidence, this place-name can hardly be taken as indicating another chapel situated within so short a distance of the parish church.

Fully a mile north of Kilmuir Church, near the shore at Calligeo in Hosta township, the site of ST. CLEMENT'S CHAPEL is marked upon the Ordnance map. This clearly represents the *Kilchalma* shown by Blaeu in 1654, and the *Kilchalman* of *Origines Parochiales*;[1] names which would rather suggest a commemoration of St. Colman,[2] although it is certain that the not far distant Priory Church of Rodil (Harris) was dedicated to St. Clement.   ✳ XII.

Slight remains of this chapel may still be found in the centre of its graveyard which has been disused for many years. So far as can be judged from present appearances, the building seems to have measured about 26 by 18 feet over walls which now show a height of about 2 feet and a thickness varying from 54 inches at the south to only 17 inches at the east, with traces of a doorway through its west gable.

In 1904 here lay an oblong fragment of stone, evidently the vertical half of a font, with a conical cavity in its top showing a depth of 7 inches and tapering downwards in width from 7 inches to 2 inches.

A mile and a half to the north-east, midway between Balamartin and Scolpaig (upon the southern face of a hillock opposite Balelone) is the site of *Cill-Pheadair* or *Kilpheder*.[3] No trace is now visible of the chapel which once stood here,[4] but we are assured upon excellent   ✳ XIII.

time a pair of horses could take shelter behind it, though now all but hidden by the accumulated soil.

Blaeu's map of 1654 shows 'Collinar skyr' as a rock lying west of Ard an Runair, clearly represented by the modern Causamul. *Colasaidh* bears much resemblance in form to the *Colosus* (Colonsay) of St. Adamnan, which is understood to be derived from a pre-Norse origin. See pp. 86-87, *antea*.

[1] Vol. ii. p. 373. The same authority suggests that there was also a chapel at Balamartin, but this seems very doubtful.

[2] Perhaps the St. Colman or Columbanus, who was for three years bishop of Lindisfarne but returned thence to Iona in the year 664 and afterwards sailed to Ireland where he died in A.D. 676 (Reeves' *Adamnan*, pp. 28, 125, 376); cf. Forbes' *Kalendars of Scottish Saints*, pp. 294, 303. The Martyrology of Donegal records no fewer than ninety-six saints of this name.

[3] Kilpheder in North Uist was evidently a minor chapel and must not be confused with the ancient parish of like name which included the southern half of South Uist;—the 'Kilpedire blisen' of *Hadinton's Collections*, ca. 1309-1320 (quoted at pp. 24-25, *antea*), and 'Keilpedder in Veist' of *Collectanea*, p. 3 (ca. 1561).

[4] It is said that the now ruined Kilpheder House (a little to the south) was built with stones taken from this chapel.

authority that its burial-ground has been recently exposed in course
of ploughing the field. Its former site is indicated as a grassy
plateau immediately to the south of Kilpheder Cross, which now
stands at the summit of the knoll, raised upon a modern square
pedestal 6½ feet high. This cross was originally within the graveyard,
having been removed to its present position by Dr. Alexander Mac-
Leod of Balelone about 1830-1840. It is of Latin form, but with
'round hollow angles' at the points of intersection by the arms and
bearing upon its (present) south face a pair of plain bosses, each with
a diameter of 5 inches and about an inch in relief. There is also
a small conical hole half an inch wide and an inch deep in its stem
below the bosses. The cross measures a width of 33 inches over its
arms, and 4 feet 7 inches in height above its rough base which is not
wholly imbedded within the pedestal, while its shaft has a width
varying from 16 inches (both at the top and immediately under the
arms) to 23 inches at the base.

The dedication of this chapel was obviously to St. Peter, perhaps
represented by the 'S. Patricius'[1] shown upon John Speed's map of
1610 at the mid-north shore of North Uist; Speed having no doubt
drawn this part of his map from hearsay evidence and not from
personal observation.

In *A History of the Clan MacLean*[2] it is noted that Sir Alexander
MacLean of Dochgarroch 'met his death in 1635 at the hands of the
MacDonalds of Sleat, who attacked him while he was collecting his
rents. He was interred in the churchyard of Kilpeter in North Uist.'
We have been unable to find any reference to this event in other
histories of the Clan MacLean, and are at a loss to conjecture what
rents Sir Alexander MacLean could draw from North Uist in the time
of Sir Donald Gorm Og MacDonald.

The next site is attested by no better authority than a traditional
place-name, MOL NA CILLE[3] or 'pebble-beach of the chapel.' This
occurs two miles north-east from Kilpheder, at Callernish upon
Griminish, close to the north shore of the main island, being
thoroughly descriptive so far as concerns the 'pebble-beach.' Proof

---

[1] Unless this 'S. Patricius' may refer either to Skellor or Ard a' Bhorain, at both of which
places are graveyards probably once associated with chapels.

[2] By J. P. MacLean, Cincinnati, 1889, p. 258.

[3] According to Professor Donald MacKinnon (*The Scotsman* newspaper, 30th November 1887)
cill or *ceall* originally meant a chapel or cell, not necessarily in association with a burial-ground.

that a chapel formerly here existed is quite another matter, and perhaps now unattainable.

VALLAY ISLAND, 2½ miles in length and situated at the north-west corner of North Uist, is said by Martin to have contained no fewer than three chapels. According to this writer (who, from a phrase in his itinerary, evidently spent at least one night upon the island)—'It hath Three Chappels, One Dedicated to *St. Ulton*, and another to the *Virgin Mary*. There are Two Crosses of Stone, each of them about 7 Foot high, and a Foot and a half broad. There is a little Font on an Altar, being a big Stone, round in like of a Cannon Ball, and having in the upper end a little Vacuity capable of two Spoonfuls of water; below the Chappels there is a flat thin Stone, called *Brownies* Stone,' etc.[1] This account evidently implies that two of the chapels were somewhat close together, one dedicated to ST. MARY and the other to ST. ULTAN;[2] and, when we come to con- ✠ xv. sider the local conditions, it is clear that both stood near the south ✠ xvi. shore of Vallay, towards its east end, where the Ordnance map shows 'Teampull Mhuire (Ruins of).' The site of the second chapel—St. Ultan's—is unvouched either by this map or by local tradition, but the third is given as 'TEAMPULL ORAIN (Remains of)'[3] upon the ✠ xvii. *Oransay* which forms a small annexe to Vallay at its north side, now separated as a distinct island only by the highest tides.

Near the west side of this Oransay are the foundations of a rect-angular structure standing east and west, its walls nearly 4 feet thick, built without lime and showing an interior which measures 24 by 17 feet. Adjoining the south of this *Teampull*—whatever has been its actual dedication—is some appearance of a semi-circular enclosure, and many large stones lie scattered at the west.

The site of St. Mary's Chapel is immediately to the south of its ancient graveyard, which latter, to the writer's knowledge, has served upon at least two occasions within the past eight years. Here are

[1] *A Description*, etc., p. 67.
[2] Dedications to St. Ultan are most uncommon in Scotland, and the fact of there being (as usual) more than one Saint of this name makes any information all the less easy to obtain. Forbes (*Kalendars of Scottish Saints*, p. 456) considers the St. Ultan commemorated in the island of Sanda (Kintyre) to have become a hermit, and in later life abbot of Peronne, dying A.D. 680. It is said that an arm of St. Ultan was preserved at Sanda, *ca.* 1600, in a silver shrine religiously kept by a gentleman of the MacDonell family ; *Origines Parochiales*, vol. ii. p. 820.
[3] It would however seem more probable that the chapel derived its name from the islet than *vice versâ*. See also at p. 86, *antea*, under the place-name Oransay.

slight traces of both nave and chancel, thus indicating a period of construction not earlier than the twelfth century. With regard to the
nave, its walls have been so completely removed that no measurements
are available, a mere trench showing the outline of their foundations.
The chancel has fortunately suffered less, as a small part of its walls
still remains, these being 3 feet thick and forming an interior about
10 feet in length by 9 feet in width, or apparently quite 3 feet
narrower than the nave.

Of the Altar and Font, as also the two crosses described by
Martin, no trace could be found, although we are informed that one of
the crosses was taken to Argyllshire within recent times. As a
headstone, in the graveyard, stands part of a small rude cross, which
however can hardly represent either of those in question.

Mr. T. S. Muir, writing in 1885,[1] notes this site 'in or near to
which are two crosses, one of them in the burying-ground, the other
forming a doorway-lintel in an outhouse, and a fragment of one of
the three chapels mentioned by Martin.' Upon the same page
✱ Mr. Muir figures these two crosses; the larger as 64 inches in height
and with four symmetrical round holes pierced near the points of
✱ intersection by the arms;[2] and the smaller as standing 30 inches
above ground, being apparently the broken cross which still remains.

A few yards west of St. Mary's is a modern square burial-enclosure,
no doubt built with stones from that chapel, and perhaps even
occupying the site of St. Ultan's. In 1904 it was found that the
✱ lintel over the doorway of this tomb consisted of an ancient cross-slab
(much the oldest relic here remaining), which measures 52 by 23
inches with a thickness of 4 inches. Its front is rudely incised with
two Latin crosses facing each other, one from each end, and measuring 9 and 10 inches in length.

According to tradition a nunnery once existed upon Vallay. This
may possibly be true, although little faith is to be placed in another
and commoner story to the effect that St. Mary's graveyard contains
the ashes of twenty priests. The latter statement evidently arises
from some confusion with the island of Boreray—distant only five

---

[1] *Ecclesiological Notes of some of the Islands of Scotland*, Edin., 1885, p. 47.
[2] No doubt the cross above mentioned as having been recently carried away, and very possibly
that to which reference is made at p. 98, *antea*, in connection with the practice of archery at
Leathad na Croise, although pierced by four holes instead of three.

CROSS-SLAB, ST. MARY'S CHAPEL, VALLAY.

SKELLOR GRAVEYARD, FROM WEST.

miles to the north-east—where all the monks who died north of Eigg are said to have been buried.

A mile to the south, near the opposite shore of Vallay Strand and little above high-water mark, is a site locally known as *Cladh Mhàrtuinn* or 'the graveyard of Martin,' where tradition records that a priest of that name was buried. This is a low sandy bank at the extreme north end of Malaclett township, and here several graves have certainly been found, although possibly of pre-Christian origin.

With regard to one of these is related the following story. It seems that more than fifty years ago the father of the present crofter built a cottage, but, that upon the first occasion of a fire being there lit, the hearth-stone and burning peats suddenly fell through the floor into a cavity which proved to be a cist containing human bones. This cottage was forthwith pulled down, to be re-erected within a short distance.

At Middlequarter, half a mile to the south-east and opposite Sollas post-office, is a slight knoll which bears the name of *Cnoc Chrosamul* —perhaps representing the Norse *kross-hólmr* or 'cross-islet.' We could glean no confirmation of any cross having existed here, but it seems certain that this hillock was an island at some not very remote period, tradition (with every appearance of truth) stating that the neighbouring low ground was formerly covered by a large loch.

Fully a mile east of Vallay, upon a sand-hill at the edge of Machair Leathann (already noted as a bent-grown waste to the north of Sollas township) is SKELLOR graveyard, still in occasional use, and ✱ xviii. once probably associated with a chapel, of which however not a vestige seems now to exist.[1]

Here, especially, in its scarped west end, are found kitchen-midden remains, including fragments of rude pottery ornamented by various simple patterns evidently of ancient origin. This site is entirely unenclosed and presents a most desolate appearance.

Upon ARD A' BHORAIN, three miles north-east of Skellor and ✱ xix.

---

[1] In *A Description of the Western Islands of Scotland, etc.*, London, 1819, vol. i. p. 138, Dr. Macculloch refers to 'an ancient chapel situated at the north-west angle of this island' upon one of a group of sand-banks, and then still showing its east gable. The circumstantial account given by that writer cannot apply to any other locality than Skellor, with which the identification is practically complete.

immediately above the shore facing the island of Boreray, is another old graveyard still sometimes used. This also shows no remains of any chapel, although in all probability one formerly existed.

It was at Ard a' Bhorain that the MacLeans of Boreray had their family burying-ground with two walled tombs, and to the north of these are many other graves with no attempt at enclosure.

On the beach, 200 yards to the west and at the base of a massive rock just above high-water mark, is a small well variously known as 'of the Priest,' 'of the Cross' and 'of the cups.' The face of this rock, directly above the well, is inscribed with a Latin cross potent measuring 14 inches in length by 7½ inches over the arms. Nine yards to the south-east, and within reach of high tides, are 24 cup-marks arranged along the twin narrow and parallel ridges of a boulder imbedded within the pebbly beach, above which it slightly protrudes. Upon the southmost edge, these cups are arranged nearly in line east and west; while upon the other, six are in line and four in a group near the east end. All are shallow and measure two to three inches in diameter, half of the total number being very well defined and the remainder more or less indistinct. The cross and cup-marks thus fully account for two of the variant names given to the well, while a neighbouring chapel (which presumably existed) would provide the third. This well has long been considered as sacred, tradition adding that the people of North Uist formerly made a pilgrimage thither 'every year about Easter, taking with them hard-boiled pasch eggs, which they inserted into the cups.'[1] Close to the west of the graveyard at Ard a' Bhorain are several patches of land tilled by the Grenetote crofters. Here, at the end of a plot of rye, was to be seen in the autumn of 1904 a peculiar small construction explained to us as serving the purpose of a 'scare-rabbit.' This consisted of an oval lump of mica-schist about a foot in length, set on end and capped by a couple of divots upon which a piece of red cloth was held in position by a smaller stone; the whole arrangement being nearly two feet high. A photograph of this modern agricultural curiosity is annexed.

---

[1] *Proc. Soc. Antiq. Scot.*, vol. xvi. pp. 400-401. This well was not easy to identify, being completely filled with large pebbles thrown up by the sea. When cleared, however, to the depth of about a foot, it was found to contain fresh water. It is said that a number of other cup-marks exist both above the well and on various stones at the north-east side of the same promontory, but the writer was unable to discover any of these, apart from a 'bait-basin' on the top of a rock close to the sea.

WELL and CROSS, ARD A' BHORAIN.

CUP-MARKED ROCK AT ARD A' BHORAIN.

SCARE-RABBIT.

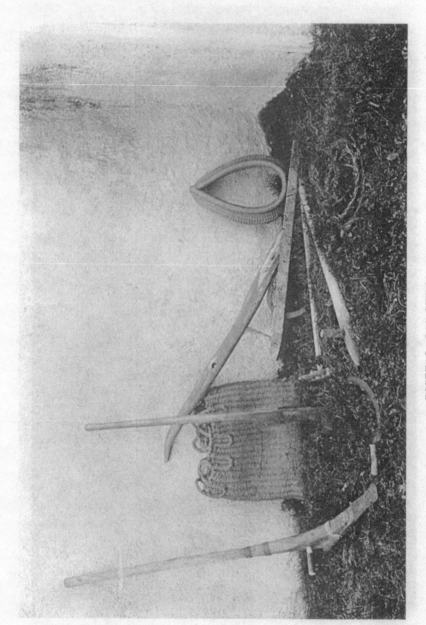

RISTEAL, CAS-CHROM, ETC.

The ORANSAY which lies north of Ahmore Strand is said to have been provided with a chapel. Of this however no trace remains apart from the name *Pàirc an Teampuill* still applied to the westmost enclosure in this island, where the foundations of a structural erection were recently disclosed upon a slight knoll when the field was being ploughed. ✳ XX.

In the island of BORERAY is an ancient graveyard, now unenclosed but left fallow in the midst of arable land. This was doubtless once accompanied by a chapel if not by a monastery, its site being shown upon the Ordnance map as 'Cladh nam Manach. Burial Ground (Disused),' with 'Sculptured Stones' marked at its west side. ✳ XXI.

This graveyard stands in an elevated position near the south-east corner of Boreray. Within its centre are two narrow oblong slabs placed on end but almost covered by the soil, one bearing upon its west face a rudely incised Latin cross 7½ inches in length. We could find no other 'sculptured stone,' these indeed being the only gravestones visible. ✳

Upon cultivated ground, 50 yards to the west of this cross-slab, is a boulder with its top just at the surface level and measuring about 32 by 24 inches, but evidently widening downwards and of considerable thickness. It is noteworthy as containing an oval basin which measures 17 by 11 inches with a greatest depth of 6 inches near its west end, the depression being curved in the form of an ogee at its opposite extremity. In general appearance this might be taken as representing a primitive font, although it seems to be so massive as necessarily to occupy its original position. No doubt it is one of the 'Vacuities . . . dug for receiving the Monks Knees' afterwards quoted upon the authority of Martin.

A few yards to the north-west, upon the face of a flattish rock outcropping in a slight knoll, is a group of three conical cup-marks, all of them well shaped and measuring 3 to 4½ inches wide at their tops, the largest with a depth of about 3½ inches.

Near this burying-ground are five or six considerable cairns, two of them standing in parallel lines on its south, and two similarly on its north. But such cairns are numerous in Boreray, and perhaps of no significance, most of them being evidently formed to dispose of the superabundant stones.

According to Martin,[1] ' The Burial place near the Houses, is called
the Monks-Field, for all the Monks that dyed in the Islands that lye
Northward from *Egg*, were buried in this little Plot, each Grave hath
a Stone at both ends, some of which are 3 and others 4 Foot high.
There are big Stones without the Burial place even with the Ground,
several of them have little Vacuities in them as if made by Art; the
Tradition is that these Vacuities were dug for receiving the Monks
Knees when they prayed upon 'em.' Martin certainly has a quaint
flavour throughout, and here quite reaches his usual standard.

It may be noted that half a mile off Boreray, to the north-west,
are the ' Friar Rocks ' covered by only six feet of water.[2]

A mile south-east from Boreray is the island of Lingay, which,
according to *Origines Parochiales*,[3] contained a chapel dedicated to
the Virgin Mary, although this is clearly a mistaken interpretation of
Martin, who wrote as follows : ' This Island was held as Consecrated
for several Ages, insomuch that the Natives would not then presume
to cut any Fuel in it. '[4]

It has already been incidentally mentioned that two of the graveyards in North Uist—those in connection with the parish and *quoad
sacra* churches at Kilmuir and Sand—are in regular use, while five
others (at Carinish, Baleshare, Vallay, Skellor, and Ard a' Bhorain)
still receive occasional interments.

[1] *A Description, etc.*, p. 68.　　　　[2] *Sailing Directions*, part 1, p. 76.
[3] Vol. ii. p. 376.　　　　[4] *A Description, etc.*, p. 69.

CHAPTER X

NORTH UIST IN POST-REFORMATION TIMES

FROM incidental references already made, it has been seen that, during the sixteenth century, North Uist was in a most unsettled state through family feuds and general lawlessness, a condition which did not show much improvement until well into the seventeenth century. Within the brief period from 1506 to 1517 five out of the six sons of Hugh MacDonald of Sleat each met a violent death: Donald Gallach at Loch Kishorn; Donald Herrach in Dun Scolpaig; Angus Collach, as also Angus Dubh, in South Uist; and finally, Archibald Dubh at Lee near Loch Maddy.[1] These murders bear all the worse aspect as having in almost every case been perpetrated by near relatives of the victim. The cause seems not far to seek, since no doubt the system of 'hand-fast marriages'[2] (coupled with a generally loose standard of morals) would contribute much to this state of matters, by giving free play to jealousy and ambition for personal advancement.

Again, we have the Battle of Carinish, fought in May 1601; and soon afterwards the affair of Dun an Sticir which terminated in the death at Duntulm Castle of Hugh, son of Archibald the Clerk, by torture from thirst.

[1] *The Clan Donald*, vol. iii. pp. 12-16. Archdeacon Monro, *ca.* 1549, in his *Description of the Western Isles* (Edinburgh, 1774, p. 35) writes—'Into this north heid of Ywst, ther is sundrie covis and holes in the earth coverit with heddir above, quhilk fosters maney rebellis in the countrey of the north heid of Ywst.' An Act of Parliament passed in 1594 refers to 'the barbarous cruelties and dalie heirschippis of the vickit thevis and lymmaris of the clannis and surnames following inhabiting the hielandis and Iles,' with a list which is somewhat significantly headed by 'Clangregour,' while 'Clandonald south and north' appears a little lower down; Thomson's *Acts of Parliament of Scotland*, vol. iv. p. 71.

[2] Described in the famous 'Band and Statutes of Icolmkill' of 1609 as 'mariageis contractit for certaine yeiris'; *Reg. Privy Council*, vol. ix. p. 27. The duration of these peculiar unions would seem to have been as irregular as the arrangement itself. Upon this point we find different statements, all of them perhaps strictly accurate. For example, the compact might be 'for twelve months and a day' and conditional upon the birth of a child within that period (*The Clan Donald*, vol. i. p. 432). Again, it is recorded that John, fourth MacLean of Ardgour, took a daughter of MacIain of Ardnamurchan 'upon the prospect of marriage if she pleased him; at the expiration of two years, (the period of her *noviciate*,) he sent her home to her father; but his offspring by her were reputed lawful children'; *An Historical and Genealogical Account of the Clan Maclean,* by a Seneachie, London, 1838, p. 265.

Two successive 'Remissions' of 7th December 1562 and 26th March 1588,[1] to the chieftains of Clan MacDonald of Sleat in connection with raids upon Clan MacLean, may be cited as proving that the Viking spirit ran strong in the veins of these successors to the Lords of the Isles. The first document was in favour of Donald Gormson, and included his uncle James 'M'coneill' of Castle Camus, together with Donald and Angus, sons of Archibald the Clerk, besides others. This bore specific reference to depredation and homicide committed in Mull, Tiree, and Coll. The second (of 1588) was granted to Donald Gorm Mor (son and successor of Donald Gormson), his brothers Alexander and Archibald (the second 'Archibald the Clerk'), his grand-uncle (James of Castle Camus, above noted), and Hugh 'alias Hucheoun M'illespeckie alias M'conneill balliuo de Oyst,' evidently son of the first Archibald the Clerk, and already mentioned as taken prisoner at Dun an Sticir ca. 1602. Upon the faith of this dispensation Donald Gorm Mor visited Edinburgh in or about 1591, but was there arrested and imprisoned within the castle for a year or more.[2]

All this took place during the full ascendancy of the clan system, which received its first distinct check through the signature of 'The Band and Statutes of Icolmkill' in 1609, the Hebrides being thereafter gradually brought under the control of law and order as prescribed by the Scottish Parliament. This agreement had been ratified—not without the exercise of some compulsion—by the Island chiefs assembled at Iona on 23rd August 1609, and became an all-important factor in the subsequent history of the Hebrides. Although its provisions were certainly drastic, and in some details so paternal as now to raise a smile, there can be no doubt that they arose from a genuine desire to forward the best interests of all concerned.

The Iona covenant marks a fresh epoch in the Western Isles, a fact which may serve as sufficient excuse for here giving a brief digest of its nine articles.[3]

I. The ruinous kirks to be repaired, and handfast marriages abolished.

---

[1] Reg. Sec. Sig., vol. xxxi. folio 48, and vol. lvii. folio 75, of the as yet unprinted MS.
[2] Reg. Privy Council, vol. iv. p. 754, of 8th June 1592, refers to the release of Donald Gorm Mor under sureties, in which connection are noted 'Archibald M'Coneill, baillie of North Ewist, and Allaster M'Coneill, sone to Hucheoun M'Coneill, baillie of Trouternes.'
[3] Reg. Privy Council, vol. ix. pp. 26-30.

II. Inns or 'oistlairis to be set doun in the maist convenient placeis within every Ile.'

III. The household retinue of each chief to be limited, this in the case of Donald Gorm Mor MacDonald (of Sleat and North Uist) to six gentlemen.

IV. All sorning and begging, 'be way of conzie as they terme it,' to be put down.

V. The 'extraordinair drinking of strong wynis and acquavitie' to be reduced.[1]

VI. 'Everie gentilman or yeaman within the said Ilandis, or ony of thame, haveing childreine maill or famell, and being in goodis worth thriescore ky, sall put at the leist thair eldest sone, or haveing no childrene maill thair eldest dochter, to the scuillis on the Lawland, and interteny and bring thame up thair quhill thay may be found able sufficientlie to speik, reid, and wryte Inglische.'

VII. An already existing Act of Parliament which forbade any subject to 'beir hagbutis or pistolletis out of thair awne housis and dwelling places, or schuit thairwith at deiris, hairis, or foullis' to be strictly enforced.

VIII. 'Vagaboundis, bairdis, idill and sturdie beggaris' to be expelled.

IX. The chief of each clan to be responsible for his kinsmen and dependents as touching all the above points.

The Scottish government did not long rest content with these stipulations, but summoned the Hebridean chiefs to appear before the Lords of Privy Council in July 1616, then imposing terms of even greater stringency 'which can be described as nothing less than a revised and extended edition of the Band and Statutes of Icolmkill.'[2] On his way to Edinburgh, Donald Gorm Mor fell ill at Fortrose, where he signed (16th August) a procuration binding himself under conditions and sureties to obey these additional clauses, and was consequently excused from personal attendance upon that occasion.

---

[1] 'Without prejudice alwyse to ony persone within the saidis Illis to brew acquavitie and uthir drink to serve thair awne housis,' etc. ; *Reg. Privy Council*, vol. ix. p. 28. So far as we are aware, the earliest notice of the distillation of whisky in Scotland is contained in *The Exchequer Rolls*, vol. x. p. 487, under date 12th August 1495—'Et per liberacionem factam fratri Johanni Cor per preceptum compotorum rotulatoris, ut asserit, de mandato domini regis ad faciendum aquavite infra hoc compotum, viij bolle brasii.' But in the fifteenth century whisky 'was probably reckoned rather among drugs than among articles of ordinary consumption,' *Accounts of the Lord High Treasurer of Scotland*, vol. i. p. ccxiv.

[2] *Reg. Privy Council*, vol. x. p. lvii.

In the main, these fresh obligations were : [1]

I. To compear personally before the 'Lordis of Secrite Counsell' on the tenth of July in each year, and also at any other time upon sixty days' warning served at the dwelling-house (in Edinburgh, being understood) of his advocate and agent specially nominated for this purpose.

II. 'That I the said Donald, sall mak my residence and duelling at Duntillim ; . . . that I sall mak policie and planting about my hous ; that I sall tak a maynes in laboring in my awne hand, and labour the same with my awne goodis, to the effect that I maybe thairby exercisit and eshew idilnes '; etc.

III. 'That I sall not haif nor keepe ony mae birlingis of xvj or xviij aires bot ane.'

IV. 'And, last, that I sall not rinn nor drink, nor suffer to be rwn and drukkine, in my hous, ony mae wynes nor be this present act is allowit unto me,—viz. four twnes of wyne'; etc.

Donald Gorm Mor was not however long spared to the temptations of 'idilnes,' as he died in December of the same year, being succeeded by his nephew, Sir Donald Gorm Og, who was knighted before 17th July 1617, on which day he personally compeared before the Privy Council and accepted all the conditions which had been imposed upon his late uncle.[2]

Although Hebridean affairs at once began to show a distinct improvement, it is but natural to find that the clans were not prepared for the immediate abandonment of usages which had become ingrained during the course of past centuries. With regard to Clan Huistein or 'Clan Donald north'—of Sleat and North Uist—we find not more than two or three serious tribal feuds recorded during the second half of the seventeenth century. One of these was in Lochaber, 1663-1665, renewed in 1676 ; [3] and another in connection with Clan Ranald of Knoydart, 1694; [4] although it would appear that in neither quarrel was the chief of Clan Huistein deserving of blame.

Sir Donald (Gorm Og) MacDonald, first baronet of Sleat, thoroughly accepted the political situation, remaining consistently loyal to the Stewart cause, as did several of his successors to their ultimate ruin.

Reg. Privy Council, vol. x. pp. 778-780. [2] *Ibid.*, vol. xi. pp. 191-192.
[3] Mackenzie's *History of the Macdonalds*, p. 218 ; *The Clan Donald*, vol. ii. pp. 636-638
vol. iii. pp. 67-68. [4] *The Clan Donald*, vol. iii. p. 78.

In 1645, his son Sir James (second baronet) provided four hundred clansmen who took part in the victory of Auldearn, and in 1651 (certainly at Worcester, and no doubt also at the battle of Inverkeithing) shared in the Royalist defeats. Sir Donald (third baronet) led five hundred soldiers to join Claverhouse in 1689, but being suddenly taken ill at Lochaber, his son (Donald, then about twenty-five years of age) assumed command of the clan at Killiecrankie.[1] It was this Sir Donald MacDonald who, as fourth baronet, led his clansmen to Perth in 1715, though he had to return through illness, being represented at Sheriffmuir by his brothers James and William,[2]—these afterwards known as Sir James (sixth baronet) and William ('the Tutor') of Vallay. Serious consequences now ensued, Sir Donald (in 1716, and for the second time) suffering forfeiture, which on this occasion proved no mere formality. He died two years later, and was succeeded in the title for very brief periods by his son Donald, and thereafter by his brother James; these again followed by Sir Alexander (son of Sir James) as seventh baronet, during whose minority in 1723 the confiscated estates of Sleat and North Uist were repurchased for him from the Crown through the intervention of friends. This Sir Alexander MacDonald of Sleat was born in 1710, dying in 1746. Sir Alexander was undoubtedly a Jacobite at heart, notwithstanding his refusal to join that party in 1745, feeling the attempt to be hopeless. His family had in the past suffered sufficiently on behalf of the Stewarts, and it must have been from prudential motives (amply justified by the event) that he now held aloof, even sending two companies of Islesmen to Inverness in nominal support of King George. These were led by James MacDonald of Aird and John MacDonald of Kirkibost, both of them sons of William 'the Tutor' and cousins of Sir Alexander himself. Only two of the gentlemen of North Uist—James MacDonald of Heisker, and Donald Roy MacDonald of Baleshare—are known to have then fought for Prince Charles; while on the other hand, it is to Sir Alexander's credit that his attitude after the Battle of Culloden was one of remonstrance

---

[1] *The Clan Donald*, vol. iii. pp. 59-63, 71. According to *The Grameid* (Scot. Hist. Soc.), p. 125, he led seven hundred men at Killiecrankie. It is interesting to note that Martin Martin (author of *A Description of the Hebrides*, 1703) acted until 1686 as 'governor' or tutor to this Donald, who underwent a nominal forfeiture in 1690.

[2] *The Clan Donald*, vol. iii. pp. 80-81.

with the Duke of Cumberland against the wanton cruelties which followed.[1]

Under the Lords of the Isles several functions were exercised by hereditary officials. The Bard was then considered a necessary attendant, who in earlier times was a member of Clan MacVurich, a sept which came from Ireland in the thirteenth century, thus first appearing in Scotland in the time of the founder of Clan Donald. After the MacVurichs, others bearing the surnames of MacBeattaig and MacRuari are found connected with the MacDonalds of Sleat, while the last clan bard in North Uist was John MacCodrum, appointed in 1763.[2]

The harper and the piper come next in order of antiquity, the harp apparently disappearing about the end of the seventeenth century, its place being taken by the bag-pipes so well suited for military purposes. Members of Clan MacArthur held the position of piper to the Lords of the Isles and their successors until the year 1800.

Another and important caste was that of the physician, evidently confined throughout the West Highlands to the sept of MacBeth, afterwards known as Beaton or Bethune. The last of the North Uist branch was Neil Beaton, who died in 1763.[3]

A rare pamphlet of thirty-six pages, entitled *An Historical and Genealogical Account of the Bethunes of the Island of Sky* (Edin., 1778), gives much detailed information as to the physicians of that surname who evidently practised not only in Skye but also in North Uist and Harris. The first to be mentioned by name (pp. 3-4) is Peter Bethune, son of Archibald Bethune of Pitlochy and Capeldrae in Fife, and grandson of John, fifth Bethune of Balfour, being also cousin to Cardinal Beaton, Archbishop of St. Andrews; although it is added at p. 35 that 'there were Bethunes in Sky before Doctor Peter came to that country, families of good esteem and repute.' Dr. Peter Bethune seems to have flourished in the second half of the sixteenth century, and 'being a famous physician, was called to Argyleshire to practise his skill there, and from thence received an invitation to the

---

[1] *The Clan Donald*, vol. iii. pp. 88-91, 495, 541; also Mackenzie's *History of the Macdonalds*, pp. 234-237. The fortunes of Clan MacDonald of Sleat and North Uist during the seventeenth and eighteenth centuries have been already touched upon in Chapter iii. pp. 32-35, *antea*.

[2] For these notes as to the hereditary officials of North Uist we are largely indebted to *The Clan Donald*, vol. iii. pp. 122-129

[3] Martin's *Description, etc.* of 1703 notes Neil Beaton as then a physician in Skye (p. 197) and James Beaton in North Uist (p. 325).

Isle of Sky from the lairds of McDonald and McLeod. The Doctor, upon condition to settle in the country, was promised as much land as he inclined to possess, rent free ; . . . It was also promised on the Doctor's side, that one of his posterity, particularly the eldest son of the family, if he had a turn for it, should be educated as a physician, without any expence to him or his successors, whilst any of them continued in that country and inclined to the study of physic or medicine. By these encouragements, he was prevailed on to take up his residence in Sky, which is far from being a disagreeable place.' Dr. Peter Bethune married a daughter of MacDonald of Moydart, and had 'a son Angus, Doctor of Medicine. He was a prudent man and of good esteem in the country, and though the McDonalds and McLeods, the most powerful clans in that country, were often at variance, yet he was loved and much caressed by both sides,' (*Ibid.*, pp. 4-5). It is unnecessary here to follow out the subject, further than to state that for at least two centuries practically each generation of the Bethune family in Skye was represented by one or more physicians.

A single trade—that of the smith or armourer—was also hereditary, being limited in North Uist, as at Trotternish in Skye, to a family named MacRuari.

Having thus endeavoured to give some account of the political and other relations of Clan Huistein from 1609 to 1745, we must now turn to the social and economic aspects of North Uist during that period, as also in still more recent times.

The first important trade development of the Western Isles seems to have been in connection with the herring fishery, which rose into prominence about the year 1566, while twenty years later we find 'Donald Gorme in the Sky' foremost in a list of Hebridean lairds against whom a complaint was lodged as to illegal exactions upon the fishermen.[1] To judge from the serious manner in which both the Scottish Parliament and the Lords of Privy Council issued regulations for the fisheries—especially those of the west coast—it is evident that during the first half of the seventeenth century much was hoped from them,

---

[1] *Collectanea*, pp. 99, 102-104. Loch Broom was an early seat of this fishery, and it is said that the MacDonalds of Clan Huistein held lands there *ca.* 1500. According to *The Clan Donald*, vol. iii. p. 114, Lochmaddy 'was the principal centre of the herring fishing in the Outer Islands for at least a hundred years from the middle of the 16th century.' The herring fishery seems always to have held primary importance, as against that for cod and ling, which was also practised.

an expectation not wholly disappointed. It appears that in still earlier days this industry had been largely monopolised by fishermen from Holland and France; but in 1632 (7th September) a national company, 'The Counsell and Commountie of the fishing of his Majesteis dominions of Great Britane and Ireland,' was incorporated by a royal charter from Charles I., provision being made to exclude foreigners, and also for reserving 'anie part of anie creik or fyrthe . . . to the necessar sustentatioun and vse' of the king's subjects dwelling there.[1]

Ten years earlier, on 1st August 1622, the Hebridean chiefs had come under an obligation that they 'sall on nawayes invade, molest, harme, nor oppres his Majesties goode subjectis hanting the trade of fisheing in the Ilis, and that thay sall not onlie protect thame fra all violence within thair boundis, bot lykeways that they salbe ansuerable for thair awne men and for all otheris personis quhatsomevir . . . and that every one of thame within thair awne boundis sall appoint some sufficient honnest man to haif a cair and to attend upoun the saidis fishearis to protect and manteene thame in thair fisheing'; etc.[2] Again, on 23rd July 1623, 'it is aggreit that nane of the fishearis sall go oute of ony loiche till thay adverteis the landislord or his baillie of thair outgoing, and acquent thame with the nomber of fisheis they haif tane, and pay thair dewtie accordinglie.'[3]

This reference to a 'baillie' seems to explain the inclusion of 'the office of baillerie of the Loches of North Ust' in a lease of Boreray, granted 17th March 1626, by Sir Donald Gorm MacDonald to Neil MacLean.[4]

For a time the west-coast fishings were distinctly successful, and Lochmaddy, as one of its centres, no doubt shared in the temporary prosperity. How these conditions ceased is not exactly known, unless it was in consequence of the Civil War. North Uist never again resumed an important position in this industry, though Martin (writing of Loch Maddy shortly before 1703) remarks, 'The

---

[1] *Acts of Parlt.*, vol. v. pp. 239-245.
[2] *Reg. Privy Council*, vol. xiii. p. 37; Sir Donald Gorm was put under a penalty of £8000 (Scots).
[3] *Ibid.*, pp. 308-309. These are merely two out of many regulations made as to the fishings.
[4] *The Clan Donald*, vol. iii. p. 650. Salmon fishing (*i.e.*, evidently by nets) was given with a tack of Oransay to Kenneth MacQueen in 1619 (*Ibid.*, p. 136), being the only definite reference to this particular industry which we can find in connection with North Uist.

Natives told me that in the Memory of some yet alive, there had been 400 Sail Loaded in it with Herrings at one Season; but it is not now frequented for Fishing.'[1] To what extent the fisheries of *ca.* 1620 to 1650 were of pecuniary advantage to the landlord can hardly be estimated, although these may partly account for the prosperous affairs of Sir James MacDonald (second baronet of Sleat) who in 1653 became security on behalf of MacLeod of Dunvegan for £6000 sterling, and before 1670 lent £40,000 Scots upon a wadset of the lands of Moydart and Arisaig.[2]

The potato was introduced to South Uist from Ireland in 1743[3] and continued to be the staple food in the Outer Hebrides for almost exactly a hundred years, even now remaining an important item in the domestic economy of these islands, notwithstanding the frequent crop failures.

At about the same period a profitable market for kelp (the calcined ashes of sea-ware) wrought even more remarkable changes upon the condition of the Hebrides. This commodity is said to have been first manufactured in North Uist *ca.* 1735, reaching an extreme price of £20 or £22 per ton in 1772, and maintaining an average of £10, 10s. throughout the years 1801 to 1822, while 'in 1812 the net proceeds of kelp in North Uist exceeded £14,000.'[4] Latterly, *ca.* 1880-1890, kelp was sold at the unremunerative price of 42s. per ton, but its value has since risen to 105s., with the natural consequence of more attention being again devoted to this industry.

In 1753, Captain Barlow was ordered to the Long Island with a company of troops to search for 'arms, priests, and the Highland dress.'

---

[1] *A Description*, etc., pp. 54-55. A note shown upon Moll's map of 1725 at 'L. Patran' is a literal quotation from Martin. It would appear that early in the eighteenth century the Shetland Isles had become a favourite resort for the herring fishery.

[2] *The Clan Donald*, vol. iii. pp. 64-65. Sir James' whole estates are recorded as yielding him a revenue of £10,133 Scots in 1644, but of only £6050 Scots in 1657—both sums representing money payments apart from rent received in kind (*Ibid.*). This discrepancy, and at so short an interval, is very marked, although in the absence of details we should hardly be warranted in attributing it to a cessation of the fees and duties exacted from stranger fishermen.

[3] Mackenzie's *History of the Outer Hebrides*, p. 547.

[4] *Ibid.*, pp. 548-549. See also *Old Stat. Acc.*, vol. xiii. p. 305; and *The Clan Donald*, vol. iii. pp. 142-143; giving the date of introduction as 1726-1735, and stating the pioneer to have been Roderick MacDonald, brought from Ireland by Hugh MacDonald, then tacksman of Baleshare, for that special purpose. It is said that stones were set in various bays of North Uist so as to artificially increase the growth of sea-ware (*New Stat. Acc.*, Inverness-shire, p. 175), although the larger tangle or *laminaria* is now chiefly utilised.

In 1755 North Uist had a population of 1909, rapidly increasing under the above conditions to 4971 in the year 1821, but since steadily reduced to 3862 at the latest census (of 1901).

In a Report (dated ' Vala,' 30th June 1753) he writes—' The People are very civil, and hitherto I have had no Complaints. They are all Presbyterians and very well affected to His Majesty King George and His Family, for they say, the late Sir Alexr. McDonald, desired them with his last breath to be faithfull and obedient, to whose Memory I find they pay great Veneration. He took a way all their Arms in the year 1746, which were restored to the Goverment, since which they have had none amongst them. . . . Here is a Linnen Manufactory Establish'd among them which at present is but in its Infancy. . . . They yearly make great Sums of Money by their Kelp.' In a later Report (of the same year) Captain Barlow adds ' Lady Margaret McDonald hath established a Linnen Manufactory, which thrives mightily, and is of infinite use in employing numbers of poor Children. All the principal Farmers of the Country are likeways keen Adventurers in this Undertaking.'[1]

This Lady Margaret was a daughter of the Earl of Eglinton, and married (as his second wife) Sir Alexander MacDonald, seventh baronet of Sleat, in 1739, being left a widow in 1746 and surviving until 1799. Of Lady Margaret's ' Linnen Manufactory' nothing more seems to be known, but it was doubtless a ' cottage industry' to encourage the erection and use of looms in separate houses all over North Uist.

With regard to the general state of agriculture in North Uist, it is evident that, during the middle ages and for a long period thereafter, the island was farmed upon very self-contained lines, thus involving a much larger proportion of arable as compared with pastoral husbandry. Before 1566 the Hebrideans had begun to attend Lowland markets, and in that year it was ordered that 'nane molest the Hieland men' in the 'interchange of the excrescence and superflew frutis growand in the Laich and Hielandis.'[2] Nevertheless, even at

---

[1] Mackenzie's *History of the Outer Hebrides*, pp. 473, 601, 605.

[2] *Reg. Privy Council*, vol. i. pp. 470-471. Donald MacIain of Eriskay—hero of the battle of Carinish in 1601, and grandson of James MacDonald of Castle Camus—was a drover or cattledealer, and is said to have been the first man to ferry cattle between Uist and Skye, *The Clan Donald* vol. iii. p. 501. Martin, in *A Description, etc.*, p. 69, remarks—' The Cattle produced here, are Horses, Cows, Sheep and Hogs, generally of a low stature. . . . Their Cows are also in the Fields all the Spring, and their Beef is sweet and tender as any can be ; they live upon *Sea-ware* in the Winter and Spring, and are fatned by it, nor are they slaughtered before they eat plentifully of it in *December*. The Natives are accustomed to salt their Beef in a Cows Hide, which keeps it close from Air, and preserves it as well, if not better, then Barrels, and tasts they say best when this way used : This Beef is transported to *Glasgow*, a City in the West of *Scotland*, and from thence (being put into Barrels there) exported to the *Indies* in good Condition.' This reference to Glasgow, so carefully explaining its locality, must seem quaint to the modern reader.

the end of the sixteenth century, traffic with the south must have
been small, so that the quantity of live-stock would be correspondingly limited. On the other hand, sufficient cereals—oats,[1] rye, and
bere, in addition to some flax—were grown for home consumption,
little money actually passing, and business transactions (rent included)
being chiefly settled in kind.

At the present day the exports of North Uist may be roughly
stated as consisting of a small quantity of kelp, with horses, cattle,
and sheep, all other farm produce (except butter and eggs) being con-
sumed upon the island itself;[2] while the imports mainly include
oatmeal, wheat-flour, tea, and sugar. It seems obvious that the
island can never have been in a position to export cereals of any kind,
but rather (especially before the potato was introduced about 1743)
that greater attention was paid to the culture of grain-crops for the
sustenance of its own inhabitants.

While, perhaps from time immemorial, North Uist contained a
few holdings large enough to deserve the name of farms, its main
cultivation, since at latest the beginning of the eighteenth century,
seems to have been carried on by crofters and cottars.[3]

Formerly the 'Runrig' system of cropping was much in vogue,
under which a township or scattered village possessed both hill-
pasture and 'machair' in common, together with a moderate extent of
arable land. This latter was allocated afresh either annually or every
third year between the various crofters, who in this way individually
owned no specific and continuous holding of arable soil, such being
changeable and regulated by comparative rental, while the acreage
itself was entirely subordinated to the question of value.

In some of the older townships of North Uist, this Runrig system
still prevails,—as at Kyles-Paible, Hosta, and Heisker,—and also
to a less extent at Boreray, Knockline, Balmore, Knockintorran, Hougary, Tighary, Balamartin, Malaclett, and Middlequarter. In the
recently revived crofter-townships of Sollas and Grenetote a similar

[1] Black oats now form the usual crop of this grain, although white oats also thrive to some
extent upon peaty soil. Barley is unsuitable.
[2] The *Old Stat. Acc.* of 1794 (vol. xiii. p. 307) mentions that North Uist was then unable to
spare any sheep, while horses were purchased 'in great numbers yearly' from Skye and Lewis.
It would further seem that at this period 300 cattle and about 1200 tons of kelp formed practically
the sole annual exports from the island.
[3] It is understood that among the earliest crofting settlements in North Uist were several near
the east shore of the main island, notably at Eaval and Liernish, districts long since wholly
depopulated. The same remarks may apply to *Bàgh a' Bhiorain*, on the south side of Loch Eford.

method has been partially adopted, although such is not the case with the new settlements at Minish, Kallin, and Knock-Cuien. This variation is no doubt due to the differing conditions of soil, which are indeed apparent to a casual observer. It may be added that, where the practice of Runrig exists, this fact is almost invariably indicated by a grouping together of the various cottages. Thus, while North Uist hardly includes a single village worthy of the name, the nearest approach (Lochmaddy excepted) is to be found at those townships where Runrig still continues either in whole or in part.

Here it may be repeated that where an old charter mentions a 'tirunga' or 'ounce-land' this affords no measurement of area, the term being a statement of annual value, not of acreage. In North Uist, as probably elsewhere among the Outer Hebrides, the 'tirunga' or 'terung' evidently consisted of 18 penny-lands, each penny-land being of distinctly greater value as compared with the average croft of to-day, and therefore (when occupied by a single tenant or tacksman) rather representing the dimensions of a small modern farm.[1]

Dr. Carmichael[2] (in connection with a raid upon the township of Udal, probably ca. 1550) states that eighteen 'seisreachan' were there at work, seisreach in the singular being the Gaelic term for a set of six plough-horses, 'the necessary team for ploughing of old in the Western Isles. There were four horses attached to the principal plough— crom-nan-gad—and two to the rustal, a kind of marking or scarifying plough, which preceded the crom-nan-gad.' Another notice of the same implement in 1794 gives it no specific name, and otherwise slightly differs :—'It is drawn by 4 horses, has only one handle, which the person who directs it holds in his right hand, as he walks beside it, having in his left a lash to drive the horses. Before this plough is a machine drawn by one horse, to which is fixed a crooked iron, of the form of a reaping-hook, to cut the ground, so that the plough may turn it up with greater facility.' Here four men and five horses are stated as the necessary complement.[3] In a volume written by a native of Paible, North Uist, and published in

---

[1] See Chapter iv. pp. 41-42, antea.

[2] Proc. Soc. Antiq. Scot., vol. viii. p. 279. Dr. Carmichael, writing in 1870, adds :—'These ancient ploughs, the crom-nan-gad and the rustal, are still commonly used in Lewis.' In North Uist the risteal is now practically unknown, though a specimen was procured from the Loch Eford district in 1905, having done service for its owner within the past fifty years.

[3] Old Stat. Acc., vol. xiii. pp. 307-308.

1811, the *risteal* or 'ristle' is both figured and described.[1] We find the same contrivance noted in *The Clan Donald*[2] as consisting of two separate ploughs, the foremost provided with a coulter and the second supplying a ploughshare which turned the furrow.

At the present day it is not uncommon to find double-stilted ploughs in ordinary use, with their frame and handles constructed of wood, thus giving the implement a clumsy appearance. We have also noticed several examples of a peculiarly formed plough, contrived for the special purpose of earthing potatoes. This has a double mould-board and is entirely composed of wood—apart from the share, three bolts, and the gearing attachment.

It would seem that in North Uist the corn was formerly pulled up by the roots instead of being cut,[3] no doubt for the purpose of securing all the straw. The writer can testify to this operation as practised at Callernish (Lewis) in September 1900, Lewis indeed being a favoured place of survival for several old customs elsewhere long obsolete.

We now come to the *cas-chròm* or *cas-tilgidh* (literally 'crooked leg' or 'casting-leg'), which still does active service throughout many parts of North Uist. During the spring of 1900, the writer found this implement in very common use near Lochboisdale (South Uist), and specially noted one with ornamental carving upon its shaft.

The *cas-chròm* may be described as a 'crooked spade' or 'foot-plough,' and is indeed a combination of both, admirably adapted to break up soil which consists of solid peat interspersed with rock and small stones. While especially suited for the cultivation of the potato, its origin may date back to a period long before that tuber was known in the Hebrides, the *cas-chròm* forming an almost ideal implement with which to prepare peaty ground for any crop whatever.[4] Wooden harrows are also common in North Uist, though not

---

[1] *A General View of the Agriculture of the Hebrides*, by the Rev. James MacDonald, Edinburgh, 1811 ; frontispiece and pp. 156-157.

[2] Vol. iii. p. 112. The *crann-rustlaidh* of MacLeod and Dewar's *Gaelic Dictionary*.

[3] A method which prevailed in the Hebrides from *ca.* 1600 ; *The Clan Donald*, vol. iii. pp. 112-113.

[4] The *Old Stat. Acc.* of 1793, vol. vi. pp. 288-289, under the parish of Edderachylis, Sutherlandshire, describes the *cas-chròm* as ' of great antiquity.' Similarly the Rev. James MacDonald (in his *General View of the Agriculture of the Hebrides*, pp. 151-156, refers to this implement figured upon the frontispiece of his volume) as the oldest known in the Hebrides, and of great value in tilling mossy or stony ground, being capable of removing 'stones of 20 to 200 pound weight.' The same writer mentions that he had introduced the *cas-chròm* into Hungary, when

often to be seen in less remote districts. Serving in the same connection is another useful tool known as the *ràcan* or ' clod-breaker,' a strong heavy rake made entirely of wood and furnished with six or seven thick teeth, its head being sharpened at both ends.[1] In an old garden the writer came across two implements, each measuring 43 inches in length and specially designed for joint service in the planting of potatoes,—chiefly perhaps in connection with ' lazy-beds.' One is a rake with a blunt-ended head and only four teeth ; the other being a long dibble[2] with a pin fixed in its side to act alike as a treader and a stop.

The flail is still in common use, being sometimes even preferred to the threshing-mill for the treatment of bere, a grain not easily separated.

North Uist has now but a single corn-mill in active operation, this being situated at Dusary, on the west side of the island. A large mill at the mid-north, between Loch nan Geireann (Geireann Mill Loch) and the shore, ceased work about the year 1893, having since been dismantled ; while another, at Hough near Tighary, was discontinued so recently as 1904-1905.

Many smaller mills have also existed, several of them evidently fulling-mills for the purpose of scouring and thickening woollen cloth. The name of Malaclett (presumably related to that of Eilean Maleit, a mile to the west) doubtless took its origin from a neighbouring mill.[3] We are further assured upon good authority that, within the past fifty

travelling there, 1805-1806 ; (*Ibid.* pp. 83, 154). Both of these notices date from a time when the potato had been under cultivation in the Hebrides for not more than fifty to seventy years, further suggesting the inference that the *cas-chròm* was invented at a much earlier period.

The *cas-chròm* consists of a wooden handle or shaft nearly six feet in length, with a lateral spur or 'head' (measuring about 30 inches) fixed at an obtuse angle upon its base and tipped by an iron blade. A strong wooden pin is inserted at the junction of the shaft and head, for the purpose of serving as a fulcrum upon which leverage is applied by the labourer's right foot. We are informed that the blade has to be renewed at the local smithy almost every second year. Without question the *cas-chròm* is a most interesting survival, and cleverly suited to its special function. Another form of this implement was the *cas-dìreach* or ' straight leg,' with a much slighter bend, and now apparently obsolete.

[1] *Ibid.* p. 159. The *ràcan-buntàta* or 'potato rake,' which we have seen in regular use upon soft ground, as a substitute for the harrows.

[2] The dibble is known in North Uist as *sliobhag*, but elsewhere (in Harris and Skye) as *pleadhag*. A somewhat similar rake and dibble are figured on p. 16 of a pamphlet entitled *A Holiday in North Uist*, being a lecture delivered at Perth and printed at London in 1865.

[3] The remains of a mill-dam still exist upon *Sruthan Ruadh*, the streamlet which flows past Malaclett smithy. If the suggested Norse derivation for Malaclett is well-founded, it would seem that a corn-mill stood here at so remote a period as the thirteenth century.

years, another mill (latterly adapted for fulling and pressing cloth) was in operation on the Backlasary Burn, where its ruins can still be seen near the roadside, midway between Malaclett and Eilean Maleit. Upon *Allt a' Mhuilinn* at Scolpaig there certainly stood a mill, while the scanty remains of a fourth are traceable at *Allt na Muile*, a tiny stream which flows from Loch Olavat into Vallay Sound. It is said that this last was planned as a fulling-mill but did not reach completion, its builder visiting Glasgow to purchase the needful machinery, and never returning to North Uist. Within the same district, a little south of Cnoc a' Comhdhalach, are the ruins of a small round corn-mill showing an interior diameter of about $7\frac{1}{2}$ feet, near the shore and once supplied with water through a narrow and clearly artificial lade which ran from Loch nan Gearrachan.

It would be hopeless to attempt a complete enumeration of the various mills which formerly existed in North Uist. We may however note the place-names *Abhuinn na Muile* (Claddach-Bale-share), *Loch a' Mhuilinn* (Bayhead), *Abhuinn an t-Seanna Mhuilinn* (Garry Hougary), *Abhuinn a' Mhuilinn* (flowing into the north-west corner of Geireann Mill Loch), and *Àrd na Muile* (at Loch Iosal an Duin), all of these obviously indicating some association with old mills of one class or another.

It is interesting to note that, *ca.* A.D. 1281, Guild Laws were framed for the express purpose of discouraging the use of hand-mills or querns, evidently in order to uphold the vested rights of thirlage.[1] We also read that 'When illicit grinding was discovered, the miller was empowered to break the querns, and it is said that about the middle of the 18th century a raid was made upon the querns in South Uist, when a large number were collected by the millers and thrown into the sea.'[2] The fact remains, however, that the quern is still found as perhaps the commonest ancient survival in the Hebrides,

---

[1] 'Statuta Gilde,' in Thomson's *Acts of Parliament*, vol. i. p. 435. One of many enactments adopted by the burgh of Berwick (though apparently also applicable to a much wider area) runs :—' XXII. Statuimus quod nullus frumentum mastilionem uel ciliginem ad molas manuales molere presumat nisi magna tempestate cogente uel penuria molendinorum hoc faciente,' etc. It is evidently this law which is quoted (*New Stat. Acc.*, Inverness-shire, p. 283) in the Scottish vernacular : 'That na man sall presum to grinde quheit, maisloch, or rye, with hand-mylnes, except he be compelled by storm, and be in lack of mylnes quhilk should grinde the samen.' Under date A.D. 1283, at p. 437 of the same volume of Thomson's *Acts*, we find : 'XLVI. Item nullus habeat nisi duo paria molarum et qui plura habuerint a molis suis per vnum annum et diem priuentur.'

[2] *The Clan Donald*, vol. iii. p. 130.

even where now dismissed from active service; although its use has not even yet been wholly abandoned in some of the remoter districts of North Uist, particularly upon the islands of Grimsay and Heisker, as no doubt also in Boreray.

The quern is known in at least two very distinct varieties—one of them, the saddle-quern,[1] consisting of two oblong stones, the upper and smaller of which was worked to and fro over grain placed within the comparatively long and wide hollow groove of the lower.   Another type is represented by the normal or circular form, which also consists of two stones, these being of equal size and the upper rotated by hand with much the same action as that of a regular mill, though upon a minor scale.   Dr. Carmichael notes a third variety under the name of *abrach*, whence he attributes its origin to Lochaber.[2]   This implement was smaller than the ordinary quern, further differing therefrom both in geological composition and in the absence of pick-marks; being roughened by setting it for a single night under a waterfall to wash out the softer material.   We are also told of a still smaller quern, made for the special purpose of grinding snuff.

The shieling must have played a prominent part in the economics of North Uist during many centuries until within the past sixty years, while we are told that the crofters of Claddach-Kirkibost continued this system at Unival until about the year 1890, and one family from Paible so recently as in 1901 at Toroghas.   Shielings are still represented by the frequent place-name *àiridh*, though their occupation has fallen into disuse, the custom having now become obsolete throughout the Hebrides, except perhaps in South Uist[3] and Lewis.[4]

---

[1] The saddle-quern was long ago superseded in North Uist, being there now practically unknown; although the writer has noted three specimens lying upon ancient sites, two of which are evidently to be classed as pre-historic forts.

[2] *Proc. Soc. Antiq. Scot.*, vol. viii. pp. 282-283.   About fifty years ago Dr. Carmichael found a quarry of these *abrach* querns in a small creek at Heisker, where 'the size of each quern, and the marks of the tools in cutting out, are quite visible. . . . Some were just begun, and the marking could only faintly be traced ; others were half cut and abandoned ; while not a few broke as they were being separated from the rock.'   Here the writer must also acknowledge personal indebtedness to Dr. Carmichael for calling attention to a remarkable mill-stone quarry on the shore near Scolpaig, immediately south of the *Allt a' Mhuilinn* already noticed.   This lies somewhat below high-water mark in a creek filled with rocks, where may yet be seen a hard bluish slab partly cut through in a complete circle measuring 53 inches in diameter.

[3] In the Loch Skiport district, where, until about the year 1898, if not to the present day, shielings were occupied each summer.   We are told that the type is here somewhat unusual, consisting of an excavated hollow with a roof little above the natural level of the surface.

[4] The writer found this system yet in vogue near Garrynahine in the summers of 1901 and 1902.

MILL-STONE QUARRY, NEAR SCOLPAIG.

SHIELING MOUND ON NORTH SLOPE OF CRAONAVAL.

The earliest mention of shielings in any document known to the writer is of ' 40 sol. terrarum de Wester Stwikis, cum silvis, piscariis, *lie schelingis*,' etc.[1] in the Atholl district, although the practice itself must be of very much earlier origin.

The normal shieling was a hut built of turf or peat and roofed with the same. Probably it had to be repaired every summer, being deserted save for two or three months from June to August, during which period the younger members of each family were accustomed to take the cattle to the hill-pasture or outrun attached to their croft, visiting home weekly, laden with dairy produce. The approach of harvest would always mark the time to leave the shieling, and in later months the cattle were pastured upon the low ground or *machair*.

Large farms were then comparatively few. It may be that in connection with these a similar custom also prevailed, although the whole tradition of shielings seems to refer to their use by crofters, each of whom had his own hut upon some knoll among the hills, its site being, as a rule, still recognisable if only by a patch of vivid green, even where the name of *àiridh* no longer survives. *Buaile* or ' cattle-fold ' seems to represent a shieling upon a larger scale, and several of this title occur in North Uist. *Gearraidh* or ' garry ' is the name applied to an enclosed strip of land intervening between the hill-pasture and the arable soil near the crofts.

It seems unnecessary, even were it possible, to enumerate the various shielings still recognisable as such in North Uist. These are scattered throughout every district of the island, and it is interesting to note that ancient burial sites were specially thus favoured, no doubt from the double reason of their comparatively elevated situations and the supply of stones there available. Shielings seem indeed to be associated with almost every known chambered cairn in North Uist, as also with the less definitely ascertained sites at Buaile Maari, Buaile Risary, and upon the north slope of Craonaval, in addition to numerous others.

Many natives left North Uist for America during the period from 1771 to 1775, and again a large proportion of its cottar population emigrated in 1828 and 1841-1842, a main cause being the depressed

---

[1] *Reg. Mag. Sig.*, 24th March 1601. This notice was observed by chance, and no doubt others exist of earlier date.

price of kelp, a commodity which lent but temporary prosperity to the Hebrides. Soon followed a total failure of the potato crop in 1846, after which the western isles continued to lose their inhabitants in an almost unceasing stream. In recent years, this tide has been partly stemmed, thanks to the successful action of the proprietor, Sir Arthur J. Campbell-Orde, Bart., assisted by the Congested Districts Board, in forming several new crofter settlements.

We have already quoted a record of 1753,[1] to the effect that Lady Margaret (widow of Sir Alexander MacDonald, seventh baronet of Sleat) had established 'a Linnen Manufactory' in North Uist. This industry can at best have enjoyed a brief existence as to any export trade, although during previous centuries a supply of linen for domestic requirements had been woven within the island itself from flax of local production, both as regards growth and spinning.[2] Hemp is another fibre which was apparently cultivated,[3] though perhaps only to a small extent; while tobacco was grown in Barra before 1703,[4] and also in other parts of the Long Island.

In North Uist, at the present day, a number of looms are employed in weaving tweeds, blankets, and drugget for petticoats; principally the first mentioned, which are of excellent quality and sold at a standard price of about three shillings per yard. This fabric is identical with the better known 'Harris tweed,' and is a purely native product in all stages from the fleece to the finished cloth. Thus, the wool is carded, spun, dyed, and woven, all within the island itself.

The older type of loom is very primitive,[5] the shuttle being passed through the 'shed' by hand instead of being driven by a mechanical striker. Upon the accompanying plate are figured four Hebridean shuttles; the smallest and crudest from Pabbay, south of Barra; another, of somewhat serpentine shape, from Tiree; and two which were acquired in the autumn of 1904 at Hougary, North Uist. The pirns used in these shuttles are even more curious, that from

---

[1] P. 312, *antea*.

[2] It would seem that the distaff and spindle have been practically disused for about fifty years.

[3] *Reg. Mag. Sig.*, 17th Aug. 1596; a charter stipulating for the cultivation of a garden 'et ad seminand. canapem et linum extra hortos caulium et non infra.'

[4] Martin's *Description, etc.*, p. 91; 'some years ago Tobacco did grow here, being of all Plants the most grateful to the Natives, for the Islanders love it mightily.'

[5] The 'upright' loom was formerly not uncommon, and we are told that at least one of this type still exists in North Uist, although now worked in the ordinary horizontal position.

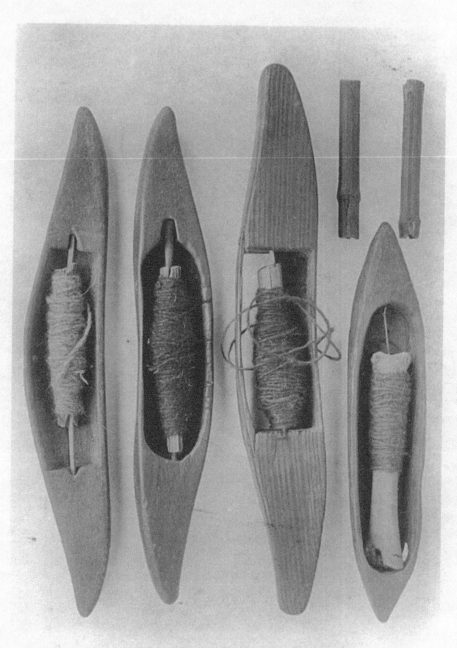

HEBRIDEAN SHUTTLES AND PIRNS.   TO SCALE OF ONE IN TWO.

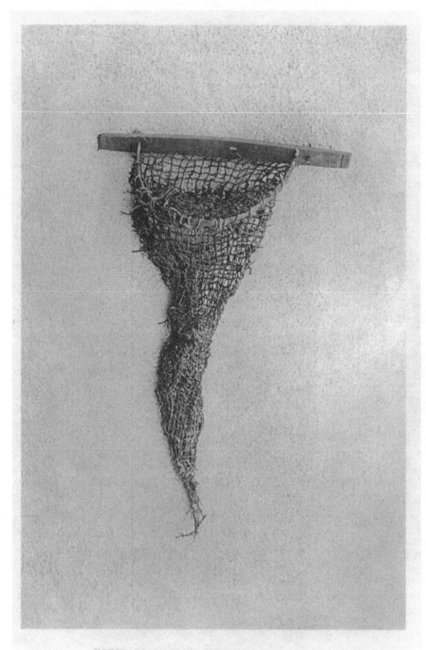

TABH, OR NET, MADE OF GRASS ROOTS.

Pabbay consisting of a hollow bone (evidently of the sheep) about 3 inches in length. All the specimens obtained in North Uist are segments of the stem of the cow-parsnip or some other similar umbelliferous plant, while we are informed that goose-quills also serve a like purpose—interesting examples of adaptability to circumstances.

The writer was given a *crois-iarna* (literally ' yarn-cross ' or yarn-reel) intended for winding thread into hanks from the balls into which it is rolled at the time of being spun, so as to make it ready for dye-ing. This appliance consists of a wooden rod about two feet long, with a cross-bar fixed within each end, and when in use is revolved by means of both hands. Sometimes it is furnished with an adjust-ment to slacken the hank after being wound—a provision necessary in the case of linen, although not required for woollen yarn on account of its greater elasticity.

In this island most of the dyes used for wool are still home-made. Lichen or *crotal* gives a reddish-brown, while the root of the iris yields a grey. Yellow is furnished by the tips of heather, green being produced from the same with the addition of copperas. Rue also gives a yellow dye, and peat-soot a dark yellow, while thyme and the roots of the docken and sorrel are utilised—the latter as a mordant. Tea-leaves yield a pale green, and blue was formerly obtained from a plant locally known as *lus-mór*, now displaced by indigo as a more effective substitute. It is not uncommon to see dyed wool and bleached or dyed yarn laid upon the top of a wall to dry.

After the woollen cloth is woven it has yet to undergo the process of being ' waulked,' or in other words, shrunk and thickened. A reference already made to ' fulling-mills ' in North Uist would show that even within the past century this was effected by means of water-power, for some reason latterly abandoned. It is curious to find that more than two hundred years ago the captain of an English vessel witnessed upon Boreray, North Uist, this operation in its cruder form (not in-deed greatly differing from the present-day practice), and his view of the matter may here be quoted.[1] This observer, ' having Landed in the Island, happened to come into a House where he found only Ten Women, and they were imploy'd (as he suppos'd) in a strange manner, *viz.* their Arms and Legs were bare, being Five on a side, and between them lay a Board, upon which they had laid a piece of Cloth, and

---

[1] Martin's *Description, etc.*, p. 57.

were thickning of it with their Hands and Feet, and Singing all the while, the *English* Man, presently concluded it to be a little Bedlam, which he did not expect in so remote a Corner.' The captain, however, on being reassured by John MacLean (then tacksman of Boreray) ' that it was their common way of thickning Cloth, he was convinced, tho' surpriz'd at the manner of it.' Notwithstanding the awkwardness of such a combination, both hands and feet seem to have been employed at some former period, although the *New Stat. Acc.*[1] (dealing with Kilmuir in Skye, under date 1840) inferentially limits this operation to the hands alone. Precisely as there described—except that the posture was one of sitting instead of kneeling—the writer witnessed this fulling process at Grenetote, North Uist, in August 1901, to the accompaniment of a Gaelic song ; and still more recently the long and shallow wooden troughs,[2]—*cliathan-luaidh*—made for this special purpose, have been noted at various townships including Malaclett, Grenetote, and Claddach-Kirkibost.

Bent-grass abounds upon the sand-hills at the north and west shores, this fibre being utilised in its natural state for making sacks,[3] ropes, horse-collars,[4] mats, and even chairs. In September 1897, while sheltering within a barn at Kirkibost Island on a very wet day, the writer saw bent-ropes in process of manufacture. Heisker formerly yielded the best supply of this raw material, though we are told that Kirkibost is now the favoured locality. Ropes made from heather are still preferred as fastenings for thatch,[5] while in the Loch Eford district these are also used to secure boats. Small poaching-nets have been quite recently made of the same material, surely a most tedious and difficult task. In this connection may be noted a net of similar type but

---

[1] *Inverness-shire*, p. 286.

[2] These usually consist of two grooved boards fixed side by side within a narrow wooden frame so as to give an interior depth of about one inch. Three specimens examined were found to measure 11 feet 9 inches by 21 inches, 10 feet 10 inches by 31 inches, and 10 feet 9 inches by 25 inches ; their bottoms formed respectively by one, two, and three boards. The first noted was of exceptional type, having ten narrow grooves, each only one inch wide and about a quarter of an inch deep, while the normal arrangement may average 8 or 9 grooves of double these dimensions.

[3] *Plàta-shìl* or *plàta-mhuilinn* were recently made in Heisker for carrying grain and meal by boat to or from the mill. These are so thick as to be nearly impervious to spray and rain.

[4] Used with wooden ' hames,' to which the harness is attached. Straw plaiting is said to have been introduced to Lewis by the last Earl of Seaforth, who was forfeited in 1716 (Mackenzie's *History of the Outer Hebrides*, p. 538). Since at least early in the nineteenth century, bent-grass (*Arundo arenaria*) has been planted for the special purpose of preventing sand-drift ; *New Stat. Acc.*, Inverness-shire, pp. 175, 191.

[5] Heather laid above bent-grass is considered the most lasting material for thatch, although rushes and iris leaves are often used.

wrought from the root of a grass, *Carex flacca*, which trails within about an inch of the surface to a length of six or eight feet. This specimen has a one-inch mesh and is of conical shape, measuring 4 feet in length by a width of 19 inches across its mouth, thence tapering to a point at the other end. It bears the Gaelic name of *tàbh*, and when in use is placed within a *cabhuil* or dam formed by small stones in the bed of a narrow burn,[1] the fish being then driven down stream. We have been told that very strong tethers are also made from the same root.

Apart from the home-made tweed commonly worn by the men, and the fact that pronounced shades of red, blue, and green seem very acceptable to the girls, perhaps the most noteworthy items of wearing apparel are the 'sole-less stockings' or *mogan*, still much affected by the older women of Lewis,[2] and also used in Skye though less frequently to be seen in North Uist. With regard to this island, if our information is correct, *mogan* are not now made for the purpose but represent old stockings from which the soles have been cut. In Lewis, on the other hand, they are specially knitted without soles, and held in position by a loop which is passed between or over the toes. Their use is obviously to protect the ankle and instep while allowing the privilege of walking barefoot.

In North Uist we have at various times noticed elderly women equipped with *mogan*, and perhaps still oftener have failed to observe the particular fact where it existed. Upon one occasion the wearer was carrying, slung across her back, a long stick with a barbed iron spike fixed into one end. This implement was a *brod-leàbag* or 'flounder-spear,' which we have at various times seen in actual service upon the fords to Vallay and Baleshare.[3]

Toll-solaidh or 'shell-bait basins' are commonly found upon rocks at each suitable fishing-point along the shore.[4] In dimensions these

[1] We are assured that the word *cabhuil* has this signification in North Uist, though in other parts *cabhuil* means a net, and *eileach* the place where it is fixed.

[2] The Lewis term being *osan*, simply the Gaelic word for 'hose.'

[3] These spears are made for the special purpose at the nearest smithy, the ordinary kind being hammered out of a plain rod which is inserted within the cleft end of a stick ; a more elaborate form being sometimes wrought with a socket to contain the handle. In either case the essential feature is a barbed spike at the end of a 5-foot staff, although a common hay-fork is occasionally used for the same purpose, and presumably not without success. This method of fishing is practised by women wading in shallow tidal runs at the ebb of spring-tide in calm bright weather, feeling with their bare feet where a flounder may lie half-covered by the sand.

[4] Dr. Alex. Carmichael, in *Carmina Gadelica*, vol. ii. p. 333, quotes a local tradition to the effect that these bait-holes were made by order of Amie MacRuari.

average 5 or 6 inches wide and from 3 to 5 inches deep. Their purpose is not however to contain the bait itself, being incidental rather
to the angler's first procedure—that of reducing shell-fish to a pulp
and casting this into the sea, so that it may serve as a lure to attract
later victims. We are further assured that the stone used as a pounder
is frequently left near the bait-cup, so that the same implement (really
a modern hammer-stone) may thus lie for a period of several years.

Coal is necessarily an expensive commodity in North Uist, and
wood—apart from wreckage—being totally absent, it follows that the
provision of a sufficient supply of peats forms a serious item in the
work of each family. As already stated, the peat is both plentiful and
of excellent quality; and of this, fifty or sixty loads are required to
maintain a single fire throughout the whole year. To cut, dry, cart,
and stack this quantity is estimated as giving full employment to one
man for at least a month. The usual practice, as we are informed, is
for two neighbours to work together at the cutting for about ten days,
after which each has to devote four days or more to the drying and a
fortnight to the carting of his own share—that is, if the peat-hag is
within average distance from home.[1]

The Heisker islands contain no peat, and the provision of fuel thus
entails a much greater tax upon the inhabitants of Ceann Ear and
Ceann Iar, to whom is allotted part of the bog near Loch a' Charra on
both sides of the Committee Road. During the month of August,
boats from these islands may often be seen lying north of Dusary at a
place known as Ardheisker, clearly so named in association with the
Monach group.

For a like reason the Boreray crofters have to cut their peats at
Stromay, an islet in Cheese Bay.

The peat-spade or *treisger* is an implement of distinctive shape,
thoroughly adapted to its special purpose, having an oblong blade
with a knife which projects at right angles to its base on one side,[2] so

---

[1] While cutting peat the crofters occasionally come upon articles buried in the moss. Of such
objects the present writer can only note from personal inspection a hazel-nut found near Langass,
a whet-stone unearthed in Bogach Backlasary, and two craggans which lay, one within the other,
about 3 feet below the surface of the Sollas peat-moss at Treacklett. These craggans are said to
have been in perfect condition when found, though afterwards only fragments were available
for examination, clearly representing two separate vessels, each of them marked with rude
patterns of different styles. One portion shows the perhaps unique feature of a number of small
dots arranged close together in a series of straight and curved lines, hardly seeming to be intended
for ornament, but suggestive rather of a mark denoting ownership.

[2] Upon measuring one of ordinary type, the main blade was found to be 10 inches long by a width

COCKLE-SHELLS BURNT FOR LIME.

OLD INN AT TIGHARY.

that blocks of uniform size can be easily cut in quick succession from the bank.

In North Uist it is still the practice to burn heaps of cockle-shells, encased within a layer of peats, for the purpose of making lime.   In some parts, especially at the north and south shores, the cockle is very abundant, once indeed having formed an ordinary article of diet.

Appliances for producing light by old-fashioned methods have long ago become obsolete in this district, so that it is difficult to find a single specimen.   Although the writer was able to obtain an ornamented steel 'striker'[1]—for use with a flint, and probably dating from not earlier than the eighteenth century—the tinder-box seems quite unknown.   Even the 'crusie' oil-lamp is now wholly discarded, common as it must have been about fifty years ago.   In the Malaclett smithy, however, there still exists an oblong iron anvil which contains in one of its faces a pair of circular hollows slightly differing as to diameter and made for the definite purpose of shaping the upper and under trays of a *cruisgein*.   We can vouch for the fact that this mould served its special use upon at least one occasion, the writer (in the summer of 1907) having persuaded the blacksmith to hammer out a complete 'crusie,' which was in due time sent home, accompanied by a good supply of its proper wick—namely, the pith of rushes.

In connection with the general use of sea-ware for manuring the crops in North Uist, some details may be here recorded.   In the first place, where loose weed is not available, it is necessary to cut it from the rocks with a small sickle rudely notched like a saw by means of a file.   This sea-weed must then be conveyed to the arable land, an operation effected by various methods, according to local circumstances.   In some cases a boat is required, although this has almost invariably to be supplemented at a later stage.   In Boreray we have witnessed a small procession of women ascending from a geo, and laden with sea-ware in sacks slung across their shoulders; while

of 3½ inches, and the knife 8 by 2 inches; while the implement had a total length of 55 inches, with a spur fixed into the shaft to serve as a treader.   This form is used for working downwards.   There also exists another and decidedly scarce variety which has a broader blade and also a broader (although shorter) knife, for the purpose of cutting peats horizontally from below.   The handle is comparatively short, and furnished with a cross-bar upon its end, this being pressed forwards from the chest against the opposite face of solid peat.

[1] It may be worth noting that in February 1908, at Saint Raphael on the French Riviera, a 'striker' of almost identical form was seen in a shop window, together with several flints.   The striker and four shaped flints were acquired at a cost of 40 centimes, the purchaser being informed that such articles are in regular demand among the country people there.

upon the same island (as also at Lieravay, near Lochmaddy) another system was observed, the manure being borne in panniers on horseback. At Boreray the tangle was filled into a basket on each side and also heaped across the pony's back which was protected by a long mat made of bents. At Lieravay the panniers were formed of wood, with a somewhat complicated attachment by which the bottom could be released at will; and here the mat was of coir instead of bent. Another and easier way is to cart the tangle in cases where both the beach and the arable ground are thus accessible. When leaving Boreray (there is no pier) we had to be driven out in one of these carts to the side of our boat. This formed in itself an unusual experience, but still more noteworthy was the fact that the harness and bridle—which were almost new—consisted entirely of strips of sealskin pieced together by the owner, who had himself killed the seals.

It may be added that, throughout North Uist, home-made stirrups of wire or of rope with a wooden sole are quite the rule, while bridles and stirrups formed wholly of rope are also common.

In North Uist, as elsewhere throughout the Hebrides, horse-racing was regularly practised on Michaelmas day, having probably originated from a religious ceremony in honour of St. Michael. These races, or *odaidh*,[1] were held upon Traigh Ear at Udal, Traigh Stir near Hosta, and Traigh nam Faoghailean at Hougary, as no doubt also in other suitable localities where a wide stretch of sand lies bare at low-water.[2] In connection with this festival, triangular cakes of barley-meal were provided under the name of *Sruan Mhìcheil* or 'Michael's cakes,' a custom which survived until within living memory.[3]

As the modern chief harbour of North Uist and its official centre, Lochmaddy has in a way reigned supreme for about a hundred years, practically monopolising the whole passenger traffic of the district. Very early in the nineteenth century (if not before the close of the eighteenth) a mail-packet station was established at Lochmaddy,[4] the

---

[1] From the Norse *etja*, 'a horse-fight'; see *The Norse Influence on Celtic Scotland*, by Dr. George Henderson, Glasgow, 1910, pp. 74-75.

[2] Dr. Alexander Carmichael's *Carmina Gadelica*, vol. ii. p. 315.

[3] Martin's *Description*, etc., pp. 79-80, enters into some detail as to these races in North Uist ca. 1700, and also (pp. 52, 89, and 100) refers to 'cavalcades' on Michaelmas day in Harris and Barra, and to the baking of 'St. Michael's cakes' in Barra and South Uist.

[4] With a post-office under the name of *Carinish*, evidently preserving that of a still earlier station near the south-west extremity of North Uist (*New Stat. Acc.*, Inverness-shire, p. 178. Written in 1837).

sloop *Perseverance* plying fortnightly thence to Dunvegan in Skye;[1] this arrangement being gradually improved upon by the successive weekly, bi-weekly,[2] and tri-weekly services of the *Skylark*, while from 1876 the cutter *Dream*[3] with great regularity made a daily round trip between the same ports, until in 1886 superseded by MacBrayne's steamers.

At a distinctly earlier period (dating from about the middle of the eighteenth century) the mails were carried by a smack sailing between Dunvegan and the south-east corner of North Uist, the regular harbour (with variations) being then at *Bàgh Seòlaid Rudh' Eubhadh*,[4] at the south side of Eaval opposite the island of Flodday More—that is, immediately within the narrow entrance to Grimsay Sound, which lies between Eaval and Ronay at the deep east end of the North Ford.

During various periods since about the year 1700, North Uist has contained at least thirteen different Inns or public-houses, perhaps not more than four or five of them, however, having been thus occupied at any one time. According to Martin in 1703:[5] 'There was never an Inn here till of late, and now there is but one,'—probably that at Carinish, which may likely be the oldest. In 1837 we read:[6] 'The inns in the parish are four. One at the packet station at Lochmaddy, another at Carinish, the opposite extremity of the island, and the other two at proper intermediate distances along the road.' These 'proper' intervals evidently point to Ahmore at Loch Aonghuis, where still remains this building of two stories; and to a humbler inn at Balamartin, afterwards given up in favour of Tighary, a mile to the

---

[1] It is locally told that, upon one occasion, a policeman had to wait patiently at Lochmaddy for this sloop with a prisoner under sentence of six weeks' confinement at Inverness, a period which exhausted itself just as the *Perseverance* at last entered the bay, so that a voyage across the Minch had become unnecessary.

[2] Bi-weekly in 1827 and 1837 : Mackenzie's *History of the Outer Hebrides*, p. 542 ; and *New Stat. Acc.*, Inverness-shire, p. 178. According to the last-mentioned authority this packet was one of sixty tons.

[3] This cutter achieved the noteworthy average of five and a half round trips per week throughout its run of ten years.

[4] Evidently 'the harbour of Rueheva' of the *Old Stat. Acc.*, vol. xiii. p. 302 ; and 'Rhueva' of Lewis' *Topographical Dictionary of Scotland*, London, 1846. Disaster overtook one of these smacks plying between Liernish (a little west from *Rudh' Eubhadh*) and Dunvegan, when the boat foundered and all on board perished, the Presbytery Records of Uist up to 1768 being at the same time lost. In 1840 (*New Stat. Acc.*, Inverness-shire, p. 214) it is evident that all the mails from Barra, South Uist, Benbecula, and North Uist passed through Lochmaddy. Possibly even then, and almost certainly in earlier times, Harris was served by the same route as the southern divisions of the Long Island—all under a subsidy from the various proprietors ; but in 1846 Harris had its separate packet, sailing twice weekly in summer and once in winter between Tarbert (Harris) and Uig in Skye : Lewis' *Topographical Dictionary*.

[5] *A Description, etc.*, p. 78.

[6] *New Stat. Acc.*, Inverness-shire, p. 180.

south.   Tighary Inn, a long thatched cottage, was itself abandoned in 1899 and soon afterwards disroofed, its licence having been transferred in 1896 to Kirkibost[1] under the same tenant.

Of the earlier Inns, that at Carinish alone survives in its original capacity; while at Lochmaddy the former erection is utilised as a bothy, this village being now provided with a commodious Hotel close to the modern pier.   In addition to those already specified, we hear of seven other old hostels—at Clachan Sand (part of a gable still remaining), Trumisgarry, Port nan Long, Grenetote, Sollas, and Hasten; while perhaps the most primitive of all was a cottage in the Eaval district, a little to the south of *Bàgh Moireaig*, this existing in connection with the packet-service at *Bàgh Seòlaid*.

The old *Statistical Account* of 1794 states—'There is not a slated house in the parish, but the church, one mill, a house at Lochmaddie, that was intended for a public house, and another in the Island of Vallay, in a ruinous condition'; and further that all North Uist then contained only eight carts.[2]   By the year 1837 matters had improved to the extent that 'The greater number of the tacksmen occupy comfortable and commodious slated houses; and many of the farm-offices are of the same description.   Besides these, the church, three mills, and three public-houses are slated.'[3]

North Uist affords good all-round sport, and that in great variety. It contains a fair stock of Red Deer, chiefly confined to Langass district in the central portion of the main island.   Rabbits are not numerous except in a few isolated places amongst sandbanks; while Hares have been turned down at Langass but do not thrive under the local conditions.   The Otter is not uncommon, though much scarcer than in former times.   On the other hand, the Seal is present in large numbers and in two varieties; the Common Seal abounding, especially in the Sound of Harris, while the Grey Seal is also fairly plentiful, its chief habitat being the Haskeir rocks eight miles west of Griminish Point, where the farmers of the north-western portion of North Uist were accustomed to club the young in late autumn.

Grouse are not numerous, as indeed is the case throughout the

[1] This is at Claddach-Kirkibost, a conspicuous square house, originally built for a doctor's residence.   It now bears the name of 'West Ford Inn,' from the adjacent but little used ford to Kirkibost Island.

[2] Vol. xiii. pp. 308, 325.

[3] *New Stat. Acc.*, Inverness-shire, p. 171.

Long Island, the heather being of poor quality, most of it either rank or stunted, according to the damp or stony extremes which prevail in North Uist. The hooded-crow and the raven are also too much in evidence to allow winged game to thrive unmolested. Woodcock are found in fair quantity, being regular annual visitors. The Common Snipe abounds, especially on the west side of North Uist, the Jack Snipe being also of frequent occurrence at its period of migration, though not quite so numerous. The Rock Dove is plentiful wherever caves exist around the coast; and the Golden Plover is specially common, being found in immense flocks during the autumn.

Geese, particularly the Grey-Lag, afford perhaps the best sport of all the wild fowl which resort to this district. About harvest-time they appear in large numbers, but are most difficult to stalk on account of a wariness not usually attributed to the species. Two other varieties, the Bernacle and the Brent, also occur, but with much less frequency. Duck are found in great variety, including the sheldrake, mallard, gadwall, teal, widgeon, pochard, scaup, tufted duck, golden-eye, long-tailed duck, and the eider—some of these not desirable except as specimens.

Bird life is remarkably abundant on the lochs and tidal waters, North Uist being at least notable for its rough shooting, which may be there enjoyed almost in ideal form, though the mixed bag exacts the hardest of work—after all, not unwelcome to the true sportsman.

To the angler, North Uist also offers many attractions. Salmon, though not very plentiful, are frequently taken in Lochs nan Geireann and Skealtar, near Lochmaddy, during the months of April and May, and have been introduced into Geireann Mill Loch on the north side of the island. Since the mill-sluice was removed, this loch is distinctly the best for sea-trout, many being taken in September and October up to a weight of over seven pounds. On the other hand, the Horisary lochs, near Kirkibost at the west side of the island, are to be preferred in March and April. In addition to the normal autumn run of sea-trout, there is certainly a minor run for a short period in early spring, but how regularly and to what extent is rather doubtful. The sea-trout frequents other lochs and also rises to the fly (though more capriciously) in sea-pools upon the tidal strands at Horisary, Geireann Mill, and Vallay.

Loch Fada, near the centre of North Uist, bears the highest reputation for brown trout, though containing comparatively small fish ; while Loch an Duin and Loch Tormosad yield a much better average in regard to size. But from May to July almost any of the countless lochs in North Uist would no doubt provide sport if thoroughly tested with the aid of a boat, the greater number being practically unvisited by any angler.

The mackerel is often to be found in Loch Eford, where it is habitually netted by the crofters. The grey mullet also sometimes occurs, this representing the *iesk-druimin* or 'Marled Salmon' of Martin,[1] who describes it as ' full of strong Large Scales, no bait can allure it, and a shadow frights it away, being the wildest of fishes, it leaps high above water, and delights to be in the surface of it.' This is a fish of ugly appearance, having a wide purse-shaped mouth and very large thick scales, and it certainly displays great agility in leaping over a net.

The lobster is both abundant and regularly fished, the difficulties of conveyance to market rendering it, however, somewhat unprofitable.

Oysters seem now to be absent, though Martin—referring either to Cheese Bay or to Loch Maddy—mentions that these grow ' on Rocks, and are so big that they are cut in four peices before they are eat '[2]—surely a coarse and undesirable variety if this account is to be taken literally.

The whole of North Uist, with its subsidiary islands, was purchased in 1855 from Baron MacDonald of Sleat by Sir John Powlett Orde, Bart., and now belongs to his grandson, Sir Arthur J. Campbell-Orde, Bart., apart from the minor exceptions of Ronay, Balranald, and Vallay, which were sold in the years 1886, 1894, and 1901, respectively.

Ronay was bought (subject to a small annual feu-duty) by Captain Allan MacDonald of Waternish in Skye. Balranald had already been held by the same family of MacDonald for nearly 150 years as tenants, until in 1894 it was purchased—together with Paiblesgarry, Penmore, and Ard an Runair—by the representative of this family, Mr. Alexander MacDonald, who died in 1901, being succeeded by his only son, Mr. J. A. Ranald MacDonald. In 1901 the island of Vallay—including its pendicles of Griminish, Scolpaig, Balelone, and Kilpheder, upon the

---

[1] *A Description, etc.*, p. 58.   [2] *Ibid.*, p. 55.

' mainland ' of North Uist—was advertised for sale ; this small portion, at the extreme north-west corner of the parish, being then acquired by the author of the present volume.

North Uist is well equipped with churches and also contains fourteen schools, one of these upon Ceann Ear in the isolated Heisker group.

CHAPTER XI

ANCIENT MAPS OF NORTH UIST, AND DESCRIPTIONS RECORDED BY EARLY TRAVELLERS IN THAT ISLAND

THE cartography of the Outer Hebrides, while furnishing some place-names of much interest, is otherwise chiefly notable for its incorrectness, a fault excusable in maps which date from the sixteenth and seventeenth centuries, representing islands then so little visited. Until within quite modern times, all these maps bear evidence of having been compiled at second hand instead of from personal knowledge; a remark specially applicable to the curious map (not earliest in date, though perhaps the first to show the name of Uist or 'Eusta') in Bishop Leslie's *De Origine Moribvs, et Rebvs Gestis Scotorvm*, printed at Rome in 1578. This includes 'Hebrides insvle. 43,' but is only too subject to criticism when we find 'Cumbra' and 'Iona' each represented as of greater dimensions than 'Ila'; while 'Schia' and 'Leuissa' are placed close together, north of Sutherland. 'Hirta' or St. Kilda is there figured as the largest of all the Hebridean isles—twice the size of Mull and north of Skye and Lewis, not far from the Shetlands.[1] 'Eusta' and 'Mula' are shown as neighbours, although the letterpress (p. 36) more correctly states 'Euste contermina est Leuissa.'

Blaeu's Atlas (Amsterdam, 1654) marks a distinct advance, notwithstanding its error in showing Benbecula as continuous with both North and South Uist, while the general outline is very fanciful. The Scottish Atlas of Hermann Moll (London, 1725) shows a still further improvement, although it is upon a much smaller scale and gives fewer place-names than appear in Blaeu's Atlas.

Apart from these old maps, we are fortunate in having two

---

[1] Bishop Leslie's map is obviously copied from Lafreri's Atlas (Rome, 1558); see Nordenskiöld's *Facsimile-Atlas*, Stockholm, 1889, p. 123.

independent accounts of the Hebrides, one of them written in the middle of the sixteenth century and the other about the year 1700, both containing details of much interest.

The earlier—'by Mr. Donald Monro, High Dean of the Isles, who travelled through the most of them in the year 1549'—was first published at Edinburgh, 1774, in a small edition said to consist of only fifty copies.[1] Although taking the form of a numbered catalogue, the instances are few in which some description is not given; and the very fact of our possessing a contemporary record dating back more than three hundred and sixty years, is of itself cause for great satisfaction.

It is not known to what extent Archdeacon[2] Monro travelled among the Outer Hebrides, and yet the duties pertaining to his office would probably bring him upon more than one occasion to North Uist with its 'twa paroche kirks,' and this in the time of Donald Gormson who had succeeded to the chiefship of Clan Huistein as a minor in 1539. There is an amount of circumstantiality in the reference to Loch Bee in South Uist which would infer that Monro writes from personal observation. From statements in his volume

[1] According to an 'Editorial Note' which appears in the Glasgow reprint of 1884. Two manuscript copies of Monro's works are preserved in the Advocates' Library (Leslie Stephen's *Dictionary of National Biography*).

[2] Theiner's *Vetera Monumenta*, pp. 69-70, shows that in the year 1256 the three ecclesiastical positions *decanus*, *subdecanus*, and *archidiaconus* were sanctioned for the diocese of Ross. Whether *archi-diaconus* or *archi-decanus* was the correct term for Monro's office in the Isles, various facts tend to prove that he had not attained this dignity before the year 1553 at the earliest. In *Origines Parochiales*, vol. ii. pp. 347, 354, reference is made to *Reg. Sec. Sig.* (vol. vi. folio 31, vol. vii. folio 30, and vol. xxv. folio 29) for the presentation of Sir Donald Monro by King James v. in 1526 to 'the vicarage of Sneisport and Rairsay, vacant by the decease of Sir Tormot McFarsane'; and by Queen Mary 'super rectoria unita de vig in trouternes, Skye,' 6 December 1552, in succession to Sir John McCrummey. *Reg. Mag. Sig.*, 13 Feb. 1552-3, confirms a Fowlis charter of 20 January 1551-2, witnessed 'D. Donaldo Monro rectore de Y.' This was evidently our traveller, who afterwards appears (*Ibid.*, 16 March 1562-3 and 31 March 1563) in two other Ross-shire charters dated 25 January 1562-3—'Test. Donaldo Munro archidiacono Insularum,' etc. 'Master Rore McClane' was archdeacon of the Isles in 1544 and then named as bishop postulate, though it would seem that he did not receive consecration until some time between 1548 and 1553, reference being made to the bishopric of the Isles as vacant in 1553 'by the decease of Master Roderic Mac Clane last bishop' (*Origines Parochiales*, vol. ii. pp. 292-294); Keith's *Catalogue of the Scottish Bishops* (Edinburgh, 1824, p. 307) further noting that the see of the Isles was vacant in 1549.

Scott's *Fasti* (vol. iii. pp. 299, 302) gives some notices of the post-Reformation career of the Rev. Donald Monro, 'formerly Archdeacon of the Isles.' A native of Ross-shire and related to the Fowlis family, he was appointed by the General Assembly, 26th June 1563, as a Commissioner 'to plant kirks within the bounds of Ross,' apparently also serving for some years as pastor of Kiltearn, until translated in 1574 to the adjoining parish of Lymlair or Lumlair, long since united with that of Kiltearn. We further learn that Monro 'was not prompt in the Scottish tongue,' evidently implying that he had but a slight knowledge of Gaelic.

(pp. 31, 37, 45) it is in any case certain that the Archdeacon visited Barra, Harris, and Lewis, and there is every reason to believe that North Uist was also included.

During the sixteenth century it is evident that several of the North Uist forts were at least in occasional if not regular use—for example, Dun Steingarry 'on Loch Paible at Balranald' and Dun Scolpaig, both *ca.* 1506 ; Dun Aonghuis, *ca.* 1510-1516 ; four duns possessed by members of Clan MacVicar, *ca.* 1580-1585 ; and Dun an Sticir in 1601-1602—all of which appear semi-historically at about the dates mentioned.

We could wish that the Archdeacon had taken some notice of these and other forts, as also of the social condition of the island, beyond his passing remark that 'Into this north heid of Ywst, ther is sundrie covis and holes in the earth coverit with heddir above, quhilk fosters maney rebellis.' Again, he might easily have given some account of the churches and chapels from personal observation.

Monro was a contemporary of two Scottish historians—George Buchanan, and John Leslie, Bishop of Ross[1]—with both of whom he had relations, being a correspondent of Buchanan's, while Bishop Leslie was his diocesan superior from the year 1566. George Buchanan's *Rerum Scoticarum Historia* was first printed in 1582 and acknowledges assistance from Monro in the geographical section.[2] Reference has been already made to Bishop Leslie's volume of 1578, with its quaint map of Scotland upon which the Hebrides are so inaccurately figured.

'M. Martin, Gent.,' author of *A Description of the Western Islands of Scotland* published in 1703, seems in most cases to deal with the various islands and their special features from personal observation. A native of Skye, and resident there for many years, Martin had great facilities for visiting comparatively inaccessible parts. It is unfortunate that the forts and pre-Reformation chapels of North Uist had not, in Martin's time, as yet acquired a flavour of antiquity, though for this very reason—little over a century having elapsed since their occupation—golden opportunities then offered themselves, both by way of current tradition and contemporary description, which have

---

[1] Leslie was a 'friend and adviser' of Mary Queen of Scots, whereas Buchanan took up a directly opposite standpoint.

[2] 'In primis autem Donaldum Monroum sequemur, hominem & pium, & diligentem, qui eas omnes & ipse peragravit, & oculis perlustravit,' folio 9.

since become lost for ever.   All the same, we must be grateful for
Martin's detailed remarks upon items which would seem only common-
place to the natives ; and, indeed, apart from his volume and Sir John
Sinclair's *Statistical Account* published in the last decade of the
eighteenth century (supplemented by the *New Statistical Account* of
1845), few definite notices of the Outer Hebrides are available until
within quite recent years.   It may be added that Martin is so full of
unconscious humour in describing peculiarities — whether social,
personal, or otherwise—as to yield some compensation for the fact
that Dr. Johnson did not include North Uist in his memorable
Tour.

Martin Martin was born at Trotternish in Skye *ca.* 1656-1660,
third son of Donald Martin,[1] who held a wadset of Beallach at Duntulm
in the extreme north-east corner of that island.   He was educated
with his elder brothers at Edinburgh, there taking the degree of M.A.
in 1681.   For some period until 1686 he was 'governor'[2] to Donald
MacDonald, younger of Sleat—afterwards fourth baronet, evidently
born *ca.* 1665, who led the Sleat men at Killiecrankie in 1689 and
died in 1718, two years after being forfeited.   From 1686 to 1692
Martin Martin acted as 'governor' to young MacLeod of Dunvegan,
the earliest receipt for his salary in this capacity being dated 13th
August 1686 and the latest 16th August 1692.   In 1698 Martin
Martin published *A Late Voyage to St. Kilda, the Remotest of all the
Hebrides, or Western Isles of Scotland*; which was followed in 1703
by his more general *Description of the Western Islands*.   Both of
these are most valuable, and the second is credited as the inducing
cause of Dr. Samuel Johnson's visit to the Hebrides.[3]

Nothing seems to be known of Martin Martin in his later years,
except that he entered Leyden University, 6th March 1710, and

---

[1] The name of Martin Martin's mother is variously stated as ' Mary, daughter of Alexander,
brother of Sir Donald MacDonald of Sleat ' (*The Clan Donald*, vol. iii. p. 560), and as 'one of the
Nicolsons of Scorrybreck' (MS. information from Husabost).   Two of his nephews (both named
Martin Martin) are said to have married daughters of Lachlan MacLean of Vallay (*The Clan
Donald*, vol. iii. pp. 560-561).   This Martin family was long seated in Trotternish, although
evidently never owning any land there.

[2] *Ibid.*, p. 560.

[3] Boswell, in his *Journal* of this famous tour, states that Dr. Johnson 'told me, in summer,
1763, that his father put Martin's Account in his hands when he was very young, and that he was
much pleased with it.'   Leslie Stephen's *Dictionary of National Biography* adds : 'Although
Johnson was interested in this work, and took the book with him to the highlands, he had a poor
opinion of its literary merit.   "No man," he said, "now writes so ill as Martin's account of the
Hebrides is written."'

there graduated as M.D.,[1] afterwards residing in London until his death, unmarried, in 1719. It has been stated that Martin was 'factor' to the laird of MacLeod, but this is wholly incorrect.

We are also much indebted to the *Old* and *New Statistical Accounts of Scotland* for the descriptions of North Uist written by the Rev. Allan MacQueen *ca.* 1794, and by the Rev. Finlay MacRae in 1837—both of them parish ministers of that island.[2]

---

[1] Leslie Stephen's *Dictionary of National Biography*, which adds that Martin contributed two papers to the Royal Society, the first (in 1697) forming the groundwork of his volume of 1703; and further, that Martin, 'mainly at the request of Sir Robert Sibbald, the antiquary, travelled over the western islands of Scotland, collecting information regarding the condition and habits of the islanders.' It would seem that Martin had begun to gather materials for his *magnum opus* before the year 1680, since, in describing Benbecula, he states (p. 82), 'This Island belongs properly to *Ranal Mackdonald* of *Benbecula*'—a chieftain who died in 1679 (*The Clan Donald*, vol. iii. p. 279).

[2] Mr. MacQueen 1770-1801, and Mr. MacRae 1818-1858.

INDEX

Printed by T. and A. CONSTABLE, Printers to His Ma
at the Edinburgh University Press